Mysterium Magnum

Volume One

Mysterium Magnum

An exposition of
The First Book of Moses
called

GENESIS

written *Anno* 1623 by

Jacob Boehme

translated by
John Sparrow

[Volume One]

Hermetica

San Rafael, Ca

Third, facsimile edition
Hermetica, 2007

For information, address:
Hermetica, P.O. Box 151011
San Rafael, California 94915, USA

ISBN-13: 978-1-59731-214-1
(Vol 1: pbk.: alk. paper)
ISBN-13: 978-1-59731-216-8
(Vol 1: hardcover: alk. paper)
ISBN-13: 978-1-59731-215-8
(Vol 2: pbk.: alk. paper)
ISBN-13: 978-1-59731-217-2
(Vol 1: hardcover: alk. paper)

Author's Preface

1. WHEN we consider the visible world with its essence, and consider the life of the creatures, then we find therein the likeness of the invisible spiritual world, which is hidden in the visible world, as the soul in the body; and see thereby that the hidden God is nigh unto all, and through all; and yet wholly hidden to the visible essence.

2. We have an example hereof in the mind of man, which is an invisible fire, that is inclined to light and darkness, viz. to joy and sorrow; and yet in itself is none of these, but only a cause thereto; an invisible, incomprehensive sourcive, fire; and yet as to its own essence is included in nothing, save only in the will of life.

3. The body cannot comprehend the mind; but the mind comprehends the body; and brings it to love, or dislike;[1] this likewise is to be understood of the Word and power of God; which is hidden to the visible sensible elements: and yet dwelleth through and in the elements; and worketh through the sensible life and essence, as the mind in the body.

4. For the visible sensible things are an essence of the invisible: from the invisible and incomprehensible the visible and comprehensible is proceeded: the visible essence is come to be from the expression or spiration of the invisible power: the invisible spiritual Word of divine power worketh with and through the visible essence, as the soul[2] with and through the body.

5. The inward spiritual soul of man was breathed into the visible image by the in-speaking, or inspiration, of the invisible Word of the divine power; (for an understanding to the created image) wherein man's science and knowledge of the invisible and visible essence consisteth.

6. Thus man hath now received ability from the invisible Word of God to the re-expression: that he again expresseth the hidden Word of the divine science into formation and severation: in manner and form of the temporal creatures; and formeth this spiritual Word according to animals and vegetables; whereby the invisible wisdom of God is portrayed and modellised into several distinct forms: as we plainly see, that the understanding of man expresseth all powers in their property, and giveth names unto all things, according to each

[1] Or sufferance and sorrow.   [2] In.

thing's property, by which the hidden wisdom is known and understood in its power: and the hidden God is made manifest with[1] the visible things, for the delight and play of the divine Power: so that the invisible might play with the visible, and therein introduce itself into the sight and sense of itself.

7. As the mind doth introduce itself with the body and by the body into senses and thoughts, whereby it worketh and acteth sensibly to itself, so also the invisible world (worketh) through the visible, and with the visible world: we are not in any wise to think that a man cannot search out what the hidden divine world is, and what its operation and essence is, for on the visible essence of the creation we see a figure of the internal spiritual operation of the powerful world.

8. And we ought not to think otherwise of God, but that he is the most internal ground of all essences; and yet so, as that he cannot be comprehended of any thing by the own-peculiar power of the thing; but as the sun doth introduce itself with its light and power into the sensible living things, and worketh with [or in] all things, and introduceth itself also into an essence; the same likewise is to be understood concerning the divine Word with the life of the creatures.

9. Seeing then this visible world is the expressed, formed word, according to God's love and anger, viz. according to the Grand Mystery of the eternal spiritual nature, which spiritual world is hidden in the visible; and yet the human soul is a spark out of the eternal-speaking Word of the divine science and power: and the body an ens of the stars and elements; and also as to the internal ground an ens of heaven, viz. of the hidden world; therefore he hath might and ability to speak of the Grand Mystery whence all essences do originally arise.

10. Since then the great Mysteries, the beginning of and original of all things, do befall us by divine grace; that we are able (as through the ground of the soul) to understand the same in real knowledge, with the inspired word of the divine science, we will write down its ground (so far as it is permitted to us) in this book: for a Memorial to ourself, and for the exercise of divine knowledge to the Reader.

11. And I. we will signify and declare what the centre and ground of all essences is.

II. What the divine manifestation (through the speaking of the word of God) is.

III. How evil and good have their original from one only

[1] In.

ground, viz. light and darkness; life and death; joy
and sorrow; and how it is in its ground; also whereunto every essence and source is profitable and
necessary.[1]

IV. How all things have their ground from the Grand
Mystery, viz. from the spiration of the eternal One.

V. How the eternal One introduceth itself into sensation,
perception, and severation, to the science of itself,
and the play of the divine power.

VI. How man may attain to the true knowledge of God, and
to the knowledge of the eternal and temporal nature.

VII. Also how man may come unto the real contemplation of
the Being of all beings.

VIII. Also of the creation of the world and of all creatures.

IX. And then of the original, fall, and restoration of man;
what he is according to the first Adamical man in the
kingdom of nature: and what he is in the new regeneration in the kingdom of grace, and how the new
birth comes to pass.

X. Also what the Old and New Testaments are, each in its
understanding.

12. And we will enlarge this exposition through all the chapters of
the first Book of Moses; and signify how the Old Testament is a
figure of the New: what is to be understood by the deeds of the holy
patriarchs: wherefore the spirit of God did give them to be set down
in Moses: and at what the figures of these written histories do look,
and aim; and how the spirit of God in his children before the times of
Christ did allude with them in the figure concerning the kingdom of
Christ; whereby then God hath always represented this mercy-seat
[or throne of grace] Christ: by whom he would blot out his anger and
manifest his grace.

13. And how the whole time of this world is portrayed and
modellised, as in a watch-work: how afterwards it should go in time:
and what the inward spiritual world, and also the outward material
world, is: also what the inward spiritual man, and then the external
man of the essence of this world, is: how time and eternity are in one
another, and how a man may understand all this.

14. Now if it should so fall out that when these our writings are
read the Reader might not presently apprehend and understand the

[1] Text, unavoidable.

same (seeing this ground which yet hath its full foundation and pregnant concordance, as well with the Scripture as through the light of nature, hath for a long time been very dark, and yet by divine grace is given to plain simplicity) let him not despise and reject the same, according to the course and custom of the wicked world; but look upon the ground of practice which is therein intimated; and give himself up thereunto; and pray God for light and understanding: and at last he will rightly understand our ground, and it will find very great love and acceptance with him.

15. But we have written nothing for the proud and haughty wiselings who know enough already; and yet indeed know nothing at all; whose belly is their God, who only adhere unto the Beast of the Babylonical Whore, and drink of her poison; and wilfully will be in blindness, and the devil's snare: But we have laid (with the spirit of our knowledge) a strong bolt before the understanding of folly, not to apprehend our meaning; seeing they wilfully and willingly serve Satan, and are not the children of God.

16. But we desire to be clearly and fundamentally understood by the children of God: and do heartily and readily communicate our knowledge given to us of God; seeing the time of such revelation is born: therefore let everyone see, and take heed, what sentence and censure he passeth: Everyone shall accordingly receive his reward, and we commend him into the grace of the meek and tender love of Jesus Christ. Amen.

Sept. 11. Anno 1623.

To the Reader

THIS book of the *Mysterium Magnum,* being an exposition of Genesis, if it be read through and weighed with good attention, will remove those mists from their eyes that have not diligently perused the other writings of the author, Jacob Behm, which hath occasioned their being offended by the stumbling blocks that have lain in their way, from the misreports and relations of others who have but superficially looked upon them, and taken up surmisings at the second or third hand, and so come to be bereaved of the greatest benefit to their understandings which they would infallibly gain, if they would follow the advice in the last paragraph of the last chapter of this book, where the author saith: We admonish the reader that when he findeth somewhat in any place of our deep sense to be obscure, that he do not condemn it according to the manner of the evil world; but diligently read and pray to God, who will surely open the door of his heart, so that he will apprehend it and be able to make use of it, to the profit and salvation of his soul.

And that I also may be helpful to the furtherance of the reader, I shall descant a little upon that which may draw him with the cords of love, and clear his thoughts from some objections that perhaps hinder his setting upon the perusal of these precious writings.

Let us a little examine, though cursorily, what is done towards the satisfaction of the desire to understand: and we may observe that whosoever will bring anything to pass, must be furnished with skill beforehand, or else have a teacher stand by to direct: wherefore are all writings, but that others at a distance either for time or place may be informed of that which else they could not so easily know; what serve the registry of arts, philosophy, and histories for, but to tell succeeding generations what was in the times of their forefathers, yet that which hath been transmitted from age to age is but a relation of things done outwardly or words spoken, and few or no footsteps mentioned of the most ancient skill, which possessed the thoughts and minds of the wise men, at least, none have expressed the original ground, ways, and proceedings of their understandings, by which they arrived to such attainments: tho' Holy Scripture is the most ancient and exact, yet it everywhere, though about most hidden depths, only makes a bare relation. For instance, at first it saith thus: In the beginning God created the Heavens and the Earth: and that God said, Let there be Light, and there was Light. But it nowhere expounds what the

xi

Beginning, God, the Creation, the Heavens, the Earth, and the Light, are, nor how God did then create, or how spake and it was done; nor how done with speaking or without; Moses knew it all; and likely some of the people in that age for whom he wrote it, did understand them, or else he would have written more particularly, for he could not intend to express that which they could not fully apprehend; I cannot but think, the same God that taught him so eminently by his spirit, had so fitted the people that they were capable to receive instruction by his words; and why not we also, by the same spirit of God, since they were written for our instruction as well as theirs: how great a gift then must it needs be, that is given to this author, to expound these things fundamentally as he hath done.

The best part of man's skill consists in the knowledge of those materials that are the subject of man's working and producing of effects; it is no direct method to go about to teach youths arts and not first sufficiently furnish them with the knowledge of matter enough, to make use of, in the exercise of those arts: in mechanic works we are able to discover that many materials happen to be spoiled in the using, so that afterwards the best use of them cannot be made, as timber, bricks, stone.

The beginnings of things are therefore to be looked into, that amendment may be made of that which is amiss, for one error there will hazard the loss of labour in all that is built upon it, and ignorance in such things doth apparently stop the bringing forth any exact work for the use and benefit of the body of man, but the minds, spirits, and souls of men, which are the materials of arts and sciences, called liberal, we scarce offer to look to the husbandry, planting and meliorating of such things; though in divine skill as well as natural, we have a pattern for doing it, in that Paul did plant, and Apollos did water, though God gave the increase.

But we spend our time and thoughts so much about wordly profit and pleasures, that we care for no more knowledge than will serve the turn of the outward man, and though we hear of deeper skill that the wise men had who first invented those most useful things enjoyed and practised by us, for the necessary support of our life; we hardly believe that was ever done which we cannot do, when it is clear, that if we had their skill we might do as they did: and if the Holy Scriptures did not mention that so great works were done by Moses, the Prophets, Christ, and the Disciples, we would not believe such things had ever been done. For we are commonly so far from thinking the great works of the skilful in Egypt to have been real, that contrary to the express words of the text, theirs are accounted not real serpents, as when Moses did bid Aaron lay down his rod and it became a serpent, and the Egyptians laid down their rods and they became serpents, but Aaron's rod devoured all the rods of the Egyptians: for all this, men will suppose that the Egyptians' rods were not turned into true serpents as Aaron's was, but that they were mere delusions of the devil; and what makes us backward to believe the truth in this, but because we know not, what the rods were, nor the serpents, nor how they were so changed: which being in Exodus, the author would have explained if he had lived to perform his purpose upon the whole five Books of Moses, as he did begin and perfect this of Genesis. Neither is the transformation of Nebuchadnezzar believed, that his hairs were turned feathers and his nails into claws, as in Dan. iv. 33.

In treatises of magic are histories of strange actions, where the particular way and manner whereby they were effected is omitted: and spiritual magic operations in nature are not at all looked into, being esteemed satisfactory to the question, What are the hidden virtues of minerals, stones, plants, beasts, men? to answer, that they are occult qualities, as the powers and virtues of the loadstone, attractive of iron, and tending to the poles of the earth, are called: and the knowledge of these is so far remote from our reach, that we must first inquire the place where, and the manner how they may be discerned.

To which end we make many outward experiments, and thereby happen to cause nature to produce her wonderful effects: but few examine how the spirit of Nature works therein, she worketh under a veil or shell, within which, the Spirit produceth all its wonders, and so spiritual things are hid from our outward eyes, though visible things are a glass wherein the resemblance and similitude of all spiritual things are represented; yet of all glasses the mind itself is the more clear and undeceiving, to behold the motions of that working Spirit; all things are there, to be seen, intimately; if we will search how things come there to be produced, and what makes so many various thoughts and representations; we shall there perceive a workmaster, the Spirit which created everything in the world, and in the mind, and he who yieldeth to that Spirit, it will make known to him its own workings within and without; that, it is, which opens our understandings when we apprehend anything; and this is the Mighty God, the creator of all things, who knows when, and where, and how, itself made everything, and wrought in all wisdom, both of angels and men, and to this Spirit we must always have recourse as this author adviseth us, or we can have no true knowledge at all.

Which way would any go that they may be able to perform an excellent thing, would they not first inquire of friends or others whether they knew of any that had attained the thing, if it were concerning a piece of fine workmanship, suppose a clock or watch, sure we would ask where such a thing may be had, and we should as readily be directed to go to those that sell, but perhaps none of them were to be seen in our native habitation; if so, we would desire some to write to a rare artist abroad beyond sea, in the Indies if it were not elsewhere to be had, entreating him to describe the making of it, in a letter to a friend of his with us, and if he should return an answer concerning the parts of it, the standing, or other defects, when it is foul, or a tooth broken, or string slipt, or any other fault; this would be prized highly from so skilful a man, and we would presently look out for his friend in our own country that understandeth the language to expound this letter, that we may have the right meaning thereof: yet when that is done, we could not thereby be instructed about the materials, how to begin, what tools to have, and many other particulars, requisite to the understanding of the thing; without still further and further directions, from him: and therefore we are desirous to speak with the party himself who was able to give such directions; but then if we should hear, that person were dead who made them best and had written that letter: what advice should we next take: we should seek out whether any books or other letters have been written by that artist, and for men most conversant in reading the writings of that nature, by which means competent knowledge what the thing is may be obtained; and the same course must be taken concerning any subject whether natural or divine; this is done with much toil and expense of time and cost; but if we could have notice where one for a pattern were to be gotten we might begin to look into it, and so imitate though but weakly at first, and by a long tract of experience come to a more exact knowledge than can be attained by all the books in the world, much more than if all the learned men were set together accurately to expound those books that could be most diligently composed concerning such a thing. This contrivance is in case the party that invented or made the thing be dead, and not to be spoken with himself, for if he were alive, he could soon teach one capable of learning, how to do it as well as himself: and then by exercise that party comes to amend the invention in every particular, and makes it exact at last: and thus are divine attainments also both sought, found and gotten: these are the tedious searches that most men wander in about mechanic things. It is frequent with men, to be apprentices seven years to learn a trade, or as they properly call it a mystery, and because it is their employment by which men get their livelihoods, they are loath to divulge it, lest thereby they come short of what else they might comfortably enjoy for the maintenance of themselves and families; yet so much pains is taken for a poor transitory benefit.

Outward things are not worth the knowing, but in reference to the sustaining our life in which we are to labour in this world to the glory of our Creator; neither is this life worthy to be compared to that which is future and endureth for ever; yet the whole learning of physic is to procure health, and prevent sickness which causeth death to the present life, but hurteth not the soul nor spirit as to eternity: but let health be wanting and all other things bestowed upon men on earth are of no value, no trading, getting of estates and gain of riches, to the settling and assuring whereof that it may be enjoyed, in which the lawyer's advice is wholly employed, hath no delight in it. Some care is requisite to provide for wife, children, kindred and friends, in leaving that they have, free from entanglements, to posterity after them: yet though the exactest course be taken that the learnedst counsel can devise, the casualty of every case is such that desperate expenses happen to the ruin of vast estates; so vain is all that part of learning without health.

And then, the riches and fullest plenty of all earthly things which set the whole world on work; honour and power of dominion, stately palaces, pleasant gardens, groves, walks, meadows, fields, prospects of land, rivers, seas; full tables, dainty fare, delicate attire, great attendance, all usefulness of convenient houses, coaches, horses, beds of down, gorgeous apparel, increase of all cattle for food and clothing, fruits of the earth, all variety of commodities fetched from all parts of the world; as Solomon's navy brought gold, silver, ivory, apes and peacocks (1 Kings x. 22), so we have the same things, and precious stones, pearls, spices of all sorts, fragrant perfumes, silks, parrots, and fine singing birds, brought in by shipping in abundance.

All recreative pleasures and exercises of body, which require much time, pains and cost to be spent in them, wherein men labour for that which is not bread: yet these have their lawful use, in that men thereby become helpful and beneficial one to another, and so necessity hath brought forth many exquisite mechanic arts. There are also rare endowments of mankind, the exercises of the minds of men, as grammar for languages, logic in discoursings, rhetoric in persuasions for reconciling different affections, to the peace and comfort of human society; delight of pleasant music; arithmetic, that fundamental requisite for accountants in all commerce and traffic, without which nothing of great moment can be managed. Geometry in surveying, architecture, geography, optics or perspective, picture, sculpture, graving. Also astronomy which regulates the order of times in the transaction of civil affairs, and in navigation, husbandry, chronology: And lastly, astrology, whereby is hinted to us the pre-discovery of the change of seasons to dearth or plenty, the inclination of years, countries or persons to sickness or health, to purity or impurity of the air, dryness or moisture. And whatsoever more the arts called liberal do furnish man with, are not esteemed where there is not health of body.

And were it not that the performances, effects and works that are wrought in this mortal life, do follow the soul in the world to come, and are represented distinctly and particularly to the soul as thoughts to the mind; and as the actions of great victors are set forth in shows of triumph: it were in vain to spend our time here in anything but drowsiness and sleep: if the enjoyment of our works were not the fruit of our labours; as in the Revelation it is said, Blessed are those that die in the Lord, for they rest from their labours, and their works follow them (Rev. xiv. 13): the manner whereof being well understood would cause such circumspection and care in men, that they would endeavour to have only such works as wherein they shall have joy, and not such as shall be burned and the person suffer loss though the soul be saved, as through fire: and this at that day when the thoughts of all hearts shall be laid open; as if they were plainly limned before us in a picture to the life, and every secret thought shall be brought to judgment: the cabinet councils of the close Cabals, of emperors, kings, princes and states, and the lustful imaginations when the mouth speaks holy things in highest devotions, and the body acting in demurest posture; the cheating intentions in fairest pretences of love and friendship; the lies and falsehoods in multiplicities of words for self-ends; for if Elisha could tell what was whispered in the secret chamber of the King of Syria (2 Kings vi. 12), shall anything be hidden, when all things shall be made manifest; and then of every idle word that a man shall speak he shall give an account at the day of judgment; also we shall be judged for all things that were done in the body, whether they be good or evil: This is easily confessed to be truth, because written in the Holy Scriptures; but who knoweth how and in what sense it shall be really so, and in what manner performed; and layeth it seriously to heart.

Such things as these are only mentioned in the Scripture; the knowledge whereof would make the soul delighted whether there be health of body or not; and it is far surpassing all other books: because they set down all things necessary to eternal salvation so plainly that the meanest capacity may learn them, and it will be the greater con-demnation that men neglect so great salvation as is there discovered; they were written by those who knew exactly the mysteries of salvation, and do direct us into the paths thereof: how excellent is the understanding of them then, and how acceptable and profitable are those writings that expound them clearly: But we are for the most part willing to let the understanding of them go, or at most desire a literal knowledge only; for, those that mention the mystical exposition of things, are suspected to be deceivers; as if, though men do not so well apprehend divine and natural mysteries as they might do, we shall judge them for offering to search after, and but complaining of the want of such learning, as doth teach the understanding of them.

Whereas our Saviour himself taught his disciples the mysteries of the Kingdom of Heaven. And the Apostle Paul taught the mysteries of the Gospel, of Godliness, of Christ, of Faith, and of the Resurrection. To them that were without, all things were done in parables (Mark iv. 11), but Christ expounded the meaning of them apart to his disciples. The Scriptures instruct us, not only as to the mere relation of things done, but so that the man of God may be made perfect and ready to every good work: This man of God is the inward man, the child of God, the hidden man of the heart; Christ in us; whose flesh and blood, except we eat and drink, we have no part in him; these words of spirit and life he spake when he was yet alive upon the earth before his suffering, which made his disciples cry out this is a hard saying who can bear it; not considering that his heavenly Divine flesh and blood was in their souls, and that they did there eat and drink thereof, for they had part in him though they knew not how, at that time; yet the mortal flesh and blood shall not inherit the Kingdom of Heaven, being the old man of corruption, which is earth, and to earth shall return. These are great mysteries, and as well after they are made known as before; for they are the hidden secret operations of spiritual things, and the spirit of man only of all earthly creatures is capable to understand them; there are indeed lying wonders, spiritual wickednesses in high places, that make up the mystery of iniquity; these only deceive the soul of man by their working in the heart in the love of them, to the bringing forth their evil fruits, and not the knowing of them in the mystery, for therein they were well known to the Apostles. If men pretend they know mysteries and are not able to teach them, they are to blame, but not those that seek after them and speak what they find, and stir up others not to rest contented with that which they have, when they may get more rich treasure by searching after it.

The history of Christ, and of all other things mentioned in the Scriptures, are infallibly true, that he was born of the Virgin Mary, that he is the Saviour of the world, was crucified at Jerusalem, rose again from the dead, ascended into heaven; the relating of this doth not fully satisfy a soul; for the devils believe and know it all, and what hath been discovered and spoken from God by words since the beginning of the world, and tremble: and so may we if we learn not the mystery, signified in and by the history, and feel that Christ is born in us, in a pure, clean, chaste heart, and understand the knowledge of Christ and him crucified, than which the Apostle Paul desired not to know anything else, among the Corinthians; this was not the bare knowledge of the history, for he sayeth in a certain place, though we once knew Christ according to the flesh: as they did that conversed with him upon earth, yet now know we him so no more; then, how did he know him, but in the spirit, in the mystical knowledge?

Infinite are the mysteries mentioned in the Scriptures concerning God, angels, men, the world, eternity, time, the creation, fall, sin, corruption, the curse, misery, death, judgment, hell, devils, damnation: Christ, redemption, justification, salvation, free grace, free will, resurrection; Paradise: the Holy Ghost, sanctification, restitution, blessedness, eternal life and glory. These all concern the soul which is the eternal part of man, which no other books do teach the assured knowledge of, but the Scriptures. How should we therefore esteem that which teacheth things so satisfactory, and necessary, for the soul to learn, to eschew, or attain, in reference to eternity. Other writers have written from observations made upon experience by the outward senses from external objects, but that skill goes no further than the shell and cover of things, the spirit in nature being invisible to the

outward eyes as well as the divine Spirit: they that wrote from the
Holy Spirit had inward senses, for it is written, That which we have
seen with our eyes,[1] which we have heard with our ears,[1] and which
our hands[1] have handled of the word of life, declare we unto you; they
also saw with their eyes, things unutterable, such as no eye[2] hath
seen, or ear[2] heard, or hath entered into the heart of man[2] to conceive,
yet things which God hath undoubtedly prepared for them that love
him: some of which that are unutterable, have been declared and left
recorded for us by the holy men, and nowhere but in the Scriptures,
which hath stirred up the industry of some to collect and transmit
those writings to posterity: and in the time of the Apostles men were
diligent in reading the Old Testament, which were the only Scriptures
then, and our Saviour bids the Jews search them, saying, For in them
ye think to have eternal life, and they are they that testify of me
(John v. 39). A little after, the Bereans searched the Scriptures daily to
see whether what Paul taught were so or no: Now if any other books
would have informed them of those things, they would have sought in
those also; but we read not that they did so. This also adds to their
excellency, that he who was not behind the chiefest Apostles tells
Timothy who was also an Evangelist, and had known the Scriptures
as a child, that they are able to make him wise unto salvation, through
faith which is in Christ Jesus: how precious is that which can make us
wise to salvation: this hath been said of the Old Testament: but concerning the epistles of Paul, the Apostle Peter testifies of them, that
some do wrest them as they do also the other Scriptures: and the
worth of the New Testament further appears, in that it was written
by the Apostles, to whom God spake by his Son, and therein have
revealed him, of whom all the Prophets of old have testified; and
therein also are expressed some of the mysteries that have been hid
since the world began, and in this it is paramount to all other books:
and this hath provoked the industry of the most able learned men for
many hundreds of years to translate them into several languages out
of the original Hebrew and Greek, and so by the variety of the idiom
of the several speeches, the sense is the more explained, as the literal
expositions out of some of those translations into any one tongue not
varying the phrase, being compared with another, will manifest: they
have also taken pains to interpret the meaning of the words, some
from one ground and reason, some from another, collected, by the
understandings of several builders of one sect or other in religion;

[1] Inward, spiritual.   [2] Outward, carnal.

causing differences of opinion in all churches of dissenting brethren, each party having several reasons for the divers meanings of the same text of Scripture, but the ground of the mistake is from the working of the faculty of reason upon the subject that is spoken of; the faculty of understanding upon the inward ideas represented in the mind is the same in all men, and if it concludes upon outward observation it is called reason, in Greek, λόγος, which signifies verbum, sermo, ratio, the word, speech, reason: things meant by these are either expressed by the tongue or letters or imprinted in thoughts either from without by the senses, or from within, from God, by the understanding: the certain meaning of the words of Scripture being the jewel locked up in them, not now attainable from the Apostles by conference with them, since their decease, therefore now we should apply ourselves to the things they spake of, which are to be inquired after in the mind, and the knowledge of them to be received from God by prayer, who will open the understanding, for there is a spirit in man, and the inspiration[1] of the Almighty giveth understanding (Job xxxii. 8), and he will then teach us as he did the Apostles: and as he did this author, who by the command of the Holy Spirit wrote his deep knowledge given to him of God, and hath therein pointed out the way to us wherein we may understand what in us is divine and what natural, the new man, and the old: which is the aim and scope of the whole Bible: these new things and old are those that the scribe learned in the Kingdom of Heaven, bringeth out of his treasury, neither can any knowledge be wanting to him who enjoyeth Christ, for in him are hid all the treasures of wisdom and knowledge.

A man would wonder why Paul should pronounce so great a curse upon those that teach any other gospel, than the Galatians had received, saying, though we [himself or another Apostle] or an angel from heaven preach any other gospel besides that which we have preached unto you, and uttereth the same, if any preach any other gospel than what ye have received, let him be accursed (Gal. i. 8); now what is this gospel? it is the Gospel of Christ which they had received: if we knew Christ we should soon understand his gospel, and how they had received it, and know how justly they are accursed that preach any other: and when we know Christ as fully as his Apostles did, we shall understand from him more than we can find from their writings, though theirs, and the Prophets, all preaching the gospel, direct us to Christ and tell us where he is and what he is. The Apostle

[1] Or, breathing in, as Gen. ii. 7.

John sayeth: The Word was God, and all things were made by it, and in it was life, and the life was the light of men, and that was the true light which lighteth every man that cometh into the world. This Word Moses calleth the commandment, which is in our hearts that we may do it. Paul calleth it Christ, the word of faith which they preach; near us in our hearts and mouths. James calleth it the engrafted word which is able to save our souls, and adviseth to lay apart all filthiness and superfluity of naughtiness, and to receive it with meekness; by this it may be discerned, that the word which enlighteneth every one is engrafted even in those that have filthiness and superfluity of naughtiness, which is to be all laid apart, or that engrafted word cannot be received though it be able to save our souls, and seeing it is Christ in us, none doth question but it will save us, being received: and this is the word by which hearing, obeying, or receiving cometh, and by that hearing cometh faith (Rom. x. 17), that is, Christ cometh to be born in us: thus we see, where Christ is, what he is, and the powerful efficacy of him; and to know this feelingly and so receive this word is receiving the Gospel, the glad tidings of salvation which shall be to all men, that embrace him; and the preaching and declaring this, is that Gospel; that sound which is gone into all the earth (Ps. xix. 4; Rom. x. 18); it is the eternal Gospel: whosoever preacheth any other besides it is accursed.

Now what this word hath and doth effect, and how, in the whole creation and in every creature, in all men, and in ourselves, is the Mysterium Magnum which this author declareth exactly upon Genesis, wherein all mysteries are couched, there is not the least jot or tittle of all the rest of the books of Scripture that want a mystery, which may be apprehended, by observing how this author lays them open in this part; and will serve as an introduction to the understanding the whole Book of God, in nature and Scripture; and then we may read how our names are written in the Book of Life, which is the best and most comfortable lesson that any can learn, and then we shall not need that this author or any man teach us, for we shall all be taught of God, as is promised and firmly expected that it will be accomplished.

These things considered, and the author's serious admonitions to walk in the ways of holiness, self-denial, resignation, the new-birth, killing of our outward will and desires which rebel against God, might perhaps satisfy, and allay the stirring thoughts of them that suppose some evil purpose was intended in the disclosing of these deep mysteries, when as it is given to none to understand such things but to disciples of Christ; neither can so great a revelation as this author hath expressed enter into any heart that is not given up to follow Christ, and to forsake his own will, living in continual repentance, and taking up his cross daily, which he hath earnestly called upon all to do, in his book of *The Way to Christ*, and here and there his writings are strewed with such counsel as with sweet smelling flowers, curious both for shapes and colours, why therefore should his books be scandalised as wicked; it cannot but be acknowledged they have appeared to be dictated by the Holy Ghost, to the apprehensions of some that desire to walk in the fear of God and in the narrow path that leadeth unto life, and have found much furtherance in that way from his writings, the comfort whereof shall never be taken from them: If his writings were thoroughly weighed, men would not need that this testimony should be given of him.

But there are some that in words are so full of reproachings and bitter terms against their brethren, whose words or writings do not please their palate; that they revile one another and return bitterness for bitterness, evil for evil; whereas Michael the Archangel when he strove with the devil about the body of Moses durst not use a railing accusation, but said, the Lord rebuke thee; yet these speak evil of the things they know not: this ought not so to be, but to return good for evil; and if we know a fault in our brother, we should tell him of it in private, and if he heareth us, we have won our brother; and it is far better so than to contemn, despise, scorn and find fault with the slips and failings one of another in any kind; moreover, to be reproached, is that which every one who would be the disciple of Christ must look for in this world, and not think to be above his master; for if they have called the master of the house Beelzebub, how much more will they call them of his household (Matt. x. 25). Also there were, that said of Christ, he hath Beelzebub (Mark iii. 22). But such names cast upon any should deter none from examining the sayings or writings of any man, that they may be discerned whether they be good or evil. It may be supposed that the persons who judge evil of this author, have received misrepresentations concerning some part of his writings, that speak of magic: as if the knowledge of magic must needs be witchcraft: when if they consider that Daniel said, Destroy not the wise men of Babylon (Dan. ii. 24); and that Daniel, otherwise called Belteshazzar (Dan. iv. 8, 9), was master of the magicians: also what the Magi or wise men of the East that came to Christ were; cannot

think but they were excellent men, and had the knowledge of the
Magia, in English, magic; not to be rejected, but to be sought after,
with all diligence; that we may be able to disclose the secret workings,
and oppose the wiles of the devil and Satan, used by his wicked magi
or magicians, his instruments in this world: that (2 Kings ix. 22) the
witchcrafts of the wicked Jezebel, may be discovered; and together
with the mistress of witchcrafts, that selleth nations through her
whoredoms, and families through her witchcrafts (Nahum iii. 4), and
such as (Gal. iii. 1) bewitched the Galatians to whom Paul wrote; may
be overthrown, and destroyed utterly.

Let us study seriously to understand the things that are expressed
in the words of the Scripture, that we may not be such as speak evil of
what we know not.

We ought not to look at the mote that is in our brother's eye,
before we have pulled the beam out of our own; much rather, ought
we to be sure there is a mote in our brother's eye before we think to go
about to pull it out; some censure this author's writings to be full of
nonsense, who yet confess they cannot understand them, why do they
then judge; for, all that I apprehend not the sense of, is not nonsense
in itself, though I think it so: another great fault is found with his
hard words; now, hard words are used in the most excellent Book, and
never the worse for being hard: deep things and mysteries cannot be
expressed in easy words; some things most excellent (Rom. viii. 26;
2 Cor. xii. 4) cannot be uttered by any words; therefore 'tis happy
some other hard things may be uttered though by hard words; better
than not at all: the words we account easy in the ordinary sense, are
hard in their true sense and meaning: even the hard words of these
writings are easier to the chimick philosophers, than $\alpha, \beta, \gamma, \delta$ to one
that cannot read Greek: so one that hath not been at the School of
Mysteries or of Pentecost, it is hard for him to read the Christ-Cross-
Row.

This author writes of the mysteries of eternity before they be
produced and made perceptible to the creature, that is, before the
Creation; also of the creation of angels, before Lucifer fell, and of his
fall, and the creation of the world; as in this book at large: and if any
will peruse him carefully they will find he mentions, three Principles
of the essence of all essences, in the book of the *Three Principles*: But in
the abstract of the *Mysterium Magnum*, at the end of this book, they
may perceive, that the Abyss and God is all one: and that the Abyss is
God ineffable, not manifested but to himself, and to whom he will

reveal himself: and that, God is the Unity, in Trinity, the three eternal Principles, manifested by creation to the creature: The knowledge of which three Principles, and of the seven properties of nature, and of the ten forms of fire in the eternity, would make his writings easy and delightful.

If we would walk humbly in the sight of God, we should brotherly exhort one another, and not judge that we be not judged, for the same measure we mete shall be measured to us again: let us judge righteous judgment, and lay open that which is evil, before the sun at noonday, that all may take notice, and beware they fall not into the ditch: God that hath shed abroad his love in our hearts, enlighten our understandings that we may see the wonderful things of his law, and then we shall not so readily despise one another, and receive accusations against our brethren and their doings, and so wound some through the sides of others.

If we were released from the virulency of the spirit of the outward man, which figured him in the mother's womb, and constellated him, when he was born, and when he first breathed the outward air as a seminal breath; which is prone to all manner of lusts, and draweth men to sin: if this were allayed by a daily temperance, and practice to mortify our members that are on the earth, by bringing down the body daily; labouring for an humble and contrite heart, a broken spirit, and a mourning soul, repenting from the bottom of our hearts, amending our lives continually, purifying, and communing with our hearts, and not suffer any iniquity or evil to lodge in the desires of our most inward thoughts: we should soon perceive, upon filling our bodies with outward food, the stirring of lust, to swelling pride, raging malice and anger, stinging envy, greedy covetousness, grudging the good of others, pleasing lasciviousness, a wandering eye after the applause, honour, and pleasure of this world; but upon fasting, this spirit is not felt almost, in the body: as we may observe in ourselves every moment: but an inclination to love, meekness, self-denial, patience, forbearance, and all virtues, the Spirit of God, reviving in us; and we may thereby somewhat perceive, why the Prophets said: The word of the Lord came unto me, saying, thus saith the Lord; whereas the word was in them before, only this spirit of life brought forth the word, from the Lord, in their hearts, into their minds and understandings that they felt it stirring or speaking anew: and further, we shall be able to discern what enemy we have to deal with in our fighting the good fight of faith: the world and the delights thereof is a great enemy, which we must overcome, or we cannot attain to the denial of ourselves, and taking up the cross of Christ, without which we cannot be his disciple; but we are subject to think, that crosses, adversities, and afflictions are our worst enemies, because we live not by faith, but by the outward spirit, which all crosses do kill in us, and by them we die daily, to that, which is the instrument of sin, whereby its desires are brought to effect: and therefore we account that our greatest friend which is our greatest enemy: it brings death, our last enemy, and is the sting thereof, but by killing the desires of the flesh we shall live and do thereby daily overcome that last enemy which we must certainly have a combat with, seeing it is appointed for all men once to die, and after death cometh judgment. If we be earnest and watchful in our fight, we shall be victorious over the first death, and on such the second death can have no power, which is the effect of the judgment: But having overcome that; then, when Christ who is our life (in the faith of the Son of God) shall appear, we shall also appear with him in glory.

How excellent a thing is it now, to understand the things expressed in the Holy Scriptures, that they may not be a dead letter having no comfort in them, for none can rejoice to die except he feel the virtue of the life of Christ, killing sin in the mortal flesh; for therefore we must serve the Lord with fear and rejoice in him with trembling, because it it not safe for us to have our outward spirit wherein is the life of sin to rejoice without trembling. How cheerful would men be in soul and conscience, to run the ways of God's commandments, if they had killed sin, that they might rejoice to die; and so were filled with assured hope to enjoy the crown of victory which is laid up for them, and which Christ, through whom we have victory, shall give us. How doth it comfort an afflicted soul to consider, that afflictions, though they be grievous for a time, are not to be compared with the eternal joys that are laid up for us. But if the transcendent sayings of the holy Apostles and Prophets be not understood, they are but dead to us and so are we to them.

To conclude, let the reader know that more than half this book was translated into English by my dear kinsman, Mr John Ellistone, who departed this life at Gestingthorp in the county of Essex, on the 22nd of August 1652, about one of the clock in the morning: and so went into the mystery, where his soul enjoyeth the fruits of his labours of love, which those shall also do that walk in the same path, and I among the rest may in my appointed time be found in Christ

TO THE READER

worthy and capable to come to the innumerable company of angels,
though now I deserve to be accounted

One of the unworthiest of the children of men,

JOHN SPARROW.

De Mysterio Magno

OF THE

GRAND MYSTERY

THAT IS

Of the Manifestation of the Divine Word through the Three Principles of the Divine Essence

The First Chapter

What the Manifested God is: and of the Trinity

1. IF we would understand what the new birth is, and how it is brought[1] to pass, then we must first know what man is, and how he is the image of God; and what the divine indwelling[2] is; also what the revealed God is; of whom man is an image.

2. When I consider what God is, then I say, He is the One; in reference to the creature, as an eternal Nothing; he hath neither foundation, beginning, nor abode; he possesseth nothing, save only himself; he is the will of the abyss; he is in himself only one; he needeth neither space, nor place; he begetteth himself in himself, from eternity to eternity; he is neither like nor resembleth any thing; and hath no peculiar place where he dwelleth;[3] the eternal wisdom or understanding is his dwelling; he is the will of the wisdom; the wisdom is his manifestation.

3. In this eternal generation we are to understand three things, viz. 1. An eternal will. 2. An eternal mind of the will. 3. The egress[4] from the will and mind, which is a spirit of the will and mind.

4. The will is father; the mind is the conceived[5] of the will, viz. the seat or habitation of the will, or the centre to something; and it is the

---

[1] Wrought, or effected.
[2] Or how God dwelleth in man, and filleth all things with his presence.
[3] Or no sundry habitation above the stars in an empyrean heaven, as reason fancieth.
[4] Efflux, effluence, the proceeding-forth.   [5] Comprehension or receptacle.

will's heart; and the egress of the will and mind is the power and spirit.

5. This threefold[1] spirit is one only essence, and yet it is no essence, but the eternal understanding, an original of the something: and yet it is the eternal hiddenness[2] (just as the understanding of man is not confined in time and place, but is its own comprehension and seat), and the egress of the spirit is the eternal original contemplation, viz. a lubet of the spirit.

6. The egressed[3] is called the lubet of the Deity, or the eternal wisdom, which is the eternal original of all powers, colours and virtues; by which the threefold spirit comes, in this lubet, to a desiring, namely, of the powers, colours, and virtues; and its desiring is an impressing, a conceiving itself: The will conceiveth the wisdom in the mind, and the conceived in the understanding is the eternal word of all colours, powers, and virtues; which the eternal will expresseth[4] by the spirit from the understanding of the mind.

7. And this speaking is the motion or life of the Deity, an eye of the eternal seeing, where one power, colour and virtue doth know each of the others, and doth distinguish each from the other; and yet they all stand in equal proportion[5] or analogy, devoid of weight, limit or measure, also undivided one from another. All the powers, colours and virtues lie in one; and it is a distinct, mutual, well-tuned, pregnant harmony; or, as I might say, a speaking word, in which word or speaking all speeches, powers, colours and virtues are contained, and with the pronouncing or speaking they unfold themselves, and bring themselves into sight and ken.

8. This is now the eye of the abyss, the eternal chaos, wherein all (whatsoever eternity and time hath) is contained; and it is called Counsel, Power, Wonder and Virtue. Its peculiar and proper name is called GOD, or JEOVA, or JEHOVAH, who is outside of all nature, without all beginnings of any essence, a working in himself, generating, finding, or perceiving himself; without any kind of source from any thing, or by any thing: He hath neither beginning nor end, he is immeasurable, no number can express his largeness, and great-ness, he is deeper than any thought can reach; he is nowhere far from any thing, or nigh unto any thing; he is through all, and in all: his birth is everywhere, and without and besides him there is nothing else: he is time and eternity, byss and abyss, and yet nothing com-prehends him save the true understanding, which is God himself.

[1] Or Tri-Une.   [2] Or mystical Mystery.
[3] That which is flown forth from the one eternal will.
[4] Or speaketh forth.   [5] Text, property.

The Second Chapter

Of the Word or Heart of God

1. THIS is now what Saint John saith, ch. 1, *In the beginning was the Word, and the Word was with God, and God was the Word. The same was in the beginning with God.* The Word is the will of the abyss: (*beginning*) is the conception [or apprehension] of the will, where it conceiveth and bringeth itself into an eternal beginning. The (*Word*)[1] is now the conceived, which in the will is a nothing, and with the conception there is a generation; this was in the beginning with the will, and in the will; but with the lubet of the will it receiveth its beginning in the conception of the will, therefore it is called [a] Heart, viz. a centre, or life-circle, wherein the original of the eternal life is.

2. And John saith further: *By the same were all things made; and without it was not any thing made that was made. In it was the life; and the life was the light of men.* Here, O man, take now this light of life, which was in the Word, and is eternal, and behold the being of all beings, and especially thyself, seeing thou art an image, life, and being of the unsearchable God, and a likeness as to him. Here consider time and eternity, heaven, hell, the world, light and darkness, pain and source, life and death, something and nothing. Here examine thyself, whether thou hast the light and life of the Word in thee, so that thou art able to see and understand all things. For thy life was in the Word, and was made manifest in the image which God created; it was breathed into it from the spirit of the Word. Now lift up thy understanding in the light of thy life, and behold the formed Word; consider its inward generation, for all is manifest in the light of life.

3. Sayest thou: I cannot, I am corrupt and depraved? Hear me! thou art not as yet born again of God; otherwise, if thou hadst again that same light, then thou couldst. Go to, then! we all indeed come far short of the glory which we ought to have in God; but I will shew thee somewhat: Have a care, and conceive it aright; be not a mocker, as the confused Babel is. Lo! when we would speak of the being of all beings, then we say, that from God and through God are all things. For Saint John saith also: *without him was not any thing made that was made.*

---

[1] *Wort* signifieth *the Word*. Which words in the High Dutch he expounds according to the language of Nature.

4. Now saith reason, Whence or how hath God made good and evil, pain and source, life and death? Is there any such will in God which maketh the evil? Here reason beginneth to speculate, and will apprehend it; but reason goeth only about the outside of the circle, and cannot enter in; for it is without, and not in, the word of the life-circle.

5. Now then, behold thyself, and consider what thou art, view what the outward world is, with its dominion; and thou wilt find that thou, with thy outward spirit and being, art the outward world. Thou art a little world out of the great world, thy outward light is a chaos of the sun and stars, else thou couldst not see by the light of the sun.[1] The stars give the essence of discrimination or differentiation in the intellective sight. Thy body is fire, air, water, earth; therein also lieth the metalline property, for of whatsoever the sun with the stars is a spirit, of that the earth with the other elements is a being,[2] a coagulated power. What the superior [being] is, that also is the inferior; and all the creatures of this world are the same.

6. When I take up a stone or clod of earth and look upon it, then I see that which is above and that which is below, yea, [I see] the whole world therein; only, that in each thing one property happeneth to be the chief and most manifest; according to which it is named. All the other properties are jointly therein; only, in various diverse degrees and centres, and yet all the degrees and centres are but one only centre. There is but one only root whence all things proceed: it severiseth itself only in the compaction, where it is coagulated: its original is as a smoke or vaporous breath or exhalation from the Great Mystery of the expressed Word; which standeth in all places in the re-expressing, that is, in the re-breathing (or echoing forth), a likeness according to itself; an essence according to the spirit.

7. But now we cannot say that the outward world is God, or the speaking Word, which in itself is devoid of such essence; or likewise [we cannot say] that the outward man is God: but it is all only the expressed Word, which hath so coagulated itself in its re-conception to its own expression; and doth still continually coagulate itself with the four elements, through the spirit of the desire (viz. of the stars), and bringeth itself into such a motion and life; in the mode and manner as the eternal speaking Word maketh a Mystery (which is spiritual) in itself; which Mystery I call the centre of the eternal nature; where the eternal speaking Word bringeth itself into a generation, and also

[1] Or receive light from the sun.   [2] Essence substance or body.

4

maketh in itself such a spiritual world as we have materially in the expressed Word.

8. For, I say, the inward world is the heaven wherein God dwelleth; and the outward world is expressed out of the inward, and hath only another beginning than the inward, but yet out of the inward. It is expressed from the inward through the motion of the eternal speaking Word, and closed into a beginning and end.

9. And the inward world standeth in the eternal speaking Word: The eternal Word hath spoken it (through the wisdom) out of its own powers, colours and virtues, into an essence, as a Great Mystery, from eternity; which essence also is only as a spiration from the Word in the wisdom, which hath its re-conception (to generation) in itself; and with the conception doth likewise coagulate itself, and introduceth itself into forms, after the manner of the generation of the eternal Word; as the powers, colours and virtues do generate themselves in the Word (through the wisdom), or as I might say, out of the wisdom in the Word.

10. Therefore there is nothing nigh unto or afar off from God; one world is in the other, and all are only one: But one is spiritual, the other corporeal, as soul and body are in each other; and also time and eternity are but one thing, yet in distinct or different beginnings. The spiritual world in the internal [Principle] hath an eternal beginning, and the outward a temporal; each hath its birth in itself. But the eternal speaking Word ruleth through and over all; yet it can neither be apprehended nor conceived, either by the spiritual or by the external world, that it should stand still; but it worketh from eternity to eternity, and its work[1] is conceived. For it is the formed Word, and the working Word is its life, and is incomprehensible; for the Word is without all essence, as a bare understanding only, or as a power that bringeth[2] itself into essence.

11. In the inward spiritual world the Word conceiveth itself into a spiritual essence, as one only element, wherein the four lie hid. But when God, viz. the Word, moved this one element, then the hidden properties did manifest themselves; as there are four elements.

---

[1] Or operation.
[2] Or worketh itself out in the essence.

The Third Chapter

How out of the Eternal Good an Evil is come to be; which in the Good had[1] no beginning to the Evil. And of the Original of the Dark World, or Hell, wherein the Devils dwell

1. Now, since light and darkness, moreover, pain and source are seen in the outward world, and yet all originally proceed from the eternal Mystery, viz. from the inward spiritual world, and the inward spiritual world proceedeth out of the eternal generating and speaking Word, thereupon we are to consider, How, out of the eternal good an evil is come to be, which, in the good, hath no beginning to the evil: Whence darkness, pain and source arise: And then, from whence a lustre or light ariseth in the darkness.

2. For we cannot say that the eternal light, or the eternal darkness, is created; otherwise they would be in a time and a comprehensive beginning; which is not so. For they are concomitant in the generation, yet not in the wisdom or generation of the Word of the Deity; but they take their original in the desire of the speaking Word.

3. For in the eternal speaking Word, which is beyond or without all nature or beginning, is only the divine understanding or sound; in it there is neither darkness nor light, neither thick nor thin, neither joy nor sorrow; moreover, no sensibility or perceivancy;[2] but it is barely a power of the understanding in one source, will and dominion; there is neither friend nor foe unto it, for it is the eternal good, and nothing else.

4. Seeing then this eternal good cannot be an insensible essence (for so it were not manifest to itself), it introduceth itself in itself into a lubet, to behold and see what itself is; in which lubet is the wisdom: and then the lubet, thus seeing what itself is, bringeth itself into a desire to find out and feel what itself is, viz. to a sensible perceivance of the smell and taste of the colours, powers and virtues: and yet no perceivancy could arise in the free spiritual lubet, if it brought not itself into a desire, like a hunger.

[1] Or hath.   [2] Finding or apprehension.

5. For the nothing hungereth after the something, and the hunger is the desire, viz. the first Verbum Fiat, or creating power: For the desire hath nothing that it is able to make or conceive. It conceiveth only itself, and impresseth itself, that is, it coagulateth itself, it draweth itself into itself, and comprehends itself, and bringeth itself from abyss into byss; and overshadoweth itself with its magnetical attraction; so that the nothing is filled, and yet remains as a nothing; it is only a property, viz. a darkness. This is the eternal original of the darkness: for where there is a property there is already something; and the something is not as the nothing: It yieldeth obscurity,[1] unless something else, viz. a lustre, doth fill it; and then 'tis light, and yet it remaineth a darkness in the property.

6. In this coagulation, or impression, or desire, or hunger, by any of which I might express it to the understanding; I say, in this compaction or comprehensive complication we are to understand two things: 1. The free lubet, which is the wisdom, power, and virtue of the colours: and 2. The desire of the free lubet in itself. For the free lubet, viz. the wisdom, is no property; it is free from all inclination, and is one with God; but the desire is a property. Now the desire ariseth from the lubet; therefore the desire doth conceive and comprehend the free lubet all along in the compaction, in the impression; and bringeth it also into feeling and finding.

7. And understand us aright and punctually here: The desire ariseth out of the will to the free lubet, and maketh itself out of the free lubet, and bringeth itself into a desire; for the desire is the Father's property. And the free lubet, viz. the wisdom, is the Son's property; albeit God, seeing that he is a[2] Spirit, is not called Father, or Son in this place, until the manifestation through the fire in the light; and there he is called Father and Son. But I set it down by reason of the birth of nature, for a better understanding of the true ground; that man might understand to what Person in the Deity, nature, and to what the power in nature, is to be ascribed.

THE CENTRE OF THE ETERNAL NATURE: HOW THE WILL OF THE ABYSS BRINGETH ITSELF INTO NATURE AND FORM

8. The desire proceeding from the will of the abyss is the first form, and it is the Fiat, or, *Let there Be*. And the power of the free lubet

---

[1] Or causeth darkness.   [2] Or one.

is God, who governeth the Fiat, and both together are named Verbum Fiat, that is, the eternal Word, which createth where nothing is; and [is] the original of nature, and of all essences.

9. ♄[1] The first property of the desire is astringent, harsh, impressing, self-conceiving, self-overshadowing; and it maketh, first, the great darkness of the abyss: Secondly, it maketh itself substantial in a spiritual manner, wholly rough, harsh, hard and thick, and it is a cause of coldness, and all keenness and sharpness; also of all whatsoever that is called essence: and it is the beginning of perceivancy, wherein the free lubet doth find and perceive itself, and introduceth the contemplation of itself. But the desire in itself bringeth itself thereby into pain and source: Yet the free lubet doth only so receive finding [or perceivancy].

10. ☿[2] The second form or property is the constringency [or attraction] of the desire; that is, a compunction, stirring or motion. For each desire is attractive and constringent, and is the beginning of motion, stirring and life, and the true original of the Mercurial life of the painful [or tormenting] source. For here ariseth the first enmity between the astringency or hardness, and the compunction or string of stirring; for the desire maketh hard, thick, and congealeth, as the cold stiffeneth and freezeth the water. Thus the astringency is a mere raw coldness, and the compunction, viz. the attraction, is yet brought forth with the impression [or close constringent desire].

11. It is even here as father and son; the father would be still, and hard, and the compunction, viz. his son, stirreth in the father, and causeth unquietness, and this the father, viz. the astringency, cannot endure; and therefore he attracteth the more eagerly and earnestly in the desire, to hold and shut in the disobedient son; whereby the son groweth only more strong in the compunction.[3] And this is the true ground and cause of sense, which in the free lubet is the eternal beginning of the motion[4] of the powers, colours and virtues, and of the divine kingdom of joy; and in the dark desire it is the original of enmity, pain and torment; and of the eternal original of God's anger, and of all unquietness and contrariety [or antipathy].

12. ♂ The third property is the anguish,[5] or source, or welling forth, which the two first properties make. When the compunction, viz. the stirring, striveth and moveth with rage in the hardness or impression, and bruiseth the hardness, then in the contrition[6] of the

---

[1] ♄ Saturnus.   [2] ☿ Mercurius.   [3] Or sting.
[4] Or manifestation.   [5] ♂ Mars. Contrition or distress.   [6] Brokenness.

hardness the first sense of feeling doth arise, and is the beginning of the essences; for it is the severation whereby, in the free lubet, in the word of the powers, each power becometh severable and sensible[1] in itself. It is the origin of distinction, or differentiation, whereby the powers are, each in itself, mutually manifest; also the origin of the senses and of the mind.

13. For the eternal mind is the all-essential power of the Deity: but the senses arise through nature with the motion in the division or differentiation of the powers, where each power doth perceive and feel itself in itself. It is also the origin of taste and smell. When the perceivance of the powers in the distinction hath mutual intercourse and entrance into each other, then they feel, taste, smell, hear and see one another; and herein ariseth the joy of life, which, in the stillness of the power of God in the liberty, could not be. Therefore the divine understanding bringeth itself into spiritual properties, that it might be manifest to itself, and be a working life.

14. Now we are to consider of the anguish in its own generation and peculiar property: for just as there is a mind, viz. an understanding, in the liberty, in the Word of the power of God, so likewise the first will to the desire bringeth itself in the desire of the darkness into a mind; which mind is the anguish-source, viz. a sulphurous-source: and yet here only spirit is to be understood.

15. The anguish-source is thus to be understood: The astringent desire conceiveth itself, and draweth[2] itself into itself, and maketh itself full, hard and rough: now the attraction is an enemy of the hardness. The hardness is retentive, the attraction is fugitive: the one will into itself, and the other will out of itself; but since they cannot sever and part asunder one from the other they remain in each other as a rotating wheel: the one will ascend, the other descend.

16. For the hardness causeth substance and weight, and the compunction giveth spirit and the active[3] life: These both mutually circulate in themselves and out of themselves, and yet cannot go any whither [parted]. What the desire, viz. the magnet, maketh hard, that the attraction doth again break in pieces, and it is the greatest unquietness in itself, like a raging madness: and is in itself a horrible anguish; and yet no right feeling is perceived[4] until the fire [ariseth, or until the enkindling of the fire in nature, which is the fourth form, wherein the manifestation of each life appeareth]. And I leave it to the

[1] Feeling or distinct.   [2] Contracteth.   [3] Text, flying.
[4] Or to be understood.

9

consideration of the true understanding searcher of nature, what this is or meaneth; let him search and bethink himself; he will find it in his own natural and paternal knowledge.

17. The anguish maketh the sulphurous spirit, and the compunction maketh the Mercury, viz. the work-master of nature: he is the life of nature, and the astringent desire maketh the keen salt-spirit; and yet all three are only one; but they divide themselves into three forms, which are called Sulphur, Mercurius and Sal: These three properties do impress the free lubet into themselves, that it also giveth a material essentiality, which is the oil of these three forms (viz. their life and joy), which doth quench and soften their wrathfulness; and this no rational man can deny. There is a salt, brimstone and oil in all things; and the Mercurius, viz. the vital venom[1] maketh the essence in all things, and so the abyss bringeth itself into byss and nature.

18. ☉[2] The fourth form of nature is the enkindling of the fire, where the sensitive[3] and intellective life doth first arise, and the hidden God manifesteth himself: For without nature he is hidden unto all creatures, but in the eternal and temporal nature he is perceived and manifest.

19. And this manifestation is first effected[4] by the awakening of the powers, viz. by the three above-mentioned properties, Sulphur, Mercurius and Sal, and therein the oil [is manifested], in which the life hath[5] its vital being and radiance, life and lustre. The true life is first manifest in the fourth form, viz. in the fire and light; in the fire the natural, and in the light the oily spiritual; and in the power of the light the divine intellectual [or understanding life is manifest].

20. Reader, attend and mark aright: I understand here, with the description of nature, the eternal, not the temporal nature. I shew thee only the temporal nature thereby; for it is expressed or spoken forth out of the eternal, and therefore do not foist in or allege calves, cows or oxen, as 'tis the course of irrational reason in Babel to do.

21. First know this: That the divine understanding doth therefore introduce itself into fire, that its eternal lubet might be majestical and lustrous,[6] for the divine understanding receiveth no source into itself, it also needeth none to its own being, for the all needeth not the something. The something is only the play of the all, wherewith the all doth melodise and play; and, that the universal or all might be manifest unto itself, it introduceth its will into properties. Thus we,

---

[1] Or poison-life. [2] ☉ Sol. [3] Feeling and understanding.
[4] Or brought to pass. [5] Text, burneth and shineth. [6] Or a light.

as a creature, will write of the properties, viz. of the manifested God, how the all, viz. the abyssal, eternal understanding manifests itself.

22. Secondly, the abyssal and divine understanding doth therefore introduce itself into an anxious fire-will and life, that its great love and joy, which is called God, might be manifest; for if all were only one, then the one would not be manifest unto itself; but by the manifestation the eternal good is known, and maketh a kingdom of joy; else, if there were no anguish, then joy were not manifest unto itself; and there would be but one only will, which would do continually one and the same thing. But if it introduceth itself into contrariety, then in the contest the lubet of joy becomes a desire and a love play to itself, in that it hath to work and act; to speak according to our human capacity.

23. The original of the eternal spiritual and natural fire is effected by an eternal conjunction or copulation, not each severally, but both jointly, viz. the divine fire, which is a love-flame, and (2) the natural fire, which is a torment and consuming source. Understand it thus:

24. One part, viz. the will of the Father, or of the abyss, introduceth itself into the greatest sharpness of the astringency, where it is a cold fire, a cold painful source; and it is sharpened by the astringent compunctive anguish, and in this anguish it comes to desire the liberty, viz. the free lubet, or meekness. And the other part is the free lubet, which desireth to be manifest; it longeth after the will of the Father, which hath generated it out of or beyond nature; and useth it for his play. This here doth again desire the will; and the will hath here re-conceived itself to go again out of the anguish into the liberty, viz. into the lubet.

25. Understand, that it is the re-conceived will that desireth the free lubet of God. But now it hath taken into itself the horrible astringent hard compunctive sharpness; and the free lubet is a great meekness; in reference to the wrathful nature, as a nothing, and yet it is. Now both these dash together in one another. The sharp will eagerly and mightily desireth the free lubet, and the lubet desireth the austere will; and as they enter into and feel each other, a great flagrat is made, like a flash of lightning, in manner as the fire or lightning is enkindled in the firmament.

26. And in this flagrat the fire is enkindled. For the astringent harsh darkness, which is cold, is dismayed at the light and great meekness of the free lubet, and becomes in itself a flagrat of death, where the wrathfulness and cold property retireth back into itself, and

closeth up itself as a death. For in the flagrat the dark mind becomes essential; it sadly betakes itself into itself, as an ownness, as a great fear[1] before the light, or as an enmity of the light. And this is the true original of the dark world, viz. of the abyss, into which the devils are thrust, which we call hell.

[1] As being afraid, or dismayed at the light.

The Fourth Chapter

Of the Two Principles, viz. God's Love, and Anger: of Darkness, and Light: Very necessary for the Reader to consider of

1. IN this flagrat or enkindling of the fire two kingdoms sever themselves, and yet are only one. But they divide to one another, the one comprehends not the other in its own source; and yet they proceed from one original, and are dependent on one another; and the one without the other were a nothing, and yet both receive their source from one original. Understand it thus:

2. When the blaze or flagrat ariseth, then it is in the punctum, and maketh in the twink a triangle **ʌ**, or a ⊕ cross, and this is the true meaning of the character ⊕̇. First, it is the keenness (*alias*, the Creator) of all things; and the manifested God in Trinity. The triangle betokeneth the hidden God, viz. the Word, or divine understanding, which is threefold in its eternal un-inchoative birth; and yet only one in its manifestation. In the fire- or light-world this trinity doth manifest itself in the birth. Not as if there were any place where such a figure did stand; no, but the whole birth is so; wherever the divine fire manifesteth itself in anything it maketh in its enkindling a triangle **ʌ**; which the children of men ought seriously to observe, and how likewise the life doth enkindle itself in a triangle: which betokeneth the Holy Trinity. And since the light of life was in the Word of the Deity, which [Word] was breathed into man (as John saith in his first chapter), and yet did disappear in Paradise in relation to God; therefore it must be born again on the **T**.

THE EXPOSITION OF THE FOREGOING CHARACTERS

3. The upper cross betokeneth the unformed Word in Trinity, outside of all nature, and the character is thus set ⚲; and this character betokeneth the formed Word ⊕̇, viz. the angelical world. See *Signatura Rerum*, Ch. 14:32.

4. But that the triangle with the three straight cusps hath changed itself into such a **T**, on which death was slain, doth point and betoken unto us the great love of God, which hath freely sunk or plunged

itself again into our humanity out of the triangle, when we were departed from the triangle in the light of life.

5. Therefore the great angle waveth downwards, betokening the great humility, and also that we have lost the fiery angle which ascends on high, in which we were the image and likeness of God. Therefore the angle in the regeneration in the **T** hath turned itself downward; and ascends not upward any more with its cusp. Betokening now unto us the true resignation under the **T**, where we in the spirit of Christ shall, through the great humility of God, be born again in the light.

6. Now the will severs itself in the fire's flagrat into two kingdoms, where each dwelleth in itself, viz. the flagrat in the darkness is God's anger; and the flagrat in the reconception to the free lubet becomes the highly triumphant divine kingdom of joy in the free lubet. For thus the free lubet is elevated [predominant], and is brought into a wrestling love-play, and so it becomes springing and working.

7. Not that we mean that God thus receiveth a beginning: but it is the eternal beginning of *the manifestation of God*, viz. how the divine understanding doth manifest itself with power in distinct variety, and worketh itself forth into a kingdom; which is an eternal generation. We only speak here how the invisible, unperceivable God doth introduce himself into perception for his own manifestation.

8. Now we are to understand by the enkindling of the fire, a twofold fire, a twofold spirit, and a twofold essence, viz. a love-fire in the free lubet, which is made essential with [or through] the impression or desire; and in the fire the spirit and essence do severise; and yet they are mutually in one another, as soul and body are one. And now, as the spirit is, so is the essence. And as, in the impression of the free lubet, there is a holy sweet essence, and a holy sweet spirit, so likewise in the dark impression there is an astringent, harsh, raw and bitter essence and spirit. As the essence is, so also is the mind of the understanding and will in the essence.

9. Albeit, in reference to the temporal the eternal [essence] is spiritual, yet the true spirit is much more subtile than that which it maketh to a substance in the conception; for out of the substance the true intellective spirit primarily proceedeth, which before the substance is only a will, and not manifest to itself: for the will doth therefore introduce itself into substance and essence that it might be manifest to itself.

10. Now we are to consider of the severation in the fire: When the

fire is enkindled, then is the fire-blaze or flagrat salnitral, where the powers do mutually unfold and display themselves, and come into division; where the eternal only power of God doth manifest itself, and in the distinction or differentiation doth sunder itself into properties, both spiritually and substantially, as is to be seen in this world, whence also the manifold salts do arise; which with the creation came to be such matter, which in the eternity was only a spiritual essence, but in the beginning of time became gross and hard.

11. Also the manifold spirits, both good and evil, do originally spring from this eternal root; and likewise the manifold stars with the four elements, and all whatsoever that liveth and moveth. But the separation in itself is thus to be understood: when the blaze ariseth, then, out of the fire proceedeth the severation; the fire-flagrat is consuming, it apprehendeth the conceived essence, both in the free lubet and in the austere impression, and consumes it in the twinkling of an eye, for here the eternal will, which is an abyss, becomes manifest in the fire; no essence can subsist before it; it devoureth all into its nothing.

12. And here is the original of the eternal death or devoration; and in this devoration is the highest arcanum or secret, for the true essential lively spirit and understanding proceedeth out of this devoration, and maketh another beginning; for the first beginning is God's, who introduceth himself from the abyss into byss to his own contemplation. But this beginning, which proceedeth again out of the devoration, is a spiritual beginning, and maketh three worlds, namely, 1. The dark fire-world in heat and cold; a rawness, wholly austere, devoid of essence: 2. The other world is the spiritual, light or angelical world: 3. And the third hath its beginning with the beginning of time. When God moved both the inward worlds, he thence brought forth and created this outward visible world into a form of time.

13. Now the separation in the fire of devoration is thus to be understood: The powers, which the first impression made essential, are in the fire reduced into a spiritualness, viz. I. From the free lubet proceedeth forth a spiritual Mysterium, which is, as to the Deity (viz. the eternal understanding), spiritual; and it is the angelical light and life, and also the real human [life]; and so of all whatsoever that is like unto them, for they are powers of God. Therefore the angels bear in themselves the great name of God: and likewise do all true men who have the divine power.

14. II. From the essence of the free lubet there proceedeth forth in the fire an oily power, which is the body or essence of the understanding; therein the fire burneth, and thence the shining lustre or glance ariseth. III. From the understanding and spiritual oil there proceedeth forth a moving lubet like an element, and it is also the divine element.

15. IV. Out of the element there proceedeth forth a watery property; and yet it is only to be understood spiritually. This is the water of which Christ said, he would give us to drink; *and whosoever should drink thereof, it should spring up in him to a fountain of eternal life* (John iv. 14). It is *the water above the firmament,* of which Moses speaketh, that God hath separated from the external waters under the firmament. This watery and elemental property proceedeth from the essence of the free lubet, which is consumed in the fire; and the Word of the understanding (which hath now manifested itself in the fire) doth express these powers from itself, as a living and moving essence: and herein the angelical world is understood.

16. In the separation which is from the dark property there proceedeth forth, through the speaking Word in the separation out of the fire, viz. out of the astringent harsh impression, First, a hellish thirsty wrathful source, being as another principle, or as a beginning of another property; which source is wholly rough, like the cold or hard stones; a mind which is horrible, like to the fire-blaze. Secondly, there proceedeth forth from this fiery spirit, from the darkness, an oil which is of a poisonful property, for it is the evil Mercurius arising from the compunction in the anxious astringency.

17. Thirdly, the anguish likewise maketh a moving mind, like the element, but altogether in an exceeding wrathful, very piercing property; in which the great fire's might and will in the anger of God, or the wrath of God, ariseth. Which Lucifer desired to be, and to rule therein; and therefore he is a devil, that is, one spewed out of the love-fire into the dark fire. Fourthly, there proceedeth forth also from the wrathful property, through the devoration in the fire, viz. from the first dark impression, a watery property: but it is much rather a poisonful source, in which the life of darkness consisteth.[1]

18. But my writing here of the oil and water is thus to be understood: In the enkindling of the fire in the flagrat (both in the flagrat of joy in the ens of the free lubet, and in the flagrat of the wrathfulness in the impression of the dark spiritual ens), the essence, which the first

[1] Text, the dark life burneth.

desire hath coagulated or amassed, is consumed in the fire-flagrat; that is, it doth, as 'twere, die to its selfhood, and is taken into the only spirit, which here hath manifested itself in the fire of the wrathfulness, and in the light-fire of the kingdom of joy; which [spirit] doth now re-express it, or breathe it forth again out of itself, as two spiritual worlds.

19. Understand it aright: There proceedeth forth out of the fiery property in the spiration the vital source; which according to the free lubet is holy and joyful, and according to the darkness is painful and wrathful. The wrathfulness and painful source is the root of joy, and the joy is the root of the enmity of the dark wrathfulness: So that there is a contrarium, whereby the good is made manifest and known that it is good.

20. And the mortified essence in the fire (which the first desire in the free lubet hath coagulated and made dark) proceedeth forth through the fire-death as a spiritual oil, which is the property of the fire and light; and out of the mortification there proceedeth a water, viz. a mortified senseless essence, as a house of the oil, wherein the fire-source or spirit hath its vital dominion; which oil is the food of the fire-source, which it draweth again into itself, and devoureth, and thereby quencheth the fire-source, and introduceth it into the greatest meekness, in which the life of the great love ariseth, viz. the good taste. So that the fire-source becometh a humility or meekness in the oil, through the mortification in the water-source.

21. For no fire-spirit can be meek without the mortification of its own natural propriety or peculiar essence; but the water, which before was an essence, amassed out of the free lubet, and yet mortified in the fire, that can change the essence of the fire into a meek desire.

The Fifth Chapter

Of the Five Senses

Love-fire ♀[1] Venus

1. THE fifth form or property is the love-desire, viz. the holy life, or the unfolded light-fire, which is awakened or raised up in the wrathful consuming fire, that is, it receiveth its lustre and shine from the fire. A similitude whereof we have in all outward fires, where we see that the light ariseth in the fire; but yet hath far another source than the fire, for the fire is painful, but the light is meek, pleasant, lovely, and yieldeth essence.

2. The fire causeth light and air, and out of the air cometh the water by reason of the meekness of the light, for the air to the fire is mortified in the fire-blaze. And so that which is mortified in the fire is a meek essence, yet it's only a spirit; but when it proceedeth from the fire in the light it coagulateth, and is the death of the fire, whereby the fire goeth out. But if it be of a spiritual nature it is the food and refreshment of the fire; and we see plainly that every burning fire putteth forth an air, and out of the air a water; which air and watery spirit the fire draweth again into itself, for its own life and lustre; else, if it cannot have it, it is soon extinct and goeth out, that is, it smothers; for the air is its life, and yet it begetteth the air.

3. Thus likewise we are to consider of the divine being, how the eternal understanding of the abyss introduceth itself into the byss and essence, viz. into an eternal generation and devoration, wherein the manifestation of the abyss consists, and is an eternal love-play; that the abyss doth so wrestle, sport and play with itself in its own conceived [or amassed] byss. It gives itself into the something, and again takes the something into itself; and thence brings or gives forth another thing. It introduceth itself into a lubet and desire; moreover, into power, strength and virtue, and mutually produceth one degree from the other, and through the other, that so it might be an eternal play and melody in itself.

4. And this we are to consider of in the fifth form of nature: When the powers of the eternal Word or understanding are made manifest through the eternal spiritual fire, in the eternal light of the Majesty (that each power or property is manifest in itself, and entereth into a

[1] ♀.

18

feeling, tasting, smelling, hearing, seeing essence, which is effected through the fire, where all things become spiritual, quick, and full of life), even then one property entereth mutually into another, for they are all proceeded out of one, viz. out of the free lubet. Therefore also this free lubet is yet in all, and they all jointly desire to enter again into this free lubet, viz. into the one. And there, when one tasteth, smelleth, feeleth, heareth and seeth the other in the essence, they do embrace each other in their holy conjunction, wherein then the real divine kingdom of joy consisteth: so likewise the growing and flourishing life of this world, as may be understood by way of simili-tude in the seven properties, and the light and power of the sun.

5. The divine kingdom of joy in the heaven of God (viz. in the manifested God in his expressed or spirated essence, as I might speak it to the understanding) consisteth in the love-desire, viz. in the power, which hath manifested itself through the fire in the light; for the fire giveth unto the meek free lubet essence and source, that it [the free lubet] is severised and moved, and becomes a kingdom of joy.

6. And thus we are to consider of the darkness: Whatsoever is a desiring love in the light, wherein all things rejoice and melodise, that, in the darkness, is an enmity; for the fire is cold and burning hot in the darkness; moreover, bitter, astringent and compunctive. The pro-perties are wholly rigorous and full of enmity and opposition; they seek not the one, but only the advancement of their own might. And the greater their elevation and inflammation is, the greater is the joy in the light.[1]

7. That which is good and holy in the light of the powers, that, in the darkness, is anxious and adverse. The darkness is the greatest enmity of the light, and yet it is the cause that the light is manifest. For if there were no black, then white could not be manifest to itself; and if there were no sorrow, then joy were also not manifest to itself.

8. Thus the joy doth triumph in itself, that it is not as the sorrow; and the sorrow triumpheth in itself, that it is a might and strength of the fire and light. Hence arise pride and self-will; because the dark fire's might giveth the essence and motive source to the light. Which did so affect and move king Lucifer, that he exalted himself in the root of the fire, to rule and domineer over the fire and light, and therefore he was cast out of the light into darkness, and the light withdrew from him.

9. Therefore understand us well here, what hell and the dark

---

[1] Kingdom of joy.

19

world or the anger of God is; of which the holy Scripture speaketh plainly that there is a hell, that is, a gulf of desperation, or pit devoid of the hope of God and all good. Now we are not to understand it to be any local place apart, but it is the first ground to the eternal nature. The place is between the kingdom of God and this world, and maketh a peculiar principle, dwelling in itself, and hath neither place nor local abode, and is everywhere, but governing itself alone; and yet it giveth essence to the light- and outward-world, that is, it is the cause to the source, viz. the fire; and is the universal essence of all God's essences.

10. In the darkness he is an angry zealous God, and in the fire-spirit a consuming fire, and in the light he is a merciful loving God, and in the power of the light he is especially, above all other properties, called God; and yet 'tis all only the manifested God, who manifesteth himself through the eternal nature in introduced [*i.e.* inducted] properties. Else, if I would say what God is in his depth, then I must say, he is outside of all nature and properties, viz. an understanding and original of all essences. The essences are his manifestation, and thereof alone we have ability to write; and not of the unmanifested God, who, without his manifestation, also were not known to himself.

THE ORIGINAL OF LIFE

♃¹ Jupiter

11. The sixth property of nature and of all beings ariseth also out of all the rest, and is manifest in the fire through the light in the love-desire; it is nature's understanding, voice, sound, speech, and all whatsoever that soundeth, both in things with life and in things without life. Its true original is from the astringent desire or impression of the first, second and third form, whence the motion and hardness ariseth. The essence of the coagulation is consumed in the fire, and from the devoration there proceedeth such a spirit, both according to the light in the love-property, and in the darkness according to the antagonising source and anxious property. And this we are to understand thus:

12. Each spirit desireth essence after its likeness. Now, there proceedeth forth from the fire no more than one spirit (which is a spiritual understanding, that is, the manifestation of the understanding of the abyss, or God) which doth re-conceive itself in the love-

¹ ♃.

20

desire, and formeth itself in the properties of the powers. And this mutual intercourse, consent, and qualifying into one another, is the pleasant taste of love.

13. But the conceived in the love-desire, wherein the desire doth again coagulate the powers and doth introduce them into forms, viz. into a substantial spirit, wherein the powers are able manifestly to move and act; that [I say] is now the natural and creatural understanding, which was in the Word. As John, i. 4, saith, *In him was the life, and the life was the light of men.*

14. This harmony of hearing, seeing, feeling, tasting and smelling is the true intellective life; for when one power entereth into another, then they embrace each other in the sound; and when they penetrate each other they mutually awaken and know each other. In this knowledge consists the true understanding, which hath neither number, measure nor ground, [but is] according to the nature of the eternal wisdom, viz. of the ONE, which is ALL.

15. Therefore one only will, if it hath divine light in it, may draw out of this fountain, and behold the infiniteness; from which contemplation this pen hath written.

16. Now there belong unto the manifest life or sound of the powers, hardness and softness, thickness and thinness, and a motion; for without motion all is still, and yet there can be no clear sound without the fire's essence; for the fire first maketh the sound in the hardness and softness.

17. Also there could be no sound without a conception, therefore all forms belong unto the sound: 1. The desire maketh hardness. 2. The compunction moveth. 3. The anguish doth amass it into an essence, for distinction. 4. The fire, in its devoration, changeth the grossness of the first amassed essence into a spirit or sound. 5. Which [spirit or sound] the desire both again receive in its softness and meekness and formeth it to a voice, tone, or expression, according to the powers. 6. The conceived or formed is the life-sound, or understanding [standing-under] of all differentiation.

18. This is now the manifested Word, which in itself is only one power, wherein all powers are contained; but thus it manifesteth itself through the eternal and temporal nature, and puts forth itself in forms, for its expression. For the formed word hath the like might in it as to reproduce its likeness, viz. such a being as the birth of the spirit is.

19. In the light of God, which is called the kingdom of heaven, the sound is wholly soft, pleasant, lovely, pure and thin; yea, as a stillness

in reference to the outward grossness of our sounds, speech and song; as if the mind did play and melodise in a kingdom of joy within itself, and did hear in a most entire inward manner such a sweet pleasing melody and tune; and yet outwardly did neither hear nor understand it. For in the essence of the light all is subtile, in manner as the thoughts do play and make mutual melody in one another; and yet there is a real, intelligible, distinct sound and speech used and heard by the angels in the kingdom of glory: but according to their world's property. For where the sound is gross, harsh and shrill, there it is strong in the dark impression; and there the fire is vehement and burning. As we men after the fall of Adam have so awaked and enkindled the fire of the dark world in our vital essence, that our vital sound is gross and beast-like, resembling the abyss: and the like is to be understood of the sound in the darkness. For as the generation of the word is, in its manifestation in the light, in the holy power, so also in the darkness; but altogether rigorous, harsh, hard and gross. That which, in the light, giveth a pleasing sound and lovely tone, is, in the darkness, a throbbing, without any true sound. And this proceeds from the essence of the astringent hard compunctive anxious genera-tion, viz. from the original of the coldness, or cold fire's source.

The Sixth Chapter

Of the Essence of Corporality

THE SEVENTH FORM OF NATURE

☽[1] *Luna and* ♄ *Saturnus*

Beginning——End

1. WE acknowledge that God in his own essence is no essence, but only the alone power or the understanding[2] to the essence, viz. an unsearchable eternal will, wherein all things are couched; and the same is ALL, and yet is only ONE, but yet desireth to manifest itself, and introduce itself into a spiritual essence, which is effected in the power of the light, through the fire in the love-desire.

2. But yet the true divine essence, (understand essence, and not the spirit of God), is nothing else but the understanding manifested, or the formation of the powers; and it consists in the desire, that is, in the love-desire, where one power doth experimentally and knowingly taste, smell, feel, see and hear another, in the essence and source of the property, whence the great ardent longing desire ariseth. In these properties the manifested God is understood, as in a fiery flame of love-desire, wherein there is a mere pleasing taste, sweet-breathing smell, ravishing melody, lovely and delightful seeing, smiling and friendly aspect, a gracious delight, pleasure or feeling: and yet it is only a spiritual essence, where the only powers (which have introduced themselves through the impression into property, and manifested themselves through the fire in the light) do mutually, as in a love-play, wrestle with and in one another, like a pleasant song, or pregnant harmony, or kingdom of joy. This is now the spiritual essence of the manifested God; [and] how the powerful all-essential word doth manifest itself in its own peculiar generation, wherein the melodious play of the divine wisdom is understood.

3. But if we would speak of the heavenly or divine essentiality, wherein the divine powers do introduce themselves again into form-ings, in an external degree, then we must say that the powers of the formed and manifested Word do again, in their love-desire, introduce themselves into an external essence, according to the property of all the powers; wherein they, as in a mansion, may act their love-play,

---

[1] ☽.   [2] Or original.

and so have somewhat wherewith and wherein mutually to play and melodise one with another in their wrestling sport of Love. And this is to be understood thus:

4. As a mineral power lieth in the earth, and is enkindled by the sun, whereby it beginneth to stir and spring, and becomes desirous of the powers of the sun, and attracts them into it, but in this longing desire it doth amass itself and form itself to a body, viz. a root, or the like, from which root there groweth forth in this hungry desire such a body or herb as the first power was. Thus likewise the manifested powers of God do form themselves into an external degree, viz. into an essence or corporality; to speak in reference to the spirit, whereas we must understand only a spiritual essence, but yet corporeal or essential in reference to the spirit of the powers: as the water is a thicker substance than the air. For the air penetrates the water: the like is to be understood concerning the divine powers and essence.

5. The powers stand manifest in an oily property, but the oily is manifest in a watery property; therefore the essence of the divine powers consisteth in a spiritual water, viz. in the holy element, whence this world with the four elements (as a degree more external) was brought forth and created into a substantial form.

6. And in this holy element or spiritual water we do understand the holy Paradise, in which the manifested powers of God do work; which holy element in the beginning of this outward world did penetrate and pullulate through the four elements; in which power there grew such fruit wherein the vanity of the wrath was not manifest; which man negligently lost. So that the lively buddings of the holy element, through the four elements and the earth did cease; for the curse of vanity was manifest in the springing and budding out of the earth.

7. Thus by the seventh form of the eternal nature we understand the eternal kingdom of heaven, wherein the power of God is essential; which essence is tinctured by the lustre and power of the fire and light; for the lustre of the spiritual fire and light is the working life in the spiritual water, viz. in the holy element; for this water (being the amassed or congealed essence of the divine powers) is moving. But yet, in reference to the divine powers, it is as an essence void of understanding; for it is a degree more external; as every substance or body is inferior to the spirit. The oily essence is the spirit of the water, viz. of the watery spirit; and the manifested powers of God are the spirit of the oil or oily spirit. And the eternal understanding of the Word is

the beginning of the manifested powers; and one degree goeth forth mutually from another; and all essence[1] is nothing else but the manifested God.

8. When we consider what kind of life, motion and dominion was before the times of this outward world, in the place of this world, and what eternity is, then we find that it was, and is unto eternity, such a life, motion and dominion as is above mentioned.

9. This outward world with the four elements and stars is a figure of the internal powers of the spiritual world, and was expressed or breathed forth by the motion of God (when he moved the internal spiritual world), and was amassed by the divine desire of the inward powers; and introduced into a creatural being, both out of the internal spiritual dark world, and also out of the holy light world.

10. This outward world is as a smoke, or vaporous steam or exhalation of the fire-spirit and water-spirit, breathed forth both out of the holy world and then also out of the dark world; and therefore it is evil and good, and consists in love and anger; and is only as a smoke or misty exhalation; in reference to and respect of the spiritual world; and hath again introduced itself with its properties into forms of the powers, to a pregnatress; as is to be seen in the stars, elements and creatures, and likewise in the growing trees and herbs. It maketh in itself with its birth another principle or beginning; for the pregnatress of time is a model or platform of the eternal pregnatress; and time coucheth in eternity: and it is nothing else, but that the eternity, in its wonderful birth and manifestation in its powers and strength, doth thus behold itself, in a form or time.

11. And now as we do acknowledge, that in the spiritual holy world there is an essence, viz. a comprehensive essence, which consisteth in the spiritual Sulphur, Mercurius and Sal, in an oily and watery byss, wherein the divine powers play and work; so likewise in the dark world there is such a property, but altogether adverse, opposed, antagonistic, envious, bitter and compunctive. It also hath essence according to[2] its desire, but of an altogether crude watery nature, wholly sharp and harsh, like to the property of the rough hard stones or wild earth; of a cold and scorching, dark and fiery property. All which is a contrarium to love, that so it might be known what love, or sorrow, is.

[1] Or beings; or all the universal created substance is only God revealed, God manifested, God expressed.
[2] Or, of.

12. In order that the fullness of joy may know itself in itself, the sharpness of the source must be a cause of the joy; and the darkness must be a manifestation of the light, in order that the light may be manifestly known, which, in the ONE, could not be.

13. But to inform or instruct the Reader's desire briefly and fully, concerning the seven properties of the eternal nature, which make three Principles or worlds, I will (out of love, for the sake of the simple) yet once more set down the forms in brief, as an A B C, for his further consideration and meditation.

I. FORM: ASTRINGENT; DESIRE

14. Lo! the desire of the eternal Word, which is God, is the beginning of the eternal nature, and is the concreting of the eternal nothing into something. It is the cause of all essences, also of cold and heat, so likewise of the water and air, and of the formation of the powers; and a cause of the taste, a mother of all salts.

II. FORM: BITTER; COMPUNCTIVE

15. The motion of the desire, viz. the attraction, is the second form of nature, a cause of all life and stirring, so also of the senses and distinction.

III. FORM: ANGUISH; PERCEIVANCE

16. The anguish, viz. the sensibility, is the third form, a cause of the mind, wherein the senses become active.

IV. FORM: FIRE; SPIRIT; REASON; DESIRE

17. The fire is a cause of the true spiritual life, wherein the holy powers of the free lubet are delivered from the astringent undigested roughness; for the fire devoureth in its essence the dark substance of the impression; and works it forth out of itself, out of the light, into spiritual powers.

V. FORM: LIGHT; LOVE

18. The holy spiritual love-desire, where the holy will of God hath sharpened itself in the harsh impression, and manifested itself through

the fire with the power of the omnipotence, that now brings itself forth through the fire in the light; and so in the powers it is introduced into life and motion, in the desire; and herein the holy generation, and the triumphant kingdom of the great love of God, doth consist, and is manifest.

VI. FORM: SOUND; VOICE; WORD

19. The sixth is the sound of the divine Word proceeding from the divine powers, which is formed in the love-desire; and introduced into an audible word of all powers; wherein consisteth the manifestation of the divine kingdom of joy, in the free lubet of God's wisdom.

VII. FORM: ESSENCE; BEING; MANSION

20. The seventh is the formed essence of the powers, viz. a manifestation of the powers: what the first six are in the spirit, that the seventh is in a comprehensible essence, as a mansion and house of all the rest, or as a body of the spirit wherein the spirit worketh, and playeth with itself: also it is a food of the fire, whence the fire draweth essence for its sustenance, wherein it burneth; and the seventh is the kingdom of the divine glory. And the seven are named or expressed thus:

21. *The Out-Birth or Manifestation is this.*

The Seaven Spirits of God, or powers of Nature; as they shew and manifest themselves in Love and Anger, both in the Heavenly and Hellish Kingdom, and also in the Kingdom of this world

Anger / Love		Hellish / Heavenly		World / Earthly Kingdom	
1	Astringent, Desire.	Hardnes cold Contrines.	Cold, Hardnes, Bone, Salt.
2	Attractio or Compunctio of Sence	Compulsion Envy	Poyson Life Growth Senses.
3	Anguish or Minde.	Enmity.	Sulphur, Perceivance, Paine.
4	Fire or Spirit.	Pride, Anger	Spirit, Reason, Desire.
		Love Fire	
5	Light or Love-Desire.	Meekenesse	Venus Sport Lifes-light
6	Sound or Vnderstanding.	Divine Joy.	Speaking, Crying, Distinguisng
7	Body or Essence.	Heaven.	Body, Wood, Stone, Earth, Mettall, Hearb.

This was received from the Author in such a forme by Abraham von Somerveldt

22. Courteous Reader, understand the sense aright and well: the meaning is not to be understood so, as if the seven properties were

divided, and one were near by another, or sooner manifest than another. All seven are but as one; and none is the first, second, or last; for the last is again the first. As the first introduceth itself into a spiritual essence, even so the last introduceth itself into a corporeal essence: the last is the body of the first. We must speak thus in part, in order to write it down and present it to the senses for the consideration of the Reader: the seven forms are altogether only the manifestation of God, according to love and anger, eternity and time.

23. But this we are to mark, that each property is also essential. In the kingdom of heaven this essence is jointly as one essence, and is a Mysterium, whence heavenly plants spring forth out of each power's property: as the earth is a Mysterium of all trees and herbs, so also of the grass and worms; and the four elements are a Mysterium of all animals; and the astrum a Mysterium of all operations in animals and vegetables.

24. Each property is to itself essential, and hath also in its essence the essence of all the other six forms; and maketh the essence of the other six forms also essential in its essence. As we see in the earth and stones, especially in metals, where ofttimes in one compaction all seven metals are couched together, and only one property is principal, which doth coagulate and captivate all the rest in itself; and always one is more manifest than the rest, according as each property hath its powerful predominancy in a thing. The like is also to be understood in vegetables, where ofttimes in a herb or piece of wood there is an astringent sour, harsh, bitter, anxious or sulphurous property, also a fiery, sweet or luscious, damp or watery quality.

The Seventh Chapter

Of the Holy Trinity, and Divine Essence

1. NATURE, both in its eternal and in its temporal aspect, is especially understood in the dark and fire world, viz. in the four first forms: as 1. In the astringent desire. 2. In the bitter compunction. 3. In the anguish or sensation. 4. In the fire, where the severation proceedeth forth in the enkindling [of the fire] in the flagrat. But the powers, both in the internal and in the external world, are all understood in the light or love-fire, viz. in the love-desire.

2. For their first ground is the eternal Word, viz. the One, wherein all things are couched. The second ground is the free lubet of the Word, viz. the wisdom, wherein all the colours of the only power are manifest in the will of the Deity. The third ground is the love-desire, wherein the free lubet with the colours and virtues of the powers hath sharpened itself through nature, and introduced itself through the fire's inflammation into a spiritual dominion; which [lubet] displayeth itself with the powers in the light in an eternal kingdom of joy.

3. The fourth ground is the oily spirit; in that the free lubet doth amass itself in the fiery love-desire in the meekness, as in its own peculiar form; and co-amasseth the lustre and essence of the fire and light, and introduceth it [the lustre and essence] into the first essence; which power of the fire and light in the meekness of the free lubet in the oily property is the true and holy tincture.

4. The fifth ground is the watery spirit, arising from the mortification in the fire, where the first spiritual essence in the astringent harsh dark desire has been consumed in the fire. Now, out of the devoration of the fire there proceedeth forth a spiritual essence, which is the oily ground; and out of the mortification a watery essence, which depriveth the fire-spirit of its wrath; so that the fire-spirit is not able to set its wrathful properties on fire in the oily ground; so that the fire must burn through death, and be only a light; else the oily ground would be inflamed. Thus the fire in its devoration must beget the water, viz. its death; and yet must again have the water for its life; else neither the fire nor the light could subsist. And thus there is an eternal generation, a devoration, a receiving, and again a consuming; and yet also it is thus an eternal giving; and hath neither beginning nor end.

5. Thus we now understand what God and his essence are. We Christians say that God is threefold, but only one in essence. But that we generally say and hold that God is threefold in Person, the same is very wrongly apprehended and understood by the ignorant, yea, by a great part of the learned; for God is no Person save only in Christ. But he is the eternal begetting power, and the kingdom, with all essences; all things receive their original from him.

6. But that we say of God, he is Father, Son, and Holy Spirit, that is very rightly said; only, we must explain it, else the un-illuminated mind apprehends it not. The Father is first the will of the abyss: he is outside of all nature or beginnings: the will to something; which will doth conceive itself into a lubet to its own manifestation.

7. And the lubet is the conceived power of the will, or of the Father, and it is his Son, heart, and seat: the first eternal beginning in the will. And he is therefore called a Son, because he receiveth an eternal beginning in the will, with the will's self-conception.

8. Now the will speaketh itself forth by the conception out of itself, as an outbreathing or manifestation; and this egress from the will in the speaking or breathing is the spirit of the Deity, or the third Person, as the ancients have called it.

9. And that which is outbreathed is the wisdom, viz. the power of the colours and the virtue of the will, which it eternally conceiveth to a life's centre or heart, for its habitation; and doth again eternally speak it forth out of the conception, as from its own eternal form; and yet also eternally conceiveth or comprehends it for his heart's centre.

10. Thus the conception of the will, viz. of the Father, is from eternity to eternity, which conceiveth his speaking Word from eternity to eternity, and speaks it forth from eternity to eternity. The speaking is the mouth of the will's manifestation; and the egress from the speaking or generation is the spirit of the formed Word; and that which is spoken forth is the power, colours and virtue of the Deity, viz. the wisdom.

11. Here we cannot say with any ground that God is three Persons, but he is threefold in his eternal generation. He begetteth himself in Trinity; and yet there is but only one essence and generation to be understood in this eternal generation; neither Father, Son, nor Spirit, but the one eternal life, or good.

12. The Trinity [*i.e.* God in Trinity] is first rightly understood in his eternal manifestation; where he manifesteth himself through the eternal nature, through the fire in the light.

13. Therein [*i.e.* God in Trinity] we understand three properties in one essence; the Father, with the fire-world; the Son, with the love-desire in the light, that is, with the light-world, or with the great meekness in the fire; and the Holy Spirit, with the moving life in the tincture, in the oily and watery life and dominion. God in Trinity is manifest in the fire and light: according to the property of the free lubet or divine property [he is manifest] as a great fiery flame of light and love; and according to the property of the dark fire-world [he is manifest] in a property wrathful and painful in its source; and yet he is the One. In the light he is the love-fire flame; and in the enkindled fire of nature he is a consuming fire, according to which God is called a consuming fire; and, in the dark, wrathful source, he is an angry, zealous avenger, in which property the spirits of the dark world consist.

14. The Father is called a holy God only in the Son, that is, in the power of the light in the divine kingdom of joy, viz. in the great meekness and love; for that is his proper manifestation, wherein he is called God. In the fire he is called an angry God; but in the light or love-fire he is called the holy God: and in the dark nature he is not called God.

15. We must make distinction: each world hath its Principle, and its dominion. Indeed all is from one eternal Original; but it severiseth itself into a twofold source: a similitude whereof we have in fire and light, where the fire is painful and consuming, and the light is meek and giving; and yet the one were a nothing without the other.

16. The fire receiveth its original in nature, but the light hath its original from the free lubet, viz. from the powers of the Deity. The will of God doth therefore introduce itself into a fire, that he might manifest the light and the powers, and introduce them into essence.

17. Albeit I have written here of the forms of nature (understand the eternal nature) yet it must not be understood as if the Deity were circumscribed or limited; his wisdom and power in divine property is without limit or measure, innumerable, infinite and unspeakable. I write only of the properties, how God hath manifested himself through the internal, and through the external nature; which are the chiefest forms of his manifestation.

18. These seven properties are to be found in all things; and he is void of understanding that denieth it. These seven properties make, in the internal world, the holy element, viz. the holy natural life and motion; but, in this external world, this one element severiseth itself

into four manifest properties, viz. into four elements; and yet it is but one only; but it divides itself into four head-springs, viz. into fire, air, water, and earth.

19. From the fire ariseth the air; and from the air the water; and from the water the earth, or a substance that is earthy. And they are only the manifestation of the one internal element, and are, in respect to the internal,[1] as an enkindled smoke or vapour. So also the whole astrum[2] is nothing else but the outbreathed powers from the inward fiery dark and light world, from the Great Mind of divine manifestation, and is only a formed model or platform, wherein the Great Mind of divine manifestation beholds itself in a time, and playeth with itself.

[1] Or before.   [2] Or constellations.

The Eighth Chapter

Of the Creation of Angels, and of their Dominion

1. THE creation of angels had a beginning, but the powers out of which they are created never had any beginning, but were concomitant in the birth of the eternal beginning. Not that they[1] are the holy Trinity, or in the same, but they were conceived of the desire of divine manifestation, out of the eternal, dark, fiery- and light-nature, out of the manifested Word, and introduced into creaturely forms and shapes.

2. God, who is a Spirit, hath by and through his manifestation introduced himself into distinct spirits, which are the voices of his eternal pregnant harmony in the manifested Word of his great kingdom of joy; they are God's instrument, in which the spirit of God melodiseth in his kingdom of joy: they are the flames of fire and light, but in a living, understanding dominion.

3. For the powers of the Deity are in them, in like manner as they are in men, as John saith, ch. 1: *The life of men was in the Word*; so also the life of the angels was in the Word from eternity. For in Matt. xxii. 30, it is written, *In the resurrection they* (understand men) *are as the angels of God in heaven.*

4. And as we understand principal forms in the divine manifestation through the eternal nature, so likewise we are to understand arch-angels, or angelical principalities, with many legions; but especially in three hierarchies, according to the property of the holy Trinity, and also of the three Principles, which cannot be denied.

5. As 1. One hierarchy is to be understood according to the dark world with the kingdom of Lucifer, who hath plunged himself thereinto; and the other is understood with the light-fiery love-world; and the third is understood with the mystery of the outward world, wherewith the internal hath made itself manifest.

6. Each hierarchy hath its princely dominion and order, viz. they in the dark world, in God's wrath; and those in the holy world, in God's love; and they which are in the outward world, in God's great wonders, according both to love, and anger.

7. They which are in the dark world bear the name (or the names)

---

[1] Viz. the powers.

33

of the great anger of God, according to the properties of the eternal nature in the wrath; and they which are in the light bear the names of the holy God, viz. of the divine powers; and they which are in the creation of the wonders of the outward world bear the names of the manifested powers of the outward world, viz. of the planets, stars and four elements.

8. They which are in the dark world domineer in the nature of the manifested wrath, viz. in the properties of God's anger, and have their princely dominions therein; and they which are in the holy world rule in the powers of the triumphant world, viz. in the great holy kingdom of joy in the wonders of the holy wisdom; and they which are in the outward world reign over the powers of the stars and four elements, and have also their princely dominion over the world, and their kingdoms and principalities for defence against the destroyer in the wrath.

9. Each country hath its princely angel-protector with its legions. Also there are angels over the four elements, over the fire, and over the air, over the water, and over the earth; and they are altogether only ministering spirits of the great God, sent forth for the service of those which shall obtain Salvation; as it is written, *the angel of the Lord encampeth about them that fear him*: they are the officers and servants of God in his dominion, who are active and full of motion.

10. For God never moveth himself save only in himself: but seeing his manifestation of the eternal and the external nature is in combat; thereupon the spirits of the dark world are against the spirits of the holy world, but especially against man, who is manifest both in good and in evil. God hath set the one against the other, that his glory might be manifest, both in his love, and in his anger.

11. For as we men have dominions upon the earth, so likewise the superior hosts under the astrum[1] have their dominions; so also the oily spirits in the element-air: the whole deep between the stars and the earth is inhabited, and not void and empty. Each dominion hath its own Principle: which seems somewhat ridiculous to us men, because we see them not with our eyes; not considering that our eyes are not of their essence and property, so that we are neither able to see nor perceive them; for we live not in their Principle, therefore we cannot see them.

12. As in the divine manifestation of the divine powers one degree orderly proceedeth forth from another, even unto the most external

---

[1] Or starry sky.

manifestation, the like also is to be understood of the angels or spirits. They are not all holy which dwell in the elements; for as the wrath of the eternal nature is manifest in the dark world, so likewise in the outward world, in its property.

13. Also, the spirits of the external world are not all external, but some are only inchoative,[1] which take their original naturally in the spirit of the external world, and pass away through nature, and only their shadow remains, as of all other beasts upon the earth.

14. Whatsoever reacheth not the holy element and the eternal fire-world, that, is devoid of an eternal life; for it ariseth out of time. And that which proceedeth out of time is consumed and eaten up of time; except it hath an eternal[2] in its temporal, that the eternal doth uphold the temporal.

15. For the eternal dwelleth not in time: and albeit it be clothed with the essence of time, yet the eternal dwelleth in the eternal in itself, and the temporal in the temporal. As it is to be understood with the soul and body of man, where the soul is from the eternal, and the external body is from time; and yet there is an eternal in the temporal body; which verily disappeared in Adam as to the eternal light; which must be born again through Christ.

16. And we are not to understand that the holy angels dwell only above the stars outside the place of this world, as reason, which understands nothing of God, fancieth. Indeed they dwell outside the dominion and source of this world, but in the place of this world; albeit there is no place in the eternity; the place of this world, and also the place outside this world is all one unto them.

17. For the beginning of the source, viz. of the four elements, together with the astrum,[3] maketh only one place; there is no place in the internal, but all wholly entire. Whatsoever is above the stars outside this world, that is likewise internally outside the four elements in the place of this world; else God were divided.

18. The angelical world is in the lieu or place of this world internally; and this same world's abyss is the great darkness, where the devils have their dominion; which also is not confined or shut up in any place; for the eternity is also their place, where there is no byss: only, the essence and property of their world is the byss of their habitation; as the four elements are the habitation of our external

[1] Having a beginning, and an end. Temporal.
[2] Eternal being, essence, property, life or Principle.
[3] Or planetic orb.

humanity. They have also in the darkness an element, according to the dark world's property, else God were divided in his wrath; for wherever I can say, here is God in his love, even there I can also say, that God is in his anger, only a Principle severs it.

19. Like as we men see not the angels and devils with our eyes; and yet they are about us, and among us. The reason is, because they dwell not in the source and dominion of our world, neither have they the property of the external world on them; but each spirit is clothed with his own world's property, wherein he dwelleth.

20. The beginning of each world's source is that limit which divides one world from the view and ken of the other, for the devils are a nothing in the heavenly source, for they have not its source in them; and albeit they have it, yet it is unto them as if it were shut up in death. Like as an iron that is red hot, so long as the fire pierceth it, it's fire; but when the fire goeth out, it's a dark iron. The like is to be understood concerning the spirits.

21. So likewise the angels are a nothing in the darkness; they are verily in it, but they neither see nor feel it. That which is a pain to the devils, that same is a joy to the angels in their source. And so, what is pleasing and delightful to the devils, that the angels cannot abide. There is a great gulf between them, that is, a whole birth.

22. For what else is able to sever the light from the darkness, save only a birth of sight, or light. *The light dwelleth in the darkness; and the darkness comprehendeth it not* (John i. 4). As the external sunshine dwelleth and shineth in the darkness of this world; and the darkness comprehends it not. But when the light of the sun withdraweth, then is the darkness manifest. Here is no other gulf between them, save only a birth.

23. Thus we are likewise to conceive of the eternal light of God, and the eternal darkness of God's anger; there is but one only ground of all; and that is the manifested God: but it is severed into sundry Principles and properties. For the Scripture saith, that *the holy is unto God a good savour to life*, understand to the holy divine life, viz. in the power of the light; and *the wicked is unto God a good savour to death*, that is, in his wrath, viz. in the essence, source, and dominion of the dark world.

24. For the God of the holy world, and the God of the dark world, are not two Gods; there is but one only God: he himself is all being, essence or substance; he is evil[1] and good, heaven and hell, light and

---

[1] In his wrath, plagues, and hell torment.

darkness, eternity and time, beginning and end. Where his love is hid in any thing,[1] there his anger is manifest. In many a thing[1] love and anger are in equal measure and weight; as is to be understood in this outward world's essence, being or substance.

25. But now he is only called a God according to his light in his love, and not according to the darkness, also not according to this outward world. Albeit he himself is ALL, yet we must consider the degrees, how one thing mutually proceeds from another. For I can neither say of heaven, nor of darkness, nor of this outward world, that they are God: none of them are God; but [they are] the expressed and formed Word of God, a mirror of the spirit which is called God; wherewith the spirit manifesteth itself, and playeth in its lubet to itself with this manifestation, as with its own essence which it hath made. And yet the essence is not sundered from the spirit of God; and yet also the essence comprehends not the Deity.

26. As body and soul are one, and yet the one is not the other; or as the fire and the water; or the air and the earth, are from one original, and yet they are particularly distinct; but yet they are mutually bound to each other, and the one were a nothing without the other. And thus we are to conceive and consider likewise of the divine essence, and also of the divine power.

27. The power in the light is God's love-fire, and the power in the darkness is God's anger-fire; and yet it is but one only fire, but divided into two Principles, that the one might be manifest in the other. For the flame of anger is the manifestation of the great love: and in the darkness the light is made known, else it were not manifest to itself.

28. Thus we are to understand that the evil and the good angels dwell near each other; and yet there is the greatest immense distance [between them]. For the heaven is in hell; and the hell is in heaven; and yet the one is not manifest to the other. And although the devil should go many millions of miles, desiring to enter into heaven and to see it, yet he would be still in hell, and not see it. Also the angels see not the darkness, for their sight is mere light of divine power; and the devil's sight is mere darkness of God's anger. The like is also to be understood of the saints, and again of the wicked. Therefore, in that we in Adam have lost the divine sight, in which Adam saw by the divine power, Christ saith, *You must be born anew; else you cannot see the kingdom of God.*

[1] Being, essence or substance.

29. In the fire-spirit we are to understand the angelical creation, where the will of the abyss introduceth itself into byss, and manifesteth the eternal speaking Word or life with the fiery birth, viz. with the first Principle, where the spiritual dominion is manifest by the fire-birth. In this spiritual fire all angels do take their original, viz. out of the forms to the fire-source; for no creature can be created out of the fire: for it is no essence; but out of the properties to the fire a creature may be apprehended in the desire, viz. in the Verbum Fiat, and introduced into a creatural form and property.

30. And therefore there are many and divers sorts of angels; also in many distinct offices. And as there are three forms to the fire-source, so there are also three hierarchies; and therein their princely dominions. And likewise there are three worlds in one another as one, which make three Principles or beginnings, for each property of the eternal nature hath its degrees; for they do explicate and mutually unfold themselves in the fire-blaze; and out of those degrees the different distinction of spirits is created.

31. And we are to understand nothing else, by the creation of the angels and of all other spirits, but that the abyssal God hath introduced himself into his manifested properties, and out of those properties into living creatures; by which he possesseth the degrees, and therewith playeth in the properties: they are his strings in the all-essential speaking; and are all of them tuned for the great harmony of his eternal speaking Word. So that in all degrees and properties the voice of the unsearchable God is manifest and made known: they are all created for the praise of God.

32. For, all whatsoever that liveth, liveth in the speaking Word; the angels in the eternal speaking, and the temporal spirits in the re-expression or echoing forth of the formings of time, out of the sound or breath of time; and the angels out of the sound of eternity, viz. out of the voice of the manifested Word of God.

33. And therefore they bear the names of the several degrees in the manifested voice of God; and one degree is more holy in the power than another. Therefore the angels also, in their choirs, are differenced in the power of the divine might; and one hath a more holy function to discharge than another. An example whereof we have by the priests in the *Old Testament*, in their ordinances; which were instituted after an angelical manner.

34. Albeit earthly, yet there was even such an angelical understanding and meaning couched therein; which God did represent

upon Jesus which was to come into the human property; and so alluded with Israel in the type, at the eternal which was to come, which Jesus out of Jehova did restore, and introduce into the human property; which the earthly reason hath neither apprehended nor understood: but seeing the time is born,[1] and the beginning hath again found the end, it shall be manifest, for a witness unto all nations: sheweth the spirit of wonders.

[1] Manifest or come about.

The Ninth Chapter

Of the Fall of *Lucifer* with his Legions

1. ALBEIT self-reason might here cavil at us, and say, we were not by when this was done; yet we say that we, in a magical manner, according to the right of eternity, were really there, and saw this. But not I, who am I, have seen it; for I was not as yet a creature. But we have seen it in the essence of the soul which God breathed into Adam.

2. Now then, if God dwelleth in this same essence, and hath from all eternity dwelt therein, and manifesteth himself in his own mirror, and looketh back through the essence of the soul into the beginning of all essences; what then hath reason to do, to taunt and cavil at me about that, wherein itself is blind? I must warn reason, that it would once behold itself in the looking-glass of the understanding, and consider what itself is; and leave off from the building of mad Babel; it will be time.

3. The fall of Lucifer came not to pass from God's purpose or appointment; indeed it was known in the wrath of God, according to the property of the dark world, how it could or would come to pass; but in God's holiness, viz. in the light, there was no such desire manifest in any such property; otherwise the holy God must have a devilish or hellish wrathful desire in his love; which is absolutely not so. But in the centre of the eternal nature, viz. in the forms to fire, there is verily such a property in the dark impression.

4. Every good angel hath the centre in him, and is manifest in a creatural property in one degree or other in the centre; whichever property is greatest[1] in the creature, according to that it hath its office and dominion.

5. Yet the angels, which were created out of the degrees of the centre, were created for and to the light; the light was manifest in all; and they had free will from the manifested will of God's will.

6. Lucifer had still been an angel, if his own will had not introduced him into the fire's might, desiring to domineer in the strong fiery might, above and in all things, as an absolute sole god in darkness and light. Had he but continued in the harmony wherein God had created him [what would have cast him out of the light?].

---

[1] Chief, most predominant or manifest.

7. Now reason saith, He could not. Then tell me, Who compelled him? Was he not, I prithee, the most glorious prince in heaven? Had he introduced his will into the divine meekness, then he could [have been able to stand]; but if he would not[1] then he could not; for his own desire went into the centre: he would himself be God. He entered with his will into self;[2] and in self is the centre of nature, viz. those properties wherein his will would be lord and master in the house.

8. But God created him for his harmony, to play with his love-spirit in him, as upon the musical instrument of his manifested and formed Word: and this the self-will would not.

9. Now saith reason, How came it that he would not? Did not he know the judgment of God, and the fall? Yea, he knew it well enough; but he had no sensible perceivance of the fall, but only as a bare knowledge.[3] The fiery lubet, which was potent in him, did egg him on, for it would fain be manifest in the essence of the wrath, viz. in the root of fire. The darkness also eagerly desired to be creatural, which drew Lucifer, its craftmaster in the great potency of fire; indeed it drew him not from without;[4] but in the property and will of his own fiery and dark essence. The original of the fall was within the creature and not without the creature: and so it was in Adam also. Self-will was the beginning of pride.

10. Thou askest, What was that which did cause it in himself? Answer, His great beauty and glory. Because the will beheld what itself was in the fiery mirror, this lustrous glance did move and affect him, so that he did eagerly reach after the properties of the centre; which forthwith began effectually to work: For the astringent austere desire, viz. the first form or property, did impress itself, and awakened the compunction and the anxious desire. Thus this beautiful star did overshadow its light; and made its essence wholly astringent, rigorous and harsh; and its meekness and true angelical property was turned into an essence wholly austere, harsh, rigorous and dark. And then this bright morning star was undone. And as he did, so did his legions. And this was his fall.

11. He should have been wholly resigned in the holy power of God; and hear what the Lord would speak and play by his own spirit in him. This, self-will would not do; and therefore he must now play in the dark; yea, his will is yet opposite; albeit now, after the fall, he

[1] In his own will, which was from the eternal will, was both the possibility and the ability.
[2] Selfhood, or selfness.
[3] Or notional theory, in the mystery of his mind.   [4] Outwardly.

cannot will [viz. to resign to the divine will of the light]; for his meekness, whence the love-will ariseth, is shut up and entered again into a nothing, viz. it is retired into its own original.

12. Now the creature still remaineth, but wholly out of the centre, viz. out of the eternal nature. The free lubet of God's wisdom is departed from him; that is, it hath hid itself in itself; and letteth the wrathful fire-will stand: as happened to Adam also, when he imagined after evil and good, then the free lubet of the holy world's essence did disappear in his essence.

13. This was the very death, of which God told him, *that if he did eat of the Tree of Knowledge of Good and Evil, he should die the very same day*. Thus it was in Lucifer: he died to the holy divine world, and arose to the wrathful world of God's anger.

14. Thou sayest, Wherefore did not God uphold him, and draw him from the evil inclination? I prithee tell me, wherewith? Should God have poured in more love and meekness into this fire-source? Then had his stately light been more manifest in him; and the looking-glass of his own knowledge had been the greater, and his own fiery self-will the stronger. I pray, was not his high light, and his own self-knowledge, the cause of his fall?

15. Should God then have drawn him with rebuke? Was it not Lucifer's purpose aforehand to rule the magical ground as an artist? His aim and endeavour was for the art, that he would play with the centre of the transmutation of the properties; and would be and do all whatsoever he alone pleased. Had he not known this, he had still remained an angel in humility.

16. Therefore the children of darkness, and the children of this world also, are wiser than the children of the light, as the Scripture saith. Thou askest, Why? [Because] they have the magical root of the original of all essences manifest in them: and [to have] this was even the desire of Adam: However [it was] the devil [who] persuaded them that they should be wiser, and their eyes should be opened, and they should be as God himself.

17. This folly caused king Lucifer to aspire, desiring to be an artist, and an absolute lord, like the Creator. The water of meekness had been good for his fire-will; but he would none of that. Hence it is that the children of God must be the most plain, sincere and simple; as Esaias prophesied of Christ: *Who is so simple as my servant the righteous one, who turneth many unto righteousness*, viz. upon[1] the way of humility.

[1] Or to.

42

18. All angels live in humility, and are resigned to the spirit of God, and are in the eternal speaking Word of God, as a well-tuned, pure-sounding instrument in the harmony of the kingdom of heaven; of which the Holy Ghost is chief master and ruler.

19. But the devil hath forged to himself a strange fool's play, where he can act his gulleries with his sundry interludes and disguisments; and demean himself like an apish fool; and transform himself into monstrous, strange and hideous shapes and figures; and mock at the image of angelical simplicity and obedience. And this was his aim and intent, for which he departed from the harmony of the angelical choirs. For the Scripture saith, that he was a murderer and liar from the beginning. His juggling feats and fictions are mere strange figures and lies, which God never formed in him; but he brings them to forms and shapes in himself; and seeing that they are contrary to his creation, they are lies and abominations.

20. He was an angel, and hath belied his angelical form and obedience; and is entered into the abomination of fictions, lies and mockeries; in his centre he hath awakened the envious hateful forms and properties of the dark world, whence wrath and iniquity springeth. He sat in heavenly pomp and glory, and introduced his hateful desire and malicious will into the essence, viz. into the water-source; and cast forth his streams of enmity and malignity.

21. His properties were as the venomous stings of serpents, which he put forth out of himself. When the love of God was withdrawn from him, he figured his image according to the property of the wrathful forms (wherein there are also evil beasts and worms, in the serpentine shape), and infected or awakened the Salniter of the centre of nature in the expressed essence, in the generation of the eternal nature; whence the combat arose, that the great prince Michael fought with him, and would no longer endure him in heaven among the fellowship of the holy angels.

22. For which cause the will of the abyss, viz. of the eternal Father moved itself, and swallowed him down, as a treacherous perjured wretch, into the gulf and sink of eternal darkness, viz. into another Principle: the heaven spewed him out of itself; he fell into the darkness as lightning, and he lost the mansion of God in the kingdom of heaven, in the holy power; and all his servants with him. There he hath the mother for his enchanting delusions; there he may play them juggling feats, and antic tricks.

23. Moreover, we are to know that he had his royal seat in the

43

place of this world: therefore Christ calleth him a prince of this world, viz. in the kingdom of darkness, in the wrath, in the place of this world.

24. His kingly throne is taken from him; and another hath possession of it in the heavenly world's property, in the place of this world: he shall not obtain it again.

25. Also (at the instant of the creation of the stars and four elements) another king was established over him, in this place in the elements; which albeit we could mention; yet at present it remaineth in silence, by reason of the false magic. Also by reason of other superstitions and idolatries we will not speak anything of it here: and yet hint enough unto our schoolfellows.

The Tenth Chapter

Of the Creation of Heaven
and the Outward World

1. IT seems strange and wonderful to reason, to consider how God hath created the stars, and the four elements; especially when reason doth contemplate and consider of the earth, with its hard stones, and very rough, indigested, harsh substance; and seeth that there are great stones, rocks and cliffs created, which are in part useless, and very hindersome to the employment of the creatures in this world. Then it thinks, whence may this compaction arise in so many forms and properties; for there are divers sorts of stones, divers metals, and divers kinds of earth whence manifold herbs and trees do grow.

2. Now when it doth thus muse and contemplate, it finds nothing, save only that it doth acknowledge that there must be a hidden power and might, which is abyssal, and unsearchable, which hath created all things so; and there it sticks, and runs to and fro in the creation, as a bird that flies up and down in the air; and looks upon all things, as an ox looks upon a new door of his stall; and never so much as considers what itself is; and seldom reacheth so far as to know that man is an image extracted out of this whole being or essence. It runneth up and down, as a beast void of understanding, which desireth only to eat and procreate; and when it comes to its highest degree, as to search out and learn something, then it searcheth in the outward fiction and artifice of the stars; or else in some carved work of outward nature. It will by no means simply and sincerely learn to know its Creator. And when it comes to pass that one attaineth so far as to teach the knowledge of him, yet then it calleth such man a fool, and fantastic; and forbids him the precious understanding of God, and imputes it to him for sin, and revileth him therein.

3. Such mere animals are we, since the fall of Adam, that we do not so much as once consider that we were created in the image of God, and endued with the right, natural and genuine understanding, both of the eternal, and temporal nature; so as to mind and bethink ourselves, by great earnestness, to re-obtain that which we have lost; whereas we have yet that very first soul wherein the true understanding lieth; if we did but seriously labour to have that light which we

have lost, to shine again in us; which yet is offered unto us out of grace.

4. Therefore there will be no excuse at the great day of the Lord, when God shall judge the secret and hidden things of mankind, because we would not learn to know him, and obey his voice; which daily hath knocked amongst us, and in us; and resign up ourselves unto him; that so our understanding might be opened. And a very severe sentence shall he receive who will undertake to be called Master, and Rabbi;[1] and yet neither knoweth the way of God, nor walketh therein, and that which is yet more heinous forbiddeth[2] those that desire to know, and walk therein.

5. The creation of the outward world is a manifestation of the inward spiritual Mystery, viz. of the centre of the eternal nature, with the holy element: and was brought forth by the eternal-speaking Word through the motion of the inward world as a spiration; which eternal-speaking Word hath expressed the essence out of the inward spiritual worlds; and yet there was no such essence in the speaking, but was only as a breath or vaporous exhalation in reference to the internal, breathed forth, both from the property of the dark world, and also of the light world: and therefore the outward essence of this world is good and evil.

6. And we are with very entire and punctual exactness to consider of this motion of the eternal Mystery of the spiritual world. 1. How it came to pass that such a wrathful, rough, gross and very compunctive essence and dominion was brought forth and made manifest, as we see in the outward forms of nature, as well in the moving things, as in the stones and earth. 2. Whence such a wrath did arise, which hath compacted and introduced the powers of the properties into such a harsh nature [or rude quality] as we see in the earth and stones.

7. For we are not to think that there is the like in heaven, viz. in the spiritual world. In the spiritual world there are only the properties of possibility; but not at all manifest in such a harsh property; but are as it were swallowed up; as the light swalloweth up the darkness, and yet the darkness doth really dwell in the light, but not apprehended.

8. Now we are yet to search out how the desire of the darkness became manifest in the power of the light; that they both came mutually into the compaction or coagulation. And yet it affordeth us a far greater and more profound consideration; that when man could not stand in the spiritual mystery of the paradisical property [and estate],

---

[1] Sir.   [2] Or hindreth.

that God cursed this compaction, viz. the earth; and appointed an earnest judgment to sever the good in this compaction again from the evil; so that the good must thus stand in the curse, that is, in death. He that doth here see nothing is indeed blind. Why would God curse his good essence, if something were not come into it which was opposite to the good? Or is God at odds with himself? as reason would be ready to fancy. For it is written in Moses, that *God looked upon all that he had made, and behold it was very good.*

9. Now man, for whose sake the earth was accursed, had not introduced anything into the earth, whereby it was now made so evil, as to cause God to curse it, save only the false and faithless imagination of his desire to eat of the evil and good: so as to awaken the vanity, viz. the centre of nature in him, and to know evil and good. From which desire the hunger entered into the earth; whence the outward body was extracted as a mass; which set the hunger of its desire again upon its mother; and awakened the root of vanity out of the dark impression of the centre of nature, whence the Tree of Temptation, viz. evil and good, grew manifest to him; and when he did eat thereof the earth was accursed for his sake.

10. Now if man, by his powerful desire, did awaken the wrath in the earth, what then might Lucifer [not] be able to do, who was likewise an enthroned prince, and moreover had many legions? Lucifer had the will of the strong might and power of the centre of all essences in himself, as well as Adam [had]. Adam was only one creature, but Lucifer was a king, and had a kingdom in possession, viz. a hierarchy in the spiritual world, viz. in the heavenly Salniter in the generation of the manifested word. He was an enthroned prince in the manifested power of God: therefore Christ calleth him a prince of this world: for he sat in the essence (understand, in the spiritual essence) whence this world was breathed forth as a spiration.

11. He it is that by his false desire, which he introduced into the essence, did awaken the wrath in the internal, as Adam stirred up the curse. He raised the centre of nature with his dark wrathful property in the like wrathful properties; for he had first awakened the wrath of God in himself. And then this awakened wrath entered into its mother, viz. into the magical generation, out of which Lucifer was created to a creature: whereupon the generation was made proud and aspiring, contrary to the right [or law] of eternity.

12. Also he sat in his angelical form in the good holy essence, as to the generation of the divine meekness; and therein exalted himself to

47

domineer in the will of his wrath above the meekness, as an absolute peculiar god, contrary to the right of eternity.

13. But when the speaking eternal Word in love and anger, for his malicious iniquity's sake, did move itself in the properties, viz. in the essence wherein Lucifer sat, to cast this wicked guest out of his habitation into eternal darkness; then the essence was compacted: for God would not permit or allow that he should any longer have these manifested powers, wherein he was a prince; but created them into a coagulation, and spewed him out of them.

14. And in this impression or conjunction the powers, viz. the watery and oily properties, were compacted; not that Lucifer did compact or create them; but [they were compacted by] the speaking Word of God, which dwelt in the manifested powers and properties: the same took away the disobedient child's patrimony, and cast him out as a perjured wretch, out of his inheritance into an eternal prison, into the house of darkness and anger; wherein he desired to be master over the essence of God's love, and rule therein as a juggler and enchanter, and mix the holy with unholy, to act his juggling feats and proud pranks thereby.

15. And we see very clearly with quick-sighted eyes, that thus it is: for there is nothing in this world so evil but it hath a good in it: the good hath its rise originally out of the good or heavenly property, and the evil hath its descent from the property of the dark world; for both worlds, viz. light and darkness, are in each other as one.

16. And therefore they also went along together into the compaction or coagulation; and that from the degrees of the eternal nature, viz. from the properties to the fire-life, and also from the properties in the oily and spiritual watery light-essence.

17. For the metals are in themselves nothing else but a water and oil, which are held by the wrathful properties, viz. by the astringent austere desire; that is, by a Saturnine martial fiery property, in the compaction of Sulphur and Mercury, to be one body [or congealed bulk]. But if I wholly destroy this body, and severise each into its own property, then I clearly find therein the first creation.

I. SATURNUS: SAL

18. As first, according to the astringent desire of the Fiat, viz. of the first form to nature, according to the property of the dark world, I find a hardness and coldness; and further according to this astringent

property, secondly a deadly baneful stinking water, from the astringent impression; and thirdly, in this stinking water, a dead earth; and fourthly, a sharpness like to salt, from the native right and quality of the astringency. This is now the coagulated essence of the first form of nature, according to the dark world; and it is the stony substance (understand the grossness of the stones and of all metals); so likewise of the earth, wherein the mortal part (or the close-binding death) is understood.

II. MERCURIUS

19. Secondly, I find according to the second form and property of the dark nature and world essence, in the compaction of the metals and stones, a bitter compunctive raging essence, viz. a poison; which maketh a strong harsh noisome taste in the earth and stinking water; and it is the cause of growth, viz. the stirring life: its property is called Mercurius; and in the first form the astringency is called Sal.

III. SULPHUR

20. Thirdly, I find the third property, viz. the anguish, which is the sulphurous-source, in which consisteth the various dividing of the properties, viz. of the essence.

IV. SALNITER

21. Fourthly, I find the fire or heat, which doth awaken the salniter in the sulphurous-source, which severiseth the compaction; and that is the flagrat. This is the original raiser of the salniter out of the brimstony, watery and earthy property; for it is the awakener of death, viz. [the awakener] in the mortal property, and the first original of the life in the fire: and even to the fire the property of the dark world reacheth, and no farther.

V. OIL

22. Fifthly, we find in the compaction of the metals and stones an oil, which is sweeter than any sugar can be; so far as it may be separated from the other properties. It is the first heavenly holy essence; which hath taken its original from the free lubet. It is pure and transparent; but if the fire-source be severed from it (albeit it is impossible wholly to separate it, for the band of the great triumphant joy consisteth therein) then it is whiter than anything can be in nature: But

49

by reason of the fire it continues of a rosy-red;[1] which the light changeth into yellow, according to the mixture of red and white; by reason of the earthy property, and predominant influence of the sun.

23. But if the artist can unloose it, and free it from the fire of the wrath, and other properties, then he hath the pearl of the whole world, understand the tincture: for Virgin Venus hath her cabinet of treasure lying there: It is the Virgin with her fair attire [or crown of pearl].

24. O thou earthly man hadst thou it yet! Here Lucifer and Adam have negligently lost it! O man, didst thou but know what lay here, how wouldst thou seek after it! But it belongeth only unto those whom God hath chosen thereto. O precious pearl, how sweet art thou in the new birth, how fair, and surpassing excellent is thy lustre!

VI. THE LIVING MERCURY; SOUND

25. Sixthly, we find in this oily property a sovereign power from the original of the manifested powerful divine Word, which dwelleth in the heavenly property; in which power the sound or tone of metals is distinguished; and therein their growth consisteth. For here it is the holy Mercurius: that which in the second form of nature in the darkness is compunctive, harsh, rigid, and a poison, that is here, in the free lubet's property (when the fire in the salnitral flagrat hath divided love and anger) a pleasant merry Mercury, wherein the joyfulness of the creature consisteth.

26. And here, ye philosophers, lieth the effectual virtue and powerful operation of your Noble Stone: here it is called Tincture. This operation can tincture the disappeared water in Luna; for here your Jupiter is a prince; and Sol a king, and virgin Venus the king's sweetest spouse. But Mars must first lay down his sceptre; also the devil must first go into hell; for Christ must bind him; and tincture simple Luna, which he hath defiled, with the oil of his heavenly blood; that the anger may be changed into joy. Thus the artist's art is born: understood here, by the children of the Mystery.

[VII. ESSENCE, BODY]

27. Seventhly, we find in the separation of the compaction of the metals a white crystalline water; that is, the heavenly water, viz. the water above the firmament of heaven; which is severed from the

---

[1] Or crimson purple-red.

oil, as a body of the oily property. It gives a white crystalline lustre in the metals; and Venus with her property makes it wholly white; and that is a silver property; and Venus in Sol, a gold; and Mars in Venus, a copper; and again, Venus in Mars, an iron; Jupiter in Venus, a tin; Saturn in Venus, a lead: Mercurius in Venus, quicksilver; and without Venus there is no metal, neither fixed nor mineral.

28. Thus understand by Venus, heavenly essentiality, which consisteth in an oil and crystalline water, which giveth body unto all metals, understand the spiritual beautiful body; its own peculiar essence, without the influences of the other properties, is the great meekness and sweetness. Its real peculiar essence is a sweet pure water; but the power of the manifested Word doth separate the holiest through the fire into an oil; for in the oil the fire giveth a shine or lustre. When the fire tasteth the water in itself, then out of the taste it giveth an oil; thus the oil is spiritual, and the water corporeal. The oil is a body[1] of the power; and the water a body[1] of the properties, which are living in the oil, and do make or use the water for a mansion. In the water the elemental life consisteth, and in the oil the spiritual life;[2] and in the power of oil the divine life, viz. the life of the expressed Word, as a manifestation of the Deity.

29. Now we see here, how, in the compaction of the Verbum Fiat, the holy entered along with the unholy into a coagulation. For in all things there is a deadly and also a living water; and also a mortal poisonful virtue, and a good vital virtue; a gross, and a subtile [power]; one evil, the other good: all which is according to the nature of God's love and anger.

30. The grossness of the stones, metals and earth proceed from the property of the dark world, all which are in a mortal [property], understand substance and not spirit: the spirit of the grossness is in the poison-life, in which Lucifer is a prince of this world.

31. But the heavenly [part] holds the grossness and poison-source captive; so that the devil is the poorest creature in the essence of this world; and hath nothing in this world for his own possession, save what he can cheat from the living creatures which have an eternal being; that they enter with the desire into the wrath of the eternal; viz. into his juggling incantations.

32. If we would rightly consider the creation, then we need no more than a divine light and contemplation: it is very easy unto the illuminated mind, and may very well be searched out. Let a man but

---

[1] Text *Corpus*.   [2] Or life of the spirit.

consider the degrees of nature, and he seeth it very clearly in the sun, stars, and elements. The stars are nothing else but a crystalline water-spirit; yet not a material water, but powers of the salnitral flagrat in the fire.

33. For their orb, wherein they stand, is fiery; that is, a salnitral fire, a property of the matter of the earth, metals, trees, herbs and the three elements, fire, air and water. What the superior is, that also is the inferior; and that which I find in the compaction of the earth, that likewise is in the astrum;[1] and they belong both together as body and soul.

34. The astrum[1] betokeneth the spirit, and the earth the body; before the creation all was mutually in each other in the eternal generation; but in no coagulation or creature; but as a powerful wrestling love-play, without any such material substance.

35. But it was enkindled in the motion of the Word, viz. the Verbum Fiat: and therewith the inflammation in the salnitral flagrat, each property did divide itself in itself; and was amassed by the awakened astringent impression (viz. the first form of nature, which is called the Fiat), and so each became coagulated in its property; the subtile in its property, and the gross in property; all according to the degrees; as the eternal generation of nature derives itself from the unity into an infinite multiplicity.

36. Good and evil is manifest in the astrum:[1] for the wrathful fiery power of the eternal nature, so also the power of the holy spiritual world, is manifest in the stars, as an essential spiration. Therefore there are many obscure stars, all which we see not, and many light stars, which we see.

37. We have a likeness of this in the matter of the earth, which is so manifold, whence divers sorts of fruit grow, viz. according to the properties of the superior spheres: for so likewise is the earth, being the grossest substance, where the mortal water is coagulated.

38. The earth was coagulated in the seventh form of nature, viz. in the essence; for it is that same essence which the other six properties do make in their desire: it chiefly consisteth in seven properties, as is above mentioned; but the unfoldment or various explication of the properties is effected in the salnitral fire, where each property doth again explicate itself into seven; where the infiniteness and great possibility[2] ariseth, that of one thing, another can be made, which it was not in the beginning.

[1] Or constellation.   [2] Or potency.

39. The being of all beings is only a magical birth [deriving itself], out of one only, into an infiniteness; the One is God, the infinite is time and eternity, and a manifestation of the One; where each thing may be reduced out of one into many, and again out of many into one.

40. The fire is the workmaster thereunto, which putteth forth from a small power a little sprout out of the earth, and displayeth it into a great tree with many boughs, branches and fruits; and doth again consume it, and reduceth it again to one thing, viz. to ashes and earth, whence it first proceeded: and so also all things of this world do enter again into the one whence they came.

41. The essence of this world may easily be searched out, but the centre or point of motion will remain dark unto reason, unless there be another light in it: it supposeth that it hath it in the circle, and can measure it;[1] but it hath it not in the understanding.

42. When we consider the hierarchy and the kingly dominion in all the three Principles in the place of this world, so far as the Verbum Fiat reached forth itself to the creation of the outward world, with the stars, and elements, then we have the ground of the punctum[2] of the royal throne, of which the whole creation is but a member.

43. For the stars and four elements, and all whatsoever is bred and engendered out of them, and live therein, doth hang [or appertain] unto one punctum; where the divine power hath manifested itself from itself in a form: and this punctum standeth in three Principles, viz. in three worlds: nothing can live in this world without this punctum, it is the only cause of the life and motion of all the powers; and without it all would be in the stillness[3] without motion.

44. For if there were no light, then the elements would be motionless: all would be an astringent harsh property, wholly raw and cold: the fire would remain hidden in the cold; and the water would be only a keen spirit, like to the property of the stars; and the air would be hidden in the water-source, in the sulphur, and be a still, unmoving essence.

45. We see in very deed, that the light is the only cause of all stirring, motion and life; for every life desireth the power of the light, viz. the disclosed punctum: and yet the life is not the punctum, but the form of Nature. And if this punctum did not stand open, then the kingdom of darkness would be manifest in the place of this world;

[1] Or mathematically describe and demonstrate it.
[2] Central fire or radical heat; the point of motion, the virtue of the light.
[3] Or eternal silence.

in which [place of wrath] Lucifer is a prince, and possesseth the princely throne in the wrath of the eternal nature, in the place of this world.

46. Therefore, O man, consider with thyself, where [now] thou art at home, viz on one part[1] in the stars and four elements; and on the other part[2] in the dark world among the devils; and as to the third part[3] in the divine power in heaven. That property which is master in thee, its servant thou art, pranck and vapour as stately and gloriously in the sun's light as thou wilt; hast thou not the eternal [light], yet thy fountain shall be made manifest to thee.

47. By the two words *Himmel und Erde* (heaven and earth) we understand the whole ground of the creation; for, in the language of nature, the understanding is couched in those two words. For by the word *Himmel* (heaven) is understood the spiration of the Verbum Fiat, which created that essence (wherein Lucifer was enthroned) with the creative Word out of itself, that is, out of the spiritual holy world, into a time or beginning. And by the word *Erde* (earth) is understood the wrath in the essence, that the essence was amassed in the wrath; and reduced out of the properties of the dark Sulphur, Mercury and Salt, viz. out of the powers of the original of nature, and introduced into a compaction or coagulation.

48. This coagulation is the syllable *Er*, the other syllable, *de* or *den*, is the element. For the earth is not the element, but the [element is] the moving, viz. the power, whence it was coagulated; this is that element which is spiritual, and taketh its true original in the fire, where the nature, which is a senseless life, dieth in the fire; from which dying or mortification there proceedeth forth a living motion; and from that which is mortified [in the fire] a dead matter, viz. earth, and a dead water, and also a deadly fire, and venomous air, which maketh a dying source in the earthly bodies.

49. When nature was enkindled, the element did unfold [and display] itself into four properties, which yet in itself is only one. The real element dwelleth in the essence which is mortified in the fire, otherwise the earth could bring forth no fruit. Those which now are called the four elements, are not elements, but only properties of the true element. The element is neither hot nor cold, neither dry nor

[1] Viz. as to thy body and outward carcase of clay thou art a guest for a while in this outward world, travelling in the vanity of time.
[2] Viz. as to thy soul, in its own self and creatural being, without the divine light or regeneration, in the abyss of hell.
[3] As to thy divine image, and spirit of love, in the eternal light.

moist; it is the motion or life of the inward heaven, viz. the true angelical life as to the creature. It is the first divine manifestation out of the fire, through nature: when the properties of the eternal nature work therein; it is called Paradise.

50. By the word *Himmel* (heaven) is understood how the water, viz. the grossness in the mortal part, was coagulated, and separated from the holy crystalline water, which is spiritual. There, with the material, time began, as an essence expressed [or spirated] out of the spiritual water.

51. The spiritual water is living, and the spirated is dumb and unfeeling, void of understanding, and is dead in reference to the living water; of which Moses saith, *God hath separated it from the water above the firmament.*

52. The firmament is another Principle, viz. another beginning [or inchoation] of motion: the water above the firmament is the spiritual water, in which the Spirit of God ruleth and worketh: for Moses saith also, *the Spirit of God moveth upon the water*: for the spiritual element moveth in the four elements; and in the spiritual element the Spirit of God moveth on the spiritual water: they are mutually in each other.

53. The heaven wherein God dwelleth is the holy element; and the firmament or gulf between God and the four elements is the death; for the inward heaven hath another birth (that is, another life) than the external elementary life hath. Indeed they are in one another, but the one doth not apprehend the other: as tin and silver never mix aright together; for each is from another [or sundry] Principle; albeit they resemble each other, and have very near affinity to each other, yet they are as the inward and outward water to one another; wherein also they are to be understood. For the inward and outward Venus are step-sisters; they come indeed from one father, but they have two mothers, the one whereof is a Virgin, the other deflowered; and therefore they are separated till the judgment of God, who will purge away her reproach and shame, through the fire.

54. Moses writeth, that *God created the heaven out of the midst of the waters*; [and] it is very right. The astrum[1] is an external water-spirit, viz. powers of the outward water; and the material water is the body wherein the powers work. Now the fiery, airy and also earthly source is in the astrum; the like is also in the material water. The superior [astrum] is the life and dominion of the inferior; it enkindleth the

---

[1] Understand by the word astrum, the whole starry heaven, with all its powers, properties, influences, and constellations, internal and external.

inferior, whereby the inferior doth act, move and work. The inferior is the body or wife of the superior; indeed the superior is couched in the inferior, but as weak, and impotent.

55. And the superior were likewise as weak and impotent as the inferior, if it were not enkindled by the light of the sun: the same is the heart of all external powers; and it is the open punctum even to the tenth number. If we were not so blind as to contemn all that we see not with our calves' eyes, it were right and requisite to reveal it; but seeing God hath hidden the pearl, and also himself, from the sight of the wicked, therefore we will let it alone. Yet hint enough to our school-fellows: we will not give our pearl unto beasts.

56. Thus we understand what the outward heaven is, namely the powers or conception of the water. The word or power Fiat, which began with the beginning of the world, is yet still a creating;[1] it yet continually createth the heaven out of the water: and the spirit of God still moveth upon the water; and the holy water is yet continually separated from the water under the firmament.

57. This holy water is that of which Christ told us, that *he would give us it to drink; that should spring up in us to a fountain of eternal life.* The holy heavenly corporality doth consist therein; it is the body of Christ which he brought from heaven; and by the same, introduced heavenly paradisical essentiality into our dead or decayed body; and quickened ours in his; understand, in the aim[2] of the covenant in the essence of Mary; as shall be mentioned hereafter.

58. In this heavenly essence the Testaments[3] of Christ do consist; and this holy essence of the heavenly holy virginity, with the holy tincture, hath destroyed death; and bruised the head of the serpent's might in the wrath of God; for the divine power is the highest life therein.

59. Thus we understand how the holy heaven, wherein God dwelleth, moveth in the Fiat or the created [heaven], and that God is really present in all places; and inhabiteth all things: but he is comprehended of nothing. He is manifest in power in the inward heaven of the holy essentiality, viz. in the element. This holy element (in the beginning or inchoation of the four elements) did penetrate through the earth; and sprang [or budded] forth in the holy power's property, and bore fruits, of which man should have eaten in a heavenly manner. But when it did disappear in man, the curse entered into the earth, and so Paradise was quashed in the four elements; and continued

---

[1] Or creating.   [2] Mark or limit.   [3] Baptism, and the Supper.

retired in itself in the inward [element]. There it stands yet open unto man, if any will depart from this world's essence and enter into it upon the path which Christ hath made open.

60. The punctum of the whole created earth belonged unto the centre of Sol,[1] but [doth] not any more, at present: he is fallen, he who was a king: the earth is in the curse, and [hath] become a peculiar centre; whereunto all whatsoever is engendered in the vanity, in the four elements, doth tend and fall: all things fall unto the earth; for the Fiat[2] is yet in the deep, and createth[3] all earthly essence together unto the judgment of God, for separation.

61. We mean not that the earth came wholly[4] from the place of the sun; but from the whole sphere, out of both the internal spiritual worlds; but it [i.e. our meaning] hath another A B C, in that the earth belongeth unto the judgment of God for separation; even then it shall be manifest wherefore it is said: it belongeth unto the punctum of Sol.

62. For the worst must be a cause of the best. The eternal joy consists in this: that we are delivered from pain. God hath not eternally rejected his holy essence; but only the iniquity which mixed itself therein. But when the crystalline earth shall appear, then will be fulfilled this Saying: it appertains to the punctum of Sol. Here we have hinted enough to the understanding of our school-fellows; further we must here be silent.

---

[1] Ad centrum Solis, to the centre of the sun.
[2] Or creation.
[3] Or draweth or concreteth.
[4] Or only.

The Eleventh Chapter

Of the Mystery of the Creation

1. THE reason of the outward man saith: How is it that God hath not revealed the creation of the world unto man, that Moses and the children of God have written so little thereof, seeing it is the greatest and most principal work whereon the main depends?

2. Yes, dear reason, smell into thy bosom, of what doth it savour? Contemplate thy mind, after what does it long? Likely, after the cunning delusions of the devil: Had the devil not known this ground, very like he had been yet an angel; had he not seen the magical birth in his high light, then he had not desired to be a selfish lord and maker in the essence.

3. Wherefore doth God hide his children, which now receive the spirit of knowledge with the cross, and cast them into tribulation and mire of vanity? For certain, therefore, that they might play the tune of *The Miserere*, and continue in humility; and not sport in this life[1] with the light of nature; else, if they should espy and apprehend what the divine magic is, then they might also desire to imitate the devil, [and do] as Lucifer did: for which cause it is hidden from them. And neither Moses nor any other dare write clearer thereof; until the beginning of the creation beholdeth the end of the world in itself: And then it must stand open.

4. And therefore let none blame us; for the time is come about that Moses putteth away his veil from his eyes, which he hung before his face when he spake with Israel. After the Lord had spoken with him, Moses desired to see it, in that he said, *Lord, if I have found grace in thy sight, let me see thy face.* But the Lord would not, and said, *Thou shalt see my back part, for none can see my face.*

5. Now the eye of God was in Moses, and in the Saints; they have seen and spoken in the spirit of God, and yet had not the intuition of the spiritual birth in them; save at times only, when God would work wonders; as by Moses, when he did the wonders in Egypt: then the divine magic was open unto him, in manner and wise as in the creation.

6. And this was even the fall of Lucifer: that he would be a god of nature, and live in the transmutation. And this was even the idolatry

---

[1] Text, *Time.*

of the heathen: in that they understood the magical birth they fell from the only God unto the magical birth of nature, and chose unto themselves idols out of the powers of nature.

7. For which cause the creation hath remained so obscure; and God hath with tribulation covered his children in whom the true light shone, that they have not been manifest unto themselves. Seeing Adam also, according to the same lust, did imagine to know and prove the magic, and would be as God; so that God permitted him, that he defiled his heavenly image with the vanity of nature, and made it wholly dark and earthly; as Lucifer also did, with the centre of nature, when he of an angel became a devil.

8. Therefore I will seriously warn the Reader that he use the magic aright, viz. in true faith and humility towards God; and not meddle with turba magna in a magical manner: unless it conduceth to the honour of God, and to the salvation of mankind.

9. For we can say with truth, that the Verbum Fiat is yet a creating. Albeit it doth not create stones and earth; yet it coagulateth, formeth and worketh still in the same property. All things are possible to nature as it was possible for it in the beginning to generate stones and earth, also the stars and four elements, and did produce them, or work them forth out of one only ground; so it is, still unto this day. By the strong desire (which is the magical ground) all things may be effected, if man use nature aright, in its order to the work.

10. All essences consist in the seven properties. Now he that knoweth the essence, he is able, by the same spirit of that essence, whence it is come to be an essence, to change it into another form, and likewise to introduce it into another essence; and so make of a good thing an evil, and of an evil thing a good.

11. The transmutation of all things must be effected by simility,[1] viz. by its own native propriety: for the alienate is its enemy. Like as man must be regenerated again by the divine essentiality in the simility; by the simility in his holiness of the divine essentiality which he lost.

12. And as the false Magus woundeth man through enchantment with the assimilate, and through the desire introduceth evil into his evil, viz. into the assimilate; and as the upright holy faith or divine desire also entereth into the assimilate, and forfendeth man so that the false desire takes no place.

13. Thus all things consist in the assimulate; every thing may be

---

[1] Assimulation or likeness.

introduced into its assimulate. And if it comes into its assimulate it rejoiceth in its property, be it good or evil, and beginneth effectually to work: as is to be seen both in good and in evil.

14. As for example: let a man take down a little poison: it will presently receive with great desire the poison in the body, which before rested; and therein strengthen itself, and begin to work powerfully; and corrupt and destroy the contrary, viz. the good. And that now which the evil is able to do in its property, that likewise the good can do in its property; when it is freed from the wrath it may also introduce its assimulate into the real true joy.

15. The essence of this world consisteth in evil and good; and the one cannot be without the other. But this is the greatest iniquity of this world; that the evil overpowereth the good; that the anger is stronger therein than the love. And this by reason of the sin of the devil, and men; who have disturbed nature by the false desire, that it mightily and effectually worketh in the wrath, as a poison in the body.

16. Otherwise, if nature in its forms did stand in the property in equal weight, and in equal concord and harmony, then one property were not manifest above the other: heat and cold would be equally poised in the operation and qualification. And then Paradise would be still upon the earth; and though it were not outside man, yet it would be in man; if his properties were in equal weight [number and measure, if they did yet stand in the temperature], then he were incorruptible and immortal.

17. This is the death and misery of man and all creatures: that the properties are divided, and each aspiring in itself, and powerfully working and acting in its own will; whence sickness and pain ariseth. And all this is hence arisen: when the one element did manifest and put forth itself into four properties, then each property desired the assimulate, viz. an essence out of and according to itself; which the astringent Fiat did impress and coagulate; so that earth and stones were produced in the properties.

18. But now we are to consider of the greatest Mystery of the outward world between the elements and the astrum. The elemental spirit is severised from the astral spirit, and yet not parted asunder; they dwell in each other as body and soul; but the one is not the other. The astral spirit maketh its bodies as well as the elemental, and that in all creatures, in animals and vegetables.

19. All things of this world have a twofold body, viz. an elemental, from the fire, air, water and earth; and a spiritual body from the

astrum. And likewise a twofold spirit, viz. one astral, the other elemental.

20. Man only (among all the earthly creatures) hath a threefold body and spirit. For he hath also the internal spiritual world in him; which is likewise twofold, viz. light and darkness; and [this] also corporally and spiritually. This spirit is the soul; but this body is from the water of the holy element, which died in Adam, that is, disappeared as to his life, when the divine power departed from him, and would not dwell in the awakened vanity.

21. Which holy body must be regenerated, if his spirit will see God; otherwise he cannot see him, except he be again born anew of the water of the holy element in the spirit of God (who hath manifested himself in Christ with this same water-source); that man's disappeared body may be made alive in the holy water and spirit; else he hath no sense nor sight in the holy life of God.

22. This twofold outward body is now punctually to be pondered and considered of, if we would understand nature; and without this understanding let none call himself a master [or learned]. For in these (bodies) the dominion of all external creatures and essences is couched; they oftentimes are contrary one unto another, whence sickness, corruption and death ariseth in the body, that one severeth from the other.

23. The sidereal body is the highest excepting the divine in man; the elemental body is only its servant or dwellinghouse, as the four elements are only a body or habitation of the dominion of the stars.

24. The elemental spirit and body is inanimate and void of understanding, it hath only lust and desire in it, vegetation is its right life; for the air hath no understanding without the astrum. The astrum giveth the distinct understanding of the knowledge of all essences in the elements.

25. But the inward light, and power of the light, giveth in man the right divine understanding; but there is no right divine apprehension in the sidereal spirit; for the astrum hath another Principle. The Sidereal body dwelleth in the elemental, as the light-world in the darkness: it is the true rational life of all creatures.

26. The whole astrum is nothing else but the external expressed Word in the sound; it is the instrument whereby the holy eternal speaking Word speaketh and formeth externally; it is as a great harmony of unsearchable manifold voices and tunes, of all manner of instruments, which play and melodise before the holy God.

61

27. For they are mere powers, which enter into and mutually embrace each other, whence ariseth the sound in the essence; and the desire, viz. the Fiat, receiveth this sound and maketh it substantial. This substance is a spirit of the stars, which the elements receive into themselves, and coagulate it in themselves, and hatch it, as a hen her eggs: therefrom is the true rational life in the elements. And thus also the Sidereal spirit is hatched and coagulated in all creatures.

28. For the male and female do mutually cast a seed into each other; which is only a sulphur of the astrum and four elements; afterwards it is hatched in the matrix, and coagulated to a living spirit.

29. For when the fire is enkindled in the seed which is sown in the matrix, the spirit severs itself again from the body, as a propriate; just as the light from the fire, according to the right of the eternal nature; and two become manifest in one, viz. a spiritual body from the astrum, and a fleshy body from the four elements.

30. And this sidereal spirit is the soul of the great world, which depends on *Punctum Solis*, and receiveth its light and life from it; as all the stars do take light and power from the sun, so likewise [they take] their spirit.

31. The sun is the centre of the astrum, and the earth the centre of the elements: they are to each other as spirit and body, or as man and wife; albeit the astrum hath another wife, where it hatcheth its essence, viz. the moon, which is the wife of all the stars (but especially of the sun). I mean it in the essence of the operation.

32. Not that we mean that the astrum is wholly arisen from the punctum of Sol, in that I call it the centre of the stars. It is the centre of the powers, the cause that the powers of the stars do act in the essence; it openeth their powers, and giveth its power into them, as a heart of the powers, and they mutually rejoice in its essence, that they are moved to act or desire in its essence.

33. And even here lieth the great Mystery of the creation, viz. that the internal, viz. God, hath thus manifested himself with his eternal speaking Word, which he himself is: the external is a type of the internal. God is not alienate: *in him all things live and move*, each in its Principle and degree.

34. The outward properties dwell in themselves in the external, viz. in the expressed Word, and are wholly external; they cannot in their own strength reach the powers of the holy world; the holy world alone penetrates them: it dwelleth also in itself. But in the punctum of Sol the eighth number is open, viz. the eternal nature, the

eternal magical fire; and in the fire the eternal tincture, which is the ninth number; and in the tincture the cross, where the Deity manifesteth itself, which is the tenth number: and beyond this manifestation is the eternal understanding, viz. the ONE, that is, God, JEHOVAH, viz, the ABYSS.

35. Not that God is divided: we speak of his manifestation alone, from what ability and power the sun hath its shining lustre, that the same is immutable, so long as time endureth; namely, from the lustre of the fiery tincture of the eternal, spiritual, magical fire.

36. For its lustre or shining light hath a degree of a more deep original than the external world hath manifest in itself. This the wise heathen have observed, and adored it for God, seeing the true God, who dwelleth outside all nature in himself, was not known unto them.

The Twelfth Chapter

Of the Six Days' Works of the Creation

1. THAT God hath created heaven and earth and all things in six days, as Moses saith, is the greatest Mystery, wholly hidden from the external reason. There is neither night, morning, nor evening in the deep above the moon; but a continual day from the beginning of the outward world even to the end of the same.

2. And albeit the creation was finished in such a time as in the length of six days, yet the days' works have a far more subtle [or abstruse] meaning: for the seven properties are also understood therewith, six whereof belong to the active dominion, to good and evil, and the seventh, viz. the essence, is the rest, wherein the other properties rest, which God hath expressed and made visible.

3. We have in the dominion of the planetic orb the figure, how the six properties of the active life (which rest in the seventh) have, in six days, out of the inward spiritual world, introduced and manifested themselves in an external visible world of four elements: For the planetic orb hath its rise from the punctum of Sol; for there was the royal place of the hierarchies, of which the whole circle (between the stars in the internal and external) is a member or *Corpus*.

4. But seeing the prince of the hierarchies (when he sat in the heavenly essence in the rest) did fall, and aspired to or for the centre of the eternal nature, he was cast into the darkness: and God by his motion created [for] him[-self] another prince out of this place (but without divine understanding) for a ruler of the essence; and that is the sun.

5. From this place proceeded, in the divine motion, the seven properties of nature (understand, the planets) which govern the essential being in good and evil (in which [essence] Lucifer sat, and whence he was cast, and lost his dominion in the essence); and as the seven properties have their dominion in the beginning of each day in the week, even so were the six days' works of the creation.

6. For Lucifer forsook the rest of his hierarchies, and entered into the eternal disquietness. Now, God hath created all things of this world in six days, and rested on the seventh day from the creation, which is Saturday, according to the Scripture; that is, from the day of rest, understand from the eternal day of rest, he hath moved himself

64

to the creation; and in the first form of nature he began the first day; that is, he hath brought it forth out of the impression, and moved himself with his Word: this was the most inward motion according to the speaking Word of power.

7. Then began, in the expressed Word, Sunday, that is, the true paradisical day, where the powers did mutually work in each other in great holiness and glory; for on Sunday the enkindled sulphur and salniter of the earthly property was created out of the great deep of the whole hierarchy, out of the spiritual worlds, into a mass (which is the terrestrial globe), and was put forth out of the austere property of the first form of nature.

8. Even then began the first hour of the first day: and the power of nature did mutually rule in great joy in the expressed Word, out of which power of joy the sun was created on the fourth day in the princely place: so that this power, whereout the sun was created, ruled the first hour of the beginning of the world; and so it began its dominion, which continueth even unto the end of the world: and therefore the sun ruleth the first hour on Sunday; and the day is rightly so called.

9. The words of Moses concerning the creation are exceedingly clear, yet unapprehensive to reason, for he writeth thus: *In the beginning God created the heaven and the earth. And the earth was without form and void; and darkness was upon the face of the deep. And the Spirit of God moved upon the face of the waters. And God said, Let there be light: and there was light. And God saw the light, and it was good: and God divided the light from the darkness. And God called the light Day, and the darkness he called Night. And out of the evening and morning was the first day*[1] (Gen. i. 1–5).

10. The whole understanding is couched in these words: for the beginning is the first motion, which came to pass when prince Michael fought with the Dragon, when he was spewed out with the creation of the earth. For even then the enkindled essence, which with the enkindling did coagulate itself into earth and stones, was cast out of the internal into the external.

11. And he, the Dragon, fell from heaven, viz. out of the holy world, upon the wrath of the earth, as lightning, as it is written: *I saw Satan fall from heaven as lightning*, saith Christ. Moreover, it was wholly dark in the deep above the earth, and the austere endkindled wrath was manifest. For hell was prepared for him, whereinto he fell, viz. into the great darkness of the first Principle, wherein he liveth.

[1] The evening and morning were the first day.

12. Here now lieth the veil before reason, that it cannot look into the eyes of Moses, for he saith: *And the earth was without form and void.* Yea, without form indeed. Had not the Spirit of God moved upon the internal water (which was amassed with the Fiat in the heaven), and had not God said, *Let there be light,* the earth would have been yet without form and void.

THE FIRST DAY

13. With the Word, when God said, *Let there be light,* the essence of the ens did powerfully move itself in the light's property, not only in the earth, but also in the whole deep: whence[1] on the fourth day the sun was created, that is, enkindled in its place. And in this word *Fiat* the earth's mass, and also the very power which is called heaven, amassed itself in the essence; all which before was only a spirit, a spiritual essence.

14. And with the speaking, as God spake, *Let there be light,* the holy power, which was amassed in the wrath, moved itself, and became light in the same essence in the power. And with this coming to be light, the devil's might and strength was wholly withdrawn from him in the essence, for here the light shone in the now anew awakened power, in the darkness; which [light] the prince of wrath could not comprehend;[2] it was also of no benefit to him, for it was the light of nature, which is useless to him.

15. And Moses said, *God divided the light from the darkness,* which is thus to be understood. The darkness remained in the wrathful property, not only in the earth, but also in the whole deep: but in the light's essence the light of nature did arise [or spring forth] from heaven, viz. from the quintessence, whence the astrum was created; which essence is everywhere in the earth, and above the earth.

16. Thus the darkness remained in the wrath's property in the essence of the earth, and also in the whole deep of this world. And the nature-light remained in the light's essence, as a working life, through which the holy element did operate and work; in which operation Paradise budded[3] through the earth, and bore fruit until the curse of God. And then the holy bloomings or growth ceased, and the holy element remained as an inward heaven, steadfast, retired in itself. And yet it doth diffuse its power through the light of nature, but not

[1] Out of which power or virtue in the light's property.
[2] Receive or perceive.
[3] Sprang.

so powerfully as in the beginning, for the curse is the cause of its withdrawing; indeed there is no total departing, but yet it is nothing now as [compared with what it was] before the sin of the second created prince, Adam.

17. Thus in the first motion of the Verbum Fiat the heaven (that is, the circle, so far as the Verbum Fiat reached itself forth to the creation) was amassed or enclosed; and the earth was amassed with the Verbum Fiat, and created to the planetic orb. Thus by the separation, viz. of the light and darkness, and by the expelling of prince Lucifer, we are to understand the creation of the first day.

18. Now the first day with the manifested Word did convey itself through the other five days, even into the day of rest; where the beginning entereth again into the end, and the end again into the beginning. For the first motion of the Word, where the light of nature hath enkindled itself in the essence, is the joy of the creation or creature; which did open itself with the other days through all the properties of nature, where each property may be called a heaven: for it hath and bringeth also its peculiar operation and efficacy along in itself into the rest,[1] and each day one property did move and manifest itself; wherein a peculiar sundry work was manifested and revealed.

OF THE SECOND DAY

19. The second day we call Monday, and therefore, because the moon ruleth the first hour of the day: and it is very likely that the ancient wise men have understood somewhat thereof in the light of nature, which they have kept secret and mystical, rather deciphering it by figures than clearly explaining it. And it is to be seen in the names of the seven planets, that they have for certain understood the same; in that they have given them names according to the seven properties of nature, which do so wholly agree and accord, as well with the creation as [with] nature, that methinks they have in part understood the ground of the creation aright, seeing the names of the planets have their rise and derivation so fully and punctually out of the language of Nature. But the reason why it hath not been made clear, plain and manifest is (as before mentioned) because of the false magic, that it might remain hidden unto the artists of juggling and collusion in nature, by reason of the great abuse. Wherefore we also shall still let it so remain, and yet hint enough to the understanding of our school-fellows.

[1] Understand, into the rest of the properties or days.

20. Now of the second day Moses writeth thus: *And God said, Let there be a firmament between the waters, and let it divide between the waters. Then God made the firmament, and divided the water under the firmament from the water above the firmament: and it was so. And God called the firmament heaven. And out of the evening and morning was the second day* (Gen. i. 6–8).

21. Moses saith, that *out of the evening and morning was the second day,* that is, out of the manifestation of the first, the second manifestation proceeded and brake forth; and saith further, that *on the second day God created the firmament of heaven, and separated the waters; the water under the firmament from the water above the firmament.* Here now lieth the hidden veil, wherein we have hitherto been pointed and directed unto a heaven situate afar off above the stars, without the place of this world. So very blind is reason as to God that it understands nothing of him; and doth not consider that the Scripture saith of God: *Am not I he which filleth all things:* and, that *time and place cannot divide him.* Much less is it understood what the water above the firmament is, which they will flatly hold to be a place afar distant, viz. above the stars, whither also we have been shewn into heaven.

22. But seeing that God out of grace doth bestow upon us the understanding, therefore we will set it down for our fellow-scholars who are able to apprehend it; and yet herein we shall write nothing for the selfish wiselings of outward reason, for they have it already in the eyes of their reason, and cannot miss it, they can judge all things: what the Spirit of God revealeth, that must be a heresy unto them, albeit they do not understand it: so that they remain without, and do not so much as once know God.

23. The firmament is the gulf between time and eternity: but that God calleth it heaven and maketh a division of the waters, gives us to understand that the heaven is in the world, and the world is not in heaven.

24. The water above the firmament is in heaven, and the water under the firmament is the external material water.

25. Here we must understand the difference between the holy [water] and the outward element-water: the water above the firmament is spiritual in the birth of the holy element; and the water under the firmament is mortal, for it is apprehended in the dark impression; the curse and the awakened vanity is therein, and yet one water is not without the other.

26. When I look upon the external water then I must also say, Here is also the water above the firmament in the water under the

OF THE SECOND DAY

firmament. But the firmament is the middle, and the gulf therein between time and eternity; so that they are distinct. And I see with the external eyes of this world only the water under the firmament: but the water above the firmament is that which God hath appointed in Christ to the Baptism of Regeneration, after that the Word of the divine power had moved itself therein.

27. Now the outward water is the instrument of the inward; and the inward water is understood [therein]; for the moving Spirit in the Word is he which ruleth the inward water in the Baptism. Dear Christians, let this be spoken to you; it is the real ground.

28. But that Moses saith, God created the firmament, and called it heaven, is the most intimate secret, of which the earthly man is not able to understand anything: the understanding is barely in the power of the water above the firmament, viz. in the heaven, or (as I might set it down) in the Spirit of God. If he be awaked in man in the water above the firmament, which disappeared in Adam, as to his life, that [man] seeth through all; otherwise there is no understanding here, but all is dumb.

29. The creating of the heaven is understood, first how the speaking Word hath amassed[1] the manifested powers of the spiritual world, wherein it is manifest, worketh, and also ruleth. Secondly, it is understood of the manifested powers of the external world, which the spirit hath amassed into the essence of four elements, and closed into the external firmament, that the devil, viz. the prince of anger, cannot reach them; by which he would work with the internal water: so that the powers of eternity do work through the powers of time, as the sun illumines the water, and the water comprehends it not, but feels it only; or as a fire doth through-heat an iron, and the iron remaineth iron. So likewise the outward heaven is passive, and the inward worketh through it, and draweth forth an external fruit out of the outward; whereas yet the inward heaven lieth hidden therein in the firmament: as God is hidden in the time.

30. And we are to understand with the second day's work the manifestation of the internal heavenly and the external heavenly essence, viz. the manifestation of the water-source, understand, the essence of the seven properties, viz. the corporality, or the laboratory[2] of the other six; wherein the soul or spirit of the outward world worketh and ruleth in the external. This working[3] in the most external or inferior heaven next the earth is ascribed unto the moon, for it

---

[1] Conceived or formed. [2] Operate or work-house. [3] Or operation.

is the manifestation of the lunar property; not of the star[1] which was first created into the external on the fourth day to be a governor therein, but this same property [is] in the inanimate outward life, viz. in the vegetative life: the vegetative life was opened on the third day.

31. And when God had ordained the water into sundry places upon the earth, then he moved the external expressed word in the vegetative life. Now Moses saith, *God spake, Let the earth put forth herbs, and grass yielding seed, and fruitful trees; each bearing fruit according to his kind; and let each have its seed in itself: and when it came to pass, out of the evening and morning was the third day* (Gen. i. 11, 12).

OF THE THIRD DAY OF THE CREATION

32. In the original of the eternal nature, which is an eternal original, the manifestation of the six days' works is very clearly to be found; how the eternal Word hath unfolded them out of the invisible spiritual [property] and brought them into the visible: also the form thereof is to be found in the planetic orb, if any hath skill to apprehend it.

33. For in the eternal nature's birth there is an eternal day. Whatsoever God hath manifested and made visible in six diversalls,[2] which are called days' works, that standeth in the eternal nature in six distinct degrees in the essence, viz. in the seventh property, in which the six degrees of nature work, and yet also do eternally rest from working; they are themselves the working, which they give in to the seventh, as into their own peculiar rest, wherein their perfection and manifestation consists.

34. And we are to understand nothing else by the creation, save that the Verbum Fiat hath amassed the spiritual birth, and introduced it into a visible external dominion and essence. For we see it very clearly in the writings of Moses (albeit we have a glass besides to see), that when God the first day had created the gross part into a mass, that he extracted the fine part out of the same first day's work, and severed and amassed the waters, viz. the spiritual essence, and produced it out of the first day, viz. out of the holy power, into a time; that is, out of the eternal day into an inchoative day.

35. Now the third accomplishment of the third day's work is the moving growing life, in which on the first day the light of nature did shine in the essence of the ens, after an external manner: it shone

---

[1] Star or planet called the moon.   [2] Or distinctions.

likewise now through the second day, viz. through the water and the heaven. And in this shining light the expressed Word did move itself in the essence, and wrought effectually; and even then the power of the expressed Word from the light of the inward nature did pullulate, and spring forth, through the external nature, out of the heaven through the earth. [And so] now the potentate who was a king and great prince hath lost his domination, for the essence of the wrath was captivated in the light of nature, and he with it. And so he lieth between time and eternity, imprisoned in the darkness, until the judgment of God.

36. In the third day's work the sulphureous, mercurial, and saltish life out of the centre was opened out of the anguish in the outward world's property; and yet there is no anguish to be understood until the fire, but only a senseless forth-driving life, viz. a growth: for the fire-blaze ariseth out of the anguish, viz. out of the third form of nature: and this is the salnitral flagrat, which severiseth the powers in the properties, which was moved in the third day's work, where the properties opened themselves, and were mutually unfolded in the salnitral flagrat, each out of itself; which the impression did again receive into itself, and made them corporeal in the water. And thence arose and proceeded trees, herbs and grass: each property became excressive[1] in the salniter, and did manifest itself with fruit: as we see plainly how the property of the dark world did mightily force itself along in the outward power: whereupon some herbs and plants are so venomous and malignant; for the earth proceeded out of both the inward worlds to a compaction.

37. Now Mars on Tuesday hath the first hour of the day in dominion, which day is the third in the creation. And this salnitral fire-flagrat is even the property of Mars: as he is wrathful and fiery, so likewise is this property in the sulphur, where we then do understand the salnitral flagrat for the poisonful Mars; which is the cause of motion and stirring and the compunction in the first impression in the eternal nature, viz. in the dark world.

38. In the third day's work God moved the third property of nature, viz. the sulphurous source, in which the fire enkindled, and in the fire-flagrat is the division of the powers; where each property became manifest in itself: Now when God said, *Let the earth bring forth grass, herb and trees*, that is nothing else, but that when he moved the expressed Word of the powers in the properties, the properties

[1] Or putting or budding forth.

found and felt the light of nature in them; whereupon they became hungry, and were impressed, that is, amassed and compacted or coagulated. Now when as the light of nature found itself in a perceivance, and the nature did feel itself in the sweet light, thereby arose in the coagulation the dominion of joy, viz. the pullulation and growth. For all growth consisteth in the light and water; when the light penetrateth the Sulphur and water-source, then Mars springeth up for great joy in the Sulphur.

39. This opening began on the third day, and continueth unto the end of the world. On the first day the earth was without form and void, for the possibility[1] to the growth was not yet opened. Here the earth was moved and the properties opened, and not only the earth, but the whole deep in the centre of the outward nature made itself external, and yet remained also internal.

[1] Or ability.

The Thirteenth Chapter

Of The Creation of the Fourth Day

1. THE fourth day Mercurius hath the first hour of the day, who causeth the sensitive life. Here we understand very fully and exactly the ground of the manifestation of the inward nature into the external; for on the fourth day the sun and stars were created, which are the right mercurial life. Here the fire's property opened itself in the sulphurous-source through the water, and the first essence became manifest through the light of nature, which is a Mercurius Salnitri, an incentive Mercurius, a quick perceptive Mercurius.

2. In the third form of nature there is a senseless life in sulphur and Mercurius, but in the fourth there is a feeling life; for the properties are made painful in the fire; and in the oleous [life] they become meek, pleasant and full of joy: therefore now the motion in the oily is feeling from the painfulness.

3. Here we now understand very fundamentally how the separation in the fire of the eternal nature hath manifested itself in the essence of the outward world with form and shape; for in the enkindling of the fire in the salnitral flagrat two essences do severise, viz. one watery from the devoration in the fire, where the fire devoureth the rough harsh source of the impression in itself; then out of the consuming there proceedeth a great meekness, which is mortified to the fire, and is insensible, and giveth the water-source.

4. Secondly, the fire-source doth sever itself [likewise into its Principle], viz. the properties to the fire-source, which now with the enkindling of the fire are full of pain and sense. This fire-source could not subsist, unless it did again devour [or take] the water into itself, whereby it doth strengthen itself; whence also the salnitral flagrat ariseth, where the wrath is dismayed at the essence of the water's meekness; whence ariseth the feeling, so also the lustre, of the fire.

5. For that water which is devoured in the fire is dissolved into a spiritual oil, in which the fire shineth; and out of the oil proceedeth the air, viz. the moving spirit of the fire which is motive in the fire.

6. The air is nothing else but the moving life, where the speaking Word doth diffuse itself in the water-source through nature, through the powers of nature, through the fire, in the oil of the nature of the light. It is the fire's life: but it is mortified to the fire, and yet it is

made manifest by the fire; it is the life of nature according to the property of meekness.

7. Thus in[1] the enkindling of the fire in the light of the fire, which is the light of nature, four properties are to be understood, viz. a fiery, an airy, and an oily (wherein the light is manifest), and a watery; all which do originally spring forth out of the first desire to nature; in that the free lubet introduceth itself into a desire and nature; and they all display themselves through the fire into a moving life; and yet there is no intellective life, but only properties to the true life. The intellectual life is the spirited Word, which manifesteth itself through the properties. These properties are impressed in the Crea T, that is, in the Verbum Fiat, and brought into an essentiality; wherefrom is come a Sulphur Salnitri, that is, a magical astrum, in manner and mode as the mind of man is; which also hath thence its real original.

8. This salnitral and sulphureous property was brought forth out of the third day's work, viz. out of the fire-flagrat; and thence the fourth motion is arisen, viz. the mercurial, which the Fiat hath amassed, and impressed it into it, and made it visible, which are the stars; which are nothing else but properties of the powers of nature. Whatsoever nature is in a little spark in itself, that the whole astrum is in its circle; and what nature is in its hiddenness, and secretness, the same the astrum is, in an open working life. Understand it thus:

9. Each star hath the property of all stars in it, but hidden in nature, and the star is manifest only in one sole property; else, if the whole nature were manifest in each thing, then all things and essences would be but one thing and essence; and therefore God hath, by his sounding Word, moved the Sulphur Salnitri according to the properties, that the distinct severation might be manifest: and this manifestation is a Mercurius; for the eternal-speaking Word, which is called God, hath manifested his voice or will through nature.

10. Therefore the whole astrum is a pronounced voice (or breathed tone) of the powers, an expressed Word, which doth again give forth from itself its spiration and speaking out of the properties. It is an echo out of God's love and anger, out of the dark-and-light-world.

11. After the astrum[2] are the four elements, which also have their original out of this fountain; which also have their spiration [or outbreathing] out of themselves; they also speak forth their properties out of themselves, and they are as a body of the stars. For they speak or breathe forth from themselves a corporeal essence; and the stars do

---

[1] Or by, or with. [2] Next the stars.

breathe forth a spiritual essence out of themselves: and this twofold essence ruleth mutually in the visible world, as body and soul.

12. And we give you this rightly to understand: In each element there lieth a whole astrum; the fire hath a whole astrum in itself, and also the air, water, and earth, but it is not manifest in them. Therefore God hath enclosed [or encircled] the place of this world with a manifest astrum, that it might enkindle the other astrum in the four elements, that the manifest astrum might work in the hidden mystery, viz. in the astrum of the four elements, and procreate wonders. For so a wonderful figure and property may be produced out of a thing, which otherwise is impossible for nature to do, in its own [naked] self.

13. Also we are to know, that there is an astrum in the divine magic, which is the fountain of the eternal mind of the abyss, whence nature and all essences are arisen. Likewise there is an astrum in the manifest heavenly world, and also an astrum in the dark hellish world. And these astrums[1] are but one only astrum, but they are severised into distinct degrees and principles; that which in the outward world is open and manifest in the figure, the same is manifest in power in the spiritual world, and not in forms.

14. And we understand, that the Verbum Fiat on the fourth day moved the fourth property of nature, viz. the fifth essence, and opened it out of the sulphureous property out of the fire-flagrat, viz. out of the third property. And thus an astrum became manifest in the air, which are the visible stars; and an astrum in the fire, which is the rational life of all creatures; and an astrum in the water, which is the vegetative life; and an astrum in the earth, which is the wrathful earthly life.

15. The fiery [astrum] giveth soul; and the airy, spirit; the watery affordeth the mansion of the soul and the spirit, viz. blood, wherein the tincture of the fire and light dwelleth; and the earthly giveth flesh. And every of the four astrums giveth a spirit and body according to its property. Only, God hath thus associated one unto another, that the one might be manifest in the other, and be jointly together one body; like as all the four elements are only one element, but they divide themselves into four properties according to the centre of nature.

16. Therefore astrums do procreate out of themselves their officer, viz. the outward nature, that is, the soul of the outward world, as a constantly enduring mind; wherein lieth the omnipotency, as a

[1] Or constellations.

manifest Great Mystery. In this officer God hath awakened and raised a king, or as I might set it down by way of similitude, a nature-god, with six councillors, which are his assistants; that is, the sun, with the other six planetic stars, which were spoken forth out of the seven properties out of the place of Sol; and in the speaking were introduced into a rolling sphere, according to the property of the eternal generation in the centre of nature. And this was opened in seven degrees out of the birth; where the first degree of the motion in the light of nature, (from the inward spiritual fire-and-light-world), was the sun, which receiveth its lustre from the tincture of the inward fire-and-light-world: it standeth as an opened punctum to the fire-world. See *Three-fold Life of Man*, ch. 4: pars. 16–49.

17. And with the spiration the sixfold life of the six degrees of the days' works and forms of the centre came forth externally and severised itself, after the kind and nature of the eternal birth. As first, Venus which is the water-source out of the meekness out of the mortification in the fire, which is a desire of meekness from[1] the fire, for the fire enkindleth the meekness whence it is desirous. This is now the love-desire according to the spirit, and according to its essence it is water; which water in the metals affordeth the noble corpus solis.

18. This Venus, seeing she (as to her own natural right) is mortified to the fire, is submissive, and giveth the holy water; understand, as to her own peculiar property; which [water] is holy in the spirit, and yet in the essence it is captivated in the wrath, where it giveth the material water according to the deadly property. It giveth body unto all the seven metals, and essence to all the six planets: which we see in the metals; for each planet maketh its essence in its property according to itself. As the Sun, in gold; the Moon in silver; Jupiter in tin; Saturn in lead; Mercurius in quicksilver; Mars in iron; and yet it is the essence of the Venus property alone: but they give their power and spirit into it, and hold the body for their own, seeing they rule the same.

19. This Venus property in the place of Sol sank downwards in the first egress; and the fire-source above it is Mars; and out of Venus property beneath, the heavy sound, and that is Mercurius, out of the Sulphur Salnitri through the water; and upwards out of Mars, the power of the fire and light, that is Jupiter; and beneath, from Mercurius, the essence of the desire, where Venus comprehends the essence in her fiery desire, as a body of the powers, that is Luna; and

---

[1] By reason of.

above Jupiter, Saturnus, viz. the expressed or spirated impression of the first form of nature.

20. These properties were spherated in the spiration, in manner as the birth of nature is in the essence, which the Verbum Fiat received and amassed into a body, and ordained it for dominion unto the four astrums, over which he hath appointed angelical rulers as a supreme council: which we give only a hint of here, seeing we have spoken thereof at large in another place.

The Fourteenth Chapter

Of the Creation of the Fifth Day

1. Now when God had opened the astrum and four elements as a moving life, wherein the superior astrum gave the distinction in the moving life, and actuated the four astrums in the four elements, then he educed out of the essence of all the astrums and elements, through the motion of his speaking Word in the Verbum Fiat, the impress or express, as the power of that same life, which was free from the pain, and amassed it through the Verbum Fiat, and spake forth that same life, by the holy eternal-speaking Word through the Fiat, into forms and shapes, according to the properties of the astrums in the spiritual corpus, in which the Fiat or the desire attracted the elements according to the outward essence unto itself, as a body.

2. And thence were creatures produced in all the four elements; in each astrum according to its property: as birds in the astrum of the air; fishes in the astrum of the water; cattle and four-footed beasts out of the astrum of the earth and four elements; likewise spirits in the fire-astrum, which also is in the other elements. And we see very exactly in the difference of the creatures that the degrees of the astrum [or constellations] are so distinct and various. For the worms of the earth live in the third degree, viz. in the fire-flagrat, in the Sulphur, Mars, and Mercury, in the life devoid of understanding; and whereas they have an understanding [or instinct] by the enkindling of the superior astrum, in which third degree in the property also grass, herbs and trees do stand, and yet they receive assisting influence from the superior [astrum] in the enkindling, by which they are otherwise qualified.

3. And we see, that each kind hath a spirit and body according to the degree of its astrum; for we understand, that out of one astrum many kinds of creatures do proceed: the cause whereof is that each astrum hath again its degrees in itself. For there is in each astrum whatsoever all the astra have; but yet in sundry distinct degrees in the manifestation; and therefore the properties in each astrum are manifold: so also divers sorts of creatures are proceeded from each astrum. The spirit of each kind is from the astrum, but all kinds must use the four elements; for they arise out of that fountain whence all the astra do originally proceed.

4. On the fifth day Jupiter hath the dominion of the first hour of the day among the planets; and that, because he hath his original in the creation of the astrum out of the fifth degree of nature, viz. out of the power of the sulphureous and salnitral oil; and that on the fifth day this Jovial property was opened and educed, out of the fourth day's property, as a pleasant powerful life out of all the constellations; unto which life God created all creatures, except man, each out of the property of his constellation, out of his degree. So that they might all live in the soul of the outward nature, and be under the government of one officer; which is the outward constellation wherein the sun is chief regent.

5. Each constellation hath its compaction of Sulphur and Mercury; the Sulphur giveth essence, and Mercurius giveth spirit into the essence; and from both these Sal is generated, viz. out of the sharp Fiat according to the property of Sulphur and Mercury. And out of these three properties, viz. out of Sulphur, Mercurius, and Sal, all creatures entered into a life and creatural being. And now such as the Sulphur was on each place in every punctum in the property, as was taken or conceived in the Fiat, in the motion of the fifth property, in all the elements, even such a creature was opened or brought forth. As the compaction was coagulated in each punctum, so each kind had its spirit and seed in itself, to generate and bring forth again.

6. The two sexes, viz. the male and its female, arise from the separation of the watery and fiery tincture in Sulphur. For the separation was in the Verbum Fiat, where, out of one sulphur, in one only punctum, two sexes came forth out of one essence, viz. the fiery property in itself to a male, and the light's or water's property to a female, where then both tinctures severed.

7. And as we see that the fire cannot burn without the water, and the water were a nothing without the fire, and they mutually beget one another, and also do again vehemently desire each other; and their right life consisteth in their conjunction, in that they have produced each other, and afterwards do enter into and mutually embrace each other as one; where also they are again changed in the fire into one; and yet do again proceed forth from the fire in one essence, viz. in an oleous property, in which they stand in the bond of the highest love-desire; for their light shineth in the oil. And as the fire-world desireth the light-world, and the light-world the fire-world, as father and son, the like also is to be understood of the two sexes.

8. The female is from the male, as the tincture of the light and

water is from the fire; and they jointly belong together in nature as one. Thus the one may not be without the other, and they have a very ardent longing after each other, for the tincture of the light, viz. Venus's tincture desireth the fire's tincture, and the fire the light's, as its pleasing[1] delight.

9. For Venus giveth essence, and the fire taketh the essence to its life, and yieldeth out of the received essence the light; and in the fiery light the oil, and out of the oil again the water and essence. And hence it is that all creatures do desire copulation, each with its own kind; and so they do generate a third, viz. an assimulate, according to two in one: every ens brings forth a similitude according to itself.

10. And we see very clearly that each kind is created out of a sundry ens, each out of a different degree; and how each kind liveth in its mother, whence it hath taken its original; and that it cannot live in another degree. As the beasts upon the earth, which are a limus of the earth and air: therein they live; and thence they take their food and nourishment; for the Fiat extracted them out of the earth's property and amassed them in the fifth manifestation of the essence, as a sulphur of the fifth ens, whereon the four depend.

11. The birds were created in the sulphur of the air, therefore they fly in their mother; also the fishes in the sulphur of the water; and the worms in the sulphur of the earth. Thus each thing liveth in its mother whence it was taken in the beginning, and the contrary is its death.

12. And the essence and life of this time is nothing else but a contemplation of the inward spiritual world; what the possibility of eternity hath in it, and what kind of spiritual play is in the ens of the inward spiritual world, accordingly it came forth into a creatural being, out of good and evil, into a time; and that, through the divine motion.

13. And hereby the kingdom and dominion of the prince of the place of this world was taken from him, for the ens hath introduced itself into another Principle, wherein he cannot be; for he was not made a creature in this Principle, and he hath no life therein, save only in the property of the awakened wrath in the vanity.

[1] Meekning.

The Fifteenth Chapter

Of the Sixth Day's Work of the Creation

1. THE sixth day in the creation is Friday, on which Venus ruleth the first hour of the day; which doth rightly signify unto us the order of the degrees, how the eternal-speaking Word hath manifested itself with nature, through the time; how the spirit hath brought forth the six properties of nature into six degrees or days into a working life, and yet hath introduced them all again into the seventh, viz. into the rest, or into the mansion wherein they should work; denoting that all whatsoever that they should work, manifest and produce out of the wonders of the eternal wisdom should re-enter into the one, viz. into the rest; which is the seventh property, viz. a house of the working life, wherein it should stand as a figure to the contemplation of the great glory of God.

2. Now, when God had educed the five days of nature through five properties or degrees, into five constellations, (all which are not indeed constellations, but a fountain of an astral property), viz. into a sundry peculiar heaven, as it might be given and expressed to the understanding, then he did, on the sixth day, educe out of the Jovial property, viz. out of the fifth constellation, the sixth, viz. he produced out of the Jovial power the fiery love-desire; wherewith he ruleth through all the constellations. Whence it is that each life doth long after its likeness; that is, it again desireth such a creature as each life hath in it.

3. Each life desireth, in this Venus-property, to generate again such a creature as it is in itself. Hence ariseth the strong ardent imagination and fiery desire, that the properties do again desire into one, viz. into the fountain whence they proceeded; for in the same they may generate the assimulate of themselves.

4. Now when God had educed this fiery love-desire out of the centre through all the properties, then nature was now desirous (in this love-property) of the likeness of God, viz. [of] a similitude according to and in the generation of the holy love-desire; that so this holy constellation of the love-desire might also be creaturised and figurised.

5. And seeing this love-desire was educed out of all the properties of nature and the heavens, viz. out of the Verbum Fiat, wherein all the creatures lay from eternity in a Mystery, and [was] introduced

into a separation, viz. into a sundry distinct degree, therefore now the property longed to be an image of all degrees and properties, viz. a living, rational and understanding image, according to the manifestation of this manifested property.

6. Now said the speaking Word in the Verbum Fiat, *Let us make man*: that is, out of the mesh[1] of all essences, out of the property of all powers and constellations, the love-desire desired a limus out of all essences for a living image: *An image that may be like* and resemble Us: *and let them have dominion over the fish of the sea, and over the fowl of the air; over the cattle, and over all the earth, and over every worm* (or creeping thing) *that creepeth upon the earth.*

7. Understand this thus: The sixth property of nature (viz. the love-desire) was produced, expressed or breathed forth out of all the properties, and was the desirous life in the joy, viz. in the light of nature. This was not itself a limus, but it was the desire to the limus; for the speaking Word which God expressed moved therein, viz. the intellectual life. God was therein manifest.

8. This manifested word of God desired, in this love-desire, a limus out of the earth and all the created essences, out of all the constellations and degrees, for a body unto itself; therefore God said, *an image that may rule over fish, fowl, beasts, worms, and over the earth,* and all the essences of the constellations. *Now, if it must have dominion therein, then it must be thereout; for each spirit ruleth in its mother whence it is arisen and proceeded; and eateth of its mother.*

9. But here we must rightly understand this love-desire in the expressed Word. The expressed Word had, in this Venus-desire, the desire of all heavens, that is, of all entities and properties in itself, viz. the properties of the inward spiritual holy heaven, which is the mansion of the power of God; and of the outward created heaven, with the heavens of all constellations and elements; yet not essentially [or in substance], but as a spiritual desire: and these properties desired, in the spiritual desire, to be essential.

10. Now the text in Moses speaketh very clearly and fully, where it saith, *And God created man in his own image, in the image of God created he him.* By the creating is understood the body, which is twofold, viz. a spiritual body and a corporeal; for the Venus-desire is a spiritual body; and that which it hath attracted unto itself in the Fiat into the desire of the spiritual body, that is a fleshly body. The Verbum Fiat itself did figurise and form it into a spiritual man, out of all the three

---

[1] Mass or mixture.

Principles, viz. according to the inward divine world, both according to the fiery-light-world and the outward world.

11. And the spiritual body is the image of God, which the Fiat clothed with the essence out of all the essences, viz. with the heavenly holy essence, the heavenly holy corporality of the inward holy love-desire. And from the outward love-desire [it was clothed] with the limus of the earth and the other elements, together with the visible constellation of the third Principle.

12. The inward holy man was in the heaven of God, and the outward man was in the outward heaven, a limus of the outward heaven, and the inward man a limus of the holy spiritual heaven. Therefore saith Moses very rightly, *God created man in his image, to the image of God:* for *in* betokeneth that he was known by the spirit of God in this essence from eternity in the Mystery of wisdom as a constellation of magical power. Into this knowledge God introduced the essence, and created the essence to the image of the magical image of God.

13. Thus understand by the inward creating the true heavenly image, viz. a holy [spiritual] man out of all the properties of the angelical divine world. Understand the inward body for the one only element, whence the four were expressed; and understand the outward man for the outward world, with the stars and four elements, viz. fire, air, water and earth, and also for the outward tincture, which is linked with the inward in the holy expressed Word, and is only severed by a Principle; where also the inward putteth forth an external life out of itself. The inward is holy, and the outward [life or Principle] in the tincture were likewise holy, if the curse were not come into it by reason of the awakened vanity; yet if the vanity be severed by[1] the tincture, then it is holy, and a paradise, which shall open itself at the end of this world.

14. And Moses saith further, *God breathed into man the breath of life, and he became a living soul:* this signifieth the living, speaking, understanding spirit, out of all the three Principles, viz. out of the inward fire-world, which is manifest through the dark world; and out of the holy light-world, and out of the outward aerial-world: this is the soul.

15. The inward fire-breath is the true eternal creatural soul; and the light-breath is the true understanding spirit of the soul, wherein it is an angel; and the outward air-breath is the rational soul in the vegetative bestial life, wherewith man ruleth over all the creatures of

[1] Or from.

this world. That is one only soul in three Principles, according to the image or likeness of God.

16. As the only understanding of the abyssal unsearchable Deity hath manifested itself with three Principles, so likewise he hath breathed into the created image the same spirit, viz. the true life out of all the three Principles. The body is a limus of all essences, and the soul is the expressed Word, viz. the power and understanding of all essences, viz. the manifestation of the divine understanding.

17. The spirit of God hath inspired or given in itself, from the properties of all the three Principles, into the created image, viz. the Father of all essences hath breathed or spoken forth the spirit, through his eternal-speaking Word, out of all the three Principles, out of the whole essence of the powers; or, as I might set it down, he hath inspoken it, viz. the egressed sound or expressed voice of the understanding which, through the motion of God, did educe and manifest itself through the eternal and temporal nature. The same [spirit] God did again in-speak or, as the text in Moses hath it, *breathed* [itself] *into* this only image, for a ruler of the body and all other creatures.

18. And the soul, in its real life and understanding, consists in three kingdoms: the first is the eternal nature, viz. the potent might of eternity, the dark and fire-world, according to which God calleth himself a strong zealous angry God, and a consuming fire, in which Lucifer hath wholly diabolised himself.

19. The second is the holy light-world, where the eternal under-standing hath displayed itself through the fire's-sharpness, in the light of the great fiery love-desire, and turned the wrathful dark-and-fiery propery to a kingdom of joy; which is the true manifestation of the Deity; and it is called the holy heaven of the angelical delight and bliss.

20. The third kingdom or world is the outward astral and ele-mental kingdom, viz. the air, with its domineering constellations, wherein all the five outward constellations rule, viz. the superior, and the inferior of the four elements, out of which the five senses take their original, wherein the vegetable and reasonable life consisteth. This is the animal soul, which ruleth in all the creatures of this world, so also in all the outward heavens or constellations, and in all the earth or essences of the outward world.

21. Understand it thus: the fire-breath out of the first Principle ruleth in its original, viz. in its own mother, whence the spirit of

God amassed (or moulded) it, viz. in the centre of the eternal nature, in the might of the dark-and-fire-world. And it is the cause of the light-life; and also of the air-life: if that were not, then none of the others would be.

22. And the light-breath ruleth in the second Principle, viz. in the holy kingdom of the manifested power of God, which is the mansion of the holy spirit of God, the temple of God, viz. in the heavenly holy essence; understand, in the holy spiritual body of the holy pure element, which, with its properties, standeth in equal weight and measure, as a fit prepared instrument of the spirit; wherein he manifesteth God's wonders out of the eternal wisdom, and introduceth them into the melody of joy, viz. into the holy harmony of the eternal-speaking Word of God, into the divine kingdom of joy, viz. into the manifestation of the divine powers; in which the holy spirit is the true musician.

23. And the air-spirit ruleth also in its mother, whence it originally stood, viz in the outward world, in the figure and similitude of the inward world, viz. in the outward mystery of time; and manifesteth its mother, which is brought forth out of eternity into a time, to the contemplation of the wonders of the wisdom of God.

24. And yet there are not three souls, but only one. But the soul standeth in three Principles, viz. in the kingdom of God's anger, and in the kingdom of God's love, and in the kingdom of this world. And if this were not, then it could not be said, the soul went into heaven or hell, if they[1] were not in it. When the air, viz. the outward kingdom of time doth leave the soul, then is the soul manifest either in the dark fire-kingdom of God, or in the holy kingdom of light, in the love-fire of the power of God; whereunto it hath given up itself in this life-time, therein it standeth when it foregoeth the outward life.

25. And we are in no wise to think that the soul is God himself, who is neither nature nor creature, also dwelleth in nothing, save only in himself; and yet dwelleth through all things, and is neither far off nor nigh unto any thing. But the soul is the expressed Word, the formed Word; *it is the spirit and the life of the three Principles of divine manifestation.* But if it were God, then it were immovable, and no judgment could pass upon it.

26. But a judgment may pass upon it, if it departeth out of that order wherein God introduced it in the beginning; if it goeth out of the divine harmony, out of the order of the manifested word of God's

[1] Heaven and hell.

power, if it doth manifest or produce another will in itself, viz. other properties out of the strong might of the eternal nature.

27. The whole man with body and soul is threefold; and yet but one only man. The body is out of a threefold essence; and the soul is out of a threefold property of the spirit. An example thereof you have in the fire, light and air: the fire hath another property than the light and air have. The fiery body is the eternal constellation, viz. the magical constellation, the Great Mystery, out of which the outward constellation was produced, and brought into a creatural being or creation.

28. The fiery spirit, viz. the fiery soul, dwelleth in the fiery spiritual body; and in the light's body (which is from the holy element, viz. from the true heavenly image, which consisteth in a spiritual Sulphur, Mercurius and Sal) dwelleth the holy soul, viz. the true spirit of the soul, which is a temple of God; and in the outward body (which is a limus of the earth and the other elements), viz. in the outward constellation of the five senses, the outward soul, viz. the real spirit of the outward world doth dwell.

29. Each property of the soul hath a corporeal property in itself, which may be called a heaven, viz. a sundry special magical astrum; as the fiery property of the soul hath a body from the inward constellation of the dark and fire-world, which is a spiritual body.

30. And the lucid[1] property of the soul hath a spiritual, oleous and watery body, wherein the two properties of the highest tincture of the fire and light do open the lustre and beauty of the colours, wonders and virtue of the divine wisdom. This water is the water above the firmament, of which Moses speaketh; and this oil is the holy oil of the divine powers; and this was a usual type in the Old Testament, in that the real oily body of the heavenly property did disappear in Adam in the awakened vanity; so God ordained the type of the new Regeneration with an unction of oil, wherein he powerfully wrought through the promised Covenant, as in a type.

31. The third outward property of the soul hath likewise every way such a body of many constellations in it, as always the inward properties; all which multiplicity of properties may be called heavens. For each property of the outward body hath a magical constellation; as there is a body of the sulphurean constellation of the earth; also a body or constellation of the mercurial, poisonful life; also a body of the

[1] Or light.

86

salt-powers of bodies; also a body of the soul of the outward world, viz. of the upper created constellation; all according as the outward powers of the outward soul are. Thus each power hath a corporeal property in it: and thus also the inward powers of the spiritual property are to be understood with the inward body.

The Sixteenth Chapter

Of the Difference of the Heavenly and Earthly Man

1. WHEN we consider the image of God which God created in Paradise unto the eternal uncorruptible life, then we can in no wise say of the gross fleshy image, that the gross property of the earthliness is the image of God, which can possess the holy world: for it is not of the same essence and ens, whereof also Christ speaketh: *The spirit is life; the flesh profiteth nothing*: also, *flesh and blood shall not inherit the kingdom of heaven*. And yet verily the true body is couched in this bestial, gross property; as the gold in the ore.

2. All that is earthly on man, that is bestial and corruptible, and not man. Albeit God created man an external body out of the limus of the earth; yet it is not to be considered of us, as now it is. For the true human body, according to the inward world, is a spiritual Sulphur, a spiritual Mercurius, and a spiritual Sal: each property of the soul hath a corporeal or essential quality on it.

3. God created such a body as the soul was in its essence, viz. in the spirated Word of the understanding; and breathed the soul there-into for the understanding; also, the outward sulphurean body is in no wise the gross beast which passeth away and returneth not again. The true, real body, which is hidden in the grossness, is a spiritual body, in comparison to the grossness: it is created indeed in flesh and blood; but in a fixed, steadfast [uncorruptible flesh and blood].

4. By the lust and imagination of Adam the grossness was manifest; the true outward body is a sulphureous, mercurial and saltish property; a pure essential power, according to the nature of the soul: That which the soul is in the spirit, the same is the true human body in the essence, as a mansion of the soul.

5. All the properties of the inward holy body, together with the outward, were (in the first man) composed in an equal harmony, none lived in self-desire, but they all gave up their desire unto the soul, in which the divine light was manifest, as in the holy heaven. The light shone through all the properties, and made an equal temperature in the properties; all the properties gave their desire into the light, viz. into the manifested sweetness of God, which penetrated all the properties; in which penetration they were all tinctured with the

sweet love; so that there was nothing but mere pleasing relish and love-desire and delight between them.

6. The inward holy corporality from[1] the pure element penetrated through the four elements, and held the limus of the earth (viz. the outward sulphureous body) in itself, as it were swallowed up; and it was really there, but in manner as the darkness dwelleth in the light, and yet its darkness cannot be manifest for the light; but if the light extinguisheth, then the darkness is manifest.

7. Thus the inward man held the outward captive in itself, and penetrated it, as a fire through-heats an iron, that it seems as if it were all fire; but when the fire goeth out, then the dark, swart iron is manifest.

8. Thus likewise was the first man when he stood in Paradise, in his fixed condition, in manner as time is before God, and God in the time; and they are distinct, but not parted asunder. As the time is a play before God, so also the outward life of man was a play unto[2] the inward holy man, which was the real image of God.

9. The outward spirit and body was unto the inward as a wonder of divine manifestation, according to the fire-dark-and-light world, a mirror of the great omnipotence and omniscience of God: and the inward was given unto it for a ruler and guide.

10. As God playeth with the time of this outward world, so likewise the inward divine man should play with the outward in the manifested wonders of God in this world, and open the divine wisdom in all creatures, each according to its property; so likewise in the earth, in stones and metals, in which also there is a twofold essence, viz. one from the original of the dark fire-world, and one from the original of the holy light-world.

11. All this was given him for his play: he had the knowledge of all tinctures: all was subject to him; he ruled in heaven and earth and over all the elements, so also over all the constellations; and that, because the divine power was manifest in him: no heat nor cold did annoy him. As a tincture penetrates a body and preserves it from sickness, and as the warmth of the sun defends the body from cold, so likewise the highest tincture of the fire and light, viz. the holy power of the inward spiritual body, penetrated the outward body of flesh and blood, and took every outward elemental property, as also the limus of the earth, into its preservation or protection.

12. For as there was a temperature in the body of the inward and

[1] Of.   [2] Before.

outward man, so likewise there was nothing without the body that could either destroy or annoy this temperature. As gold endures in the fire, and as a tincture penetrates all things, and yields or gives way unto nothing, so likewise man was not subject unto any thing, save only and alone to the only God, who dwelt through him, and was manifest in him with the power of the holy essence: and this was an image and likeness of God, in whom the spirit of God inhabited.

13. Reasons will understand us amiss, and say, I speak of a two-fold man. But I say no! I speak only of one only man, who is a likeness according to God, viz. according to the manifested God, according to the expressed formed Word of the divine power, of divine under-standing.

14. As all things are in God essentially,[1] and yet he himself is not that very essence; and yet that essence ruleth every essence according to its property; so likewise the inward spiritual man is an image of the formed Word of divine power, and the outward an image of the inward, viz. an instrument of the inward. As a master must have an instrument wherewith to finish and perform his work, so likewise the outward man from the limus of the earth and four elements, with its outward constellation, is only an instrument of the inward, where-with the inward frameth and maketh what the inward spirit of the soul willeth.

15. As we see that the will is the master in all purposes and under-takings; and [we] see further, that the inward man hath divine will and desire, but the outward [hath] only a bestial [will], which is so by reason of the fall. The whole man is but one only man, but his property lieth in sundry degrees, according to the inward and out-ward heavens, viz. according to the divine manifestation through the seven properties of nature.

OF THE CREATION OF THE SEVENTH DAY

16. God created all things in six days out of the seven properties, and introduced the six days' works of the manifestation of his creature into the seventh, wherein every life should work as in one body; for the seventh day and the first belong mutually to one another as one. For the six properties of the eternal nature are all couched in the seventh, as in a structure[2] of the other six; the seventh property is a

---

[1] Text, in essence.   [2] Operate or work-house.

mystery or essence of all the others; and out of the seventh day the first day hath taken its original and beginning.

SEVENTH DAY, SATURNUS

17. For on the seventh day, viz. Saturday, Saturn hath the first hour of the day [under] his dominion in the planetic orb; which is a figure of the sevenfold generation of the eternal nature. For like as the first form of the eternal nature is the astringent desire, viz. the Fiat, which in the desire impresseth the free lubet (which is as a thin nothing in the eternal will of God, in the divine understanding) and introduceth it into a spiritual essence, in which desire-essence all the properties do arise, as is above mentioned.

18. So likewise Saturn, or the seventh property of the seventh day, is the rest or mansion of the other six days works, wherein they work as a spirit in the body: the seventh property standeth still as a senseless life.

19. But that now Moses saith, *God rested on the seventh day from all his works, and sanctified the seventh day* for rest: this hath a very peculiar emphatical deep meaning; and yet it were but plain and child-like, if we were in Paradise, and dwelt in the Sabbath. Understand it thus:

20. Out of the Verbum Fiat, viz. out of the divine Word, and out of the divine desire (which is the Fiat in the Word, wherewith the Word formeth itself, or introduceth itself in the spiritual essence to the dark fire-and-light-world), the six properties of the eternal and temporal nature proceeded; and each hath introduced itself into a sundry degree of a sundry property, which degree may be called a heaven, or a magical spiritual-constellation.

21. For each property is a spirated essence, viz. a heaven: for heaven[1] doth properly and exactly denote and signify, in the Language of Nature, a spiration or formation, where the Fiat formeth what the Word speaketh or breatheth forth; and thus the spiration or speaking was introduced into six degrees or days'-works.

22. Each spiration continued [for] a time, viz. the length of a day and night in the formation and conception, and each property of a day was mutually spoken or breathed forth out of the other, even unto the sixth, in which the formed Word was manifest, which in the fifth form, viz. in the love-desire, did receive its aspect or illustration

---

[1] Text, *Himmel*, expounded in the Language of Nature.

through the fire from the light; and amassed or formed itself in the sixth form of nature; in which formation the image of God (man) was created, as an image of the formed Word, which God introduced into the Sabbath, viz. into the seventh day, understand, into the Verbum Fiat, viz. into the first divine desire to nature, wherein Paradise and the eternal day was.

23. For in the seventh property lieth the eternal day, whence the days of time are proceeded; and the ancients have called it *Sonnabend*;[1] but it is rightly called *Sönnabend*,[2] wherein God's love doth appease and atone the anger; as, when the six properties in the operate do enkindle themselves in the impression in the wrath's property, they are atoned and reconciled in the seventh property, viz. in the manifested holy power of God in the love-desire; (which holy power manifesteth itself in the fifth and sixth property, and doth encircle the operate of all the rest as a holy heaven) and so are introduced into one only essence, wherein they rest, as in the Word of the Lord;[3] which hath introduced itself with the seven properties into nature and essence; and thereof Moses speaketh rightly, *God rested on the seventh day from all his works, and hallowed the seventh day.*

24. Understand it here aright: God rested with his formed Word (which he first introduceth into darkness and fire, viz. into the first Principle, according to which he is called a consuming fire), in the second Principle, viz. in the formed holy Word, where he educeth himself through the fire in the light in the love-desire, viz. in the holy Fiat: and resteth eternally with his manifested Word therein. His rest therein is a dominion of joy, where the anguish-source of God's wrath, of the eternal nature, is changed into a divine kingdom of joy.

25. And this rest is the holy heaven in the natural heaven, where time worketh in itself, and setteth forth its operate for the day of rest, viz. the day of separation, where, at the end of the days of this world, the evil shall be separated from the good, and each thing shall possess its own heaven, viz. the property of its original [or sourcive] spirit, whence it was generated.

26. But in this time God's love and anger must mutually work in one another, and manifest the wonders of God, both according to the fire-[world] and light-world, and the Verbum Domini resteth in the seventh manifestation of the properties, and shineth with its power

[1] As to the word: Sun-evening, or the evening of the sun. In our English, Saturday.
[2] The Evening of reconciliation: or Saving-day.
[3] Text, *im Verbo Domini.*

and virtue into the operation of the six days, viz. into the six properties; and affordeth aid and help to every life.

27. In the seventh property all things are brought into their end,
viz. into the first day of the beginning of all essences. For the seventh
day, viz. the seventh property of the eternal nature, is *the transparent
glassy sea before the throne of the Ancient*, in the *Revelation of St. John's*,
whence, as out of the Grand Mystery,[1] this world was created into
sundry peculiar heavens and forms, and formed in the Verbum Fiat.
The seventh day was from eternity without and beyond all time, for
it is the formed Word of the divine understanding; in it the eternal
wisdom of God is manifest, viz. the powers and wonders of the divine
understanding, in which the Deity worketh.

[1] Ex Mysterio Magno.

The Seventeenth Chapter

Of Paradise

1. **M**OSES saith, that *when God had made man*, that *he planted a garden in Eden, and there he put man, to till and keep the same: and caused all manner of fruits to grow, pleasant for the sight and good for food: and planted the Tree of Life, and the Tree of Knowledge of Good and Evil in the midst* (Gen. ii. 8, 9).

2. Here lieth the veil before the face of Moses, in that he had a bright shining countenance, that sinful Israel cannot look him in the face. For the man of vanity is not worthy to know what Paradise is; and albeit it be given us to know it according to the hidden man, yet, by this description, we shall remain as dumb to the beast; but yet be sufficiently understood by our fellow-scholars.

3. The Garden Eden was a place upon the earth, where man was tempted; and the Paradise was in heaven; and yet was in the Garden Eden. For as Adam, before his Eve [was made out of him], before his sleep, was as to his inward man in heaven, and as to the outward upon the earth; and as the inward holy man penetrated the outward, as a fire through-heats an iron, so also the heavenly power out of the pure element penetrated the four elements, and sprang forth through the earth, and bore fruits, which were heavenly and earthly, and were qualified [sweetly tempered] of the divine power; and the vanity in the fruit was held as it were swallowed up, as the day hideth the night, and holdeth it captive in itself, that it is not known and manifest.

4. Paradise was nothing else but the seventh day's property. The heavenly essentiality of the second Principle is couched or shut up in the earth, the curse of God hath hidden it; it budded (in the beginning of the world) through the earthly essentiality, as the eternity is in the time, and the divine power is through all things; and yet is neither comprehended nor understood of any earthly thing in selfhood.

5. But in Paradise the essence of the divine world penetrated the essence of time, as the sun penetrates the fruit upon a tree, and effectually works it into a pleasantness, that it is lovely to look upon and good to eat: the like also we are to understand of the garden in Eden.

6. The word *Eden*[1] is nothing else but what Moses saith of the

[1] *Eden*, expounded according to the Language of Nature.

earth: that it was void and empty; that is, it should not manifest its might according to the wrath of vanity, it should be still, as a mother to bring forth. For the internal would rule through the external, as the spiritual world through time, [and] heaven through the earth. The earth was empty without fruit; but the heaven was its husband, which made it fruitful, and bore fruit by it until the curse, where heaven did hide [disappear or withdraw] itself from the earth.

7. The whole world would have been a mere Paradise, if Lucifer had not corrupted it, who was in the beginning of his creation a hierarch in the place of this world. But seeing God knew well that Adam would fall, therefore Paradise sprang forth and budded only in one certain place, to introduce and confirm man therein; whom (albeit God saw that he would again depart thence), he would again introduce thereinto by Christ, and establish him anew in Christ, to eternity in Paradise.

8. For Lucifer poisoned the first Paradise with his false and wicked desire, therefore God promised to regenerate it anew in Christ; for the seventh day, which God appointed for rest, is nothing else but Paradise regenerate anew in the spirit of Christ, in the human property, wherein the poor soul shall rest eternally from the source of the six days'-works, viz. of the six properties of the life.

9. Also it is the seventh time or manifestation of God, in which the Mystery of God's kingdom shall be finished, when it shall be again pure in the place of this world; when heaven shall be again manifest in the world, and the devil driven out with his wickedness:[1] whereinto no unclean thing shall any more enter; for this world, in which Adam was, before his Eve, must again return, as it was before the curse, in which righteousness shall rule: but the vanity shall be purged away through the fire of God's anger, and given to the dark world.

10. But that Moses saith, *the Tree of Life stood in the midst of the Garden,* and presently next after setteth down, *and the Tree of Knowledge of Good and Evil.* Here lieth the veil before his eyes, that the earthly sinful man cannot behold him; for he is not worthy of it; for his earthliness in the curse of the bestial vanity shall not inherit Paradise.

11. The precious pearl lieth in [the knowledge of] *the difference of the two Trees:* and yet it is but *only one,* but manifest in two kingdoms. For the Tree of Life standeth wholly in the midst of the Garden; for

[1] Text, evil essence.

95

it standeth in two Principles, in the midst, viz. in the holy world, between the eternal dark world of God's anger, where God is an angry zealous God and a consuming fire, and the outward visible world.

12. The holy power of God in the Tree was the middle-most kingdom, and Paradise was the outermost kingdom; for the middlemost penetrated the outermost, and manifested itself with the outward. This was the knowledge of the Good, which Adam should have as little known, in its original, as the Evil: he was created for an instrument of God, with whom God would manifest his wonders in figures; he should keep only a child-like mind, and be resigned unto God.

13. Now the Tree of the Knowledge of Evil was the dark world, which also was manifest on this Tree; likewise the vanity, as now[1] it is; all earthly fruit was manifest therein. Therefore Moses distinguisheth the Tree, and saith, *the Tree of Life*; thereby he understandeth the property of the eternal life in the Tree, viz. the second Principle. And by the words, *of the Tree of Knowledge of Good and Evil*, he understandeth[2] the wrath of the anger of God, which was manifest by the essence of the outward world, in earthliness in this Tree, of which Adam should not eat; for he should have eaten[3] with the inward mouth, and not with the earthly desire but with the heavenly; for he had such fruit growing for him which the inward mouth could enjoy; indeed the outward mouth did also eat thereof, but not into the worm's carcass.

14. For as the light swalloweth[4] up the darkness, so the celestial swallowed up the terrestrial, and changed it again into that whence it proceeded; or as the eternity swalloweth up the time, and in it is as a nothing. So likewise there were two centres in Adam's mouth. For the kingdom of God stands in power; and Adam also, before his Eve, stood in the kingdom of God, for he was male and female, with both divine heavenly tinctures; and neither the fire's nor the light's tincture or desire should be manifest in him, for they should stand in equal weight [in the true temperature] resigned in[5] God.

15. But in the Tree of Knowledge of Good and Evil the properties, viz. of God's love and anger, and also the earthliness (as it is at this day in the curse), were peculiarly manifest, each in itself, and did eagerly put themselves forth; that is, they were departed out of the likeness, out of the equal harmonious accord. And all the three

[1] At this day. [2] Or meaneth. [3] Or eat. [4] Avalleth.
[5] Or to.

96

Principles were each of them in an especial manner manifest in this Tree, and therefore Moses calleth it, *the Tree of the Knowledge of Good and Evil*.

16. Reason saith, Wherefore did God suffer this Tree to grow, seeing man should not eat thereof? Did he not bring it forth for the fall of man? And must it not needs be the cause of man's destruction? This is that about which the high schools contend, and understand it not; for they go about to seek and apprehend the inward in the outward, and it remaineth hidden and dead unto them, they understand not what man is.

17. Man, according to body and soul, was created out of all the three Principles; and was placed in the Principles, in the properties of the inward and outward world, in equal number, weight and measure; none of the Principles did exceed the other; there was an agreeing harmony; the divine light temperised all the properties, so that there was a mutual melody and play of unanimous love between them.

18. The fiery dark-world rejoiced in the holy light-world, and the light-world in the outward [world], as in its manifestation. Again, the outward world joyed itself in both the inward worlds; as in its life; and there was a mere pleasing harmonious will, pleasure and sweet delight between them. The Mercury, viz. the sounding, hearing and feeling life, viz. the manifestation of the divine Word in the Fiat, did mutually penetrate all essences, in a very exceeding joyful property.

19. The property or essence of all the three worlds reached with the desire after the light;[1] and in the light the expressed Word was holy. This holy Word gave its power and virtue to the sound of the inward dark fire-world; and also into the sound of the outward elemental world, viz. it gave itself into the inward fiery Word or life, and also into the outward earthly life.

20. Thus the holy divine Word was predominant through all the three Principles of the human property, and there was an equal accord; and no enmity or opposite will was manifest between the Principles, but a mere harmonious affection and inclination of will, pleasing relish, ravishing melody, sweet smell, a friendly smiling, and most pleasant aspect, a meek and kind sense, and mutual fruition of delight.

21. For man was, on the sixth day, taken and created unto a divine likeness and image in the sixth manifestation of the seven properties

---

1 Or set their desire upon the light.

of the divine harmonious manifestation in the expressed power, which hath diffused and manifested itself through the fifth property, viz. through the fiery love-desire. His true life's-centre was the fifth property of the eternal nature, viz. the fiery love-desire; which held the fire and darkness hidden [or shut up] in itself, and used it to its joy and delight.

22. But it is very needful for us to understand aright in this place, whence the desire to fall away from the equal accord did arise, both in the hierarch Lucifer, and also in Adam, the second hierarch or royal prince in the divine image.

23. When the eternal only God once moved himself through the eternal spiritual nature, viz. in the eternal great abyssal Mystery, and comprised [or amassed] this Mystery into a circumference or place, to manifest his great wonders; and introduced the eternal wisdom into a formal visible contemplation, and manifested all the seven properties of the inward eternal spiritual world, and introduced them into a creation of the angels; then all the properties were moved and affected and each desired to be in a creatural form, in the place, so far as the Verbum Fiat had put itself forth[1] to motion and manifestation.

24. And the angelical princes also, with their legions, were taken and created out of the properties in the Verbum Fiat, even from the first centre where the eternal lubet betaketh itself into a desire, and introduceth itself into nature, unto the most external manifestation, each hierarchy in its heaven or property.

25. But seeing Lucifer was, in his creation or formation of the properties, apprehended in the Principle of the property where the enkindling fire ariseth, where the light is manifest, thereupon he became so aspiring in himself, as the most mighty prince; and being in the root of his creatural original he understood the great magical constellation, viz. the Mystery of the ground of all being, but yet in the dark property, which yet was now moved and affected; which magical constellation also desired to be[2] manifest and creatural in the dark world, thereupon it set its desire upon this mighty prince and hierarch.

26. And he, Lucifer, turned himself away from the divine light into the fiery Mystery, towards the darkness, whence the fire ariseth. And so the magical astrum of the Grand Mystery of the dark world apprehended him; for his desire, which the Verbum Fiat had extroduced through the fire in the light, turned itself back again thereinto,

[1] Or given itself in. [2] Or would be.

and would be like the creator of all beings, and change himself and the essence according to his own pleasure.

27. Thus he contemned the meekness in the light, viz. the second Principle, which [ariseth] through the fire-death, (where the wrath, of the spiritual essentiality of the wrathful dark property, dieth in the fire; and out of which death of devoration the second Principle, viz. the holy love-world of great meekness and humility, is generated), and went back into the first Principle, viz. *in magiam naturae,* into the original of the eternal nature; and would be an omniscient artist: he would rule and domineer in and above the whole creation, and be a co-former in all properties.

28. Thus the light was extinct to him, for he made his angelical essence, which stood in great meekness and in fiery love-desire, wholly rough, austere, cold, wrathful and fiery, in the dark wrathful property; and the properties of enmity instantly arose in him, for in the light they could not be manifest; but when the light extinguished they were manifest, and he became a devil; and was driven out of the angelical world, out of his own heaven of the second Principle.

29. Thus we are to know, that the fall befell him from his creature, for had he not turned away his creatural desire from the divine meekness and love, in pride and stubborn will, to rule in the matrix of the pregnatress, which took him as a player, he had remained an angel. Had he continued under God's love-spirit and will, then his anger-spirit and will had not captivated him.

30. But seeing he hath freely and willingly broken himself off from God's love-will, he hath now God's anger-will in him, wherein he must be a manifestor and worker of the dark world's property, for it also would be creatural. Here it hath a right captive, that can artificially act in ape's-sport; and now, as the dark world is in its property in its desire such also is its hierarch or creatural prince.

31. And here it is very requisite for us to know aright how man came to fall. Man was created in the stead and place of extruded Lucifer, understand the inward spiritual man. He was created in the same heaven, according to the inward human soul, and should possess the hierarchy which Lucifer had lost; and hence the devil's envy against man is arisen.

32. But seeing God did well know that the devil would tempt him, and not beteem him that honour, the deepest love of God (viz. the high name *Jesus* out of *JEHOVAH*) hath freely given itself herein, to regenerate this hierarchy which Lucifer had defiled; and to

purge it through the fire, and to introduce his highest love thereinto; and to overcome the wrath (which Lucifer had awakened) with love, and change it again into divine joy, viz. into a holy heaven; in which place the Last Judgment standeth.[1] And this is that which Saint Paul saith, *Man was chosen* [or elected] *in Christ Jesus before the foundation of the world was laid.*

33. And for this end God created man out of three Principles in one, that [being] he did not live wholly in the place of Lucifer, that so he might help him. For God saw very well, according to the property of his wrath, that man would fall; but he would bring him again through and in the name *Jesus* through the corruptible death, into the royal kingdom whence Lucifer was fallen; in whose stead the man Christ, God and man in one person, should sit as a hierarch, high priest, or the great prince of men, in the name and power of *Jesus* out of *JEHOVAH.*

34. Therefore we are here rightly to consider of the fall of man, how he stood in Paradise and was tempted, and what the Paradise was. Man stood in three Principles, which indeed stood in man himself, viz. in body and soul, in equal accord and harmony; but not [so] without him, for the dark-world hath another desire than the light-world; so also the outward world hath another desire than the dark-and-light-world. Now the image of God stood between three Principles, all which three did set their desire upon this image, each would be manifest in Adam, and have him in their dominion for a ruler, and manifest their wonders through him.

35. But he, man, should have introduced his desire only into the sixth property of the divine manifestation, wherein he was created to an image of God; he should be wholly resigned to God; he should live only in the manifested divine Word, obedience to God, and not enter into [his] own will, but introduce his desire into God's will, viz. into the sixth property; that so the manifested Word of God might be his will, knowing, and doing: even as the holy angels do so live and rejoice only in the divine will, and melodise in the Holy Ghost, as he doth open and manifest himself in them, according to the divine wisdom; and thus they live, will and act with a child-like mind and will.

36. Paradise, or the garden in Eden, did indeed stand with its properties in equal concord as to man. But the properties were in themselves an awakened hunger, each in itself; which verily the

---

[1] Or unto which end the Last Judgment is appointed.

divine light did again introduce into a temperature. But the devil, in his enkindled envy, opposed man, and insinuated his venomous imagination into the human property, and enkindled the human properties in the centre in the first Principle of the soul's property, wherein the soul standeth in like essence and being with the angels and devils.

37. Whence Adam's imagination and earnest hunger did arise, that he would eat of the evil and good, and live in [his] own will. That is, his will departed out of the equal concord into the multiplicity of the properties; for he would prove, feel, taste, hear, smell and see them. As the devil did persuade them also in the Serpent, *they should be as God, and their eyes should be open* in the properties; which also happened unto them in the fall, that they knew, tasted, saw and felt evil and good: whence arose unto them sickness, disease, pains and corruption [or the dissolution of this carcass].

38. And seeing the divine providence did afore know that the devil would tempt man, and bring him into strange lust; lest he should long after the centre of the dark world, and become a devil, as Lucifer did, God did represent unto him the Tree of Life, and of the Knowledge of Good and Evil, wherein the dissolution of the outward life was manifest.

39. For Adam was guilty therein, seeing he was yet in Paradise when he lusted after vanity, and brought his imagination into the earth, viz. into that essence whence the limus of the outward body was extracted; and desired out of his mother to assay of the enkindled vanity which the devil had inflamed. Thereupon the Fiat drew him forth such a plant out of the matrix of the earth, whence also it had extracted Adam's body, so that Adam, in his hunger, had to eat.

40. For the essence in the Tree of the Knowledge of Good and Evil, and the hunger of the desire in Adam, were alike; what he desired was represented unto him by the Fiat; Adam's imagination was the cause of it.

41. Reason saith, wherefore did God suffer it to come to pass? Christ said, *If you had faith as a grain of mustard-seed, and should say to this mountain be cast into the sea, it should be done*: [I prithee], was not the soul's spirit [sprung forth] out of the great divine omnipotence out of the centre of the eternal spiritual nature, whence all beings were created, and should it not then be potent?

42. He was a fire-spark out of God's might. But when he was

formed into a creatural being of the creatures, he withdrew into self-lust, and broke himself off from the universal being, and entered into a self-fullness. And so he wrought his own destruction, and this he had had, if God's love had not redeemed him.

43. The soul's power was so potent before the vanity, that it was not subject to any thing; and so it is still powerful, if the understanding were not taken away from it. It can by magic alter all things whatsoever that are in the outward world's essence, and introduce them into another essence; but the vanity in the outward air's dominion hath brought a darkness thereinto, so that the soul doth not know itself. The curse of God hath cast the defiled child into the dirt, that it must pray for a laver; and must be in this lifetime its own enemy, that it may learn to be humble, and continue in the divine harmony, and not become a devil.

The Eighteenth Chapter

Of the Paradisical State[1] showing how it should have been if *Adam* had not fallen

1. I KNOW the sophister[2] will here cavil at me, and cry it down as a thing impossible for me to know, seeing I was not there and saw it myself. To him I saw, that I, in the essence of my soul and body, when I was not as yet I, but when I was in Adam's essence, was there, and did myself fool away[3] my glory in Adam. But seeing Christ hath restored it again unto me, I see, in the spirit of Christ, what I was in Paradise; and what I now am in sin; and what I shall be again. And therefore let none cry it out as a thing unknowable; for although *I* indeed know it not, yet *the spirit of Christ knoweth it in me*; from which knowledge I shall write.

2. Adam was a man and also a woman,[4] and yet none of them [distinct], but a virgin, full of chastity, modesty and purity, viz. the image of God. He had both the tinctures of the fire and the light in him; in the conjunction of which the own love, viz. the virginal centre, stood, viz. the fair Paradisical rose-garden of delight, wherein he loved himself. As we also, in the resurrection of the dead, shall be such; as Christ telleth us, that *we shall neither marry, nor be given in marriage, but be like the angels of God*.

3. Such a man, as Adam was before his Eve, shall arise and again enter into, and eternally possess Paradise; not a man, or a woman, but as the Scripture saith, *they are virgins, and follow God, and the Lamb, they are like to the angels of God*, yet not only pure spirit, as the angels, but in heavenly bodies, in which the spiritual angelical body inhabiteth.

4. Seeing then Adam was created in Paradise to the life eternal in the image of God; and God himself breathed his life and spirit into him; therefore we can well describe him, how he was in his innocency, and how he fell, and what he is now, and shall again be at last.

5. If God had created him unto[5] the earthly, corruptible, miserable, naked, sick, bestial, toilsome life, then he had not brought him into Paradise; if God had desired [or willed] the bestial copulation and propagation, then he would instantly, in the beginning, have created man and woman, and both sexes had come forth in the Verbum Fiat,

---

[1] Dominion, life or condition.   [2] Or Sophist.   [3] Negligently lose.
[4] A husband and also a wife.   [5] Or for.

into the division of both tinctures, as it was in the other earthly creatures.

6. Every creature bringeth its clothing from its mother's body; but man cometh miserable, naked and bare, in deepest poverty, and un-ability; and is able to do nothing; and in his arrival to this world he is the poorest, miserablest, forlornest, and most shiftless creature amongst all kinds, which cannot at all help himself; which doth sufficiently shew unto us that he was not created of God unto this misery, but in[1] his perfection, as all other creatures were; which [perfection] the first man fooled away [or lost] by false lust; where-upon God afterwards, in his sleep, did first figurise him in the outward Fiat to the natural life in man and woman, according to the property of all earthly creatures; and hung upon him the worms'-carcass, with the bestial members for propagation, of which the poor soul is to this day ashamed, that it must bear a bestial form on the body.

7. Two fixed and steadfast essences were in Adam, viz. the spiritual body from[2] the love-essentiality of the inward heaven, which was God's temple; and the outward body, viz. the limus of the earth, which was the mansion and habitation of the inward spiritual body, which in no wise was manifest according to the vanity of the earth, for it was a limus, an extract of the good part of the earth; which at the Last Judgment shall be severed in the earth from the vanity of the curse, and the corruption of the devil.

8. These two essences, viz. the inward heavenly, and the outward heavenly, were mutually espoused to each other, and formed into one body,[3] wherein was the most holy tincture of the divine fire and light, viz. the great joyful love-desire, which did inflame the essence, so that both essences did very earnestly and ardently desire each other in the love-desire, and loved one another: the inward loved the outward as its manifestation and sensation, and the outward loved the inward as its greatest sweetness and joyfulness, as its precious pearl and most beloved spouse and consort. And yet they were not two bodies, but only one; but of a twofold essence, viz. one inward, heavenly, holy; and one from the essence of time; which were espoused and betrothed to each other to an eternal [being].[4]

9. And the magical impregnation [or conception] and birth did stand in this fiery love-desire, for the tincture penetrated through both essences, through the inward and outward, and did awaken (or stir up) the desire; and the desire was the Fiat, which the love-lubet

[1] Or unto.   [2] Or of.   [3] Text, Corpus.   [4] Or eternally.

[or imagination] took,[1] and brought into a substance. Thus the likeness of the express image was formed in this substance, being a spiritual image according to the first. [Just] as the Fiat had conceived and formed the first image, viz. Adam, so also the likeness was conceived out of the first for propagation; and in this conception the magical birth was also forthwith (effected), where, in the birth, the spiritual body became external.

10. Understand, if it had been that Adam had stood in the trial, then the magical birth had been thus [effected]: not by a sundry peculiar issue from Adam's body, as now, but as the sun through-shineth the water, and rends or tears it not. Even so [in like manner] the spiritual body, viz. the birth, had been brought forth, and in its coming forth had become substantial, without pains, care and distress, in a great joyfulness and delight, in a manner as both seeds of man and woman do receive in their conjunction a pleasant aspect. Even so also the magical impregnation and birth, had been a virgin-like image, wholly perfect according to the first.

11. Which afterwards, when Venus's matrix was taken from Adam, and formed into a woman, must be done through anguish, trouble, smart, pangs and distress; as God said to Eve, *I will multiply thy sorrows when thou conceivest, thou shalt now bring forth children with sorrow, and thy will shall be subject to thy husband.* Wherefore? Because it was sprung forth from the man's will. Eve was half the Adam, viz. the part wherein Adam should have loved and impregnated himself; the same, when as he stood not, was taken from him in his sleep, and formed into a woman: therefore when Adam saw her, he said, She shall be called woman, because she is taken out of man.

12. Man should have walked naked upon the earth, for the heavenly [part] penetrated the outward, and was his clothing. He stood in great beauty, glory, joy and delight, in a child-like mind; he should have eaten and drunk in a magical manner; not into the body, as now, but in the mouth there was the separation; for so likewise was the fruit of Paradise.

13. All things were made for his sport and delight; no sleep was in him; in or to him the night was as the day; for he saw with pure[2] eyes in peculiar light.[3] The inward man, viz. the inward eye, saw through the outward; as we in the other world shall need no sun, for we [shall] see in the divine sight, in the light of the peculiar nature. No heat nor cold had touched them; there had also no winter been

---

[1] Conceived.   [2] Glorified, illustrious.   [3] In his own genuine innate light.

manifest upon the earth, for in Paradise there was an equal temperature.

14. The tincture of the earth had been their delight and pastime; they had had all metals for their play, until the time that God had changed the outward world: no fear or terror had been in them, also no law from anything or to anything; for all had been free unto them. Adam had been their chief prince; and they had lived in the world and also in heaven, inhabiting in both worlds at once; Paradise had been through the whole world.

15. But seeing the divine providence did well know that Adam would not stand, seeing the earth was corrupted by its former prince; in that the wrath of God had moved itself, and amassed[1] the essence into an impression; therefore God created all manner of fruits and beasts, also all sorts of medicines[2] for the future sickness of man; and likewise all kinds of meat, that the man might have food, and raiment also in this world.

16. For he had determined to send another prince, by whom he would redeem man from his sickness and death, and purify and purge the earth through the fire of God, and introduce it into the holy (being), as it was when Lucifer was an angel, before it came into such a creature.[3]

17. And Adam was created only unto[4] the divine image, which should be eternal; and though it was known in the wrath of God that man would fall, yet the Regenerator[5] was also known in God's love; to[6] whom this hierarchy should be given for a royal possession, in Lucifer's stead.

18. But that the fall might not proceed (or come)[7] from the divine appointment, God made man perfect, and created and ordained him unto Paradise, and forbad him the false lust, which the devil stirred up through the limus of the earth, in Adam's outward body, with his false imagination and hungry-desire.

19. And Adam was, before his Eve, forty days in Paradise in the temptation, before God made the woman out of him; if he had stood steadfast, then God had so confirmed him to eternity.

20. But that I write of forty days, contrary to the custom [and opinion] of other writers, is, that we have certain knowledge and sufficient ground of the same, not only by conjecture, but from

---

[1] Or took.   [2] Or sovereign healing.   [3] Or creatural being.
[4] Or in.   [5] Or Restorer.   [6] Text, for.
[7] Or might not so much as appear to arise from the divine decree.

another knowledge; of this also we will shew you the types. As (first) of Moses upon Mount Sinai, when God gave him the Law; this was done in forty days, and Israel was tried whether they would continue in divine obedience; but seeing they made a calf, and an idol, and fell from God, therefore Moses must break the first Tables of the Law, signifying the first Adam in the divine law, who departed from it: therefore the same was broken from him, and he fell into the breaking[1] of his body, as Moses broke the Tables in pieces.

21. And God gave Moses another Scripture or writing upon a table[2] of stone; which signifieth the Second Adam (Christ), who should restore the first, and again introduce his Law into his table of the heart, viz. into the life, into the humanity, and write it with the living spirit in the sweet name JESU; thus the other law was also written, how God's love would destroy or break in pieces the anger; of which the Covenant in the Law was a type, as shall be hereafter mentioned in Moses.

22. The second figure of Adam in Paradise are the forty years in the wilderness; where Israel was tried in the Law with the heavenly manna, whether or not they would be obedient to God, that the anger might not so much devour them. The third figure is the true, real one, viz. Adam's hard encounter[3] with Christ in the wilderness, where he stood in Adam's stead before the devil and God's anger, where he did eat forty days magically, viz. of the word of the Lord;[4] in which Adam also was tempted, whether he would remain wholly resigned unto God's will. Christ was, in Adam's stead,[5] tempted in Adam's temptation, and with all that whatsoever wherein Adam was tempted, as shall be mentioned hereafter.

23. The fourth figure are the forty hours of Christ in the grave, where he awakened Adam out of his first sleep. The fifth figure are the forty days of Christ after his resurrection in the last proba, where the humanity was last of all tried, whether it would now stand, and be wholly resigned in God, being that death was destroyed, and the inward human life was new-born in God.

·24. These five figures belong unto the five degrees of nature; from the first form of nature even to the fifth, viz. to the holy centre of the love-birth. If it were not too large we would set it forth very clearly. It shall be shewn in its place.

25. These forty days Adam was tried in his innocency,[6] whether

---

[1] Destruction.   [2] Round ball or globe.   [3] Combat.
[4] Text, of the *Verbo Domini*.   [5] Place or lieu.   [6] Or stood in the proba.

or no he would or could stand, to possess the throne of Lucifer, as a hierarch and prince of God. But seeing God knew that this would not be, he determined to move himself with his deepest love in this Adamical, angelical image of the inward holy man, which did disappear[1] in Adam, and to regenerate him anew, viz. in the seed of the woman, understand in the love-desire's seed, wherein Adam should have impregnated, generated or brought forth himself in a magical manner. In this seed the mark or bound of the promised Covenant in[2] Christ was set; who should restore the angel's image, viz. the divine man, as it is effected.

26. These forty days Adam, viz. the soul of Adam in the flesh, was tempted between three Principles; for each Principle drew the soul in the flesh, and would have the upper hand or dominion.

27. This was the right proba[3] of what the free will of the soul would do; whether it would remain in the divine harmony, or whether it would enter into the selfhood. Here it was tried in soul and body, and drawn by all the three Principles; each would accomplish [or work forth] its wonders in him.[4]

28. Not that the three Principles did stand in unequal measure and weight in Adam, they were in equal weight in him, but not outside him; moreover the devil was very busy in God's anger in the first Principle, with his false desire; and introduced continually his imagination into the soul, and into the outward flesh, viz. into the limus of the earth, and insinuated it into the first Principle, viz. into the fiery property of the soul, even into the eternal nature; whereupon the first Principle in the soul was moved to speculate itself in the devil's imagination (or glass of fancy), viz. to contemplate in the magical birth how and what evil and good were, how it would relish and be, in the unlikeness of the essence:[5] whence the lust did arise in the soul.

29. Namely, the earthly lust to eat of the manifold properties did arise in the outward part of the soul; and in the inward fiery part of the soul the lust of pride did arise, to know and prove evil and good; desiring to be like God, as the devil also did, when he would be an artist[6] in the magical birth; after which Adam here also lusted.

30. Albeit Adam did not desire to prove the first Principle, as Lucifer hath done, for his lust was only bent to taste and prove evil

---

[1] Vanish or withdraw.　　　[2] Or with.　　　[3] Trial.　　　[4] With or by him.
[5] In the dissimilitude or various disparity of the properties which were without itself.
[6] Or craftsmaster.

and good, viz. the vanity of the earth. The outward soul was so awakened, that the hunger entered into its mother wherefrom it was drawn, and introduced into another source.

31. And when this hunger entered into the earth to eat of evil and good, then the desire in the Fiat drew forth the Tree of Temptation, and set it before Adam. Then came the severe command from God, and said to Adam, *Thou shalt not eat of the Tree of the Knowledge of Good and Evil, in that day that thou eatest thereof, thou shalt die the death.*

32. And Adam also did not eat thereof in the mouth, only with the imagination or desire did he eat thereof, whereby the heavenly tincture disappeared, which stood in a fiery love; and the earthly one did awake in the outward soul's property, whereby the heavenly image was obscured.

33. Thus the magical birth was spoiled, and it could not then be; although Adam stood[1] in Paradise, yet it had not availed him;[2] for in the imagination or hunger after evil and good the outward man did awake in him, and obtained the dominion. Then Adam's fair image fell into a swoon, and drew near to the cessation of its operation;[3] for the heavenly tincture was captivated in the earthly desire; for the outward desire impressed into it its essence out of the vanity, whereby the man was darkened, and lost his clear pure steady[4] eyes and sight, which was from the divine essence, from whence before he had his sight [or seeing].

34. Now Moses saith, that *the Lord God said, it is not good that this man should be alone, we will make an help meet for him.* When God had created all creatures, with the whole creatural host, Moses saith, *and God beheld all things which he had made, and lo! it was very good;* and confirmed all to its propagation. But here he saith of man, *it is not good that he should be alone,* for he saw his miserable fall, that he could not magically propagate himself; and said, *we will make an help for him.*

---

[1] Or had stood.   [2] Or them.   [3] Or rest.   [4] Constant, permanent.

Of the building[1] of the Woman; Shewing how Man was ordained to the outward Natural Life

1. AND Moses saith, *God caused a deep sleep to fall upon the man, and he slept: and he took one of the ribs of his side, and built a woman thereof, and closed up the place with flesh* (Gen. ii. 21). Moses saith, the woman was made of a rib out of Adam's side: who will understand this, without divine light? But here lieth the veil before the brightness of Moses' face, by reason of the unworthiness of the bestial man.

2. For we find that the woman was taken and formed in the Fiat out of Adam's essence, both in body and soul.[2] But the rib betokeneth Adam's dissolution or breaking, viz. that this body should, and would, be dissolved;[3] for in the place of this rib Longinus's spear must afterwards, when Christ was crucified, enter into the same, and tincture and heal the breach in the wrath of God with heavenly blood.

3. Now when Adam's hunger was set after the earthliness, it did, by its magnetic power, impress into his fair image the vanity of evil and good; whereupon the heavenly image of the angelical world's essence did disappear; as if a man should insinuate some strange matter into a burning and light-shining candle, whereby it should become dark, and at last wholly extinguish. So it went also with Adam, for he brought his will and desire from God into selfhood and vanity, and broke himself off from God, viz. from the divine harmony.

4. Even then he forthwith sank down into a swoon,[4] into sleep, viz. into an unability, which signifieth the death: for the image of God, which is immutable, doth not sleep. Whatsoever is eternal hath no time in it; but by[5] the sleep the time was manifest in man, for he slept in the angelical world, and awaked to the outward world.

5. His sleep is[6] the rest of Christ in the grave, where the new regenerate life in Christ's humanity must enter into Adam's sleep, and awaken it again to the eternal life, and bring it out of time into the eternal [being].

---

[1] Or framing.   [2] Or out of his body and soul.   [3] Or destroyed.
[4] Faintness or impotency.   [5] Or with.   [6] Signifieth, or was the real type of.

6. But the breaking [or dividing] of Adam's essence, when the woman was taken out of him, is the breaking or bruising of Christ's body on the cross, from the sixth hour unto the ninth; for so long was the Fiat in Adam's sleep in the separating of the man and woman;[1] for in such a space of time the woman was completely finished [or brought forth] out of Adam into a female [person or] image.

7. And when Christ on the cross had again accomplished this redemption of our virgin-like image from the divided sex of male and female,[2] and tinctured it with his heavenly blood in the divine love, he said, *It is finished*: for before, he stood in Adam's thirst. As Adam did thirst after the vanity, so Christ did now fill or satiate this thirst of vanity with the holy divine love-thirst, and turned about the will of the soul, that it might again introduce its thirst into God. And when this was brought to pass, he said, now, *it is finished* and converted. Christ turned back Adam in his sleep from the vanity, and from the man and woman, again into the angelical image. Great and wonderful are these Mysteries, which the world cannot apprehend; for it is as blind in them, as a man that is born blind, is, to behold this world; but he that regardeth and findeth them hath great joy therein.

8. Eve is the right magical child,[3] for she is the matrix in which the love-desire stood in Adam, viz. the magical impregnation[4] and birth; she was Adam's paradisical rose-garden in peculiar love, wherein he loved himself; for the amassing [or conceiving] of the magical impregnation, or incarnation, or divine formation of propagation, was [or did stand] in the conjunction of both tinctures.

9. And, after the eating of the apple, God said unto them, *The woman's seed shall bruise the Serpent's head*. The ground and corner-stone lieth here in this matrix; for the woman's matrix wherein the divine formation stood, was, as to the right life, heavenly, being out of the heavenly essentiality, wherein consisted the right paradise.

10. But Adam with his imagination brought earthliness and vanity thereinto, viz. self-will; and then the holy part, viz. Venus's desire, which was the divine centre in the humanity, viz. the manifested love-word in the image of God, did disappear in this matrix; therefore

---

[1] Or a making the sex of male and female.
[2] Text, from the man and woman.
[3] Understand, as to the right life which was then manifest, but afterwards disappeared, for in her lay the woman's seed, which was to break the monstrous serpent of the earthly Eve.
[4] Conception.

Eve, from[1] this strange will introduced into the matrix, brought forth at first a self-willed proud murderer; for Adam, with his false imagination, had introduced this vanity, so also the devil's desire [thereinto].

11. But the divine love-will would not forsake this disappeared angelical matrix; and gave himself by promise thereinto with the dear and precious name of Jesus, who should again awaken it in the holiness's property; and bruise the head of the devil's insinuated desire and false rebellious will; that is, destroy, and take away the might of its life, and introduce it again, through divine love, into the first life. And even in this holy matrix, which the word and power of God did again awaken in the sweet name [of] Jesus in the seed of Mary in the bound[2] of the Covenant, the Serpent's poison in the soul and flesh was destroyed.

12. And this is the seed of the woman: dear brethren, observe it, it is highly known. The aim of the Covenant of Promise[3] was pight [or set] into this matrix: but Eve was not the same child; for the part of the heavenly matrix stood disappeared in her; but [yet it was] in the Covenant of God, as the dry rod of Aaron (which budded forth afresh) did typify unto us.

13. She was indeed the whole matrix of Adam, but the holy part was shut up in her; and [there] lived only the outward part of the outward world with evil and good, viz. the matrix of the third Principle, which had indeed a half soul-like property, but [captivated] in the prison of God's anger. The holy Covenant of love rested in the disappeared part, in the midst of the awakened anger; from which Covenant the prophetical spirit in the Old Testament spake, and prophesied of the future opening (or manifestation) in the Covenant.

14. The greatest Mystery is to be understood in the formation of Eve; for a man must very entirely and intimately understand and apprehend the birth of nature, and the original of man, if he will see the ground; for she is the half Adam; not taken only and wholly out of Adam's flesh, but out of his essence, out of the female part: she is Adam's matrix.

15. The woman received no more from Adam's flesh and bones, save the rib in his side, and the half cross in the head[4], which was the life's birth-cross, whereon Christ destroyed death. The matrix of the heavenly part was in Adam, magical,[5] that is, moving in the essence;

---

[1] Out of, or by reason of.   [2] Aim, mark or limit.
[3] Text, the promised mark of the Covenant.
[4] Or skull.   [5] Or magically.

but the outward part of the outward world was made fleshy; and both were mutually bound [or espoused] to one another; as the time with the eternity. The holy part was in heaven, and [was] the heaven itself; and the outward fleshy part was in the outward world in *Matrice Mundi*.[1]

16. Thus the female property was, in the Fiat, extracted out of Adam's essence, as his dearest rose-garden, and he kept the limbus, heavenly and earthly [celestial and terrestrial], according to the eternal Father's manifested property, viz. the fire-soul's matrix's property; and the woman [kept] the part of the spirit's soul's property; the woman had the centre of the angelical world in her disappeared part of the soul-like property, viz. the manifested love-word, viz. the fifth property of the eternal nature; and the man had in his limbus the divine fire-world, viz. the centre of[2] the light-world, the centre of all essences.

17. The man's limbus, which he kept when the woman was made out of him, was the Father's property, according to all essences; and the woman out of [or proceed from] the man was the Son's property, according to all essences, understand, the heavenly part [both of the limbus and matrix]. Therefore Christ became man in the woman's part, and brought the man's part again into the holy matrix, so that the limbus and the female matrix were again one image,[3] viz. a manly virgin, above and in all the three Principles, as a creatural-formed God, in whom the eternal unformed God dwelt, with universal fullness, both in the formed, and outside the formed [divine creature or God-man]. For thus was Adam also, before his Eve, and so must we also be in Christ, if we would be the image and temple of God.

18. Now when the pregnant matrix was taken from Adam, the woman was every way formed with such members for propagation as she is at this day; and so Adam also. For before, when Adam was male and female, he needed no such members; for his birth was magical, his conception moving in the matrix [was to be] done through imagination; for the Fiat was manifest in him.

19. And the bestial worm's carcass of the bowels, with the formation of other inward principal members pertaining to the earthly life, was hung upon Adam instead of the female matrix, and the like worm's carcass was also hung upon the woman, instead of the heavenly

[1] In the matrix of the third Principle.   [2] Or to.
[3] Or person.

limbus, that they might stuff in a deal of vanity, and live like the beasts, seeing they did so eagerly lust after evil and good.

20. Reason will object against me, and say: God created Adam in the beginning such a man, and even with all members, as he now is. Which, notwithstanding, it cannot make out or demonstrate, seeing the soul is ashamed of this bestial property. Also I would fain know of this self-full reason, whether or no such an Adam (if he were created so miserable, destitute, naked and bare, unto this bestial life) were created to eternal life, without defect, and also without need, distress, and death? And whether this sink [or filthy carcass of earthly flesh and blood] were the Paradise and temple of God; and how could he have been able to defend himself from hurt and ruin? For such a beast-like man may be drowned in the water, and burnt in the fire, and also crushed to pieces with rocks and stones.

21. But sayeth thou, God did well know that it would be so with Adam, therefore he created him so at the very first? Against this the Scripture declareth, saying, *God created man in his image, yea, to the image of God created he him*; not to the bestial image. What sin would God have imputed or charged upon man, if he had created him in a bestial image? what then would the new birth avail him [to what end then should he be born again]? The new birth contains in real sum, this: That the angelical image must be born again, which God created in Adam. God formed Adam in the image of God, and though he knew that he would not stand, yet he appointed him the Saviour, who would bring him again into the first image, and therein establish him for ever.

22. Now it plainly appears that Adam stood in the divine image, and not in the bestial, for he knew the property of all creatures, and gave names to all creatures, from their essence, form and property. He understood the Language of Nature, viz. the manifested and formed Word in every one's essence, for thence the name of every creature is arisen.

23. Now, seeing he knew how the word of power was formed[1] in every creature, thereupon we cannot esteem him bestial;[2] he was without doubt angelical; for none other man shall arise, but such a one as Adam was before his Eve. God created him perfect, but he stood not in the proba; whereupon it must now follow, that God

---

[1] Text, stood in the form.
[2] Or make a mere animal of him, as the schools in their brutish reason do who understand not what Adam was, before he lost the image of God.

suffered him to fall into the outward magic; and ordained him to the image of this world; and set him into the natural life, viz. into the corruption and the new birth.[1] For in heaven there is neither male nor female, but all one kind, in peculiar love, without further propagation, in an eternal confirmation.

24. This therefore doth set forth unto us that Adam died in Paradise, as God said unto him, *if thou eatest of the Tree, thou diest*: He died to the holy [heavenly] image, and lived to the awakened bestial image. For now, when Adam did awake from sleep, he was indeed still in Paradise, for the vanity in the flesh and soul did not yet actually and effectually work, and was yet dumb, still, and senseless, until they did eat of the forbidden fruit; and then the earthly dominion began to rise; then the vanity awakened, viz. all the forms of the life, each in its selfhood, and forsook severally their mutual harmony, and forthwith heat and cold fell upon them [Adam and Eve]; for the outward [image or being] did assimulate [or ensource] with the inward, and the heavenly image at last quite disappeared; which in Adam's sleep, and also in this awakening, did yet live both in Adam and Eve, but in a very obscure and impotent manner.

25. Adam, in his perfection, while he was man and wife, and had the magical conception in him, did amuse himself on (or imagine after) the beasts, and introduced himself into bestial lust, to eat and generate according as the beasts do: And so, likewise, the Fiat took in the same lust, and formed him in his sleep even as the lust was; and every member was formed in its place to the conjunction of the beast-like copulation; for each desire hath obtained its mouth to manifestation. Thus the image of God formed itself in the Verbum Fiat into such a beast as we are still to this day; and this same (was done) in itself, viz. man's own Fiat (viz. the first form of nature, which is the desire of God's manifestation), did effect it, and none other maker from without him.

26. We are not to conceive, that there was anything else upon Adam, which made his Eve out of him, or that formed them both to the outward natural life, save only the Verbum Fiat in them, their own very propriate, and not any alienate (or anything strange) from without them. As the first creation of Adam and all kinds of creatures was so brought to pass, the Verbum Fiat coagulated each ens, and the manifested word severed itself in the ens according to its property, and formed the creature according to its astrum and kind; where

---

[1] Degeneration, and regeneration.

also, in every ens, the matrix was separated from the limbus, and formed into a male and female [into a he and she].

27. The picturing of God as a man in making Adam, and afterwards standing over Adam as he sleepeth, and making a woman out of him, is more idolatrous than real; and God hath earnestly forbidden, in Moses, to make the likeness of any God. For he is no image, save only in the creatures, according to the expressed formed Word, both according to the creatures of eternity, and of time: he is no [such] maker, but a former of the properties, a creator, and not [such a] maker.

28. The creating is the Fiat which amasseth [or formeth], and the Word in the power of the amassed [or conceived being] gives the distinction according to the ens. As the ens is, in the generation of the spirit, so a thing is formed; for the body or substance of all things is nothing else but a signature or mansion according to[1] the spirit. As the birth is in the ens, where the spirit formeth itself, so is likewise the body of all kinds of creatures, both in animals and vegetables. As we plainly see, that the first Creator, who hath moved himself and brought himself into a creatural manifestation, hath left in all creatures a power to their self-multiplication or increasing, propagation, and procreation;[2] and incorporated the Fiat in them as a maker, for their own propriety [or most innate instinct].

<hr/>

[1] Or of.   [2] Text, making.

The Twentieth Chapter

Of the Lamentable and Miserable Fall and Corruption of Man

1. Now when Adam did awake from sleep he saw his wife Eve standing before him, and took her unto him, for he knew that she was his own, that she was his matrix; and [he] cast the property of his desire upon her, as he had done before when he loved himself. So now also the fiery tincture of Adam's soul entered into the spirit's or light's tincture in Eve.

2. But they both stood yet in Paradise, in the garden in Eden, and knew neither evil nor good; for they lived yet in joy and delight, in the kingdom of heaven; and it was Eve's first longing to eat of good and evil: for Adam's desire had introduced and imprinted it into the magical image, while it was yet in Adam's essence; as a child receiveth a mark [or impress] in the womb, which the mother imprints on it.

3. Thus also Adam had impressed the false desire into his essence, whence the woman was made; therefore the woman so soon lusted after the vanity; as to this day, mere earthly lust of the flesh is found in most of them. So soon as this sex comes but to any years, the selfish lust [and will] doth predominantly appear in pride and glistering shows of fleshly desires; and they soon long after the forbidden tree, contrary to the virgin-like modesty, chastity and angelical humility.

4. The abomination which Adam introduced into his matrix is so exceeding strong in them, that they are as 'twere in naked shame[1] before the image of God, which [image] God himself created in Adam. Therefore they must be subject to the man, in that they are the cause that the vanity was enkindled, to which the devil also was a strong promoter.[2]

5. For when he saw Eve, he then knew his insinuated desire in her, which he had introduced into Adam; the same did shew forth and discover itself in Eve's lust. Therefore the devil came now in a strange form, viz. in the Serpent's essence, which was the most subtle beast, and laid himself on the Tree of Temptation towards Eve, that the introduced concupiscence in Eve, which the devil had also infected, did amuse itself upon[3] the outward Serpent, and so one lust took another; whereupon Eve did strongly imagine and long after the

---

[1] Or very weak and poor.   [2] Solicitor.   [3] Was much taken with.

forbidden fruit, which the devil persuaded her to eat; *and then her eyes should be opened, and she be as God, and know evil and good.*

6. Which indeed was true: this knowledge did stick in the fruit, for the essences were discordant and unlike therein; but he told her not that the enmity would awaken in the essences of her body, and that heat and cold, moreover sickness and death, would force into her. Herein he was silent, and fairly coloured it over, and drew her in by collusion; as if God had withheld some great thing from them, which she might find as a treasure; so craftily did he deceive Eve.

7. And when she yielded to discourse with the Serpent she was taken in the voice; for the devil infected the same with false delight, until he persuaded her she should be wise if she did eat thereof.

8. For the devil thought that if Eve should bring forth children in Paradise then his design would miscarry:[1] they might then possess his angelical kingdom.

9. Now the question is, Wherefore the devil did deceive Eve by the Serpent only, and not by some other means? Could he not do it in his own form: why did he even speak through[2] the Serpent to Eve? And wherefore did the Serpent address itself to the Tree, to persuade her against God's prohibition?

10. Here the veil lieth before Moses his clear eyes, for he sets down the history very right. But how can an unilluminated mind understand it, in that he writeth of the Serpent, saying, *that the Serpent spake with Eve, and deceived her*, whereas indeed it cannot speak. And also is only a beast, without divine understanding, and in its selfhood cannot know the image of God; much less did the Serpent understand the heavenly powers, or the prohibition.

11. But hear what Moses saith: *The Serpent was more subtle than any beast of the field, which the Lord God had made*: Here the first question is, whence its subtlety came, that even the devil would choose to speak through its subtlety, and deceive Eve? Herein sticketh the Mystery.

12. When God moved himself according to his expressed Word in the Verbum Fiat, according to both the inward worlds, viz. according to God's love and anger, according to the eternal nature of the darkness, and according to the eternal nature and power of the light, then all the properties in evil and good did amass themselves;[3] for the Fiat was the centre in all those properties, as well as in those wherein the divine power was manifest in holiness. Now, according as each

---

[1] Text, his cause might prove naught.   [2] Or in.
[3] Or were brought into a compaction.

[central] point was opened, understand, according as the lubet to the manifestation of the Grand Mystery of all essences [was in every punctum], even so the Fiat, viz. the first form to nature did apprehend and bring forth an ens or limus out of the earth, and so also above the earth, in each magical astrum,[1] according to the degrees of severation. And so in the same ens there was a spirit according to the same degree or magical astrum, and the Fiat did figure and shape even such a body or corpus as the same spirit was.

13. Now, seeing that prince Lucifer did sit as a hierarch in divine pomp, and would domineer in divine power in the fire's might, above and in all, and contemned God's love and humility, and entered with his false desire into the essence of the expressed Word in the Fiat, as a juggler[2] or wicked impostor, that would also form and make [according to his proud perverse will], thereupon he infected that same essence, according to the dark world's property, which came forth also in the Fiat into a compaction, viz. into an ens, wherein evil and good are mutually linked together. For he, the devil, as an apostate rebellious juggler, did desire the greatest subtlety [proceeding] from the centre of nature, and would domineer in the revealed magic in the Fiat.

14. And out of the like ens, [proceeding] from this infected ens (where evil and good was manifest in great power), the Serpent was created in the Fiat. Therefore Moses saith very right, *it was more subtle than all the beasts of the field*; for the devil's will, viz. his desire, which he introduced into that ens, whence it was created, was in it; it had the devil's subtlety and will. And as the devil was an angel in the beginning, and was from a good essence, and yet introduced himself into an evil one, so likewise the Serpent's ens was good before the devil's infection, before its creation; but in the devil's desire it was brought into a property of subtlety and craft.

15. For the devil's desire drew forth the compunctive stinging thorny sharp subtlety out of the centre of nature, and introduced it through the enkindling of the fire into the heavenly salniter, viz. into that property wherein he sat and was an angel; and here that very craft came forth along in the same ens into a compaction in the Fiat.

16. For the Serpent's ens was, as to one part, viz. as to the heavenly, a great power; as also there was a great heavenly power in the devil, for he was a prince of God; and so he brought his extracted

---

[1] Star.   [2] Or false magician.

subtlety and lies into a powerful ens, desiring to play his enchanting feats thereby as a peculiar [uncontrollable] god.

17. This the learned searchers of nature do in like manner understand, viz. that there lieth excellent art, and also virtue, in the ens of the Serpent. If the devil's poison be taken from it, the greatest cure doth then lie in it for the healing of all fiery venomous hurts and distempers; also [the best antidote] against poison, and all whatsoever that hath the semblance of a fiery poison; for therein the divine power lieth in a fiery hunger, but hidden in the curse of the anger of God.

18. As God doth dwell hiddenly in the cursed earth, so likewise is it here. Notwithstanding, it is given to the wise godly searcher of the art, and he need not be astonished or afraid of the curse; for he shall rule in divine power in faith over all creatures. If he were not so much captivated in a bestial and proud manner in the Serpent's essence our sense and meaning might be opened unto him, and he might here well find the arcanum [or secret] of the world.

19. This crafty Serpent was now in external show and semblance an exceeding well-favoured, comely, handsome, neat, fine, brave, pretty beastling, accurately dressed, and set forth according to the pride of the devil. Not that we are to conceive that the devil was a creator of the Serpent; but the Fiat was manifest in it according to God's great good power, and also very potently manifest according to the power of his wrathful anger.

20. This Serpent was a living figure of the Tree of Temptation; like as the Tempting Tree was a dumb power [or lifeless resemblance], so the Serpent was a living power. And therefore the Serpent applied itself to this Tree, as to its likeness, even the likeness of its essence. Which the devil saw, and possessed the Serpent in the part of his infected and introduced poison, and armed its tongue, and spake out of its great subtlety to Eve, so that she knew not the horrible enemy, and very hideous ugly guest, the devil.

21. And the devil therefore brought the Serpent to the Tree of Temptation, seeing he saw that Eve was taken much with beholding of the Tree, and fain would eat of its fruit, that so he might make Eve monstrous by the Serpent;[1] and the true eye-mark [to reach the real understanding of the Serpent's deceiving Eve] is this:

22. Eve did now long after the fruit of the Tree of the Knowledge of Good and Evil; for Adam had introduced this lust into his ens whence Eve was created. But now the command stood against it, and

[1] Or, form strange imaginations of pride, in seeing the fair Serpent.

she feared God, and would not do contrary to the prohibition; therefore the devil cunningly insinuated into the Serpent's ens, viz. into the greatest subtlety; and yet craftily put forth the great power and wit in the Serpent's essence, that Eve might see and know how prudent, wise and subtle the Serpent was; and hung there upon the forbidden tree, and it did it no hurt; and she looked upon the Serpent and set her mind amusing after it, in manner as a woman with child doth amuse herself and strangely or monstrously form herself [in her mind] and bringeth such a figure upon the child. Even so did Eve amuse herself upon the wit and craft of the Serpent, and also upon its nimble agility and art, whereupon she longed to eat of the Tree; for the Serpent persuaded her by the devil's voice and speech, and pretended that it had its craft and art from the Tree.

23. Eve's essence was heavenly, but already somewhat poisoned and infected by Adam's imagination. Now, Eve's good desire of the good essence in her entered into the Serpent's great power and inward virtue, which it had from the heavenly essence, viz. from the good part of the ens of the earth; and the infected property of Eve, which Adam had insinuated and let in by imagination, entered into the Serpent's craft, viz. into the centre of the dark world, into God's anger. And on the other side, the devil's strong desire and imagination entered through the essence of the Serpent into Eve's essence; both by the sound and voice in their intercourse of speech, and also by the conjunction of both desires.

24. And here Eve's desire and the devil's desire were espoused [or united] in this conjunction; for the devil's desire made Eve's lust wholly monstrous, and did so egg or force her on in the lust till he overcame her; and she gave full consent thereto in her desire; she would fain also eat of the Tree of understanding and wise subtlety; and desired likewise to be, or to be made, so wise, prudent and crafty, as the Serpent.

25. For the devil said the fruit would not hurt, but the eyes of her sharp understanding would be opened; and they should be as God. This, Eve did like very well; that she should be a goddess, and wholly consented thereunto. And in this full consent she fell from the divine harmony, from the resignation in God, and from the divine desire, and entered with her own desire into the craft, distemper and vanity of the Serpent, and the devil.

26. Here, in this juncture [or point of time] the devil's desire took full possession of Eve's will, and introduced it into a serpentine

substance; and even here Eve became monstrous in her own essence [according to the essence of the Serpent]; and here the devil built up his fort, rampart and stronghold in the human essence; and here is[1] the death of the heavenly essence, viz. of the heavenly essence or being; here the Holy Spirit of God departed from Eve her essence: thus in this point [of time] the heavenly part of man, viz. the heavenly limus, in the flesh, did disappear; and this is it which God said, *in the day that thou eatest thereof thou shalt die the death* (Gen. ii. 17).

27. When Eve had turned her will from the obedience of God, and introduced it into the Serpent's craft, then the power of the heavenly meekness and humility in the heavenly limbus did disappear; not that she fully received the dark world's essence into her essence; no, but as God said to her, thou shalt die, that is die or disappear, in[2] the kingdom of heaven. For the kingdom of heaven receiveth no true death; only, when the light of the divine Principle extinguisheth, then that essence wherein it did burn, and from whence it shone, is dumb, and as 'twere dead, without feeling and understanding, as a nothing. Like as a candle burning in a dark place maketh the whole room light, but if it goeth out there is not the print or impression of it to be seen; its power entereth into the nothing, in manner as God made all things of nothing.

28. Not that we are to understand that man's heavenly ens became a nothing; it remained in man, but it was as 'twere a nothing to man in its life; for it stood hidden in God; and to man was un-apprehensible, without life. Nothing dieth in God; but in the human life the holy ens did disappear.

29. Now when Eve did reach to the Tree, take the fruit, and pluck it off, [it was] the same she had already done by the earthly limus, and by the will of the soul, which desired the subtlety from the centre of nature; which subtlety [or discretion] she already perceived in her, in the centre, and yet [it] was not manifest in the divine power and in the resigned humility. In this essay the devil's desire reacheth along in her monstrous image to the fruit; and when she took the fruit into the mouth, and did eat thereof, that her body's essence received this essence into itself, the human essence took the essence in the Tree.

30. And seeing she did not forthwith fall down and die, she thought it would not hurt her, for the anger-source still rested in her; and she persuaded Adam, that he also did eat thereof, seeing he saw that it hurt not Eve.

---

[1] Or was. [2] Or as to.

31. But now when they had eaten, the wrath of God's anger did awake in the monstrous image, viz. the properties of the dark world, viz. the devil's introduced desire, which now had its seat in the monstrous image, in the Serpent's essence. In this instant all the forms of subtlety and craftiness did awake in the human mystery;[1] for so long as man stood resigned in God, in the equal accord in the divine harmony, the heavenly part, viz. the life of the heavenly limus, penetrated the earthly limus; and the properties could not be manifest, for they were all in equal measure and weight; as the time is in God and God in the time.

32. But when man's own will began effectually and actually to work, then also the properties of the universal magical astrum began also to work in him, each [astrum or star] in its selfhood; for the universal magical astrum lay in man, for he was created on the sixth day, in the sixth manifestation of the divine Mystery, as a limus of all beings; a limus or extern [or extracted] birth, whence all the creatures were created; an astrum of the universal astrum; for he should rule above all creatures of this world, and be lord over all creatures, and yet not be ruled or lorded over by any.

33. For he stood in equal essence; but now, every astrum of every essence of all the creatures in man do depart from their mutual accord, and each steps into its selfhood; whence the strife, contrariety and enmity arose in the essence, that one property doth oppose itself against the other. Thus likewise the outward spirit of the outward astrum and four elements did presently domineer in them [Adam and Eve], and heat and cold were also manifest in their body; moreover, the property of all evil and good beasts: all which properties, before, did lie hidden.

34. Here the craft and subtlety of the Serpent was manifest, and the precious image was corrupted, and became, according to the limus of the earth, a beast of all beasts. Whereupon there are now so many and various properties in man, as one a fox, wolf, bear, lion, dog, bull, cat, horse, cock, toad, serpent. And, in brief, as many kinds of creatures as are upon the earth, so many and various properties likewise there are in the earthly man; each of one or other; all according to the predominant stars which make such a property in the seed, in the time of the seeding, by reason of their predomination or [potent influence]. That astrum which is most predominant in the constellation, that hath its desire in the seed; and if the seed be

1 Or hiddenness.

sown, such a property is hatched forth *in the earthly part of man.*

35. Not that the whole man is such [a very brute beast in outward shape], but there is such a figure of the desire *in the earthly essence*; and the man must bear such a beast in the body, which stirs him up and drives him to the bestial property. Not that he hath this form according to the outward [person]; but [he hath it] really, in the earthly essence: according to the outward [personal shape] he remains in the first formation [or platform].

36. Yet this beast doth somewhat put forth its signature externally in everyone; if one do but heed and well mind the same, he may find it. Hence Christ called the Pharisees *a generation of vipers, and the seed of serpents*; also others he called wolves, ravening wolves, foxes, dogs and the like; for *they were such in the earthly essence.* And he taught us, that we must be born anew, and forsake this bestial property, and become as children, *or we should not possess the kingdom of God.*

37. For as the essence is, in the body, even so the spirit doth figure and form itself internally, and the poor soul stands in this prison, bound and married to such a beast, unless that a man be born anew: for which ground [and end] God ordained the Circumcision in the Old Testament; and in the New the Baptism in the spirit of Christ.

38. Here we are highly to consider, what horror, lamentation and misery, anguish, fear and distress, did arise and awake in man; and was manifest as a false life and will in man. Of which we have a type in the death of Christ, when he, upon the cross, destroyed the death in our human awakened property, and overcame [it] with the great love in his heavenly blood, which he introduced thereinto; that even then the earth, viz. the limus of the earth, whence Adam's outward essence was extracted, did tremble and shake at it. Now, when the great love forced [itself] into the human earth, wherein the anger of God, in the curse, was living and effectually working, [I say] when it now was to die, and to be changed into another source, it did tremble before this great love-fire; like as the love-fire in Adam and Eve did tremble in the awakening of the anger in them; whereby they were astonished, and crept behind the trees in the garden, and were afraid. For the dread and horror of God's anger was awakened in their essence, and they knew their bestial properties.

The Twenty-First Chapter

Of the Impression and Original of the Bestial Man; and of the Beginning and Ground of his Sickness and Mortality

1. WHEN Adam and Eve were become monstrous, the Holy Spirit, proceeding from the part of the heavenly limbus, departed; for the part of the heavenly property disappeared in the soul, in which [part] the divine light shone, and in which the divine power of the holy tincture dwelt.

2. Understand, the power of the light departed[1] from him into the centre, in manner as a shining light which flameth forth from a candle, extinguisheth, and only the fire-source of the light remaineth; even so likewise only the magical fire-source of the soul's property remained, viz. the centre of the eternal nature, viz. the fire-world, and darkness.

3. And on the outward part of the soul the air-spirit, with its astrum, remained, wherein the light of the outward nature shone, which now the fire-soul must make use of; for the Fiat was enraged in the wrath of God, viz. in the fiery property of the soul, and also of the body; and in a fiery hunger, in the awakened flagrat of God's anger, had entered into and taken possession of the essence in soul and body, and with hard attraction did impress itself in the essence of the substance,[2] in the limbus[3] of the body; whereupon the flesh became gross, hard, thick and corruptible.

4. For in the flagrat of the wrath all the properties of each astrum, according to the property of all the creatures, did awake in the essence, whence the enmity, antipathy and contrariety did arise in the essence of the body and soul, so that one property is against another, one taste against another's,[4] for all departed out of the temperament; thence arose in them pain, tormenting malady, and sickness.

5. For if an opposite essence entereth into another, it makes an enmity, and a hateful overmastering and destroying, each the other. One property annoys, weakens and destroys another, whence the death and dissolution of the body is arisen.

6. For whatsoever stands not in the temperature cannot subsist

---

[1] Or withdrew.   [2] Or matter, outward essence.
[3] Or limus.   [4] Or a loathsomeness to another.

eternally; but whatsoever standeth in the temperature, that hath no destroyer; for all properties do [there] mutually love one another: and in the love is the growth and preservation of the life.

7. And we are here fundamentally to understand how the gross properties in the wrath of the Fiat in the essence of the body have obscured and wholly shut up the heavenly essentiality in the Sulphur, so that the heavenly man was no longer known; as lead doth hold the gold's-spirit avalled[1] in itself, that it is not known [or discerned].

8. For the desire, viz. the first form of nature, which is the Fiat, hath swallowed, in[2] the grossness, the heavenly part both in man and metals, as also in all herbs, and all other fruits. All the sovereign power of [or from] the holy world's essence lieth shut up in the wrath and curse of God, in the dark world's property in the earth; and springeth forth by the strength of the sun, and the light of the outward nature, in the essence, through the curse and wrath; which budding or pullulation giveth a sovereign power and healing virtue for the malignant essence in the living bodies, whence the physician is arisen, who seeketh and learneth to know the virtue [and temperature thereof], that he may resist and remedy the opposite essence in the body; which, notwithstanding, is only a lukewarm and faint sparkle thereof, if he be not able and skilful first to separate the gross raw wildness (which is from the dark world's property) from his cure.

9. For if the captivated essence of the heavenly world's property may be redeemed from the curse and wrath of nature, then it standeth in the temperature; and if it then so cometh into a living body it doth awaken also the shut-up [or imprisoned] life of the heavenly world's ens,[3] if that likewise be in the body; and expelleth the wrath, whereby the sickness is destroyed, and the essence entereth into the temperature.

10. That this is certainly thus, we may see by Adam and Eve, when the wrath did awaken in their essence, and the Fiat did impress the bestial properties, and formed (them) in the essence, that when the soul, viz. the image of God, did experimentally know this, it was ashamed of the bestial deformity, and of its being in a bestial vessel, viz. in another Principle.

11. For the outward part of the soul, viz. the air with its astrum, did arise and obtain the upperhand; as we may plainly see that amongst the greatest part of men the outward part of the soul beareth the sway and domination over the whole body, in that the bestial man

---

[1] Or blended.   [2] Or with.   [3] Essence or substance.

doth seek and labour only after the pleasure of this world, viz. after external honours, authority and beauty, and also how to pamper, fill and gluttonise the beast; and so to vapour and proudly prank with the beast, as with a god, and yet it is only a corruptible, evil beast, in which the real true man lieth shut up, without life.

12. Also this gross beast *shall not possess the kingdom of God*; and also *it profiteth not at all* (John vi. 63). But [the kingdom of God profiteth] the hidden man [alone], which lieth shut up in this beast, as the gold in the gross ore. Which [hidden inward] man the gross beast scarce regardeth or gives any respect unto, save only that it doth sometimes a little play the hypocrite with it, and comforteth it with devout words, but exalteth itself in its place, as a proud peacock; and bravely trimmeth, adorneth and fatteneth his beast, that the devil may have a horse to ride upon, and thereby mock God: and he rideth thereupon in the vanity [of this world], in the kingdom of God's anger, as upon a false whore which desireth to live in its own self-full might and wit.

13. For such a [beast] the Serpent's craft did awaken and stir up in Eve, in her awakened bestial, monstrous property; that now almost every man carrieth a beast in the body, which doth plague, molest and burden the poor captive soul, whereby it doth make itself also monstrous, and amuse itself on the beast, and brings itself into a bestial figure; which, so long as it hath this image and figure in it, cannot see or feel the kingdom of God. It must be again transmuted into an angel's form, or else there is no remedy for it; therefore saith Christ, *Unless ye be born anew, you shall not see the kingdom of God.*

14. The enclosed body of the heavenly part must be again born anew in the water of the heaven, viz. in the pure element's water, in the matrix of the water, and in the spirit of Christ out of the heavenly essence; that the soul's holy part of the angelical world may be revived and quickened, and live and work in its disappeared, and again new-born, body in the divine heavenly essence; and therein receive its food from the divine power of the second Principle. Otherwise the heavenly image, which God created in Adam, is not capable of the kingdom of God; and without the same also it cannot possess it. No glistering shows of devout hypocrisy, flattery [seeming holiness, or soothing the mind with an outward application of Christ's merits] or tickling consolations, do avail anything; it must be born [anew] or [be] quite forlorn; for the pearl-tree is withered in Adam and Eve, it must re-obtain divine essence, and die to the beast; or else it cannot spring forth and bear fruit for the soul to eat.

15. Now when Adam and Eve were awakened in the bestial property the beast stood then naked and bare; for before, the heaven's image did wholly penetrate the outward man, and clothed it with divine power; for the beast was not afore manifest. This property lay hidden in the temperature, as likewise it is so, outside the creature; but now, when the image of the heavenly essence did disappear, then the beast, viz. the bestial property, was manifest; so that now the poor soul, which was from the first Principle, stood forth encompassed with this beast, wholly naked and bare.

16. But if the beast had been manifest in the beginning of man, then it had also brought its clothing along with it from its essence, as other beasts did. But the man was not created unto the bestial life; and though God knew that it would so come to pass (for which end he created so many kinds and sorts of beasts for his food and raiment), yet he created man in and unto the true image of God out of the heavenly essence; so that if this image fell he might again bring it, through a new motion and regeneration, into its first state, as it is brought to pass in Christ.

17. The scope and eye-mark of our writing is, to search out the image of God; how it was created, and how it is corrupted, and how it shall come again into its first estate: thereby to understand aright the new birth out of Christ, and to know the inward and outward man, even what the mortal and immortal [man] is, and how he is become mortal; and what he is to do that he may come again into his first estate.

The Twenty-Second Chapter

Of the Original of Actual Sin,
and the Awakening[1] of God's Anger
in the Human Property

1. THE Scripture saith, *God hath made all things by his Word, and without the same, nothing was made which was made.* Out of his expressed Word (which was essential in the Verbum Fiat) all things came forth into formings: first into an ens, or desire of a property, and out of the same property into a compaction of Sulphur, Mercury and Salt, as into a formed nature; and out of the same ens in the formed nature the Word becomes a creatural life; and brings itself forth out of the compaction of Sulphur, Mercury and Salt out of the body,[2] that is, it manifests itself in a plain, visible being; to which end God hath created nature and creature.

2. Thus each creature hath a centre to its re-expressing, or breathing forth of the formed Word, in itself, both the eternal and the temporal creatures; the unrational, as well as man. For the first ens was spoken forth out of God's breath through the Wisdom, out of the centre, to fire and light, and taken into the Fiat, and brought into a compaction.

3. This same ens is out of the eternity,[3] but the compaction of the four elements is out of time. Thus an eternal [ens] lieth hidden in everything in the time, in all things with life or without life, in elements and creatures, in vegetative and un-vegetative. The first ens is in every thing, whence the form of compaction (which is arisen from the time) was spoken forth out of the spiritual world's being, as an eternal ens out of the eternal-speaking Word, through the Wisdom, into a time, viz. into a formed essence according to the spiritual ens; which ens cannot be destroyed by any element or thing whatsoever.

4. And although the elemental compaction, viz. the body (which the ens hath attracted to itself, that is, breathed it forth from itself as an external degree) doth vanish and come to nothing, (for it hath a temporal beginning), yet the first ens cannot perish. As we also see that all things enter again into their mother from whence they are arisen and come forth, viz. into the four elements.

1 Endkindling, stirring up or provocation.   2 Or into a body.
3 Or eternal being.

5. Now in this consideration we find the true ground of sin's original: Seeing that the living, powerful, understanding, speaking Word was breathed forth out of all the three Principles into the ens of man's image, for his understanding,[1] that he should and could rule the properties of the compaction of Sulphur, Mercury and Salt; but he hath now introduced this understanding, viz. the speaking, powerful Word again into the compaction of time, viz. into the earthly limus; where also the Fiat of time is awakened in the body, and hath taken the understanding, viz. the inspired breath,[2] captive in itself, and placed itself master over the understanding.

6. So that we do now see, by woeful experience,[3] how it is now with us; that when we would speak (albeit the understanding Word doth [idea or] conceive itself in the inward ens, and desires to manifest the truth), yet the awakened vanity in the earthly limus of the body doth soon forthwith catch it, and [cunningly blends] and works it forth into its own property [or serpentine subtlety]; so that the word of the human understanding doth breathe forth lies, iniquity, malice, falsehood, and such cunning vanity and foppery, in which voice the devil's desire doth mix itself, and makes it to a substance of sin, which the kingdom of God's anger doth receive.

7. For in what property every word doth form and manifest itself in man's speech, when he speaks it forth, let it be either in God's love, viz. in the holy ens, or in the ens of God's anger, of the same it is again received when it is spoken. The false word proceeding from the false ens being infected by the devil, and sealed to destruction, is also taken into the Mystery of the wrath, viz. into the property of the dark world. Every thing entereth with its ens into that whence it takes its original.

8. Seeing then the speaking Word is a divine manifestation, wherewith the eternal Word of God hath manifested itself, and that this same speaking Word is inspired into man, we are therefore here to consider what man doth manifest with this speaking Word. Understand it thus: if the human lubet and desire (which is the Fiat or the creating of the human word) doth conceive the form of the word in the holy ens, viz. in the heavenly part of the humanity, then the word soundeth[4] from a holy power, and the mouth speaketh truth.

9. But if it be from the vanity, from the Serpent's craft, which Eve imprinted into herself, and thereby awakened its subtlety, then the word sounds from the ens of the dark world, viz. it proceeds from the

---

[1] Intellectual faculty. [2] Sound or harmony. [3] With great lamentation.
[4] Or speaketh.

centre to the fire-word; and thereinto also it entereth (in its end)[1] when it goeth forth out of the form, viz. out of the mouth, and whithersoever it goeth it bringeth forth fruit.[2]

10. If it entereth into another man's hearing,[3] in whom the hunger of craft and vanity stands in open desire, it is soon received as into a fruitful soil, and takes deep spreading root, and brings forth such evil fruit; whence also such sharp words and stinging taunts[4] of the devil are hatched in the devilish essence.

11. But if it proceeds forth empty and bare only, into the false imagination, then it ascends into the will of the mind, and conceives itself in the mind into a substance, for a seat of the devil's desire, even for his murdering fort which he hath in man.

12. But if the false word be uttered against a holy man, in reviling and reproaching him, and the holy man will not let it take place in him, and not stir or move himself in the evil part of his property with the like evil word, then the wrath of God receives it from without the man, and is thereby mightily enkindled. And not only the inward ens of God's anger according to the spiritual dark-world's property is thereby enraged, but also the outward ens of the wrath in turba magna is inflamed, and hangs over the wicked man's head, and doth even encompass him; and he is therewith taken and possessed, as if he sat in the hellish [flames of] fire.

13. Of which Christ said, *that when the wicked did curse us we should bless him*, that is, echo forth the word of love against his fiery word, and not suffer his malicious word to enter into us, for to take root; and then it goeth back again and apprehends the wicked reviler himself, for Paul said, *we heap fiery coals upon his head*.

14. For every word of man proceeds from an eternal ens; either from the ens of God's love, or from the ens of God's anger; and if now it be brought forth out of the ens, viz. out of its own place or mother, it will have again a place of its rest, wherein it may work.

15. Now if it cannot take rest and work in its likeness, outside the wicked man, (who hath awakened and brought it forth out of his ens, and introduced it into a sound, or wordy[5] substance), then it catcheth or surrounds its expressor [or author] who hath brought it into a substance, and entereth again with its root into its mother whence it did arise; that is, with the enkindled spirit, and with the substance

---

[1] Ens.   [2] Worketh.
[3] Text, into the mansion-house of his tone or hearing faculty.
[4] Text, thorns, or jerking taunts.   [5] Vocal.

(of its contrived matter) it doth lay hold of and apprehend the inventor's[1] body; viz. the outward essence of the outward sulphur.

16. For every word, when it is expressed, is outwardly made and formed; for in the expressing or pronouncing thereof the outward spirit, viz. the outward part of the soul, receives it to its own substance; and afterwards, being enkindled in the wrath, and infected by the devil in its coming forth, in its witty glancing subtlety of the Serpent, doth enter again into the soul and body of the monstrous image; and worketh according to its property, enkindled and infected by the devil, and continually bringeth forth such evil fruits and words: as we plainly see that out of many a wicked mouth nothing but vanity proceeds.

17. Moreover, we have a very great and weighty point here to consider of, concerning the Serpent's craft: that if the devil hath infected the word (when it is born in the heart and formed in its ens, and hath taken possession of the will, and made it substantial) this Serpent's craft doth then hold and entertain the same in the devil's murdering fort, as a fine adorned pleasant brat; as the Serpent, lying on the Tree, spake very pleasingly and takingly with Eve, until it could, by its friendly intercourse, catch her in the desire. Even so likewise the false, crafty, conceived Serpent's-word, which proceedeth from the false heart, doth hold forth itself as a very lovely eloquent persuasive syren, and calls itself holy, till it can discover man's desire set open for it; there it lays open its very heart, and entereth into the desire [of him], and maketh itself a place to work [in], and to reprocreate [its like].

18. Therefrom now do come the false close backbiters, talebearers, perverters and wrong interpreters of other men's sayings, secret liars, who are very fair before, and behind are a serpent; revilers, and foul-mouthed slanderers who take away a man's good name from him; and in this false, smooth, and well-coloured and adorned Serpent's-property, the devil hath his Council Chamber, his school, where he teacheth the children of Eve his art, viz. juggling delusions, foppery, pride, covetousness, envy, anger, and all vices and abominations proceeding from the abyss of the dark-world's property.

19. Thus the devil ruleth man in body and soul by the crafty essence of the Serpent, and worketh abomination with abomination, iniquity with iniquity, sin with sin. And this is even the first original of actual sin: that Eve and Adam did introduce the Serpent's crafty

[1] Or expressor's, speaker's.

essence (which the devil had infected) into their [will and] desire; and
so made themselves forthwith monstrous in the Serpent; whereupon
the dark-world's essence did awake in them, that so soon as this was
brought to pass, the will did imagine into this monstrous property,
and formed itself into a substantial word.

20. Even thus the word was now also manifest in man in the
property of God's anger, viz. in the dark-world's ens; and thus man
doth now speak lies and truth; for there is a twofold ens in him, viz.
one from the dark world, awakened and stirred up by the desire of the
Serpent and the devil; and one from the heavenly limus which is now
stirring in man, wherein the free will taketh the word, that is, whence
it doth generate a fruit out of the divine expressed and formed word,
which is again received of the likeness, either in heaven or hell, that
is, in the darkness or light.

21. For the two worlds are in each other as one. The wicked
formeth and maketh [for] God a good word in his wrath unto death,
viz. unto the sting of death and hell; and the holy man formeth and
maketh [to] God, out of his good ens, a good word unto the holy life
and operation. As the Scripture speaketh very clearly, *the holy is to God
a sweet savour unto life, and the wicked a sweet savour unto death*, viz. to the
dark world.

22. Now every man is a creator [or framer] of his word's powers
and doings; that which he maketh and frameth out of his free will, the
same is received, as a work of the manifested word, into each property,
in the likeness.

23. For God's Word is also manifest in the dark world; but only
according to its property, as the Scripture saith, *such as the people is,
such a god they also have*. God's word is manifest in all things, in each
thing according to its ens, whence the free will proceedeth; the free
will is the creator or maker, whereby the creature maketh [formeth
and worketh] in the manifested[1] Word.

24. There is no herb or thing whatsoever that can be named,
wherein there lieth not an ens from the manifested Word of God, an
ens both according to God's Love and Anger, according to the dark
and light-world; for this visible world was breathed forth out of this
same Word. Now each ens of the forth-breathed Word hath a free will
again to breathe forth out of its ens a likeness according to itself.[2]

25. But this is now the greatest evil, that the ens in its centre is
departed out of the likeness [and harmony] of the property into an

[1] Or revealed.   [2] Its own likeness.

elevation, viz. out of one only ens into many entities, into many properties; of which the devil, being a hierarch of the place of this world, and also the curse of God upon the earth, is [a] cause, which curse man stirred up and awakened.

26. For now, an evil ens, which is from the awakened property, doth infuse[1] itself into a good vessel, and corrupteth the vessel whence the free will should draw[2] from a good property; but the evil doth mix itself into the good, and both come forth again in the formed word, into a substance; as an evil man doth oftentimes stir up an evil word and work in a good man, which he never before conceived [or purposed] in his will.

27. For the anger is become stirring [or quick] in the human ens, and adhereth to the good ens, and the will of the fire-soul is free, it conceiveth[3] as soon in the ens of anger as in the ens of love; nay, in many a one the love-ens is wholly impotent and as 'twere dead or extinct. He worketh only from the craftiness of the Serpent, fruit unto God's anger, and though his mouth doth flatter in the Serpent's craft, and make a devout show of the holy Word, and sets forth itself as an angel, yet it is only the ens and form of the crafty Serpent in the light of the earthly nature, and the man deceiveth himself.

28. Therefore Christ saith, *unless that ye be converted, and become as children, ye cannot see the kingdom of God.* The free will must wholly go out from the ens of the Serpent, and enter again, in the spirit of Christ, into its heavenly ens, which did disappear in Adam, and again awaken and stir up this ens in the hunger of its desire, that it also may be again awakened and born unto a living ens in the new regenerated Word in the humanity of Christ, and which did arise and powerfully quicken itself in the great love-property, in the man's property in the person of Christ: where also the free will becomes a new innocent child, and neither willeth nor letteth-in the Serpent's craft, otherwise the free will cannot form and manifest God's holy Word in itself, the free will must draw only out of the good ens, if it will work and live in the holy Word.

29. Now understand aright our writing concerning the Serpent's craft, and its adorned art and false virtue, [I say] understand our very profound and high meaning, opened out of the counsel of God, thus: The Serpent's ens and original was a virgin of heavenly pomp, a queen of heaven, and princess of the beings of God, apprehended and formed

---

[1] Text, or is borne, carried in, etc.　　　[2] Or create.
[3] Formeth, createth or draweth forth.

in the Fiat of the divine desire, through the fire in the light. In like manner the hierarch Lucifer was so, and prince Lucifer sat in heavenly pomp in the Serpent's ens, who had infected the ens out of which the Serpent was created, and therein awakened the dark-world's property, viz. the centre of the eternal nature, whence evil and good do take their original. But when the good did in the fire sever itself into the light, and the evil into the darkness, the Serpent's ens, which was good, was then infected, filled and possessed with the darkness; and from hence cometh its craft.

30. For even such a craft the devil desired, which also took him in the eternal-speaking Word, in such a property, and confirmed him therein to eternity.[1] For it is also a wonder in God how an evil could come to be out of a good, in order that the good might be known and manifest; and the creature might learn to fear before God, and hold still to[2] the spirit of God; that he alone might act and work in the eternal-speaking Word, and make and do what he please with and by the creature.

31. And to this end Lucifer was swallowed up in the wrath, seeing his free will went forth from the resignation and departed from God's spirit, into the centre, to be its own self-full maker and creator; that the angels now have an example[3] in this revolted fallen prince and puissant hierarch; for the kingdom of God, which is [peculiarly and properly] called God's kingdom, stands in the deepest humility and love, and not at all in the wrathful fire's-might, but in the light fire's-might, viz. in power.

32. But the devil's kingdom, after which he longed and laboured, stood in the wrathful fire's-might, but the same was, essentially,[4] taken from him in his place, and he was spewed out into the eternal hunger of the darkness.

33. And that he had infected and possessed the ens of the Serpent, which was so crafty, may be seen in its body, which is only a dry hungry skin, and fills itself with poison in the tail, in which property the great craft ariseth; and therefore the Serpent carrieth the poison in the tail (which may soon be pulled off), in that the same in the beginning was introduced into its virgin-like ens.

34. For the Serpent is therefore called a virgin according to the right of eternity, because it hath both tinctures, which is in no kind of earthly creature besides; but it is now in the curse of God. Yet if the

---

[1] For ever.   [2] Willingly submit to.   [3] Warning, Text, looking-glass.
[4] In the being, essence or substance.

artist knew what its pearl was, he would rejoice at it: yet by reason of the world's false desire, which seeketh only the false magic, it remains hidden; also [it is not manifest] that the wicked may bear his rebuke.

35. For the pearl of the whole world is trodden under foot; and there is nothing more common than the same, yet it is hidden; in order that the holy ens might not be introduced into an ungodly one, which is not worthy of it; and so God's power and Word in the virgin-like essence be thereby brought into a serpentine [ens], as it is to be understood in the Serpent: enough, here, for our school-fellows.

36. Thus we do fundamentally understand the original of sin's birth; how sin was borne and opened in the human word; and how God is provoked to anger in his expressed Word by the human re-expressing. For man beareth the Word, which created heaven and earth, in his ens, for the same Word is brought to substance.

37. Now God hath inspired into man's ens, viz. into the formed compacted Word, the living soul, viz. the original[1] out of all the three Principles, as a spirit of the formed Word. This understanding hath now power and might to re-conceive, and to generate again, a formal voice in the ens, viz. in the formed compacted Word.

38. But seeing the Serpent's craft, viz. the devil's introduced desire, became manifest in the ens of Adam and Eve, viz. in their compacted and formed word; thereupon the free will doth now draw forth from this Serpent's essence mere adder's poison and death, and formeth its word therein, unless the holy ens or seed of the woman be again awakened in the new-born love of God in Christ; then the free will may conceive in this same holy ens, and bruise and tread under foot the head of the Serpent's-and-devil's-ens in the anger of God; that is, reject and abhor the evil will, which desireth to idea and imprint itself, from the Serpent's ens, in the formation of the words, and bruise it in the will of the thoughts, with the ens of the woman, viz. of Christ, and esteem it as the devil's mire and dirt; which, in the children of God, is a continual combat and strife between the ens of the Serpent in the flesh, and between the regenerate ens of the heavenly part.

39. Also know this: Every thought which is formed in the will, so that a man consenteth unto lies, or anything else which is false, or if his will hath conceived [and contrived] anything that is unjust, and he bringeth that contrivance into the desire, that he would very willingly do it, or express it in the false evil-formed word, if he could

1 Or understanding.

or knew how, and yet must let it alone, either for fear or shame; this same is all sin, for the will hath formed itself in the Serpent's ens.

40. But understand it well: if a good will doth conceive[1] in a good ens, and yet the evil desire doth adhere to it, and willeth to poison the good; if then [I say] the good conceived will overcometh the evil, and casts it out, that the evil cannot also be formed or received into the compaction or substance; it is no sin. And though the evil desire which adhereth to the good be sin, yet if the good will doth not close with it and bring it into substance, but rejects it out of the good will, as an evil, then the sinful desire cannot come into essence, and the good will hath not hereby wrought any evil, if it hath not consented to the craft of the Serpent.

41. Every sin is born of the strange ens, if the free will departs from the ens, wherein God hath created it. The sin which is conceived in the will in false desire, and brought to essence in the ens of the will, so that man would fain do wickedly or unjustly if he could but bring his intent to pass, is also great in the sight of God; but if it proceeds so far as to hurt and injure anyone by word or deed, then the sin is double; for it is formed in its own ens, and formeth itself also in that whereinto it introduceth the false word, so far as the false word in its speaking finds a place of rest to work [and bring forth its evil fruit].

42. And therefore the holy word shall judge the false; as also at the end of this time the holy word shall cast out from itself all false idol opinions,[2] and all whatsoever that hath been formed in the Serpent's ens, and give them to the dark world.

43. All those that take or conceive the word in them, in their devilish and serpentine ens, and use it against God's children, in whom the holy ens is manifest, and do stir up also an offence [or occasion of stumbling] in the children of God, that the free will in them doth also conceive itself in the Serpent's ens, viz. in anger and averseness, where always the holy ens doth likewise form itself, and the spirit of zeal ariseth: these false authors, beginners and causers do all sin against the Holy Ghost.

44. For they do extremely despite and defy Him, that He must even proceed forth, through the anger of the children of God, whereby He is stirred up, and oftentimes shews Himself in the turba of the children of God, and falls upon the neck of the wicked. As may be seen by Elias, and Moses, and also by Elisha, who cursed the boys, that the bears came out and tore them to pieces. For thus the sword of God

[1] Or form itself.   [2] Carved work of fancy.

comes forth through the mouth of the saints. If the Holy Spirit be extremely displeased, and set into a fiery zeal, then He awakeneth turba magna, which draweth the sword against a wicked people and devoureth them.

45. Thus understand it in its full scope and meaning: Man hath God's Word in himself, which created him; understand, the Word hath imprinted and formed itself with the creating, both in its holiness and also in the anger; and that also in[1] the outward world. For the limus of the earth, or the earth itself, was amassed and compacted through the Word, so that the formed Word, which took its beginning in the divine desire, viz. in the Fiat, is an exhalation forth-breathed from the spirit of God out of love and anger: therefore it is evil and good, but the evil was hidden, and as it were wholly swallowed up in the light, as the night in the day.

46. But the sinful desire in Lucifer and Adam hath awakened the anger, so that it is become manifest essentially. Now the gates of the formed Word, both in love and anger, do stand open in the earth, and also in the limus of the earth, viz. in man, and also in the free will of man; whatsoever he doth now form and amass in his free will, that [same] he hath made, be it either evil or good.

47. But now the evil shall, in the judgment of God, be separated from the good; and in what part [either of the evil or the good] the human understanding, viz. the soul, shall be found, thereinto it must enter, with all whatsoever it hath done, as into its own made habitation. And therefore Christ saith, their works shall follow them, and be purged (or proved) by the fire. Also at the end, when the books of the essence shall be opened, *they shall be judged according to their works.* For the work, be it evil or good, doth embrace the soul, unless the soul doth wholly depart [from the evil] and destroy it again, by reconciliation of his offended and wronged brother, and drown the substance in the blood and death of Christ, else there is no remedy.

48. Therefore a man must well consider what he will speak; for he speaketh from the formed ens of God's manifestation; and well bethink and ponder with himself before he intendeth [or conceiveth in the will] to do anything; and by no means consent unto any false back-bitings, nor approve by a yea, neither privately nor openly.

49. For all forged tales and sharp taunts proceed from the Serpent's ens; all cursings, and swearings, and stinging girds, proceed from the Serpent's ens; yea, though they be but in jest, yet the

---

[1] Or out of.

Serpent's ens hath stuck itself with them to the good, and compacted them with the word. Therefore Christ saith, *swear not at all: let your speech be, yea, yea; nay, nay; for whatsoever is more than these cometh of evil*; that is, it is born of the Serpent's ens.

50. All cursers and swearers have introduced their free will, and will introduce the poor soul into the vanity of the Serpent's ens, and form their curses and oaths, with all their lewd wanton talk, which is wrought in the Serpent's ens, and sow into God's anger; and on the contrary, all God's children who are in right earnest do form their words in the holy ens; especially the prayer, when the free will of the soul doth amass or conceive itself in the holy ens (which is opened by Christ's humanity), then it formeth the true essential word of God in itself, so that it comes to substance.

51. Therefore Saint Paul saith, the *Spirit of God doth mightily intercede for us in the sight of God, as it pleaseth Him*; for the Spirit of God is formed in the desire of the holy word; He is taken (or apprehended), and this taking or receiving is that which Christ said, *He would give us his flesh for food, and his blood for drink.*

52. The soul's will taketh Christ's ens, and in Christ's ens the Word of Christ became man, which the soul's desire or Fiat doth receive or impress into its holy ens [that] disappeared in Adam. And here Adam ariseth in Christ, and becomes Christ [the second Adam or the Anointed one] according to the heavenly ens and divine Word, and from this ens of Christ proceeds forth divine knowledge, out of the Word of God.

53. Thus the children of God are the Temple of the Holy Ghost, which dwelleth in them, and so they speak God's word; and without this there is no true knowing or willing, but mere fable and Babel, a confusion of the crafty Serpent.

54. Therefore Christ called the Pharisees, *a seed of serpents, and a generation of vipers*, and although they were the High Priests, yet he knew them to be so in their essence, for they had formed their will in the Serpent's ens. They carried the words of Moses in their mouth, and therein they mixed the Serpent's ens; as many still do to this day; where the incarnate devil carrieth God's word upon his tongue; and yet doth only hide the Serpent's ens thereby, and introduceth the diabolical ens into the literal word, whence Babel, the mother of all spiritual whoredom, is born, a mere verbal contention and wrangling about words, where the ens of the devil and the Serpent doth oppose the divine ens in the formed divine Word.

55. But so it must be, that the formed and conceived word in God's children may be stirred up, whetted and exercised, and the truth come forth to light. Dear brethren: this is the inheritance which we have received from Adam and Eve; and that is the cause that the body must die, and wholly putrify, and enter again into its first ens; for the Serpent's ens must be wholly done away: it cannot inherit the kingdom of God.

56. The first ens in the limus of the earth, which was coagulated in the Verbum Fiat, must be wholly renewed in the spirit of Christ, if it will possess the kingdom of God. But if it remaineth captivated in the Serpent's ens it shall never be any more manifest: understand the holy ens, which disappeared in Adam, and was captivated in the Serpent's ens, whereby death came into the flesh.

57. Therefore a man must consider what he speaketh, thinketh and doeth, lest he conceive his thoughts in the Serpent's ens, and frame a will in the mind, in the ens of the Serpent; for else the devil doth set himself therein, and hatcheth a basilisk, viz. a hellish form in the word.

58. For all wrath which is conceived in man for revenge doth primarily arise in its centre out of the nature and property of the dark world, viz. in God's anger, and forms itself further in the Serpent's ens to substance. Let it be what zeal it will, if it brings itself into a wrath to its own revenge it is formed in the ens of the Serpent, and is devilish.

59. And though the same were a prophet and an apostle, and yet would bring himself in the wrath to his own revenge, then this substance is formed from the anger of God in the Serpent's ens, and goeth into the wrath of God; and the anger of God is therein zealous, which oftentimes doth so stir up and form itself in the holy children of God, that they[1] must, against their purposed will, bring down the turba upon the house of the wicked, also upon his body and soul. As may be seen by Moses, upon Chorah, Dathan and Abiram, whom the earth swallowed up; so also by Elias in the fire, concerning the two captains over fifties, whom the fire devoured; also by Elisha, and many other prophets.

60. And there are many remarkable examples to be found concerning this in the holy histories, how, oftentimes, the children of God have been forced to carry the sword of the turba in them. A great example whereof we see in Samson, and also in Joshua, with his wars, and likewise in Abraham; how the zeal of God did enkindle itself in them, that they, in their spirit of zeal, have oftentimes awakened the

---

[1] The saints.

turba magna in the anger of God, and raised great rebukes, judgments and plagues upon whole countries; as Moses in Egypt did, with the plagues upon the Egyptians.

61. But we must here distinguish. If the zeal of God should awaken itself in a holy man without his purposed will, and give him the sword of God's anger, such a one differs much from those who in their own thoughts contrive and plot in the wrath, and introduce the conceived or purposed will into the Serpent's ens, and make it to substance; for that is sin, yea, though the most holy man[1] should do it.

62. Therefore, in the new birth, Christ so emphatically and punctually teacheth us love, humility and meekness; and would that a Christian should not at all revenge, also not be angry; for he saith, that *whosoever is angry with his brother is guilty of the judgment.* For the anger is a conception in the Serpent's ens, which must be cut off by the judgment of God from the good being. *And whosoever shall say unto his brother, Raca, shall be in danger of the council.* For the desire of Raca[2] ariseth in the centre of the dark fiery wheel of the eternal nature; therefore in the fire-soul there is a form of the fire-word, [in manner] of a wheel, like a madness; and the soul's fiery-form stands in the Raca, as a mad furious wheel, which confounds the essence in the body, and destroys or shatters in pieces the understanding; for every Raca desireth to destroy God's image. Thus the soul hangeth on the wheel of the eternal nature, viz. on the centre of the horrible anxious birth; as is before mentioned concerning the centre of the birth of nature.

63. Moreover, Christ saith, *Whosoever saith to his brother, thou fool, shall be in danger of hell fire.* This is thus wrought: when the conceived will hath formed itself in the furious wrath of God's anger, and introduced it into the Serpent's ens, then it standeth in the furious wheel, as mad; and if it doth now purposely go on, and so form the word, and casts or speaks it forth against its brother, and enkindles in him also a hateful enmity in the Serpent's ens, the same burneth in his expressed word in the fire of God's anger, and he is guilty of it, for he hath enkindled it in his Raca.

64. Therefore said Christ, *if thou wilt offer thy gift, go first and be reconciled to thy offended brother* or neighbour, for otherwise he bringeth his wrath into thy offering, and withholdeth thee in thy desire towards God, that thou canst not reach the holy ens, which else washeth away the turba in thy enkindled vanity.

---

[1] Greatest saint.   [2] Or revenge.

65. For the word fool is, in itself, in the essence, nothing else but an enkindled wrathful fiery wheel, an outrageous madness; and he that so calleth his neighbour without a cause, he hath brought forth a word in the fire-wheel, and in the wrath of God, and is guilty of it; for the forth-produced word is arisen out of the ens of the soul and body.

66. Every word, when it is formed, doth first awaken its own ens, whence it taketh its original; then it leads itself forth through the council of the five senses against its brother. Now whosoever useth such a wrathful devouring fire-word against his brother, he soweth into the anger of God, and is in danger to reap the fruit which he hath so sown, when it springeth up and groweth.

67. Therefore take heed, and beware, O man, what thou thinkest, speakest, or desirest to do. Look well always in what zeal thou standest, whether it be divine, or only of thy own poisonful nature! Thou father, thou mother, thou brother, and thou sister, which proceed and come from one blood, from one ens, and mutually assimulate each with other, as a tree in its branches: think and consider what kind of sound [or tune] thou introducest into the vital ens of thy fellow-twigs and branches, whether it be God's love-word, or his word of anger! If ye do not destroy the introduced evil again with love, and introduce again the love-ens into the anger [to overcome and reconcile it], then the substance must come into[1] the judgment of God, and be separated in the fire of God, like as the devil is severed from the good ens; and so shalt thou [be], O wicked man, with thy wicked formed word [which thou hast conceived] out of the ens of God's anger.

68. And therefore God hath introduced his holy Word out of his deepest love again into the human ens, seeing the same was introduced into Adam and Eve in the anger, that man might conceive [or form his will and doings] again in the introduced love of God in Christ Jesus, and in him destroy the wrathful anger. And therefore Christ teacheth us that he is the Gate which leads us into God, that he is the Way and the Light, whereupon we may again enter into God, and in him regenerate [or quicken again to life] the holy ens.

69. And therefore Christ forbids us to be angry, or to conceive our will and word in revenge; but if anyone did curse us, we ought to bless him; and if any did strike us, him we should not resist; lest our turba should be stirred up in the new-born holy ens of Christ, and introduce the Serpent's craft, iniquity, and ens, thereinto.

70. But we should in love be as children, who understand nothing

[1] Or before.

of the Serpent's craft. Therefore we declare, in divine knowledge, as a dear and precious truth, that all contention, covetousness, envy, anger, war, false desire, or whatsoever may be of the like name [and nature] doth take its original out of the centre of the revenge[1] of the wrath of God, out of the dark world, and is brought in the Serpent's ens to a substance, wherein the false Serpent's ens will behold and contemplate itself in pride.

71. Whatsoever doth strive and contend in this world about self-hood, selfish interest, temporal honour, its own profit for its own advancement, the same is bred and born of the Serpent's ens; be it in either rich or poor, in superior or inferior, no order, rank or condition whatsoever excepted. All men who would be called Christians, or children of divine love, they must be born again in their first ens (which disappeared and corrupted in Adam) out of the divine love in the holy and heavenly ens, or else none of them can be a child of the love of God. All the greediness and covetousness, of all places and politic powers, under what name or title soever, doth wholly proceed from the Serpent's ens.

72. I speak not of the offices, but of the falsehood of the officers. The office in its place and station is God's ordinance, if it be carried on in holy desire, and ariseth out of a divine root, for good; if not, but that it riseth only out of a root for selfhood and pride, then it is from the Serpent's craft, and goeth into destruction.

73. All war, however blanched over and under what pretence soever, taketh its original out of God's anger; and he that beginneth it, doth it from a self-full desire to selfish interest, from the Serpent's ens: unless that war ariseth from the command and injunction of God, that a nation hath brought forth (itself) in his wrath, that he would his anger should devour it, and ordain a holier in the room, as was brought to pass by Israel among the Gentiles, otherwise it is wholly born in the self-full turba in selfhood. It doth not belong to any true Christian born of Christ to raise the sword of the turba, unless the zealous spirit of God doth stir it up in him, who often will rebuke sin. Whatsoever exalts itself in the wrath about its own honour and pride, and brings itself to revenge [or bloodshed] is from the devil, be it either by nobles or ignobles, none excepted; before God they be all alike.

74. Earthly dominion and government hath its original from the fall, in the Serpent's craft; seeing man departed from the love-will,

1 Or devouring property, or wolfish gulf.

from the obedience of God, therefore he must have a judge to rebuke the false desire in its substance, and destroy the false substance. Therefore magistracy and superiority is ordained of God for a defence of the righteous substance and will, and not for its selfish interest and its own perverse will, to break down and destroy governments at its pleasure, and to oppress the poor and impotent. Whatsoever doth that, is arisen from the Serpent's ens, let it glister and colour over itself with what hypocrisy it will; and though it were clothed with gold and pearls, yea, even with the sun, it is bred and born out of the Serpent's ens, and hath the Serpent's ens in its government, and tendeth into destruction, unless it be born anew [in the ens of Christ].

75. Whatsoever is not born out of the ens of love, and beareth forth a will of righteousness and truth, to work something that is good upon the earth for the service and profit of his neighbour, the same is idolatrous; for in Adam we all are one tree; we are all sprung from one only root.

76. And God hath begotten us in his love, and brought us into Paradise. But the Serpent's craft hath set us at variance, so that we are departed out of Paradise, and come into its [the Serpent's] villainous subtle craft, into selfishness; whence we must again depart, and enter into a child's coat.

77. We have nothing in this world for our own propriety but a shirt, whereby we cover our shame before the angels of God, that our abomination may not appear naked; and that is our own, and nothing else; the other is all common: Whosoever hath two coats, and sees that his brother hath none, the other coat is his brother's, as Christ teacheth us.

78. For we come naked into this world, and carry away scarce our shirt with us, which is the covering of our shame; the rest we possess either by necessity of office, or else out of covetousness, out of the Serpent's false desire. Every man should seek the profit and preservation of his neighbour, how he might serve and be helpful to him; as one branch of a tree giveth its power, essence and virtue to the other, and they grow and bear fruit in one desire. Even so we are all one tree in Adam.

79. But we are in Adam withered in the Serpent's ens, as to the love-will; and we must all be new-born in Christ's love-ens and will; without that, none is a child of the love of God; and though there may be something of the divine love in many a one, yet it is wholly covered

with the Serpent's ens; which devilish ens doth continually spring forth above the love, and beareth fruit.

80. There is not any who doth good in selfhood and own will, unless that he forsake in the own (appropriating) will all whatsoever he hath, except the infant's shirt; that he must keep for his own and give it to none, for it is the covering of his shame. The other is all common, and he is only a servant and steward of the same, a guardian and distributor to every one in his place.

81. Whosoever suffereth the poor and miserable to be in want and distress under his charge, and gathereth into his mind temporal goods for his own property, he is no Christian, but a child of the Serpent; for he suffereth his under branches to wither, and keepeth away his sap and power from them, and will not work forth fruits by his fellow-branches.

82. We do not hereby mean the wicked idle crew which will only suck, and not work and bring forth fruit themselves in the tree, that they should be pampered to exercise pleasure and vanity; but we speak of the twigs which stand in the tree, and co-operate, and would fain grow and bear fruit, from whom the great branches of this world do withdraw the sap, and hold it in themselves, that they, as lean overdript twigs, do wither, by and under their charge. Such are the rich potentates and nobles; with them the spirit of zeal doth here speak; so far as they do keep and hold their sap within themselves, and suffer their small branches to dry up and wither, and wholly withdraw the sap from them. They are branches on the tree of the Serpent, which is grown up in the curse of God's anger, and is reserved for the fire of God's anger; saith the Spirit of Wonders.

How God re-called *Adam* and his *Eve* when they were entered into Sin and Vanity, and awakened in the Serpent's Ens; and laid upon them the Order[1] of this toilsome laborious world, and ordained the Serpent-Bruiser for a Help (or Saviour) to them

1. N o w, when Adam and Eve had eaten of the Tree of the Knowledge of Good and Evil, and were become monstrous by the Serpent, Moses writeth of it thus: *Their eyes were opened, and they knew that they were naked, and they sewed fig leaves together, and made themselves aprons* (Gen. iii. 7). Here the soul did even now know the monstrous image, and was ashamed of it; that such a gross beast, with gross flesh and hard bones, should awaken [or shew itself] with a bestial worm's carcass of vanity in their tender delicate body; and they would have covered the same from the eyes of God, and for shame crept behind the trees. So very ashamed were they of the soul-deformity of the beast; for the bestial ens had swallowed up the heavenly, and got the upper hand, which before they had not known; now they could not tell for shame what they should do.

2. The Serpent's craft would not here cover the shame, but did lay it only more open, and accused them, as revolting, faithless rebels; for God's anger did awake in them, and arraigned them now before the severe judgment, to devour them into itself, as into the dark world, as happened to Lucifer.

3. And this is the place[2] whereby the earth trembled in the death of Christ, and the rocks clove in sunder: Here God's anger shut up in death the holy ens of the heavenly humanity; which Christ, when he destroyed death on the Cross, did again open; at which the wrath, in the curse of the earth and rocks, shook and trembled.

4. And here was the sore combat before God's anger, in which combat Christ, in the Garden (when he prayed, and was to overcome

---

[1] Estate or calling, or ordinance.
[2] State, condition or thing which caused the earth to tremble, etc.

this anger), did sweat drops of blood, when he said, Father, if it be possible, let this cup pass from me; but if it be not possible, but that I must drink it, thy will be done.

5. Christ, on the Cross, must drink down this wrathful anger, which was awakened in Adam's essence, into his holy heavenly ens, and change it with great love into divine joy; of which the drink of gall and vinegar, being a mixed draught which the Jews gave him, was a type, signifying what was done inwardly in the humanity of Christ.

6. For the outward image of man should also be redeemed from the anger and death, and again arise out of the earth. Therefore Christ's outward humanity from the kingdom of this world must also drink of this cup, which God the Father had filled to Adam in his anger. The same, Christ must drink of, and change the anger into love. Therefore said Christ, Is is possible, then let it pass from me: but it was not possible to overcome the anger, unless the sweet name Jesus drink it into itself, and change it into joy: Then said Christ, Father! thy will be done, and not the will of my humanity.

7. God's will should also have been fulfilled in Adam; but he exalted his own will by the Serpent's craft: now the humanity of Christ upon the Cross must give this own self-will unto the anger for to devour it. But the holy name Jesus brought it into the death of selfhood, that it must die in the wrathful death, and enter again through death in his resurrection into the true resignation, viz. into the divine harmony.

8. Adam, when he had awakened the anger in him, stood in Paradise in great shame and scorn before God and all holy angels; and the devil did mock and deride him, that this image of God, which should possess his royal throne, was become a monstrous beast. And into this scorn Christ must enter, and suffer himself to be reviled, mocked, spit upon, whipped, crowned with thorns, as a false king; for Adam was a king and hierarch, but become false and rebellious.

9. Here Christ stood in his stead, and was condemned to death; for Adam also should have been judged by God's anger. Here Adam, that is, Christ in Adam's humanity, stood in his stead. Adam should have been rejected as a curse, even as a scorn before heaven and earth. And in sum, the whole process of Christ, from his Incarnation unto his Ascension, and sending of the Holy Ghost, is Adam's estate. What Adam had merited as a malefactor, Christ himself must take upon him in Adam's person, and bring again the life out of death.

10. Adam was made by the word of God, but he fell from God's

love-word into his anger-word. Thus God, out of mere grace, did again awaken in Adam's wrathful image his love-word, in the deepest humility, love and mercy, and introduced the great love ens into the ens of the awakened anger, and in Christ changed the angry Adam into a holy one.

11. Moses describeth it very clearly, but the veil lieth before the bestial man, that he doth not know him, for he saith, *And they heard the voice of the Lord God, which walked in the Garden when the day grew cool, and Adam and his wife hid themselves amongst the trees from the presence of the Lord God* (Gen. iii. 8).

12. Moses saith, *they heard the voice of the Lord God, which walked in the Garden.* What is now this *voice* which was [or stirred] in the Garden? for Adam's ears were dead to the divine hearing, and were awakened in the wrath; he could not in his own might hear any more God's holy voice, for he was dead as to the kingdom of heaven, as to the divine holiness; as God told him: *in that day that thou eatest of this Tree, thou shalt die.*

13. The voice was God's anger, which forced in to Adam's essence, when the day became cool; understand, the eternal day in Adam's essence was awakened in cold and heat; therefore now they heard the voice of God, the Lord, in his anger in their essence; for the turba was awakened: the tone or hearing of the dark world did sound [or ring its sad knell].

14. But that which walked in the Garden, and re-called Adam, was another voice, which brake forth out of the anger, and walked [or moved] in the Garden, for the word *der im Garten ging* is the difference, or note of distinction, and signifieth the voice *JESUS*, proceeding from *JEHOVAH*;[1] the voice was *TETRAGRAMMA*.[2] But that which walked in the Garden was *TON*, viz. the centre of the light world; and the voice *TETRAGRAMMA* is the centre to the fire-world, viz. the First Principle, and the *TON*, the Second Principle. As fire and light are one, but they sever themselves in their coming forth to manifestation into a twofold source: the like also is to be considered concerning this.

15. The voice of the fire-world entered into the essence of Adam and Eve; the same they heard, therefore they were afraid, and crept among the trees: but the voice of the light-world is this, whereof Moses spake, *Der im Garten ging*; the holy voice walked in the Garden

1 יְחֹוָה

2 *Τετραγράμματον.* Nomen Quatuor Literarum, that name of four letters.

of Paradise, for the word *Der* denoteth the Person of Christ, who walked in the spirit, in the Garden, and went forth from the fire's centre, who took possession of Paradise, and would invest Adam again with it.

16. Therefore saith Moses now: *and the Lord God called unto Adam, and said unto him, Where art thou?* (Gen. iii. 9). Wherefore said he not, *Adam and Eve where are ye?* No, he called to Adam, viz. to the first image which he created in Paradise, and not unto the man and woman; for he that called was he which walked in the Garden, viz. the Word of the light-world, the voice of the Second Principle, which called back again in [and from] the enkindled anger, and espoused itself again unto the disappeared heavenly ens, that it would arise and stir up itself again therein, in the name JESUS, viz. in the deepest love of the Deity, and unite and manifest itself, in the fullness of time, in the disappeared ens, with the introducement of the holy divine ens of the heavenly world's essence thereinto, and open Paradise again; and in the meantime bruise the head of the Serpent's ens; this Serpent-Bruiser said to Adam, *Where art thou?*

17. Now saith reason, He saw him well enough, wherefore said he then, *Where art thou?* He did indeed see Adam,[1] but Adam did not see him; for his eyes were departed from Adonai,[2] from the divine world, into time, viz. into the outward world, into the Serpent's ens, [both] evil and good, into the death and corruptibility. Out of these monstrous eyes Adam saw in the property of the fire's tincture; but the property of the light's tincture, which he had wretchedly lost, said upon him, *Where art thou, Adam?* Which is as much as if he had said, Seek me, and see me again: I am come to give myself again unto thee. And Adam said, *I heard thy voice in the Garden, and was afraid, for I am naked* (Gen. iii. 10).

18. This calling him was nothing else but the voice or sound of the holy word introducing itself again into the vital light, else Adam could not have heard this voice: therefore he said, *I am naked, and afraid.*

19. Of what was he afraid? He felt in him the world of God's anger, and feared that it would wholly enkindle itself, and devour him, as happened to Lucifer. Therefore he trembled at the call of the holy voice, as the anger trembleth at the love, as may be seen on the Cross of Christ. For even here was the fear and dread of the Serpent; for it knew the voice which called into Adam's ens, and feared before the

<hr />

ארם [1]   אֲדֹבִי [2]

face of God; for it knew [or perceived] the falsehood which was in it, which it would hide.

20. And God said, *Who told thee that thou art naked?* (Gen. iii. 11). That is, the Serpent's ens hath told thee, that thou shouldest imagine after the bestial property, and awaken the same.

21. And we see here very clearly, that Adam knew nothing of this naked bestial property in his innocency; but if it had been manifest in him, surely he had then known it. But now God saith to him, *Who hath told thee it; hast thou eaten of the tree whereof I commanded thee that thou shouldst not eat?* Did not I charge and command thee that thou shouldest not awaken the property of nakedness in thee? Wherefore hast thou by lust brought thyself into the bestial property? Did not I create thee in the angelical property? Wherefore art thou then become a beast in my power? Have not I made thee in and through my word? Why hath thy own free will changed my word?

22. And he said, *The woman which thou didst join with me, gave me, and I did eat of the tree. And God said to the woman, wherefore hast thou done this? And she said, the Serpent beguiled me, and I did eat* (Gen. iii. 12, 13). Herein it is plainly and clearly laid open, that the devil, in the ens of the Serpent, did deceive man, as it is before mentioned; and that they both, Adam and his wife, were made monstrous by the Serpent.

23. For God said to the Serpent (by whose property the devil had made himself a seat and habitation in man's image): *Because thou hast done this, be thou accursed above all cattle, and above all the beasts of the field; upon thy belly shalt thou go, and dust shalt thou eat all the days of thy life* (Gen. iii. 14).

24. But here the veil lieth before the face of Moses, who passeth by the Serpent, and doth not describe what it was. But seeing how God said unto it, that it should go upon the belly, and eat earth, and no law was given to it in the beginning, thereupon we are here well able to find what it was; seeing it was the most subtle beast among all the beasts, and slew Eve her virgin-like chastity, that she lusted after the bestial copulation. Thereupon we understand in the Serpent's property the desire of [carnal] brutal copulation, and all unchastity, wanton uncleanness, and bestial whoredom of man.

25. For it, viz. the Serpent in its inward limus whereinto the devil introduced his desire, was[1] a virgin-like ens; understand, in the good part of the heavenly ens, which was taken in the Verbum Fiat, and

---

[1] Or had been.

brought into a creatural image according to each property; as also the devil's ens, before his creature[ship], was a virgin-like ens of angelical property.

26. This Serpent's ens was modelised and engrafted in Adam and Eve, for the desire of Eve took hold of this bestial property, and imprinted it into herself, as a blemish [or foul mark], into the right pure virginity, into the pregnant matrix. Therefore God cursed the image of the outward Serpent, and bid it go upon the belly, and eat earth; and herewith also the mark [or blemish] of the impressed monstrous Serpent [was enstamped] in man.

27. For as now the outward Serpent must go upon the belly and eat earth, which had brought its figure into the matrix in Eve's belly, so must now the belly of Eve eat of the cursed earth, and the matrix goeth as a subtle Serpent upon its belly, and beguileth the limbus of the fire's tincture. Thus it longeth after its belly and Serpent-creeping, whereas it is only that this Serpent's matrix might exercise whoredom, and effect a bestial work. As Eve did deceive Adam, so that he did eat of the fruit, and as the outward Serpent was cursed, so also the Serpent's matrix of the bestial property in Eve [was accursed], from whence all her children are corrupted, and are all born of a monstrous matrix, which is a deflowered maid[1] in the sight of God; for Adam had already corrupted it when as he stood in both tinctures; but when Eve was separated from Adam it came with her into act.

28. And God said, *I will put enmity between thee and the woman, between thy seed and her seed; it shall bruise thy head, and thou shalt sting it on the heel* (Gen. iii. 15). Now the ground doth lie herein; for God did not mean hereby the outward bestial serpent without man,[2] which hideth itself in holes and crannies of the rocks, and inhabiteth in the rude solitary places [of the earth], but the monstrous bestial Serpent in man, which was figured in the woman's matrix.

29. For when God called Adam when he hid himself among the trees, and was ashamed and feared, then the voice of the holy Word entered again into the vital light. And here, when God said, *I will put enmity, the seed of the woman shall bruise the Serpent's head*, then the holy voice of God went forth out of *JEHOVAH*, (which would once more move itself in time, and manifest *JESUS*) in the woman's matrix, in the disappeared heavenly ens, and incorporated itself anew with the holy Word [therein], as into an aim[3] of an eternal covenant.

30. And this word, which did promise, inhest and incorporate

---

[1] Text, a whore.   [2] Extra Hominem.   [3] Mark, limit or bound.

itself into the woman's seed, was that same word which did move itself in Mary's seed, and opened the name JESUS out of the centre of the deepest love in the word, and quickened the disappeared heavenly ens with the introducing of the holy living ens into the disappeared ens of Mary.

31. Understand, the heavenly chaste virginity was again revived in the name of JESUS in the seed of Mary in the motion of the incorporated Word; and this incorporated [or engrafted or in-spoken] Word stood in Eve her seed in the matrix as an aim[1] of a certain Covenant; and was all along propagated in Eve's seed, from man to man in the heavenly part, as a sound or incentive of the divine holy light's-fire, wherein the name JESUS was all along propagated in an aim and Covenant, as a glimmering incentive, until the time of the awakening [or manifestation] of it in Mary, where the Covenant was fulfilled,[2] and the doors of the shut chamber were again opened. And this is that holy fire out of which the name JESUS was manifest, which holy fire did burn in the Jewish offerings, which appeased [or atoned] the anger of God, and bruised the head of the monstrous Serpent in man, viz. the monstrous fire-spirit, and will.

32. The bruising of the head is nothing else but to destroy the abomination of the Serpent, to take away its power by a right desire of faith; and *by such a strong importunate imagination of faith on the promised Word*, to take the same Word and introduce it into the Serpent's ens, and therewith destroy and ruin the devil's theft-fort; and thereby *kill the matrix of the whorish desire*, and introduce the matrix with its desire into the virgin-like ens, into the aim of the Covenant.

33. In which Covenant the woman and the man[3] shall and must die; and the chaste virgin must be born out of the death in the Word of the Covenant, with both tinctures of peculiar love; and then the Serpent, in its desire in the anger of God, will sting on the heel the virgin-child of the new-birth in the faith.

34. For all this lifetime the virgin-like child is fast bound by the heel with a strong chain unto the nonstrous image; and is not able to get quite rid of the Serpent's chain all this lifetime. This chain is the brutal bestial monstrous man, in whom lieth the monster of the whore and Serpent; a figure whereof we have in the *Revelation of John*, where the woman standeth, with the crown and twelve stars, upon the moon.

---

[1] Butt, limit, the eternal love's eyemark.   [2] Text, stood at the end.
[3] The female and the male property.

35. The moon signifieth the bestial man, and the woman signifieth the virgin-like matrix in the aim of the Covenant, out of which the virgin-child is born.

36. When as Adam was man and woman, and yet none of them both, the virginity according to the light's tincture in the holy ens was poisoned and infected in him by false desire, for the fiery property of the soul carried [or directed] its lust into the earthliness; and out of that virginity the woman, by the adjoining of all the three Principles, was made; and the woman made herself monstrous by the Serpent, and corrupted the virgin-like matrix, and by her lust did introduce a bestial monstrous serpentine [matrix][1] thereinto, infected with the devil's will and desire.

37. Now this holy virgin-like matrix in Eve was captivated by the monstrous property, and the image of the heavenly ens did disappear in her. And in this heavenly ens, (understand, in the right virgin-like seed of chastity, sanctity and purity, which was captived in Eve by the monstrous Serpent and bestial whore's-desire), the Word of God did inhest[2] itself with the dear, precious and holy name JESUS; that it would again introduce [a] living heavenly ens into this captived disappeared ens, and bruise the head of the Serpent's ens, viz. the whore's monster, and mortify its desire, and cast away the whore's image [or bastard] and overpower and allay the enkindled anger of God in this virgin-like matrix with the deepest love of God, and wholly kill and null[3] the monster [of the Serpent in flesh and blood]. And this is that which God said, *the seed of the woman shall bruise the Serpent's head.*

38. Understand it aright: The virgin-like seed of Eve in the Word of God should do it in the name and sweet power of JESUS: the seed included in the Covenant of God, whereout the virgin-child is born as the dew out of the morning, that (I say) should and must do it.

39. For the child which is from the blood of the man and woman shall not inherit the kingdom of heaven; but that which is [born] of the virgin-like ens, in the aim of the Covenant, out of the promised Word of God. The child of the man and woman is a monstrum, and must die, and putrify and rot in the earth; but the virgin-like ens which lieth hidden in this monstrum is the true seed, of which the

[1] Or whorish property.
[2] Inspire, infuse or recall or apply itself as a balsam, that is, put on promise itself.
[3] Or do away.

children of Christ are born; yea, even in this life-time, for the life of this child is the true faith and great divine desire.

40. This virgin-like child doth live in Christ's children in the spirit and flesh of Christ, in a spiritual body, outwardly covered with the monstrum in the child of the whore and Serpent; there is no man which doth not outwardly carry on him the Serpent's child.

41. But the virgin's child, born of the divine virgin-like ens of JESUS, doth not live in all: there is indeed in many a one a glimmering incentive thereunto, viz. a weak faith and divine[1] desire; but the true, holy and precious life of the virginity is not born: it standeth captivated in the judgment of God.

42. Yet well for those who have but an incentive in them; to those we give this direction: that their soul's desire should in the spirit of Christ dive[2] itself into the divine incentive; and with the fire-desire enkindle that incentive, and also forsake and hate the Serpent's monster and bastard, and introduce their great hunger and thirst into the virgin-like ens, into the Word of God's Covenant, and into the fulfilling of the Covenant, viz. into the humanity of Christ; and ever mortify and trample under foot the whore's monster in the will of the desire, as a venomous stinging evil Serpent, a false bastard, that cannot inherit the kingdom of God, and is only a hinderance to the virgin's child.

43. For the Word of the Promise in the Covenant would not incorporate itself into the man's tincture, viz. in the soul's fire-ens, but into the woman's, viz. into the light's tincture, into the virgin-like centre, which should have brought forth magically in Adam; even into the heavenly matrix of the holy pregnatress; in which light's tincture the fiery soul's ens was weaker than in the man's fire-ens.

44. In this light's ens God would arouse the fire-ens, viz. the true soul, and as it were beget it anew, as may be seen in the person of Christ according to the humanity, who in this virgin-like ens did assume a manly fire-soul from the woman's property, from the female virgin-like seed, wholly contrary to nature's proper and peculiar ability, for the image of God is a man-like virgin, neither woman nor man.

45. And if a man will rightly consider both properties according to the divine property, then let him ascribe the male to God the Father, viz. to the first Principle, where God's Word doth manifest

[1] Or godly.   [2] Dip, plunge baptise.

itself with the fire-world, which is the first centre of the creature; and the female let him ascribe to God the Son, viz. to the second Principle, where the divine eternal Word doth manifest itself in the light of love, and openeth another centre in the love-desire, and cometh into the fire's centre; in manner as the fire produceth a light; and the light [is] a great meekness of an oily, watery and aery property, which property the fire draweth in again, whence it receiveth its shining lustre, and also its life to burn, else it would smother and suffocate.

46. And as these three, viz. the fire, light and air, have one only original, yet they give a very evident distinction in their property. The like also we are here to mind: into this property in the life of man's soul the most sweet name JESUS hath incorporated itself in the Word of Promise, as into the likeness which stood in the light's centre of the heavenly matrix, viz. in the right virgin-like ens, inspired out of the light's property into Adam; and hath awaked [itself] in the same limus, as a true centre of the second Principle, viz. of the angelical world, a real temple of the spirit of God; an open, and wide[1] gate of the divine wisdom, in the highest beauty, excellency and love, wherein the holy angelical life consists, and beareth therein the name of the great holy God, viz. the holy Word of the Deity.

47. Into this property the Word of God did betroth and espouse itself in the Covenant; for it was opened out of the holy Word in Adam. God would not forsake his holy manifested Word, which, with the creating of Adam, had introduced itself into an ens, which the devil obscured and darkened in in the Serpent's ens from the anger; but would again open the same, and thereby bruise the head of the Serpent's ens, and beget the human soul out of this divine ens, to a manlike virgin, viz. to an angel, servant and child of God.

48. We do not mean that this holy ens did receive the Serpent's desire into itself when Adam and Eve became monstrous. No, but it disappeared; yet the soul, according to the first Principle, took it into the fire's property, viz. into the Fiat, and introduced the Serpent's ens, with the desire of the Fiat, into the earthly limus, whereupon out of the one only element four elements were manifest in man.

49. Therefore the virgin-like ens of the one only element must now bruise the head of the introduced Serpent's ens in the four elements; and the man of the four elements must die and putrify, and

___
[1] Or stirring.

the first [man] must return at the last day clothed with the virgin-like ens in the one only element wherein all things lie in equal weight [or perfect harmony].

50. For this virgin-like ens, new-born in the spirit of Christ, dieth not any more, although the four-elements man, viz. the image of this world, dieth; but it liveth in God's kingdom, and shall in the resurrection[1] of the dead embrace and put on the limus of the earth, viz. the third Principle, as a garment of the wonder-deeds of God. But the Serpent's ens remaineth in the earth, and shall be burnt away at the last day through the fire, from the pure limus of the earth, where the dark world shall devour it with all its works.

51. Thus we herein understand very clearly, how God out of great love hath promised the Serpent-Bruiser to the fallen man, and espoused and betrothed it unto the virgin-like and disappeared centre, and given in itself therewith for a help and companion. For when they were fallen from God, and had made themselves monstrous, then the image out of the limus of the earth became wholly brutal, and lived in opposition, in distemper, in sickness, and also in heat and cold, as all other beasts.

52. Now therefore God told them what their labour, work and employment should be in this world, viz. that they should bring forth children in sorrow, with painful smart, in trouble and distress, and eat the herb of the field, and now clothe their bestial image in turmoil and cumbring care, in toil and labour, until the four-elements man in the bestial Serpent's image should again be broken and dissolved, and return unto the earth, from whence it was taken and extracted as a limus.

---

[1] Note what shall rise again at the last Day.

The Twenty-Fourth Chapter

Of the Cause and Rise of the Curse
of the Earth, and of the Body of Sickness

1. G OD'S cursing of the ground for man's sins' sake, that it should bring forth thorns and thistles, and commanding man not, till after sin was committed, to eat of the herb of the field, and in the sweat of his face to eat his bread, doth plainly and sufficiently shew us that this had not been in Paradise. The ground should not have borne thorns and thistles and other evil herbs, which are poisonful; but in the curse all these properties became manifest; for as the body was, after the fall, so likewise its food: the half-serpentine man must now eat such food as his desire required [or coveted].

2. The curse is nothing else but the holy element's hiding of itself, viz. the holy ens, which budded forth through the earth and bore fruit, and held the property of the four elements as 'twere captive in itself [did withdraw or closely conceal itself]. The heaven in the earth hid itself from the earth; the holy tincture, from the awakened vanity, viz. the heavenly part, which was from the heavenly ens [did keep itself secret] from the part in the curse, viz. in the ens of the dark world.

3. Thus the heavenly part was a mystery unto man, and so remained in the curse between time and eternity, half dead as to the heavenly part, yet anew embraced with the promise in the aim of the Covenant; and as to the earthly [part] strongly bound to the band of the stars and four elements, infected with the distemper of the Serpent and the devil; very hard tied with three strong chains, from which he cannot get free till the total dissolution of his earthly body; for the curse of the earth and the Serpent forced also into the earthly man, viz. into the limus of the earth.

4. For God's said, *thou art earth, and unto earth thou shalt return*; for when the desire of the limus of the extract of the earth (viz. of the outward man) did enter again into the earth, and imagine after the earthly fruit, then the devil infected his desire by the property of the Serpent; and in each desire is the Fiat, which doth impress[1] and make the desire essential. Thus the earthly hunger became at this instant wholly earthly; therefore God said now unto him: *thou must turn*

[1] Or amass it into fashion, form and figure.

157

again to earth, from whence thou wast taken; for the heavenly disappeared in the earthly, as the gold is disappeared in lead.

5. Thus an earthly body is now sown into the earth, and the earth receives it as its own property. But the ens which is from the eternity (which cannot be destroyed) lieth in this earthly-sown[1] body. Nothing is broken or dissolved but the gross beast, viz. the being [or substance] of time. As a fixed metal is not destroyed [or corrupted] in the earth, even so also the fixed part of the human body; and as the artist brings forth an excellent gold out of the earth, so likewise the human gold lieth buried in the earth, and waiteth only for the artist to raise it up.

6. And as there is a various and manifold diversity of metalline property in the earth, so likewise of the ens of human property. Therefore all things shall be proved through the fire. What kind of property every one hath in this time assumed to himself, and impressed on his body (viz. with the desire of the Fiat), that shall be tried in the fire, whether or no he hath impressed a fixed steadfast property from the divine ens into himself, or a hellish bestial one. All this shall be tried and proved in the fire of God; and as the ens is, in each body, such a fire also shall be enkindled in the same ens.

7. And as quicksilver doth evaporate in the fire, even so shall all the wicked devilish serpentine works, which have been impressed[2] out of the dark world and devil's desire.

8. Now if a man hath in this lifetime impressed into himself [a] divine ens, by earnest faith and divine desire, (understand, introduced [this] by the human soul into the mortal part of the limus of the earth), then it lieth shut up in the mortal part, yet as a glimmering incentive which longeth and laboureth to burn and shine, or as the precious gold lieth shut up in a gross drossy ore, or in lead, and waiteth only for the artist to come and release it, even so likewise shall be the delivery and releasement of man's body out of the earth.

9. Now also we do herein understand the body of sickness, and also the physician [or curer thereof]; for when the heavenly ens did disappear and was captivated with the earthly, as the gold in the lead, then the outward astrum awakened in the body. And now as the outward astrum doth mutually destroy and ruin one another's ens, and change it into another ens, according to the greatest and most predominant power; so likewise the human mind (which is a magical astrum) is hereby governed and ruled, and the body also; and is

[1] Or entered.   [2] Brought forth or formed.

thereby brought into strange desire and lust; whereby man doth weaken, plague and perplex himself; and one introduced ens doth martyr, weaken and annoy another, both through meat, and thoughts, or cumbring molesting care.

10. As we plainly see that man for the most part doth rack and plague himself in the astral mind with the desire about that which cannot be his own, which stands not open in his astrum; and his astrum cannot apprehend, take, or receive it. About this the false introduced desire from the strange astrum doth plague, perplex and spend itself day and night, whence the great covetousness doth arise, that man doth desire and introduce that into his astrum which is a hurtful poison and plague unto him; and yet with such [infoisted] strange matter cannot make any fixed steadfast [thing or being] in him which may subsist in eternity.

11. All whatsoever the own peculiar astrum (viz. the life's right astrum) doth impress [or foist] into itself from [or of] a strange astrum, is false, and an adverse will; whence enmity (viz. the great envy in nature) doth arise, that the human mind willeth to domineer over the strange ens; and if he cannot get it, yet that strange in-foisted, introduced ens burneth in him in a spiritual manner, as a poisonful hungry fire of envy, that doth not freely beteem[1] that to any, that it willeth to possess itself.

12. And though it comes about that it may, through the Serpent's craft, draw it to itself, or possess it, yet it hath no fundamental seat [or true root] in its right life's astrum; for it is not capable of it. But the desire doth advance and set it up as a king, and vaunt itself therewith as an absolute peculiar god, which hath taken upon itself might over others, and sets itself upon strange authority and domination. Whence the pride of riches and self-assumed honours and domination doth arise; and yet in its ground and original it hath taken its rise from the devil (through the Serpent's ens), who also departed with the free will from his own peculiar ens into strange desire. Whereby he hath introduced and awakened in himself (by reason of his strange in-foisted ens) the hellish torment, pain and sickness, so that his life's astrum is wholly departed from its mutual accord and harmony, and entered into an enchanting sorcering property: and so likewise it goeth with the fallen man.

13. But now man hath his cure, and the devil hath not; for when the divine providence knew that he would not stand, he caused all

[1] Or vouchsafe.

manner of medicine [for hunger and health] to grow out of the earth, to resist and withstand the strange introduced property, both from the astrum and elements. And for the cure of the mind God hath given his Holy Word; that the mind should immerse itself into the Word, and through the power of the Word continually cast away the introduced strange abomination.

14. And if it doth not this, but continueth in the strange introduced ens (which the devil continually introduceth through the Serpent's image), then the strange ens becomes substantial, and surrounds the hidden ens of the heavenly world's being or substance; and even then that ens which is from and of the divine property remaineth disappeared in death and cannot attain the place of God. And hence cometh the eternal death; as is to be seen in Lucifer, in whom also his divine ens is included or shut up into the Nothing, viz. into the greatest hiddenness [or privation], so that he, in his magical astrum in the creatural property, cannot reach or obtain the place of God.

15. Therefore it is very necessary for man wholly to sink and dive himself into the promised incorporated Word of God; and continually and fully reject and cast away the strange introduced ens, which the devil insinuates into his mind (whereby he desireth strange things); and only take for his corporal necessity and livelihood that which he may obtain with good truth and real upright honesty which befalleth him in his calling;[1] the same his right life's astrum doth bring unto him, and he is capable of it; and it creates him no vexation, trouble, discontent and pain, if he doth not let in the Serpent's covetousness, pride, envy and anger thereinto.

16. And it is the greatest folly that man doth eagerly and tearingly strive and hale for strange things,[2] and bring that into his desire which doth only discontent and disturb him, and at last cast him quite from God; which doth shut up his heavenly ens in body and soul. What profit is that unto him, which he sees without him, and doth exalt himself in an outside lustre [as in a specious shadow and resemblance of a looking-glass], and yet is not capable of the same? And if he doth get to be capable of it he turns it to his temporal and eternal vexation and disquietness.

17. God hath created man naked, and given him nothing in this world that he can or may call his own, saying this or that is mine. Indeed all is his, but it is common; for God created only one man: to

---

[1] Employment, business, or affairs.   [2] Heterogene, and hurtful to his soul.

that one only man he gave all whatsoever is in this world. Now all men are proceeded out of this only man, he is the stem or body, the other are all his branches, and do receive power from their stem, and bring forth fruit out of one root, and each twig enjoyeth the tree's ens, also they do all alike enjoy the four elements and the astrum[1] alike.

18. What folly [and madness] is it then, that the twig willeth to be an own [selfish] tree; and grows up of itself as a strange plant, as if its fellow-twig did not stand also in its stem. It is the Serpent's introduced ens which seduceth and divideth the branches on the life's tree of man from the only life of man, bringing each twig into a peculiar sundry hunger, desiring to be a tree by itself, in self-full power and domination. And therefore it desireth the muchness[2] of this world for its own property, that it might greatly enlarge itself in the Serpent's ens, and be a great, thick, strong, fat, well-spread tree.

19. O thou self-exalting vapourer, of what dost thou smell and savour? Even of the Serpent's wantonness, lust, concupiscence and poison, and the temporal and eternal death. And this thou art in thy own self-tree, and not a whit better, and though thou wert a king, yet that which is under thy jurisdiction is only for thy office, and not thine own.

20. If thou wilt enter again into the life-tree, and be a twig on the only life of man, then thou must utterly forsake in thy mind and desire all whatsoever that is in this world; and become as a little child; and look only upon that which thy own life's astrum doth cast upon thee in thy estate, calling and place; and therein thou must work, and not say, It is mine alone! Albeit thou art a steward therein, yet thou servest therein the root alone upon which thou standest. Thou bearest fruit to the root in thy labour, which thou must let stand free, and therewith be diligent and careful in preserving thy calling and place, to serve thy brother, and help to increase his sap, that he may grow up with thee, and bear fruit.

21. In all self-hood and own-hood[3] there is a false plant; one brother should be the sovereign cure and refreshment to another, and delight or content his mind with the insinuation of his love-will. There were enough and enough in this world, if covetousness drew it not into a selfish property, and would bear good will to his brother as to himself, and let his pride go, which is from the devil.

22. He runneth, with great pride and belly-carking, only to the

---

[1] Or stars.   [2] Or abundance.
[3] Selfish interests, minehood, and thine-hood, meum and tuum.

devil in the bottomless pit.[1] He will be noble, and better than his brother. But whence will he have it? Did not God give but one life to man, and out of that one cometh the life of all men?

23. But that he fancieth to himself that he is more noble and genteel therein [than others] and vaunteth therewith, that is an apostacy and fall from God and his Word. For in the Word of God was the only life of man, which the Word breathed into the created image; and this same one only life is from eternity, and never had any beginning. Wherefore doth man then bring in a strange life thereinto, that doth disquiet and disturb the only life? Now it must come to this pass: that he doth either with his will and desire enter again into the only childlike life, and forsake all whatsoever he hath introduced, or else remain for ever in disquietness in that, his in-foisted, essence or [life].

24. Now then, seeing I must forsake all whatsoever I have introduced into myself for property, and that the same is only my hurt,[2] wherefore then do not I forsake this false desire, which bringeth death and hellish vexation and torment into me? Better it is to quash and destroy the *desire*, then afterward the *substance* with great anguish and sadness; as it is a very difficult and painful combat when a man must come to destroy the substance in him, by an earnest conversion into the child-like life.

25. But if the free will doth in the beginning break and quell the desire and lust, so that the lust does not become substantial, then the cure is already produced; and afterward there need not be such an earnest purpose and endeavour, as he must have who is to depart from his contrived abominations, and forsake and destroy that substance [or matter] which he hath forged and made in his mind. And yet it must come so about, or else he cannot attain the gates of the eternal only life which God gave to man; and if he reacheth it not, then he also reacheth not the gates of God.[3]

26. For the only eternal life must be introduced into the Nothing, without [or beyond] every creature and being;[4] for it hath its eternal original out of the Nothing, viz. out of the divine understanding, and it is in a disquiet source in the Something; unless that its Something be also bent and set with its desire into the Nothing; and then the Something is a joy to the life; that the life of the Nothing in itself may dwell and work in Something.

---

[1] Into the abyss.   [2] Loss, or damage.   [3] Or enters not into Paradise.
[4] Substance or thing.

27. For God, in reference to the creature, is as a Nothing, but if the creature introduceth its desire into him, viz. into the Nothing, then the creature is the Something of the Nothing, and the Nothing moveth, willeth and worketh in the Something of the creature, and the creature in the Nothing; and in this working no turba can arise, for it is its own love-play, a mutual loving [of] itself, and it stands at the end of nature with its life.

28. Thus we understand what inheritance Adam hath left us, viz. the curse, and the vain desire; and we consider the outward man in its life as a monster of a true human life: unless that the precious noble mind be born again in the spirit of Christ, else the outward centre in the mind is a serpent.

29. And in this serpent the gross beast which is from the astrum and four elements doth sit, and holds possession in the house of the mind. And according to its bestial property produceth various desires, one desiring this, another that, and causeth manifold figures in the minds of men. One maketh in his mind a fixed substance,[1] another a [shattered] ruinable [matter], that which he maketh to-day, that he breaks down to-morrow, and hath an inconstant beast in the mind, falleth sometimes upon this, sometimes upon that [and often changeth his mind].

30. But he that brings up a fixed beast, he holdeth it in him for his treasure, and vaunteth therewith as if it were the virgin-child, and gathereth up earthly treasures for his bestial pleasure, and yet before God he is only a fool with his beast, for he must leave it to the earth and the judgment of God.

31. But he in whom the virgin's child is born, he treadeth the beast in the mind under foot. He must indeed suffer it outwardly upon him, to creep and falter as a laden ass that must carry the earthly sack. But he hath enmity with it, as God said to Adam, *I will put enmity between thee and the Serpent, and between the woman's seed and the seed of the Serpent, which shall bruise the Serpent's head*, viz. the Serpent's beast. This monster of the beast in the earthly mind the true man doth bruise the head ot its desire and might.

32. Thus a godly man must have enmity in himself, and trample under foot the monster, viz. the Serpent's child, and continually kill it, for if this bestial Serpent's Seed were[2] not impressed and wholly incorporated in us, God would not have said, *I will put enmity between the seed of the woman and the seed of the Serpent*. The enmity is within

[1] Project, device, or matter.   [2] Or had not been.

man, and not without man with the creeping Serpent; this Serpent's seed in man is the devil's riding horse, his stronghold and fort, where he is able to dwell in man.

33. And therefore because the devil was a prince of this world, and still is so, in the anger, it is his will and aim to possess the image of God, which God created in his stead, and to rule it under his jurisdiction, and bring it into his kingdom; and this the curse of God's anger hath brought along with it, which now worketh mightily unto destruction.

34. And on the contrary the Serpent-Bruiser worketh unto eternal life, and the human mind stands in the midst of these in the free will; to which the free will doth engraft[1] itself; therein the mind worketh. It bringeth up a beast, and also an angel, or a beast and a devil; according to the outward world a beast, and according to the inward spiritual world an angel or a devil.

35. Here a grain of seed is sown, which standeth in three Principles, and is fit or pregnant to bear a creature in and to all three; for the divine possibility from God's manifested Word in love and anger, viz. the Verbum Fiat lieth therein. As the free will conceives itself, so it begets (or generates) an ens; and in the ens the spirit ariseth which formeth it a creature out of the ens, and the spirit signeth itself in the body what it is: and so stands its figure.

---

[1] Inoculate, or incorporate.

The Twenty-Fifth Chapter

How God drove *Adam* out of Paradise, and laid the Cherub before the Garden

1. WHEN God had cursed the Serpent, and the earth, then the beast-man was no longer profitable in Paradise, for he could not any more enjoy the fruits of Paradise; therefore God laid upon him the labour and toil of the world; and drove him out of the Garden of Eden, and placed the Cherub with the fire-sword of judgment before it, that if the new born virgin-child of the seed of the woman would again return and enter into Paradise, this angel with the fire-sword should cut away the Serpent's beast from it, and not any more suffer it to come into Paradise.[1]

2. The angel with the fire-sword is the right destroying angel, who carrieth death and life in his sword; he hath therein God's love and anger, and when man dieth in this world, then he cometh before the gates of Paradise, before this angel: and even there the poor soul must pass through this [garden] judgment.

3. Now if it be captivated in the anger of God, then it cannot pass through this judgment; but if it be a virgin-child, born of the seed of the woman, then it can pass quite through this sword, and then the angel cutteth off the beast begotten of the Serpent's ens. And even then the soul is an angel of God, and serveth him in his temple, in Paradise, and expecteth the Day of Judgment, viz. the resurrection of the outward body. When this angel with the fiery sword shall sever the earth from the curse, then the right human body returns again, for it must also pass through this sword, and the sword will cut off its beast, that he may be only a man, and no more a beast.

4. The speech of Moses concerning this Mystery is wholly hidden to the earthly man; for Moses speaketh of an angel and a sword; and albeit the outward figure was even just so (for so was Adam driven out) yet it hath far another A B C internally. The natural man without God's light understands nothing thereof.

5. This sword is in man. When man converteth and entereth into sorrow for his committed sins, and casteth away the vanity, and steppeth into the infant's shirt, then the Morning-Star ariseth in the

---

[1] Understand the beast.

spirit of Christ, in the virgin-like, occluse ens,[1] in the true, woman's seed.

6. And in this anxious sorrowful gate of true Repentance, the angel standeth with the fire-flaming sword, and the virgin-bud forceth quite through this fire-sword into Paradise, viz. into the light, into the life of Christ, and groweth forth through this sword.

7. And now the virgin-child standeth with its fair rose in the new plant in Paradise, and the poor soul which begetteth this child standeth the whole time of this life under the reach and swing of this fire-sword, and is fast bound with a band to the gross beast in the outward world. Where the virgin-child is sufficiently thrust at and wounded with this fire-sword; for the fire-soul, which in the fire-sword of God's anger is bound to the Serpent's monster, doth daily amuse itself upon the Serpent-monster, and sinneth. And even then this fire-sword doth cut away the sins, and devours them into God's anger, where they are examined and judged.

8. Therefore the poor virgin-child which is born out of the soul must stand under Christ's cross, in Christ's death; and the piercing sword of tribulation and grief passeth quite through it. It must suffer itself to be drawn quite through this flaming sword; and the fire burneth away the abomination which the soul continually brings into itself from the Serpent's monster.[2] And even then it is in a sore strait, when that is cut off from the fire-soul which it fain would have from its monster.

9. Then must the virgin-child supplicate the fire-soul, and tender it the love, that it should only forsake the monster of the Serpent. Here then ariseth strife and opposition; for the part of the fire-soul hath introduced the Serpent's monster into it, and desireth also to have its joy therein, and loveth the evil beast.

10. Then Sophia, viz. the second Principle, viz. the part of the light-world, doth speak against it. And hence cometh up the strife betwixt the seed of the woman and the seed of the Serpent; and then man goeth up and down in sorrow and sadness, trouble and perplexity; sometimes the virgin-child prevails, and sometimes the Serpent-child.

11. And then the devil stirs up and incenseth all monsters against the virgin-child, to strike it, to mock it, scorn it, revile, and laugh it to shame, and make it ridiculous; that it may by no means be known, lest the devil's kingdom should become manifest.

12. Thus the virgin-child must be exercised by this, in the spirit

[1] Or shut up ens.   [2] Or false image.

of Christ, and suffer itself to be whipped, persecuted and injuriously reproved, and often called 'one possessed by the devil'; be cursed, and continually accounted an off-scouring of the world, until the outward beast hath finished its course in its constellation. And then the Cherub cutteth off the gross beast, and lets it fall even unto the judgment of God. And then the part of the fire-soul must forthwith force through the judgment of this sword.

13. Now if the fire-soul hath taken in[1] much vanity into itself, viz. much of the Serpent's craft and lust, then the part of the fire-soul must stand under[2] this sword, until the fire of God's anger consumes this introduced vanity, which to many a one is purgatory[3] enough; which this present too, too wise world will not believe, and will be only an adopted child from without, and so have an external washing away of sins in grace; but it hath another A B C here: God will not let the Serpent's ens, neither in body nor soul, come into Paradise.

14. The fire-soul must subsist in the fire of God, and be so pure as the clear refined gold, for it is the husband of the noble [virgin] Sophia, [which is] from the woman's seed; it is the fire's tincture, and Sophia the light's tincture. If the tincture of the fire be wholly and thoroughly pure, then its Sophia will be given to it; and so Adam receiveth again into his arms his most precious and endeared bride, which was taken from him in his sleep, and is not any longer[4] man or woman, but a branch on Christ's pearl-tree, which standeth in the Paradise of God.

15. To the description whereof we need an angel's tongue, and yet we are understood well enough by our school-fellows. We have not written this for swine; for none but those only who have been by and at the marriage of the lamb do understand what kind of entire inward great joy and love-delight is therein; and how dearly[5] the bride receiveth her bridegroom in his pure, clear and bright fire's-property; and how she gives him her love-kiss: unto others this is dumb.

16. When reason heareth one speak of Paradise, then it understandeth only a certain place apart: and it is even so. There was a certain place which was called the Garden in Eden, where Adam and Eve were tempted, and from which place they were driven, after the fall. But yet the whole world was such a Paradise before the

---

[1] Impressed.   [2] Or in.   [3] Refining fire.
[4] Or, from thence forward.
[5] Excellently with surpassing beauty, glory and delight.

curse; yet, seeing God knew the fall, the holy Paradise was only opened unto them in one certain place. For to what end should the whole world bring forth paradisical fruit, seeing there was no creature upon the earth that was capable to enjoy the same?

17. But Adam and Eve were, however, brought into Paradise, that, although this first body should fall and come to ruin, yet they and their children might, by the new regeneration in the spirit of Christ, enter in again through this fire-sword. This mystery is exceeding great.

18. For prince Lucifer, before the time of the created earth, sat in the heavenly ens in the angelical world *in the place of this world*, wherein the ens of the earth was comprehended in the Fiat, and brought into a compaction; his false imagination had tainted[1] the limus before the compaction: *it was the place of his hierarchies*. Now the outward body of man was taken out of the limus of the earth in the Verbum Fiat, and formed according to the property of the human life, which was in the Word. The Word formed (by or through the Fiat) the ens or limus of the earth according to the form of the human soul-life which was in the Word; and seeing God had set himself, through his Word, to be judged against the false infection and desire of the devil, to judge him and his enkindled [wickedness which he had brought to] substance, the judicial sword[2] was already in the limus of the earth whereof Adam was made.

19. For when God created the earth he founded its time[3] when he would keep the judgment, and sever the evil from the good, and give the evil for a habitation to the apostate prince. But seeing the good in the occluse earth was without heavenly creatures (seeing its prince was cast out); God created Adam [as] another hierarch out of this good ens, to be a ruler of this place. And hence came the devil's envy against man and all good creatures of this world.

20. But now we are here to consider of the apostacy of man, with the sword of the Cherub. For Saint Paul saith: *we are chosen in Christ Jesus before the foundation of the world was laid*; and even here this saying of Paul doth belong. God knew that this ens, of which Adam was to be created, was already somewhat subject to false lust by reason of the devil's introduced desire. Therefore God chose[4] this limus in Christ Jesus before the foundation of the world, out of which he would make man; that he would, through the judgment of the flaming sword,

---

[1] Made it subject to infection and pollution. [2] Or sword of execution.
[3] Certainly appointed and set a time. [4] Foresaw or provided for.

bring it through death, and through the fire, and wholly burn away the false infected desire of lust; and regenerate him anew in Jesus, in his deepest love in his Word in Jehovah, that is opened out of Jehovah, and introduce a new limus into the tainted one; and bring them together, quite through the judgment of the fire-sword, and purge and purify them wholly and thoroughly.

21. And here also is Christ's descension into hell, where the love of God in Christ entered into this fire-sword and changed the wrath into love; and did also destroy the sting of death which was insinuated into the limus of the earth, out of which Adam was created according to the outward humanity; and this fire-sword had its raising and original in the corruption of Lucifer.

22. For albeit Adam was created as to one part out of the heavenly essentiality (that was in the Word of man's life, which was inspired and breathed into his outward and inward limus), yet this fire-sword lay hidden as a glimmering incentive in the earthly limus of the outward body, which also assaulted Adam, so that he lusted against the command of God and the kingdom of heaven. In which incentive the devil also introduced his desire into him, and provoked him to fall; [for] which [fall], seeing God well knew that the poor man would not stand, God ordained a help and Saviour in Christ, to guide and bring him into that holy ens, whereinto he should be brought, viz. into the true sabbath and eternal rest.

23. Indeed Adam was set wholly perfect, in equal harmony and accord, and brought into Paradise, [to try] if the soul could have overcome the incentive [of vain lust]. And therefore the Tree of Temptation was represented to him, to see if it were possible for the soul to overpower this contamination of lust, and remain wholly and fully in the likeness [and harmony].

24. But it was not possible: therefore Christ must afterwards come into this place,[1] and be tempted forty days in the wilderness, in Adam's ens, and in his new introduced heavenly ens, to see whether the fire-soul would stand in perfect purity. And seeing it did now stand in Christ, the new introduced heavenly ens did destroy the sword in the death of the outward body of Christ, and brought the outward body which he, in Mary, received from her seed, quite through this sword of the anger of God, into the holy ens. And in this power the outward body did arise from death, and got victory over death and this fire-sword, and took the fire-sword into its power;

---

[1] Undergo this proba.

wherewith, at the end of the world, he will purge his floor; as a judge over devils and men, as well as of the earth.

25. For the main ambition was about the fire-sword, for king Lucifer had changed it from the pure clear light into fire, wherewith he willed to domineer and rule as a God. But God sent to him another prince and king, who took it from him, and thrust him from this throne, and should turn this sword in the ens of the earth again into the divine property, and cast out and judge the devil with this sword.

26. And there is not such a silly and narrow meaning of the fire-sword as hitherto hath been generally understood. Although it hath been hidden by the counsel of God, yet we should now open our eyes and deeply consider what this manifestation importeth; that it doth even foretell and signify the judgment of this sword; that he will come, who carrieth it in his mouth; and it is also a messenger [declaring] that Babel shall [soon] come to its end by this sword, and be given to this sword to be devoured.

27. Now saith reason. Wherefore did not God examine this ens afore, out of which he created the earth, and man out of the same earth, before he created the earth and man? Forsooth, dear reason, here thou hast hit the matter right; God's omnipotence and omniscience must serve thy turn, whereby thou art able to bring all things into God's will, as rational fancy dictates. Hearken, O reason, dost thou know whence the earth is generated? Thou sayest, through the Word, viz. in the Verbum Fiat, I say so too. Now, what was this Word? Here look upon the earth and the whole creation, and thou wilt see what the desire of the Word hath brought into being or essence out of the spiritual ens. Thou wilt everywhere see good, and evil, and find out God's love and anger.

28. The Word was a full spiration from the spiritual fire- and light-world, according to which God calleth himself a strong, jealous, angry God, as to the fire, and a merciful, loving God as to the light.

29. Now if God should have quelled[1] the first Principle, viz. the fire-source, in the ens of the earth (out of which it was created), whence should the light have its might? Doth not the Father, viz. the fire-world, beget the Son, viz. the light-world? But now, seeing the Word in the fire-world was vehemently enkindled by God's motion to the creation, as we may see by the coagulation of the stones, (if we were not blocks, and had only calfish understandings), wherewith then should this fire, but especially the enkindled ens in the

---

[1] Nulled, abolished or taken away.

coagulation, be reduced and brought again into the light, into the equal temperature and harmony? God's love alone must then do it.

30. Now, how will [or can] a creature, viz. a fire-soul or angel, come into a creatural being or formation, if the fire-source were not moved and stirred in an especial manner. Like would only then remain in like; and if it be only a mere likeness, then it hath its sport with and in itself, as it was from [and in] eternity. And therefore the unchangeable God hath moved himself according to the fire and light, and stirred up the fire's property, that he may make him a play and melody, viz. a formed Word out of himself, that there might be a play before and in the unformable Word.

31. Now we do here understand this, that if God should have again introduced the enkindled ens, out of which the earth and man were created, into the unformable Word, viz. wholly and fully into the likeness, into the love, then no creature might have been produced or brought forth; for every soul's spirit, yea the angels, and whatsoever liveth, must be a stirring [or working] fire.

32. Now no fire-source can be generated out of the perfect likeness, unless the likeness doth move itself. Yet the eternal likeness, viz. God, had before moved himself in his Mystery with the creation of the angelical thrones. Now if he should have changed this motion (which was enkindled, and also poisoned by the hierarch Lucifer with false distemper) into love, before he had created the earth and man, then he must yet once more have moved himself according to the fire's property, if he would have created another hierarch and angelical prince.

33. But seeing that might not be, he created the earth, and out of the earth, man, out of the first motion; and breathed into man the light- and fire-soul, out of that breath of his manifested and moved Word, viz. out of the first motion. For out of the first motion of the Word another prince should come into the princely created throne of Lucifer, *and take in and possess the first motion.*

34. And God appointed the judgment to the first motion, and took away Lucifer's domineering fire-sword, and gave it unto Adam; and afterwards introduced the deepest love of God in Christ into Adam, and brought the moved Word again into the likeness, viz. into an eternal confirmation, and gave Adam in Christ the fire-sword over the fallen prince Lucifer.

35. For Adam, viz. the corrupted limus of the earth, should, in

Christ its first enjoyed prince, judge with this flaming sword; as Paul hath told us, that *the saints shall judge the world*. Understand, the enkindled ens of man and of the earth should judge the false prince of lies, who had perversely changed the truth in the holy ens into lies, and corrupted it with such [false desire].

36. But seeing the ens of man was corrupted, and could not, God, out of his deepest hiddenness, introduced the most holy ens into the corrupt ens of man, viz. into the heavenly part, and brought the outward [part] also through the sword of the fire and death into the inward, into an eternal likeness [or temperature]. And thus there is here a looking-glass for reason. If reason be illuminated of God it will then understand us here; but if it be not, then there is not any possibility to understand this.

37. And we faithfully and seriously warn the caviller and carper, not to say it is a blasphemy. Let him first put away his calfish and bestial eyes; and look us here in the face, before he takes upon him to censure and cavil at us; it hath far another A B C than reason hath. *It must have its birth a degree deeper*.

38. Thus we are able very well to understand the casting out of Adam, wherefore he was tempted, and driven out of Paradise. Seeing his ens was somewhat enkindled by the devil's poison he could not possess Paradise; and therefore God drove him out from thence with the sword of judgment into death and corruption. And yet gave the promised Word of his deepest love to be with and in him in the ens of the heavenly world's being, for a sure and certain Covenant; wherein Adam and his children should trust, and believe that at the end and accomplishment of this time he would in this incorporated Word bring them again, with the introduction of the holy ens, out of death through the fire-sword; and clean cut off the false infection and lust with the sword of judgment, and set them as angels of God in the place of fallen Lucifer: And this is the mystery of the angel and sword of Paradise.

39. The angel did bear the name of the Covenant, out of which God would manifest Jesus, viz. the high and almighty prince. And it was even this angel which afterwards wrought many wonders upon the earth, who was with Abel, Shem, Enoch, Noah, Abraham, and Moses; who appeared to Moses in the fire-sword of flame in the bush, and brought Israel out of Egypt, and went before them in a fiery pillar [by night], and in a cloudy pillar by day; who gave them the Law in the fire, and at last brought them by Joshua (being the type of

Him who was to be born out of the fire-sword) into the Land [of] Israel.

40. This fire-angel turned its internal light outwards, and manifested itself in Christ's person in the humanity, with whom[1] Christ, viz. the holy anointing oil of the deepest hidden love, changed the fire-sword of the angel into a love-sword and holy dominion.

41. And this is the true Cherub which drove the false Adam out of Paradise, and brings him in again by Christ, the virgin's child, new born out of Adam in Christ; and it hath no other ground or meaning.

[1] Or in which.

Of the Propagation of Man in this World, and of *Cain*, the First-born, The Murderer of his Brother

1. WE are here to consider this weighty point in right earnestness; and not to make conclusions with fictions and fables, as hitherto hath been done as touching the election of Grace; whereas it hath been handled only in a very blind and absurd manner, and no right [fundamental] understanding hath been found thereof.

2. Seeing that men have sought only in reason, and have not been able through true repentance to force through the fire-sword, and see with divine eyes, thereupon the fire-sword of God's anger and severe purpose and decree of judgment hath remained in the eyes of [their] reason alone; and further they have not seen. Therefore they have made dreadful and dangerous conclusions, without fundamental and plain understanding.

3. But Christendom is hereby faithfully and truly admonished, once throughly to awake, and shake off the conclusions of reason, and to see God's clear countenance, which desireth no evil, nor can desire it; but hath also set himself to be judge against all wickedness, and will destroy all such conclusions in the sword of his anger, and do away the Cherub.

4. Now it doth here offer itself to our consideration, how it came to pass that Adam and Eve at first brought forth an evil child and a murderer. To this, reason saith that it was from God's purpose, who hath made to himself an Election, and chose one company of men to damnation, and the other unto his love.

5. Forsooth! dear reason: Whence art thou born? and from whence dost thou speak under the cover of the Scripture? Dost thou not speak from the ens and words of the Serpent? Who brought the false ens into Eve her matrix, wherein Cain was apprehended? Did not the devil do it through the Serpent, and make the matrix of Eve monstrous?

6. Dost thou not understand how the Word of Promise did forthwith incorporate itself into the matrix of Eve in her seed, and that the contest between God's anger and God's love did presently begin;

for God's love had incorporated itself [and betrothed itself] to bruise the head of the Serpent's monster in the anger of God; and thereinto the fire-soul, which lay captivated in God's anger, should give its free will.

7. For the fire-soul is a root proceeded from the divine omnipotence, and therefore it hath free will, and nothing can deprive it thereof: It may conceive either in the life or in the light.

8. But if thou askest why the Serpent-Bruiser did not forthwith bruise the head of the Serpent's ens in the first seed, and not suffer the Serpent's murderous, poisonful will to get the upper hand in the soul's ens, it is just as if I should ask, Wherefore did not God, when he saw that Adam became evil, wholly reject him, or make him to nothing, and create a new Adam? Thus likewise will reason judge of the devils, saying that it hath pleased God that there should be devils, that it might be known what an angel is.

9. Hearken reason! I have above already answered thee, that if God should once more have moved himself for man's sake, and introduced the first motion in the human and earthly ens into a stillness, then the six days' works of the creation must have retired back; and have been brought into a workless rest. And this, God would not; the whole creation should and must subsist in its first motion; its first formed ens in the Verbum Fiat must stand, be it either in love or in anger, let who will, apprehend either: the anger was open, and so was the love also.

10. Only the love is called God: the anger is called his strength and might. Now what the free will would desire, therein it should be confirmed, either in the love or in the anger.

11. For the free will was born or sprung forth from the love and anger, viz. from the fire- and light-world: and so likewise it might choose itself a place for its working life. If God's love should have drowned the free will in the ens in Eve's seed in the love, (in which [seed] it was enkindled in the anger),[1] then the fiery motion in the matrix must have ceased. Now, out of the light's ens only and alone no soul may be brought forth.

12. Also the corrupt ens of the earthly limus must have then been presently judged through the fire, which could not be; for the motion of the new regeneration, and the opening or full explication of the divine sweetness, and the overcoming of the fire, viz. of the anger of God, did belong only to the name of Jesus.

[1] The free will.

175

13. The Word which had incorporated itself had [done this] from without the fire-sword, viz. the Cherub, and from within the Jesus, who should overcome the fire-sword with love. Thus the name Jesu stood hidden in the fire-sword, and was not manifest until the time that God would move himself therein, and manifest the same.

14. Thus the insinuated ens of the Serpent, that Eve had introduced through imagination into lust, must be wholly cast away; for in Cain the murdering image[1] of the Serpent was manifest, which cannot inherit the kingdom of God. But on the contrary, the mark of the Covenant in the promised Word was in the free will, and in the heavenly disappeared ens of the soul, into which [Covenant of the promised grace] the soul should enter.

15. And although the Serpent's ens should have been rejected (as it must be, in all the children of Eve), yet the part of the heavenly world's being lay hidden in the Covenant of the Word in the disappeared ens, as a possibility to the new regeneration. Therefore God said to Cain, when the murdering spirit persuaded him, *Rule over the sin.*

16. If thou sayest, Wherewith? He could not! But wherefore could he not? The Serpent's desire held him, and brought him to kill his brother: Wherefore? The free will had given itself up into the Serpent's ens which held him captive.

17. Now saith reason, God would have it so, else he had turned away his will. No. Indeed God's anger-will in the Serpent's ens which had captivated the free will would have it. But yet God's love-will said in him, *Rule over sin,* that is, over the wrath and anger of the Serpent, and let it not have its power and prevalency.

18. And here we are rightly to know how God's love and anger are in continual contest, understand, in the manifested Word in the limus of the earth, and in the ens of the human property out of the earth. For the anger-ens is stirred up and driven by the devil, and desireth continually to devour the love-ens, and possess this kingdom in the anger-ens.

19. The anger-ens desireth to have man; for it hath its king in Lucifer. And the love-ens desireth also to have him; for it hath its king in Christ. And therefore Christ must bring the human love-ens through death and the anger-ens, and open another Principle, viz. another kingdom; and leave prince Lucifer in his own anger, for his free will had chosen it him.

[1] Or the evil corrupt nature and property.

20. Thus also the free will in Cain did choose the false, viz. the devil's will. But thou sayest, Was then the murdering-will wholly rejected? It did reject[1] itself; but if the free will had again conceived in the love-ens it would have been again born anew, yea even after the murder: which we leave unto the judgment of God, whether it were so or no, seeing the text in Moses doth give him so bare a name in despair. For the Word, out of which the name Jesus was made manifest, was given to call poor lost sinners to repentance, and not the righteous ones, who were apprehended in the love; as Christ said.

21. Cain was a type of the first corrupt Adam in sin, and Abel was a type of Christ, the second Adam, viz. of the virgin-child; for the tree of evil and good began in Adam. And so likewise the fruit did forthwith appear, viz. Christ's children, and the children of the devil and the Serpent.

22. Now reason saith, Was Cain then wholly conceived of the Serpent's ens in the anger of God, and predestinated to damnation? No. He was [conceived] of the ens of Adam's soul and body; and so also of the seed and ens of Eve her body; but the monster in the matrix of Eve did environ the sown seed; and it was that which did seduce and beguile him; but the mark [and aim] of the Covenant lay hidden in the ens of the soul and body. For the ens of the seed of Adam and Eve was out of the heavenly disappeared [limus], and then also out of the earthly awakened limus; but the will of the Serpent and of the devil took possession of the house, as the like was in the devil, who was an angel; but the will of the dark world took possession of the house in him, and got the upper hand: so also it was here, in Cain.

23. But thou askest, How came this so to be? Hear and see, thou fair child in the will of Adam and Eve, what their desire was before and after the fall: They desired the earthly kingdom, as we see that Eve was so wholly and only minded; for when she brought forth Cain, she said, *I have gotten a man* [who is to be] *a Lord* (Gen. iv. 1). She thought him to be the bruiser and breaker of the Serpent; he should take in and possess the earthly kingdom, and expel the devil; she did not consider that she should die to her false earthly fleshly will, and be born anew in[2] a holy will. And such a will she also brought into her seed; and the like did Adam also.

24. And hence now the will in the soul's essence did arise: the tree brought forth a twig out of [or like] itself. For it was Cain's

---

[1] Reprobate or abandon.   [2] Or with.

desire only that he might be lord upon the earth; and being he saw that Abel was more acceptable in God's sight than himself, his free bestial will in him did elevate itself to slay Abel; for Cain's aim and endeavour was alone about the outward world, to domineer and be lord and master therein; but Abel sought God's love.

25. Thus there are yet two such Churches upon the earth; one which seeketh only worldly pleasure, might, honour, and the outward god Mammon and Maüsim (see Ch. 36, 32), and therein it lodgeth the Serpent's child. The other, which seeketh the virgin-child and God's kingdom, and must suffer itself to be persecuted, reviled, reproached, and killed by the Cainical Church, as Cain did to Abel.

26. For the devil will yet be continually a prince of this world in the Serpent's child; and so it is that if the virgin's child (which bruiseth the head of the Serpent) be not manifest in the Serpent's child, then the devil is and remaineth prince and host in the house of the soul: as happened to Cain.

27. And do but understand the ground aright: In the birth of this world two kingdoms lie manifest, viz. God's Love-kingdom in Christ, and the kingdom of God's anger in Lucifer: these two kingdoms are in contest and strife in all creatures, for the original of all spirits is in the contest, and in the combat of the fire the light is made manifest. The fire is a cause of the light: God's anger is a cause that God did yet once move himself in his deepest love in the name Jesus, and thereby vanquish the anger.

28. Now what can the love do, if the free will espouseth itself to the anger? Or what can the anger do against it, if the free will conceiveth in the love, and destroyeth the anger? Must it not hold still and suffer it to be done; and though it doth oppose and rage against it, yet the love pierceth quite through it, and changeth it into joy. The anger is the root of love, as the fire is the root of the light; but in the free will is the understanding, which maketh itself to what it pleaseth.

29. Dost thou not see this in the earth, that the free will in the ens of the Word hath made itself stones, metals and earth. The stones and earth are not the free will; but the free will hath introduced itself into such an ens, and by its lubet and motion introduced the ens into a compaction or coagulation; there was no other maker there but the free will in the formed and manifested Word: thou mayest indeed see wonders enough.

30. Behold the irrational creatures, as worms, toads, spiders and other wild venomous and horrible beasts, and thou shalt see somewhat in very deed, if thou beest not dead. But thou sayest, God hath created it so. Yea, right! his desire in love and anger hath amassed the ens with the motion, and compacted each ens according to the free will into a form. There was no other maker there, but the free will in the Word.

31. The desire in the Word was the Fiat, which introduced the free will into an ens. Thus the same manifested Word *is yet in all things*, and hath the Fiat, viz. the desire in itself. As the free will in every thing introduceth itself into a spirit, even so the Fiat formeth and signeth each thing. Every root bringeth forth from itself a branch of its own likeness; but when the branch or sprout is to be born and receive its beginning in the ens of the root, the ens doth then form itself to such a twig as the root at that time is apprehended in its power and free will, both by the superior and inferior constellation.

32. The like is also to be understood in man. As the will is, in the seed, that is, as the desire of the father and mother are, at the time (together with other influences from the stars and elements), yea, oftentimes from the devil's assaults and insinuations, even such a spirit is formed in the ens of the seed; sometimes an angel, if the parents be in holy desire [or in the true faith of the engrafted Word]; sometimes also a beast, a serpent and image of the devil, both according to the ens of the soul and of the outward flesh.

33. The power of the manifested Word doth give in itself into all things, into everything according to its will, according to the desire in the ens; for the desire in the ens is that which formeth the word, viz. the sound of life; as it is written, such as the people is, such a God they also have, *with the holy thou art holy, and with the perverse thou art perverse*. This is wholly to be understood concerning the expressed Word in the Fiat, viz. in the desire of nature. And therefore God hath espoused and betrothed another Word out of the centre of his love to the image of man, that, although he be arisen out of an evil property, yet the free will hath power and information to disclaim its selfhood, and die to its self in this holy incorporated Word; and then the Fiat begetteth and formeth another new creature in the free will out of the ens.

34. The possibility lieth in all men, but the making or forming of the child of God belongeth now to the holy Fiat in the new introduced

179

Word, for it lieth not on any man's self-willing, contriving, running, and toiling, but on God's mercy. He hath mercy upon whom he please, viz. upon those alone who with their free will die to their selfhood in his grace, and resign up their selves to him. And he hardeneth whom he please, viz. those alone who run with selfish Cain, and would themselves take the kingdom of God in their own evil will, and will not die to their own self-full will.

35. Now saith the Scripture, Hath not a potter power to make of one lump of clay what he please; a vessel to honour; or a vessel to dishonour; that is, will the self-full will be angry, if it be evil, that the Fiat in the Word makes it to be a vessel of the anger; or will it therefore be angry, if the holy Fiat (in the holy Word) maketh that will, which diveth itself into the love and mercy of God, and dieth to its selfhood, to be a vessel of honour. Hath not this Potter power to do with his clay, viz. (with the ens or seed) what he please. *Whereunto every seed is good and profitable, thereunto he maketh him a vessel,* either to the use of his anger or to the use of his love.

36. The holy is unto God a sweet savour to life, and the wicked a sweet savour to the death in his anger; all must enter into his glory, and praise him; one in the property of his anger, who must call the evil good; the other in the property of his love, who must call the good, good. For so it must be, that the difference of the good and evil, of the light and darkness, of the life and death, may be known; for if there were no death, then the life were not manifest to itself; and if there were no darkness, the light were not manifest to itself.

37. And therefore the eternal free will hath introduced itself into darkness, pain, and source; and so also through the darkness into the fire and light, even into a kingdom of joy; that so the Nothing might be known in the Something, and that it might have a sport in its contra-will, that the free will of the abyss[1] might be manifest to itself in the byss,[2] for without evil and good there could not be any byss [ground or foundation].

38. For the evil maketh pain and motion, and the good causeth essence and power; and yet both essences are only one essence, as fire and light are only one essence, also darkness and light are only one; but it severs itself into two mighty distinctions, and yet there is no sundry separation, for one dwelleth in the other, and yet doth not comprehend the other; the one doth deny the other, for the one is not the other.

[1] Ἄβυσσος.   [2] Βύσσος.

39. God dwelleth through all, and that all is not God, also it doth not reach him; but whatsoever quitteth itself free of its free will, that falleth into his possession: that he must have, for it is willless, and falleth into the Nothing; and he is in the Nothing. Thus the resigned will may dwell in the Nothing, and there is God's mercy; for he will have Something out of the Nothing, that he may be manifest in the Something, and therefore he hath mercy upon the Something which is fallen into his Nothing, and maketh it in himself to be his Something; which he himself ruleth, driveth and acteth with his merciful spirit.

40. And herein lieth the precious pearl, dear brethren who are driven too and fro with contention; if ye did but know it you would leave off from strife and call reason a fool. No searchings of self obtaineth it, but the will freely resigned into God's mercy, which entereth in by the way of earnest repentance, and mortification of its own evil will: that [will] falleth into God's mercy, and doth apprehend [and obtain the right understanding]. And without this there is mere self-running, walking, and willing; and yet nothing can be obtained, save only in the will freely resigned into God's mercy.

41. We have a very excellent and notable example and type of this in the first birth, which opened the womb, that it was to be sanctified and offered up to the Lord; and yet the true living offering proceedeth from the second, new birth, as we may see in Abel, Isaac and Jacob. Cain, Ishmael and Esau were the first-born, the inheritance belonged to them; but the lot and mercy fell upon Abel, Isaac and Jacob; for the first ens of man was infected and made crazy by the devil. Therefore it must be given to the fire for an offering and food; and out of the offering, viz. out of the fire of God's anger, the love of God was made manifest in mercy; and the first Adam was the sojourner[1] of the second in Christ, for the second redeemed the first.

42. The devil's desire and the bestial ens of the Serpent had got the upper hand in the matrix of Eve, and apprehended the first seed in the desire. Now the kingdom of God did yet belong to the first man, but seeing he did lose it by his negligence the first Adam must be offered to the earth, and also its first seed [must be offered] to the anger.

43. And after this first seed Abel came forth in the holy Covenant, and offered his sweet blood, to the anger for the sinful seed, that the

---

[1] Inmate; or of his family, servant.

anger might let its flame fall, and suffer the first birth to press through in the blood of the second.[1]

44. The first birth was a murderer, which signifieth the devil in man. The second was the offering of [or for] the first, that the anger-devil in the first Adam might be appeased in the offering of the second.

45. Not that we would exalt or take in the wicked into the offering of Christ, so long as he is wicked; the devil devoureth most of the wicked crew: only, the wicked sinner hath an open gate made for him in the offering of the second [Adam], if he did convert and turn himself (from his wickedness).

46. But that some write, there was a twofold seed which did sever itself in Eve, viz. one wholly devilish from the ens of the Serpent, and the other from the ens of Christ [or the promised seed of the woman] in the Covenant [is nothing so]. These have not at all learned the A B C in this school. They have only a dreaming shadow and fiction of the Mystery, and not the true sight. Thus they build the election of grace upon this; but they are much mistaken; they speak only the Serpent's words, which desired to have it so. Observe it thus:

47. Adam had only one limbus to his seed, and Eve only one matrix for her seed, but they both stood in three Principles. The Principles were in contest, as still they are at this day. The second Principle, viz. the kingdom of God or the angelical world, did disappear in the soul's seed, and God espoused his only, most holy Word again therein, unto the new birth.

48. And this espousal or betrothment stood as well in Cain's ens as in Abel's ens. But in the striving wrestling wheel, in the contest of the three Principles, Cain's ens was apprehended in the anger, and covered with the Serpent's monster. Not so, to an impossibility, as if he were born to condemnation; but even to a possibility of the free will, whether he would lay down the self-full, assumed, and self-appropriated right in Adam, and live in God's will, or whether he would live unto himself. Upon this was the election set.

49. Now God knoweth whereinto the free will is entered: If it be entered into iniquity and selfhood, then God's anger establisheth or confirms it in its choice to condemnation; but if it be entered into the Word of the Covenant, then God confirms it to be a child of heaven. And here that saying hath its proper signification and applica-

---

[1] Viz. through death and the anger into life.

tion, *I have mercy on whom I will, and whom I will I harden.* God knoweth his children even in the ens in the mother's womb; to what end should he give his pearl to him whom he yet knoweth would turn himself away from him? The pearl's ground lieth indeed in man, but hidden and shut up; *if he brought his will into the pearl it would open itself in him.*

50. All men proceed from one only seed; but in one the holy fire glimmereth, and in another it lieth as 'twere shut up and cannot [glimmer] by reason of the mire of the Serpent.

51. Thou sayest, Then is the Serpent's ens more mighty than God's love? I have already answered thee, that love and anger are in contest. Whereinto the ens doth espouse itself, of that it is apprehended and confirmed; yet so, that the will is free to go from the evil into the good, and from the good into the evil; and that while it liveth upon the earth both doors stands open unto it: for the free will is not bound: but if it were bound then no judgment could with righteousness pass upon it. It hath laws and instructions, which are given it, not unto death but unto life; but if it transgresseth these, and continueth in the transgression, now the judgment passeth upon it; for every judgment [or sentence of condemnation] ariseth from the transgression of the command.

52. Thou sayest he cannot keep them, he is drawn [to transgression]. Yea, very right. Doth not the truth rebuke him even to the face, that he is a faithless wretch, that suffers himself to be drawn to evil. The law to do right is in his vital light as a continual looking-glass: he seeth and knoweth it very well, that he is a liar, and walketh upon the way of the devil: it sheweth him the way of truth, but the free will rejecteth it; at present he is predestinated to condemnation, yet so, that the will is free so long as he is in this cottage. But the heavy band of God's anger, in the drawing of the devil's desire, draws many a one to the damnation of death.

53. Reason saith, If a man hath free will, then God is not omnipotent over him, to do what he please with him. The free will is not from any beginning, also not amassed or taken out of any ground into any thing, or formed by any thing. It is its own peculiar original out of the Word of the divine power, out of God's love and anger. It formeth itself in its own will a centre to its seat; it begetteth itself in the first Principle to the fire and light; its right and genuine original is in the Nothing, where the Nothing, viz. the $\triangle$ (or as a man might unfold it, A. O. V.) doth introduce itself into a lubet to contemplation;

and the lubet brings itself into a will, and the will into a desire, and the desire into a substance.

54. Now the Eternal Original, viz. God, is a Judge over the substance; if the lubet (which is departed from him) hath introduced itself into an evil being, then he judgeth that being or substance in its Principle. In what source and property soever, or in what ens soever, the lubet, proceeding from the departed △/, hath introduced itself into a Principle, therein the universal eternal free will, which is the abyss, and cause of all byss, doth confirm and settle it.

55. The abyssal judgeth that which doth introduce itself into byss, and severs the good (which hath introduced itself into a good ens) into the good, viz. into the divine love; and the evil (which hath brought itself into an evil ens, and set and formed itself into a centre to an evil spirit and will) into his wrath and anger.

56. For how can he judge a thing whose own it is not? How would God judge the will of the creature, if it were not sprung [or arisen] from him? Or rather, how can a judgment pass upon a thing which is bound, and not free in its willing and working?

57. The human and angelical will is arisen with the motion of the abyss (when the Deity once moved itself in its contemplation and sensation, and with the motion introduced itself into a beginning of the spirits) [the will of men and angels did spring forth] out of this beginning. Now every beginning goeth into its end; and the end is that which was before the beginning; and there is the trial of the beginning, [which shews] whereinto the beginning hath introduced itself.

58. Now God is before and without all beginnings, and from him every beginning proceedeth; also he is the end of all beginnings. Now the middle of all inchoated things standeth between the beginning and the end; for it must with its beginning enter again through the end into that whence it did arise.

59. Seeing then that God is a jealous God, and a consuming fire, and also a merciful God, every free will with its introduced centre hath its own judge born in itself; either divine love, or divine anger; for when a thing beginneth, it goeth into a time, but when this time is apprehended of the end, viz. of the eternity, then it is in its own eternal [beginning and end], whence it hath introduced itself into a compaction, so confirmed to eternity.

60. Therefore, the free will hath its own judgment, either for the good or [for the] evil, in itself. It hath its own judgment in itself: it

hath God's love and anger in it; what it amasseth and desireth, that it formeth in itself; and doth so form only its own self in its own lubet into a centre.

61. For thus the world hath likewise its original, namely, in the free will of the two eternal Principles, both from the dark fire-lubet, and also from the divine light fire-lubet. The free will introduced itself in the Verbum Fiat into distinct and several entities; and that even according to the possibility of the eternal pregnatress. As the will in the Verbum Fiat conceived itself in each place in the pregnatress, even such an ens was brought forth, and out of the ens arose its spirit according to the ens, viz. from God's spiration or motion[1] in the Principles.

62. But seeing the Principles were together as one, no thing was ever amassed or formed in the free will but the same hath a good and an evil in it, according to the nature and power of the eternal pregnatress, to light and darkness.

63. But now every spirit ariseth with its free will first out of the compaction of its centre, and is, after its effected birth, free, and may draw into itself either out of God's love, or anger, and introduce its will as it pleaseth. But this is the main thing: as the mother (viz. the ens) is, whereof the spirit is born, even such a lubet ariseth also in the spirit.

64. Now the spirit hath understanding, and the ens hath none; also it[2] hath a law, for it knoweth what is evil and good, what is right and wrong. Also God hath given it laws, that it should break the lust [to evil], and with the understanding of the light rule over the lubet of the darkness.

65. Now if it doth not, but departeth with the lubet out of the understanding into a self-lubet, then the lubet or lust doth amass itself into a substance, whereof a new, false will is again born. And this same is a bastard before God and the eternal nature; for it ariseth not out of the law and right of the eternal nature, but out of self. And upon this the judgment of the eternal nature doth pass; and at its end (when the centre of the spirit shall step again into the beginning) it will be spewed out from the free will of eternity.

66. Understand us but aright: The first free will, which was breathed into Adam, was good; indeed it was both from God's love and anger, viz. from the centre of the eternal pregnatress, of the

---

[1] Breathing or stirring up.
[2] Viz. the spirit.

eternal spiritual nature; but it had the understanding in it to rule and govern itself, so it might stand and subsist eternally.

67. But the crafty distemper or infection introduced by the devil was in the ens of the earth whence[1] Adam's outward body was formed. Into this earthly ens the devil brought his desire by the Serpent, viz. by the Serpent's crafty ens, so that the lubet arose in the ens of the body, whereinto the first free will of the inspired soul entered, and assumed the lubet of the body, and introduced this lubet into a desire to substance.

68. And out of this substance another new self-full will did now arise, viz. a bastard, a false serpent-child; and this bastard, Adam did originally propagate to his Eve, and Eve to her son Cain, and so one man to another. Thus we have now in this earthly flesh this same false will proceeded from the Serpent's substance, whereinto the devil introduceth his desire, and tempteth us, and continually makes us lust and long after the devilish property [viz. pride, covetousness, envy, and anger], *that so his desire, which he insinuateth into the false bastard in us, might become substantial and essential*; out of which such a whorish and devilish serpentine seed is continually begotten; and out of the same false ens [or seed] a devil's will [is begotten].

69. Thus the devil rideth in and upon man, in and upon body and soul. But now the first introduced free will, which God breathed into Adam, lieth yet in all men, for it is the true real soul, the centre of the fire and light, a spark of the divine power and omnipotence, but wholly hemmed in and captivated in this wicked introduced bastard.

70. Therefore God hath again in-hested[2] and incorporated the aim of his new Covenant, in the Word of the divine holy power, in the name of Jesus, into the property of the lightful fire (viz. into the dis-appeared heavenly holy ens, which did disappear in the darkness), that the first free will (which now lieth captive in the child of the whore and Serpent) should introduce its desire into this aim of the promised Covenant (which he hath fulfilled in Christ's humanity), and with the desire of the soul's free will re-introduce the holy ens of Christ (which he [Christ] in the seed of Mary introduced into our disappeared ens) into its disappeared heavenly ens. And if it doth bring it so to pass, then out of this introduced ens of Christ ariseth Christ's spirit, which destroyeth the false will of the Serpent's bastard in the flesh, and trampleth upon its head.

---

[1] Or whereof.
[2] Imputed, introduced recalled or really promised into the soul.

71. Now saith reason, God giveth this holy new ens of Christ to whom he will, and suffereth whom he please to harden and remain captive in the Serpent's ens. Yes, very right: He giveth none this holy ens into the self-will of his Serpent's child; there belongeth far another earnestness thereto; for selfhood cannot now any more take any thing of God.

72. *But this is the process which the free will must go, if it will receive the holy ens*: it must wind itself out of the Serpent's desire (out of its selfish-self and somethingness), and wind itself into God's mercy; and become a deadly mortifying enemy to the fleshly desire in itself. It must wholly forsake and depart from the self-full desire of the flesh; and bring its hunger wholly and only into the mortification of its selfish somethingness, desiring and endeavouring continually and willingly to die to its iniquity and false desire (which sticketh in the flesh, in the Serpent's child), and in Christ's ens arise with a new will.

73. *This desire*, which departeth from the Serpent's ens, and hungereth after God's mercy, *receiveth Christ's ens into itself, whence a new will is born*, which bruiseth the head of the Serpent in the flesh, for *it is the new birth* out of God in Christ Jesus.

74. But if thou wilt say, Thou canst not desire any good, that is not true. [We reply:] Thou alone sufferest the Serpent's will in thy right eternal soul's will to hold thee; and with the soul's will dost play the whore with the Serpent's will in the flesh; from whence ariseth God's election.

75. God knoweth the false whorish soul which doth only woo and wantonise with the Serpent, (with the idol Babel), and will still live in the lust and will of the flesh and of the Serpent; and yet willeth to be an outwardly adopted child: God should forgive it its sins by an outward word-speaking, but it willeth still to hang and cleave to the wanton love of the Serpent in its false lust. This, God chooseth to judgment.

76. For the free will which was inspired into Adam, and which it[1] hath inherited from Adam, hangeth on Lucifer; and therefore God confirms it unto the kingdom of darkness with Lucifer; but the gate of grace standeth yet open unto it [during] this time of the outward life.

---

[1] The soul.

The Twenty-Seventh Chapter

Of *Cain's* and *Abel's* Offering and of the False and Antichristian Church, and also of the True Holy Church

A LOOKING-GLASS FOR THE WORLD

1. HERE again, the veil lieth before the face of Moses, in respect of the offerings of both these brothers; wherefore God willed to have them offer, whereas the reconciliation and atonement consists only in the earnest will toward God's mercy, in prayer and supplication to God, that a man depart and turn away from his evil will, and repent, and introduce his faith and hope into God's mercy.

2. They must verily needs know wherefore they offered incense; what pleasure and delight God took therein; which Moses hath not once so much as mentioned, and that from God's purpose; and yet it hath not been hidden to the children of the Saints, and also not to Moses; but he hath a veil hanging before his eyes.

3. Israel (seeing for the most part they were evil children, and also idolatrous, as soon appeared by making them a Golden Calf) might not know it by reason of the false magic; and we also shall write only to those that are of our tribe, and yet plain and easy enough to be understood. Observe and mark it, thus:

4. The soul's free will is as thin[1] as a nothing; and though it be in its body indeed encompassed with the something, yet its amassed or conceived something is in a false distempered essence, by reason of the original of sin.

5. Now if the free will would approach to God with the desire, then it must depart out of its false something, and if it now doth so depart, then it is bare and impotent, for it is again in the first nothing: for if it will come to God, then it must die to its false selfhood, and forsake it; and if it forsakes the same, then it is barely and merely as a nothing, and so it cannot go, work, or move. If it will shew its might, then it must be in something, wherein it doth imaginate and form itself.

6. An example hereof we have in faith. If faith would effectually work, then it must immass [or imaginate] itself into something

[1] Or subtle.

188

wherein it may work; God's free will hath conceived [or immassed] itself with the inward spiritual world, and worketh through the same; and the inward world's free will hath conceived itself in the outward world, and worketh through the same. Even so the soul's free will, which also hath its original out of the abyss, immasseth itself in something, that it might be manifest, and thereby be able to move and act in God's sight.

7. Seeing then Adam's body was out of the limus of the earth, and also out of the limus of the holy heaven, which limus of heaven in Adam was now disappeared, wherein the free will had power to immass [or conceive] itself into a holy form, and act, work, pray and supplicate before God, therefore they made burnt-offerings of the fruits of the earth. As Cain, he brought of the fruit of the ground, and Abel also brought of the firstlings of his flock, and these they enkindled with fire.

8. But understand a magical fire, as that of Moses, for Moses declareth so also. God looked graciously upon the offering of Abel, and not upon Cain's; that is, they brought offerings before God, and the free will of the soul should earnestly press with its prayer in to God. Therefore it would have a substance,[1] when it would go out of the human house of corruption into God, that it might work in something; therefore the imagination of the will did immass [or imaginate] itself through the offering, and God enkindled the offering of Abel with the holy fire in the aim of the Covenant, which in the fullness of time should again enkindle itself in the soul's fire.

9. In this the will of Abel's soul did enform[2] itself into a holy substance, and pressed, with the desire of the enformed free soul's will, before and into God's free will, and this the will of the devil and the Serpent could not brook; and even this the will of the Serpent and devil in Cain did well understand; that the aim of the Covenant did open itself in the holy fire in Abel's desire and prayer.

10. And therefore he [the devil] would kill the body of Abel according to his [Abel's] earthly limus; lest such children should be begotten of him, and so he [the devil] might lose his kingdom in man. But God would not enkindle the offering of Cain. Now Moses maketh a veil here before it, and saith, God would not look graciously upon[3] Cain's offering.

11. The enkindling of the external offering was a figure of the internal spirit. For the soul's spirit in the free will (as to the centre of

---

[1] Subject or means.   [2] Fashion or idea.   [3] Or have respect to.

the light) was enkindled with God's love-fire; and the imagination of the body (also understand, of the heavenly part) was enkindled in the offering with the fire of the holy part of the earth (which lieth hidden in the curse). And therein the free will of the soul, and the free will in the ens of the heavenly part of the body, did immass itself into a substance; and therewith did press in before the holiness of God.

12. And here the Serpent's head was first bruised, for it was a figure of the new birth out of Christ. Not that Abel had at this time put on Christ in the flesh, but indeed in the spirit of Jehova, in the aim of the Covenant. In which the name of Jesus stood hidden in God (as a regenerator), which would move and manifest itself in the fullness of time in this aim [of the Covenant], and introduce a heavenly holy ens into the disappeared ens of the heavenly part, and quicken it to life again in the opened power of Jesus.

13. If a man would rightly and fundamentally understand the offerings,[1] he must consider that whereof the offering consisted, and what severed itself with the enkindling in the fire, out of the fire, viz. out of the enkindled offering. For in the enkindling nothing is seen or perceived, but 1. The wood to the fire. 2. The matter of offering. 3. The fire and light. 4. The smoke of the fire, which ariseth from the burning wood and matter of the offering. All this, without the faith and divine desire, is as an abomination, and indeed nothing in God's sight, and attaineth not the gate of God.

14. But if man brings his faith's-desire thereinto, then he resigneth the free will thereinto, and will thereby, as by a means (in which fire the free will of the introduced sinful abomination doth burn and consume away), press into God's eternal free will. And now how this is effected and comes to pass, understand as followeth:

15. God's imagination or lubet meeteth the free inspired will of the humanity, and the human free will meeteth the Deity: here is now the conjunction.

16. But now man's free will is become sinful, and God's free will (from whence the human free will did first take its rise in its inspiration) is holy and pure. As yet the human free will cannot press into God's will, unless it also become pure before God.

17. But seeing God will, out of free grace, receive it into himself for the delight and harmony of his praise, there is no other way or remedy but that God move himself in the centre of the eternal nature,

[1] Sacrifices.

according to the fire of the second Principle, viz. according to the holy fire, and devour that enkindled anger and vanity of man's free will; and annihilate it in the mortification of death, viz. in the anger-fire of God, that the human will might become pure before God's will, and so might enter into God's love-will. And therefore God's love-desire did itself enkindle the offering of Abel and Moses, that so the holy-and-love-fire might devour and swallow up the turba in the human free soul's-will, in the anger-fire of the eternal nature, in the Father's property.

18. But that there must be an earthly offering thereunto is thus to be understood: The body of man as to one part is a limus of the earth, and as to the other part a limus of heaven; and into this body the free will was inspired, and body and soul is only one man.

19. But seeing in the fall the earthliness and false subtlety of the Serpent (by the insinuation of the devil's desire) was awakened in the flesh of man, and so the earthly bestial property got the upper hand in his ens, and devoured the right human will in the bestial property, that is, took it captive, thereupon the earthly will which was from the limus of the earth must also be offered up in the fire.

20. For the limus of the earth shall arise again out of earth; but for to make it an offering it must also be offered in an earthly elemental fire of its likeness; so that a heavenly fire, and an earthly elemental fire, might be in one another; and each will in the offering might respectively find a place for its own comprehension and capacity, viz. the will proceeded from the earthly limus of the earth from the kingdom of this world, and the heavenly will, out of the heavenly limus, viz. out of the ens of the Verbum Domini;[1] each property of the free will went into the offering, and from the offering into the fire, where the atonement was.

21. For the Covenant of the Promise touching the Serpent-Stroyer did manifest itself by the holy fire, which holy fire enkindled the elemental fire, for the holy fire shall awaken and raise up from death the elemental man out of the limus of the earth; and in the holy fire man (who hath taken his original from time) shall be purged and tried in the Resurrection; who verily must first go through the fire of the anger, but the power and might of the holy fire shall bring him through the anger-fire, and cleanse and purge away his introduced abomination of sin (in the Serpent's and devil's ens [in him]) from the limus of the earth, that the limus of the earth may be no more earthly,

---

[1] Of the seminal and central love of the Word of the Lord.

but as a fine purified gold, which subsists in the fire.

22. Even thus the earthly man shall be purified in the Resurrection, through the fire, of which the offerings were a type, and yet they did really subsist in their power, as to the spirit. But the body must die, and the true corporality and regeneration must come forth [or begin to spring afresh] in the opened body of Christ, who, with his entrance into and manifestation in the humanity, did again open the heavenly disappeared limus in the human ens, which did disappear [or fade] in Adam and Eve.

23. Thus understand us aright: Abel and Moses offered the fat of beasts, and enkindled that with the holy fire, which fire was first enkindled by God; for the bestial property became manifest in the outward earthly man of the limus of the earth. The human limus of the earth was turned to a beast, and was moreover sinful and evil, full of the Serpent's poison and cunning subtlety.

24. The free will did immass itself in the Serpent's craft and devil's desire; and formed to itself such a figure in the ens of the flesh as the desire was; whereupon the body was more vain in God's sight than a beast.

25. But seeing the heavenly ens lay hidden and shut up in the earthly property, God would not utterly forsake the whole image; which Abel and Moses did understand, in the spirit of God, by their offerings. And therefore they offered the fat, viz. the oil of the beasts, and other earthly good fruits, that so the desire of the true man, created out of the limus of the earth, who shall arise from death, might, in the enkindling of the offering in the fire, have a substance whereinto it might give itself and imaginate itself; and so in the property of the holy fire it might be able to enter with its will into the aim of the Covenant, which stood before God in the figure, until [the promise] of the woman's seed was fulfilled and accomplished.

26. In which seed the dear and precious name of Jesus did open itself out of Jehovah, and did again awaken the heavenly life in the disappeared ens in the humanity, and offered up this whole image, in the Person of Christ, to the anger-fire of the Father, and with the holy love-fire regenerated and enkindled in the human life, did bring it quite through the anger, viz. through the fire of the eternal nature of the Father's manifestation, and changed the anger-fire into a love-fire. And this was just thus pre-figured in the offering; for the love-fire enkindled the offering, and in the offering was yet the curse of the earth, as well as in the human free will; and when the offering was

offered, it was a sin-offering, whereby the free will of man's soul was propitiated before God.[1]

27. Now if sin shall be reconciled and appeased, then it must be brought into the anger, viz. into the judgment of God, into the sword of the Cherub, that it may cut off the same, which [Cherub] is the sword of God's anger: and if then the human will be wholly sinful and altogether capable of the fire of anger, then God enkindleth the sin-offering (in which the anger-fire lay hidden in the curse), with the holy fire, that the human will, which was apprehended in the anger-fire, might be atoned in the love-fire.

28. For the love-fire of God tinctureth the soul's desire in the offering, as a tincture tingeth brass and iron and changeth them into gold. Even thus the human soul's free will, which was inspired wholly pure and spotless into man, was tinctured and again purified before God, that so it might enter into God's mercy. For the mercy was hidden in the love-fire, viz. in the aim of the Covenant, in the name of Jesus in God; in which Covenant and name the anger of God was reconciled and atoned in the offering, and laid down its anger-burning flames, and suffered the soul's free will to pass quite through it.

29. But as touching the offering in itself, with the wood, fire, light, and smoke, understand it thus: Abel offered of his flock, without doubt, sheep, or oxen, as Moses did the like, namely, the fat of them; now the offering (viz. the wood and smoke) on the outward part as to the matter was earthly; and so was man, as to the outward body, earthly; and in the earthliness lay the curse, both in man and in the offering.

30. But when the offering was enkindled it was spiritual, for from the wood proceeded the fire which took the offering and consumed it; and out of the consumptiveness went forth first from the fire the smoke, and afterwards the light. This was the figure whereinto man's and also God's imagination entered, as a compaction or conjunction.

31. In the enkindled consuming fire was the desire of the angry Father, viz. a conjunction of the eternal nature's fire with the temporal fire; the eternal is magical, and the temporal is the substance and matter of the magical, viz. its reception.[2] And in the enkindled light was the holy love-fire, which is also magical, as subtle as a will, which did also immass itself in the enkindled light; and in the forth-proceeding smoke, which is an elemental sulphur and mercury, viz. a life of the quality, the smell or taste went forth also, which signifieth

[1] Reconciled with God.   [2] Or amassment.

the human power of the body, and the outward spirit of nature.

32. In this power which proceeded forth from the offering, out of the fire and light, the spirit of God which proceedeth forth from the Father and Son did amass itself in the amassment of the human faith's desire, and so took the human faith's desire into itself, and did amass itself into a substance of the fire, light and power proceeding forth from the offering; and brought it through the gates of God's anger, upon the holy altar, in the aim of the Covenant, upon which the Lamb of God should be offered for the sins of the whole world.

33. For this Lamb of God, viz. Christ, should complete, perfect, and make this introduced offering fully acceptable upon the great altar of the angelical world; that it might be to God an eternal sweet savour of his deepest love, which he represented in mankind in his introduced offering in the Lamb of God, Christ, and mankind in this representative offering.

34. The human offering was the sojourner of the true Lamb and offering of God in Christ. And now where the offering is, there also is the spirit of man; for man's spirit is gone forth and departed from God into time, and in the time it hath defiled itself; therefore it must forsake the pollution, and enter in again through this offering to God.

35. But if it will enter, then *it must do it in manner and form as it went out*; for it brought itself into false desire and lust. Even so likewise it must introduce itself again by a returning into a sorrow and conversion, and in the sorrow or repentance again [introduce itself] into a divine desire, which is called faith.

36. But that it might apprehend or lay hold on the divine desire, it did bring the faith or the believing desire into an offering; and so amassed or formed the believing desire in the offering into a substance or essence, that the faith also might become essential; and this essentiality of faith received the holy fire of God, which would in the fullness of time open itself in the essentiality of faith, and bring the human substance thereinto; and also bring it forth in itself through God's anger, and change it in itself into a love-fire; for all the words of prayer in the offering were also received into the substance of faith.

37. For as all things were formed, amassed and introduced by the word of God into a substance, so likewise the words of the prayer of Abel and Israel in the offering were formed and amassed to substance, viz. unto an incorruptible essence. In which essence, Christ, God's Son, in the fullness of time brake forth out of the Covenant, and took upon him this same essence, together with the human essence, and as

a potent Champion and mighty Conqueror destroyed the kingdom of death and the devil.

38. And to this faith's essence, in the spirit of Christ in all his children and members, was given the judgment over the world, yea, over the kingdom of the devil and of death; thereby to destroy and bring to naught their works, and possess the royal throne.

39. This was the real offering of Abel, for the spirit of the holy love-fire in the aim of the Covenant had opened itself in him, so that he understood it. And therefore he offered, that so his believing desire might be accepted before God, and be brought into a substance to the new regeneration; for he looked upon the promise of the Serpent-Stroyer, and introduced the desire of his faith into him; and desired that his faith, spirit and life might be confirmed in the Serpent-Stroyer who was promised. He would fain be therein accepted before God; as it was granted him, so that the fire of God did enkindle his offering, and received his prayer in the love-fire; and in the sweet savour of the offering it was brought by the spirit of God in the power of the light into a holy substance, and it is rightly said, His offering was acceptable before God.

40. The offering alone could not have been able to have done it, only the faith which did idea or lay hold on the promised Messiah in the offering, which apprehended the Covenant, and the true, very precious and dear offering, the same did effect it. *The offering was only a figure of that which was therein accomplished and performed*, as the outward world is only a figure of the inward spiritual world, whereby the spiritual world doth introduce itself into a figure and essence, and beholds itself therein, as in a looking-glass.

OF CAIN'S OFFERING

41. By Cain's offering we rightly understand the verbal Christendom, the titular Christians, in the spiritual Babylonical harlotry, the type and image of whom is Cain. And as Cain in his offering sought only the outward world, might and pleasure, and would be an outwardly adopted and received child, God should permit his evil beast to be accepted and offered up; he desired to be God's acceptable child with the selfhood in the Serpent's ens and falsehood; he was an impenitent proud man, who thought to be a lord of the world, and to domineer over Abel and his posterity. And just thus is the anti-christian Church upon the earth; it also buildeth churches and altars,

preacheth, singeth and tinkleth, and doth likewise offer in the bequeathed Covenant and Testament of Christ, and so covereth itself with the offering of Christ, and will be an outwardly accepted and adopted son, notwithstanding that its offering is not accepted in the Covenant and Testament of Christ, nor brought to substance.

42. The cause and ground of it is this: Men depend and rely only barely and nakedly upon the offering, and teach that the offerings take away sin, [and teach that] Christ's Testaments do absolve sin. But as little as the offering of Cain was acceptable before God and took away *his* sin, and as little as *Cain's desire* was introduced into the divine substance, so as to have the divine fire to enkindle in *his* offering and receive *his* faith's desire into it, even so little also doth the verbal [lip-labouring] Christendom enjoy the offering of Christ in *his* humanity. It must be an Abel alone that doth enjoy it; the titular mouth-Christian attains only the smoke of the true offering. It must be only a right, hungry, thirsty, converted soul, which desireth wholly and fully to depart from the Serpent's ens and all vanity of this world, and striveth to mortify the Serpent and all vain will, in the death of Christ, and desireth to arise in a new will, totally resigned in all submission in God.

43. This true hungry will offereth rightly with Abel, and its offering is received into the holy fire of Christ, and formed [or amassed] in Christ's humanity into a substance. There must be earnestness and power, which earnestness stirreth the love-fire of Christ in his Testament, so that it doth enkindle itself in the desire; and then the desire becomes a true right faith, for there is no right faith without divine taking.[1]

44. When man's desire introduceth its hunger with earnest sighing and prayer of introversion, resignation, and departing from vanity into the offering of Christ, even then the soul's desire doth, in the heavenly essentiality, in the humanity of Christ, upon the high altar of God, form itself into a substance. The hungry desire becomes in the Word of God, in Christ's Testaments, flesh, a heavenly supernatural flesh; and this flesh is the true offering of God, which God taketh to his habitation, and not the bestial mortal man.

45. In this holy substance alone is the true faith of Abel, without this there is only an historical painted and feigned faith, a Cain's offering, which doth not take away sin: for sin must always be brought into the judgment of God wherein it was born, and the holy love-fire

---

[1] Comprehension, amassment or formation.

of God must drown and wash it away, else there is no forgiveness. Neither offering nor Covenant doth avail anything without it; also no going to church, neither singing nor devout shewing doth attain it. Nothing else at all doth it but only the hungry, desiring faith through the alone offering in the blood and death of Christ, where the desire doth wholly die to its selfhood in the death of Christ, and arise in Christ's resurrection with a true faith and Christianity, not in a specious shew of holiness, but in essence, in words and works.

46. For he is yet far from a Christian, who merely calls himself a Christian [or is only so termed], but he is one *who is born in the offering of his humanity in him.* Neither Covenant nor laws avail anything before God, but *a new creature.* No cathedral, stone church, meeting-house or hypocrisy, or whatsoever it be called, can inherit God's kingdom, but only and alone the true living offering of the new regeneration, arising from the Covenant of Promise in Paradise, through the quickening Word in the offering of Christ.

47. It only and alone is the temple of the holy Spirit, where God's word is taught and taken; without that, is Cain, with his glistering stone church, full of pride and stinking ambition, the great building of Babylon, where the language of God's word, viz. of the written word, is confounded and divided into manifold contentions and languages, where there is nothing but wrangling, jangling and snarling about the letters, and no true, real, living, effectual and powerful knowledge.

48. Now where the living knowledge of Christ is, there is the altar of God in all places, where the hungry soul may offer the true acceptable holy offering, in prayer; there it may introduce the prayer in the Word, in its hunger, into a substantial faith.

49. Not that we would hereby wholly abolish and raze down the stone churches; but we teach the Temple of Christ, which ought to be brought along [in the heart] into the stone church, or else the whole business of the stone church is only a hypocritical antichristian whoredom, a Cain's offering, both of the preacher and the hearer: so that one is not a whit better than another, unless he enter through the true door, Christ, in spirit and power in the Temple of Christ, into the stone church, or at least resolve to fix, betake and fasten himself there into such an earnest desire [that he will take and hold fast only that which is good for the amendment of his life]. Else Cain goeth to church to offer, and cometh out again a killer of his brother.

50. As it often appears, that when men in the stone churches have taken and amassed [to their minds a deal of] revilings, reproaches and

censures [that have fallen from the false smoky Cain-like fury and pretended zeal of the preachers], then they forthwith come withal and murder Abel, and Christ's members: as this spirit hath many hundred times found by experience; and that, only for the sake of the Temple of Christ.

51. Now if we would rightly consider of the offering of Cain, then we must look into the very essence of his will and desire, for he also would offer and be acceptable to God. But he loved only his ownhood and self-full self; his aim and endeavour was not to be or become a new creature, that God should so take away his sins in the offering from him, but he would still remain the old Cain; and so offer to God, that he might be so accepted with him: the devil came before God in the form of an angel.

52. Cain knew not[1] his evil serpentine property, the poor soul was captivated therewith, and had set itself up in the Serpent's wit and pride, it would needs be an outwardly adopted child and heir of God, the offering must make reconciliation for him; as Babel doth, which taketh also the mantle of Christ upon her, and saith, Christ hath undertaken and suffered for all my sins upon the cross, I cannot purchase or do anything for myself, my works avail nothing before God, I need only believe that Christ hath done it, and comfort myself therewith, and then I am already justified and acquitted from all my transgressions.

53. Thus she cometh before God, and thanketh God that he hath paid the reckoning and score, in his Son, and offereth with Cain and the Pharisee in the Temple, and remaineth in herself a brother-slayer with Cain: and this is the Babylonical fruit. Like as Cain would take the offering upon him for a cloak and covering, so also his succeeding Church taketh on it the offering of Christ for a cloak and covert of its sins and false murder; and covereth its murderous spirit, so that men must call it a holy devout Christian.

54. Saint Paul must serve their turn thereto, when he saith, *I do that I would not, now if I do it, it is not I, but sin that dwelleth in my flesh*; but that he saith, *Now then, with my mind I serve God, but with the flesh the law of sin*. The same, Cain will not understand, how the mind must, without intermission, rule and reign over the sinful will and desire of the flesh, and mortify the lust.

55. Saint Paul speaketh of the heavenly Abel-like desire, how sin must be mortified in the flesh, and not rule over the mind, as it did in

---

[1] Or did not acknowledge.

Cain, when he saw his brother was accepted before God, and that he himself was not. Then the murdering spirit arose in his mind, which should have been mortified in the offering by true repentance and conversion.

56. Thus also goeth Babel under the mantle of Christ, which offereth also to God, and thanketh him for the offering of Christ; but itself remaineth in the mind of the Cainical brother-slayer, in pride, covetousness, envy and anger, in persecution, in war and contention. It fighteth about the offering, and about the outward covering, lest it should be stripped thereof; and doth [in the meantime] fatten itself under it, with the bestial offerings of the fatness of the earth, and still remains the Cainical beast, and doth also continually murder Abel in Christ's members, and comforteth itself with the death of Christ: the same must be a covert for the false murdering spirit.

57. The heart and mind is far from the new creature. It is only the old Cainical brother-slayer, which bemantles itself with Christ's offering, and offers with Cain; such, and nothing better, remains now of Christianity[1] among all sects, except the children of Christ, who are here and there hidden with Abel.

58. Cain's Church was never more potent and predominant upon the earth than it is even at this time, whereas, notwithstanding, men cry out with full mouth-cry and great ostentation, Come all hither: we have found the offering of Abel in Christ. Yes, forsooth, dear Babel, thou hast indeed found the mantle of Christ; but behold thy Cain-like heart, and thou wilt see whether thou offerest with Abel from the new creature, or from the false brother-slaying spirit. Where are thy fruits? where is love and righteousness? where is truth? where is patience and meekness? Where is the mind that with Paul serveth God? Where art thou, thou fair Christian Church upon the earth? art thou not become a murdering den of the devil? Now shew thy Christian virtues; art thou not full of contention and murder, both in the Church and without the Church? Thy mouth is only a prater of God's kingdom, like as Cain's mouth prated of the offering, but his heart was a murderer.

59. Thus likewise men do prate in the stone houses of the mantle and offering of Christ, and yet in the meanwhile, in this prate and babble, do murder the children of Christ, condemn and judge them, and make a whole heap and crew of reviling devouring wolves, that do all cry out, snarl and snap; and none knoweth where the hind is

---

[1] Or Christendom.

which they hunt, save only that the devil doth thus act and drive on his sport by them; so that the true, real offering of Christ may remain covered and hidden, and be only as a mystery in this world.

60. For we poor children of Eve do sojourn here in this cottage in a strange lodging,[1] wherein the devil in God's anger is host. We dwell upon the cursed earth, where the devil rideth over our soul and body, and at all times tempteth us: we had need be wary and watchful, and at no time secure: it costeth body and soul.

[1] Or harbour.

Of *Cain's* Killing[1] of his Brother, viz. of the Proud, Haughty, Antichristian, Hypocritical Church upon the Earth; and also of the True Christendom hidden under this Antichristian Church

1. WHEN the devil in God's anger, in the wrath of the eternal nature, had introduced his throne and seat into the human property, and awakened the centre of the wrathful nature in him, there forthwith arose up such a desire out of the awakened anger's property in the human ens or seed, in the propagation; out of which property Babel, viz. the antichristian Church, is begotten and brought forth.

2. And now as God had incorporated and promised the Serpent-Bruiser of this false property (who should bruise the head of the Serpent's ens and will or desire) unto the heavenly ens of man, which disappeared in and to Paradise, which word of promise was a mystery, and a very secret hiddenness to the earthly man; even so also the false Cainical Church of hypocrisy and seeming holiness, whose heart and desire is only [of] the outward world, hath gotten aloft this whole time, and hath the outward dominion and name as if it offered to God. But the true, real Christian Church is hidden under it, as a very secret Mystery, and is not known of the Cainical Church.

3. Cain's Church sets forth itself very devoutly, and glisters on all sides with specious ceremonies and pompous ostentation; giving forth that it is holy, righteous, and good; that it also offers in the Covenant of Christ; but its heart is only a glozing, soothing, bravely attired harlot, full of Cainical murder, reviling and blasphemy, full of censure and self-speculation in pride, in covetousness and high mindedness. But Abel's Church is hidden under it in great plainness, and with no respect and reputation, and is accounted but foolish in reference to the glittering show of Cain; and is continually slain by Cain in its simplicity.

4. Now saith reason, What, had God any pleasure herein, that he

[1]Fratricide.

suffered Cain to kill Abel; and why is it still to this day that the children of God are slain, despised, contemned, reproached, mocked, scorned, and cried down for false by Cain, viz. by his posterity? One cause hereof is this:

5. Prince Lucifer was a hierarch in the kingdom or place of this world (as Christ even calleth him a prince of this world, viz. in the kingdom of darkness in the anger of God), and was cast for his pride's sake out of the light into the darkness.

6. But seeing God then created another prince, viz. Adam, in and for this place, with whom he bound himself even with his deepest love before the foundation of the world in the dear and precious name Jesus, that he would break down and destroy the throne and kingdom of proud prince Lucifer in the human property, and overcome and be predominant with love; thence forthwith arose his envy and wrath against man.

7. Secondly, the cause is this: In the fall of man the wrath of the eternal and also of the temporal and inchoative nature obtained the superior sway and dominion in the human property. For the kingdom of heaven did extinguish in Adam and Eve when as they became earthly; and in the room and stead thereof the kingdom of the devil did awake in the Serpent's wit and pride in them; for the human will[1] had broken itself off from God, and was entered into selfhood, and no longer understood anything of the Mystery of God's kingdom.

8. But seeing that the kingdom of God did again bud and break forth in the aim of the Covenant in Abel and the children of God, the devil's kingdom and will, in the Serpent-monster, could not brook it. Also the love-kingdom is a great enmity against the wrath of the eternal nature according to the dark property, for the human essence was become, according to the dark world's property, as to the soul a half devil, and as to the outward world's vanity a half beast, in which beast the false, subtle, crafty, wicked, lustful, proud, covetous, envious and angry Serpent's worm did sit, infected with the devil's will.

9. This wrathful, vile, malicious, monstrous beast would live in its own self property; therefore the angelical virgin-child, which should destroy and possess the kingdom of this evil beast, did appear against him in Abel. This was now a great enmity, for the anger of God had captivated man, and would work and rule in him; therefore God's love broke forth out of the anger, as a light out of the fire, and would

1 Man's will.

kill the anger, and change it into love, and help again poor man's image, and redeem it from the eternal anger and death.

10. But seeing the anger had got the upper hand and sway in man; and yet the virgin-child of the angelical world's essence should spring forth and grow out of the Covenant of God, out of the disappeared ens, through the anger, as a clear delightful light shines forth out of the candle, through the wrathful fire, which depriveth the darkness of its power and prevalency; therefore the outward body in [Abel, and] the children of God must suffer itself to be slain and persecuted by the wrath of God; for it[1] was a strange figure on the virgin-child.

11. For Abel in his outward flesh had the awakened vanity lying in him, as well as Cain; he was also sinful as to the outward man, but internally the angelical world and image of Paradise did spring and bud forth again in the Covenant. This was now a great enmity against each other; the inward man bruised the Serpent-monster upon the head of its false desire, and the Serpent-monster stung him on the heel of his angelical will, and openly mocked the angelical image; as it is so still to this day. So soon as the virgin-child is born in the spirit of Christ, the outward earthly body, together with the virgin-child, is, by the children of Cain, persecuted, contemned, reviled, and accounted as a strange child of the world.

12. For the Serpent's monster is as a fool before God, and seeing the noble and precious virgin-child must bear such a monster on it in the outward flesh, to which the devil hath yet continual access, therefore this body is strongly assaulted and struck at by the devil in the anger of God and its children; they would continually slay it, for the virgin-child worketh through the outward man, as a light through the fire, and manifesteth itself. It teacheth and reproveth the wicked sort; and this the devil cannot endure, for it is against his kingdom, as the offering of Abel was against Cain's.

13. For Cain offered in the proud Serpent's desire as a hypocrite, and would be an honest, demure, devout and godly child in his Serpent's desire; but Abel humbled himself before God, and set his desire into God's mercy. God's love-fire took his offering, and penetrated through the earthly offering and fire; and the like also is to be understood in the body of Abel; as the incorruptible [being] shall swallow up the corruptible, so also the heavenly took the earthly captive in itself.

14. But that Cain slew the outward body of Abel hath this type[2]

---

[1] The outward body.   [2] Signification.

and figure: that the outward body shall be slain[1] in the anger of God. The anger must devour and mortify the outward image which is grown up in the anger; and out of death springeth forth the eternal life.

15. Abel was a figure of Christ; the children of God's anger must execute the right of God's anger upon the outward earthly and also [upon the] bestial image of the children of the holy one. Even as the Pharisees (who before God were only false serpent-children, as Christ called them) must persecute and kill the humanity of Christ; so likewise was Cain a type of these serpentine wolfish Pharisees, and also of the verbal titular Christendom.

16. As the false Serpent's child is a monster and fool before the angelical world, so likewise the children of darkness do account and esteem the children of the light for fools; for there must be a contrary, that the one might be manifest in the other. If the anger had not taken hold of the humanity, and devoured it into itself, then the deepest love of God would not have been manifest in man.

17. But thus the love taketh cause, by the anger, to overpower and prevail over the same with its motion and manifestation; as the same may be known in Christ. The true Son of God gave himself into our image, which was awakened in the anger, that so he might be made manifest with his love in the anger, and change the same into joy.

18. Christ gave our human image to the anger of his Father to be devoured in death, and brought his life into death, and yet manifested his love in the life which death had devoured, and brought forth the life in love through the death. As a grain of corn which is sown into the earth, the same must die in the earth, but out of that mortified grain grows a fair new body; even so the corrupt body of Adam shall and must be offered to death and the anger; and out of the death and anger the body of the divine love shall be manifest.

19. It was exactly typified and prefigured in Cain and Abel how it would be in the succeeding and future generations. Seeing Abel outwardly did bear the earthly image, and yet in the spirit he was an image of heaven, his outward body in the corruption was only a visard[2] before the outward world; for there was another spirit hidden therein, which was not of the outward world's essence and property; therefore because he was not wholly a right child of the earthly world, it would not suffer him (being as a strange child) in it; for the devil was prince in the wrathful essence in this world, who would not that a

---

[1] Or mortified.   [2] Text, Larva or strange disguised person.

child of the light should spring forth through the wrathful essence [and be in his garden].

20. Thus the image or person of Cain and Abel is a true figure of the false, and then also of the holy and true, children of God; of the outward sinful corrupt and mortal man, and of the inward new regenerate holy man. When Christ with his love-kingdom ariseth from death out of the disappeared ens, then Adam's earthly image must die in Christ's death; and if it now be that the outward body must yet live, it is only a scorn and fool before the heaven's image, and so also before the natural life of this world.[1]

21. For so soon as Christ is born, the sinful life is condemned to death; and standeth in scorn and open shame before all the false children in the anger of God, as a whore in Bridewell,[2] whom other whores likewise help to deride and scoff at; and yet they do but only judge and condemn themselves thereby. For if Christ be born, then the judgment passeth upon the false bestial life, and that man must stand in the judgment of God as a malefactor, and be termed a fool, a heretic; and be jeered, scoffed and reviled, yea, even utterly defied and slain, that the monster may be judged before God's anger. But those that do it are the children of the lusty, pampered, and well-fattened anger of God, whom the wrath of God useth for its instrument; for God is a spirit, therefore he accomplisheth his judgment by a material image.[3]

22. For so soon as Abel did, in his offering, put on or attract the love of God in the Covenant anew into his human desire, and comprehended [or amassed] the same into his essence, then forthwith the judgment passed upon the external mortal man; and God's sword of anger took him, which Cain executed, and slew the outward body of Abel. And at this time also the judgment passed upon the false image of the anger in Cain, for he stood there, and cried, My sins are greater than can be forgiven me.

23. This doth now hint and point at the figure of Christ, how the anger of the Father must devour[4] the life of Christ in death, and when as the anger had devoured the life in death, then the holy life of the deepest love of God moved itself in the death and the anger, and devoured the death and anger into itself; whereat the earth trembled, and the rocks clove asunder, and the graves of the saints opened.

[1] All natural men.
[2] At the house of correction or whipped through the streets.
[3] By some outward substantial means or persons.
[4] Or swallow up.

24. And so likewise the love-fire and the anger-fire[1] in the place of this world (which wrathful fire was enkindled in the creation when The Apostate [Lucifer] fell) shall at the Last Day be again changed into the divine joyfulness, and be avalled or swallowed up in the love. Understand, it shall be thus in the third Principle, where love and anger do strive [during] this time one with another: but he[2] remaineth in the darkness in the first Principle.

25. The true cause wherefore Cain murdered Abel was by reason of their offerings and worship of God, viz. religion; as this contention continueth still to this day; the Cainical Church is not yet one with the Abelical.

26. Now saith reason, I see it well enough, that all contention and strife ariseth from religion, but what is the ground and most un-doubted cause and reason thereof. Behold! this is the cause: set before thee the false Serpent's child, which is evil and good, and then set before thee the virgin's child, born of Christ, and then thou hast the fundamental cause, exactly drawn to the life, before thine eyes.

27. The Cainical Church drives a subtle trade with external ceremonies, and will appease God with some external thing or other; it will be outwardly an accepted and adopted child, it must down right be called honest, godly, holy and heavenly, it adorneth and trimmeth up itself very finely, and standeth mightily upon its calling, which it hath itself ordained and instituted; it makes a very specious and renowned show in the white sheep's clothing; and therein lodgeth the high priest of selfhood, without Christ's spirit, and rules and masters the work of the outward letters; and whosoever learneth to transpose and compose the same boldly and bravely [according to their form of forged opinions] he is a high priest in their office and order; he putteth Christ's garment of innocency on him for his cloak and covert.

28. The other party of the confused Cainical Church crieth out, and holdeth forth the goodly glistering child to sale for money;[3] and hath bound the kingdom of heaven to its ceremonies, and will sell it for money; so that the man may but fat himself in this world under the white garment [of its hypocrisy].

29. The third party giveth forth that they have so holy an order that it doth even sanctify and save them, and they, above all others, will be esteemed holy.

---

[1] Good and evil now mixed and in contest one with the other.
[2] Lucifer.   [3] Makes good merchandise of its religious ceremonies.

30. The fourth party [or sect] will obtain the kingdom of God by their lip-labour,[1] with muchness of speaking, reading, singing, preaching and hearing, and it rebukes, censures and reviles all that will not approve of, praise, and give diligent attention to its lip-labour [and fine conceited long prating].

31. This party hath clothed itself with the white garment, and set itself upon the letter [or writings] of God's children, and therewith it doth so lustily bestir and lay about it, as a beggar that casteth stones at the dogs; and sometimes hits a churlish[2] one, sometimes a quiet[3] one. And he that is hit at makes him hear of it, and then others fall on, pell-mell, and bite and worry him; and there is a continual biting, tearing, confounding, reviling, reproaching, cavilling and jangling about the letter, a mere external work, whereby men [blindly zealous] suppose to serve God, and obtain grace: a very Cainical offering.

32. The Cainical Church is in the outward world, evil and good; it buildeth, and breaketh down; and is only a figure of[4] God's love and anger. What one party buildeth and calleth holy, that, another pulleth down and revileth. With one mouth it buildeth, and with another it teareth down. What one hypocrite praiseth, that, another dispraiseth. And thus there is only a confused [shattered] Babylon, evil and good; a wonder of nature and time.

33. All these run on in their self-contrived and devised orders, and rely upon their received orders. And so they offer the letter of the word, and the work of their own hands, before God; and will needs be outwardly adopted and accepted children before God. God must have respect unto their offering, and forgive them their sins by a word-speaking; as a lord out of favour and clemency freely gives a malefactor his life. Such an unmeasurable matchless heap of grace they have brought into their literal offerings, and into the works of their hands; so that their teaching, and the hearing of them, is accounted for the most holy way wherein salvation is to be had. And whosoever doth not worship and honour this their way with exceeding diligence, and subject himself thereunto, him they reproach, persecute and kill, or else hold him for a heretic.

34. But Abel's children in Christ have far another worship and service of God. They dwell indeed among Cain's children, and do also appear in their orders and offerings; [but] they offer to God a broken and bruised heart, and a humble, contrite mind, in true sorrow for,

---

[1] Text, mouth-cry.   [2] Or evil.   [3] Or good.
[4] Or according to.

and conversion from, their committed sins; and with their spiritual will do go out from and forsake all their creatureself-fullness and selfish interests and arrogation, and die to their selfhood in the death of Christ; and become as children, who neither know (nor will) anything, but only their mother which hath brought them forth; they cast themselves into her bosom, and they take in patience whatsoever she pleaseth to do with them.

35. For their internal will is quite mortified to the outward world, with all its glozing show and alluring glory; they account themselves very unworthy before the great grace of God, and their vanity, which the flesh desireth, is always in their sight; and to this the inward spiritual will is a deadly opposite enemy, and yet it cannot be wholly separated from it in this lifetime. Their whole course through this world is a mere work of repentance, for their sins and impurity do appear continually in their sight.

36. There is a continual and constant combat in them, of the flesh in the earthly desire against the divine desire, and of the divine desire against the lust of the earthly flesh; for the divine desire doth amass[1] itself into God's grace and mercy, and brings itself into a centre of a working life, and penetrates through the earthly false lustful life, and striketh the false lust [and imagination] down; and then the false imagination falls into great sadness, when as it contemplates and beholds the voluptuous, pompous, stately, brave, glistering course of this world, and finds itself so mean and foolish that it must forsake and forego that wherein it might have its chief joy, pleasure and delight.

37. Also the devil he cometh forthwith with his temptation, and bringeth his desire into the false imagination; and shews him the fair kingdom of the world, and rebuketh his intent as a false fancy and mere conjecture; stirreth up the crew of the wicked against him, who scorn, jeer, reproach and contemn him; and then sometimes the sprackling glimpse, and divine desire, doth even lose itself, for Christ, viz. the virgin's child in the spirit of Christ, is lead into the wilderness, and is tempted of the devil and of the anger of God, and also of the carnal world's spirit, and oftentimes the spirit of Christ doth hide itself, as if the virgin's child were quite gone, and past hopes, also the devil makes his address thereto, and brings him into doubt as if the virgin's child were not born.

38. For the virgin's child is hidden in the desert, and then the poor captivated soul is in great sorrow and lamentation, sigheth and crieth

[1] Betake.

to God; also it cannot love, nor away with, the bestial image, but it doth stir up itself as a great assaulting storm in the body, and seeketh the gates of the deep in its original; and forceth with might [or holy violence] into that Word which hath formed it to be a creature, and diveth itself thereinto, as an impotent, will-less child, and desireth its first mother, whence the first soul was born, for its nurse; and makes itself wholly will-less in this mother, and lieth only at her breasts, and sucketh her love and grace into it; the mother may do with it what she please. This is the true meaning, and the right manner, of dying to selfhood and self-full imagination and lust in oneself, and becoming, as to the will of the soul, as a child in oneself; as Christ saith, *Unless ye be converted, and become as children, ye can in no wise see the kingdom of God*; self, and self-full reason in the lust of the flesh, can neither taste nor see it.

39. From this mortification of the self-full will, and earnest resignation into God's mercy, the virgin's child doth again spring forth out of the desert, with its fair and glorious pearl-blooming tree, with very excellent and new fruit; for so it must be tried in the fire of God's anger, that the abomination of the introduced earthly will may die in it.

40. For the fire-soul, viz. the first Principle, hangeth upon the band of the outward world, and continually and eagerly introduceth something of vanity into it, whereby the virgin-child of the angelical world's essence, viz. of Christ's essentiality, is defiled, obscured and darkened, therefore it must be so refined, purified and purged again; and many a cold, piercing, rautish wind of tribulation, anguish and great perplexity bloweth upon this child. It must be continually as an off-scouring of the world, for its kingdom is not of this world; as Christ said, *My kingdom is not of this world.*

41. But the effect is this: when the fair Morning-Star doth dawn and arise in the virgin-child, then the outward life is even illuminated in this time;[1] and it giveth itself up unto the obedience of the internal [life], as an instrument and servant of the internal.

42. And then the holy spirit of God shineth forth through the virgin-child, and preacheth Christ crucified, and reproveth the world for its sins and wicked malicious doings, and shews them their false hypocritical erroneous way, that they will needs be the children of God in the outward kingdom, in their self-contrived and devised ways, and will seek an external forgiveness of sin in their own conceited and received ways; and yet will still remain in the vanity, and

---

[1] Or while it lives here.

in the pleasure of their flesh. And desire only to make devout shows before God, and give good words in a soothing glozing gloss of fine hypocrisy, as if they served God in their contrived conjectures and opinions; but still they will continue in selfhood, in the outward show and ostentation.

43. These the Holy Ghost doth rebuke and reprove by the virgin-child in Christ's spirit, and calls them hypocrites, and wolves in sheeps' clothing, and crafty foxes born of the Serpent's ens, in whom there is the very property of toads, dogs and wild beasts; and shews them, that they draw near to God with their lips, but their heart is full of murder, gall and serpent-desire, and hath no true upright love-desire in it; also it shews them that they are but mere flatterers and dissemblers in their office, who only seek pleasure and temporal honour and respect thereby, that so they might be able to domineer and lord it over men's bodies and souls, goods and estates, and thus they serve God only from without, with hypocritical mouths: Their heart hangeth to the whoredom of Babylon, full of devilish murder and poison against him that doth but touch their conscience.

44. Such children in the Serpent's craft, who are best able as cunning craft masters in sophistry to turn this subtlety most takingly and artificially, the children of the world do set up unto themselves for teachers, and will learn the way of God from them.

45. These teachers do assume unto themselves [and presume upon] the writings of the saints, and proclaim with open mouth that they teach God's word, [and that] the Holy Spirit is poured forth by their teaching and preaching; and though their conscience doth even convince them that they are not capable of the office of the ministry, and that they are in no wise the temples of the Holy Spirit who should teach in and by them, yet they care not for that: it brings them money and honour. Christ is gone up to heaven, and hath placed and ordained them to be stewards and vicars in his office; they must compose and contrive their doctrine out of the writings of the saints, and out of their reason, upon the letter of the Scripture. Their heaping together and composing of the words [in the form of their subtle reason] must be the voice of the Holy Spirit; they say the Holy Spirit is thereby poured forth into the hearts of men.

46. And though they themselves be only Cain, and in their literal and bookish rhapsody[1] in their sermons do cast forth a great deal of light, lewd, Cainical scorn and brother-slaughter, and oftentimes mix

[1] Or composing of the texts, or bare letter of Scripture.

lies and truth together; yet the Holy Spirit must have taught, and the congregation must thank God for such holy, [sound, orthodox, evangelical] doctrine, as they call it. And after their killing of their brother there, they must also help, with boldness, courage and zeal, to murder and slay Abel, and the little child Jesus, in his members, with words and deeds.

47. Such teachers the world sets up, to learn the kingdom of God from: and whosoever can but lustily cavil, censure and condemn others in their gifts, and propose it with fine distinctions and subtle arguments, and clothe them with the mantle of reason, and hide the wolf (which thereby murdereth and devoureth Christ's flock) under the purple mantle of Christ, to him they give diligent attention; for the fleshly Serpent's heart doth therewith sooth up and flatter itself in its evil property; it hath even such an artificial nature and constitution.

48. Such seed these teachers, chosen of men, do sow, who only desire the calling for temporal honour and pleasure, but are not called of God, and are also without divine knowledge [and understand not what true divinity is]. They enter not by the door of Christ; but they come into place by the election and favour of men, through the means of their own willing, walking and running: these can no way be acknowledged for the shepherds of Christ, for they are not born of Christ, and [are not] chosen to this function and divine calling.

49. They are only the great master-builders of Babylon, where the languages are confounded, and men thereby set at odds and variance, and they set up war and contention upon the earth. For they wrangle and jangle about the mere husk, viz. about the written word and letter; and they have not the living word of God dwelling in them, from which they ought to teach. The Spirit of Christ itself must be the teacher in the word, with the living voice [or expression]; the spirit of man[1] must know and feelingly find Christ in it, otherwise none teacheth the words of Christ, [but] only dumb [senseless] words, without power and spirit.

50. Now the Spirit of Christ in his children doth reprove these, and shews them the true way how we must die wholly in Christ's death to the selfhood and the false self-full desire of temporal pleasure and honour; and be born again of Christ's Spirit, with another new will and desire out of Christ's love, in peculiar real knowledge, and preach and teach Christ from our [own peculiar and singular knowledge of him in our] selves.

[1] The human spirit.

51. This, Babel in Cain cannot endure, that one should teach: that Christ himself must be the teacher in the human spirit. They plead their cause from the forewritten Apostolical word, and say, if they teach the same then the Spirit of God is poured forth. Yes, forsooth! very right, I say so too: If the same be taught in Christ's spirit and power, then 'tis so, indeed.

52. But the Spirit of Christ in his children is not bound to any certain form, that it need not [or ought not] to speak anything which stands not in the Apostolical letter; as the spirit in the Apostles was free, and they spake not all one and the same words, but from one spirit and ground they did all speak, every one as the spirit gave him utterance. Even thus likewise the spirit speaketh yet out of its children, it needeth no form aforehand composed and gathered together out of the literal word. It indeed doth put man's spirit in mind of what is comprehended and contained in the letter; for Christ said, *The Holy Ghost shall take of mine, and declare it unto you.*

53. Christ is alone the Word of God that teacheth the way of truth through his children and members. The literal word is only a manuduction and manifestation of Christ; that we should have the same before us, as a testimony and witness of Christ, [shewing] what he is, and what he hath done for us, that we should conceive, let and fasten our faith therein; and yet with the desire enter into the living Word, Christ; and be ourselves born to life therein.

54. None is a shepherd of Christ but he that hath Christ's Spirit, and teacheth from him. No art nor university makes one a shepherd of Christ, unless he be capable of the office in Christ's Spirit. If he hath not that, living and working in him, then man hath only chosen him to be a carver and builder of the great Babylon; a letter-changer [a verbal jangler and wrangler], without divine understanding and knowledge; for the Scripture saith, *The natural man perceiveth nothing of the Spirit of God.* How then will he teach the way of God, who himself understands nothing thereof.

55. And Christ saith, He that entereth not into the sheepfold by him, viz. by the door of his spirit, but climbeth up some other way, as by art and reason, or by the favour of man, into the same: whosoever setteth up himself, not being called of God's Spirit, to be a shepherd of Christ, for human and temporal repute and revenue's sakes, he is a thief and murderer, and the sheep hear not his voice, for he hath not Christ's voice, and cometh only that he may rob and steal.

56. But they say, the written word is Christ's voice. Yea, it is indeed the cabinet thereof, viz. a form of the word: but the voice must be living which opens the same, and likewise acts it in due motion as a watch-work. The letter is as an instrument thereunto, as a trumpet; but there must be a true and right breath and air which agrees with the air or tune in the letter.

57. The word of the letter is a prepared instrument:[1] what kind of trumpeter takes it in hand to play thereon, even such a sound it gives. Is not, I pray, the great Babel built out of this work? Every one hath sounded the trumpet of the letter as his own air and tone hath been in him; and so it hath been approved and received by each trumpeter, and brought into a substance; and this same substance is the great Babylon, where evil and good are built into a building.

58. But if men had not introduced any exposition upon the Apostolical word, and [had not] brought or contrived the same into other forms, then the instrument had remained pure. But the un-illuminated mind hath set itself up to be a master therein, and bowed the same according to its own imagination and well-liking; for the human pleasure hath thereon set itself, and formed and expounded the same according to the [rule of] fat [benefices for the] belly ['s sake] and worldly pleasures. And thus the spirit is extinct; and 'tis turned to an antichristian order and custom. Men have taken and formed the word as an organ, and so they have brought it into a fashion and custom, thàt a man must play thereon, and others must hear the sound and tune which he makes; and thus for the most part such organists are only used who strike the organ from without, and make a fine con-trived and composed piece, which they willingly and readily hear. But the organ soundeth only as the master strikes it.[2]

59. But to this Christ saith, *Every plant, which my heavenly Father hath not planted, shall be rooted up.* Also, *Whosoever is of God, he heareth God's word.* Christ said, *The Son of man speaketh nothing but what he heareth the Father speak in him.* So likewise must a teacher of Christ hear the Father's Spirit in Christ speak in him; he must hear God's word in the Spirit of Christ in him; as David saith, *I will hear what the Lord speaketh in me.* He must be a temple of God, in whom God dwelleth, and from whom he speaketh, being only an instrument thereto. For Christ said, *We will come to you, and make our abode in you.* Also, *I will put my word into your mouth,* saith the prophet. Also, *The word is nigh thee, namely in thy*

---

[1] Or work.
[2] Or plays on it.

mouth, and heart. Here the Spirit of God speaketh of the living Word; and not of a bell without a clapper.

60. This, the Spirit of Christ in his children doth teach, and reproves the wooden clapper in the right bell, which hath hung itself up to be a clapper in the bell of the divine word, and yet hath no power to make the bell sound. This, Cain, in his offering, can by no means brook, that one should tell him his offering doth not please God.

61. He setteth forth himself with very fair glozing and glistering outside shows, and hath made himself such a brave glorious form; moreover, he is chosen of the high schools and worldly might thereto. And if a mean layman, without human calling, should come thereinto (as Christ, who was accounted for a carpenter's son), and offer to reprove such a high priest in such great dignity, honour and respect, the same the world believeth not that it is from God that he is sent.

62. The great bear thinketh presently, This is only a sheep, which I will take into my mouth and devour him. What, shall a sheep reprove me, who am a bear? Will a disesteemed sheep nullify my reputation and esteem among men, and dare to quetch at me? I will soon rid him out of the way, and so defile him that he shall not be known that he is a sincere and single-hearted lamb of Christ, and speaketh from Christ's Spirit. I will so wallow and mire him in the dirt, disgrace, and scorn, that he shall be held for a filthy beast, or a very defiled swine.

63. In the meantime I live in my delicious days of pleasure, and remain lord over soul and body. But if the sheepling shall offer to stir, and shew more than a sheepling of Christ, then I will help the butcher drive it to the slaughter-house.

64. Thus it goeth with the simple, single-hearted children of Christ, whom the Spirit of Christ driveth, and out of whom he teacheth here in this world, etc. They are only as sheep among wolves; as Christ said, *I send you as sheep among wolves.* The earthly man is a serpentine wolf, under whom the virgin-child, viz. Christ's lamb, must dwell; and then beginneth and ariseth murdering, slaying,[1] and killing.

65. But it doth not at all hurt the virgin-child; *its external wolf is also by this means bitten off by another*: for the outward wolf of all men is grown from the anger of God, and arisen with the sin in Adam; therefore it must be given for food to the anger of God, that the virgin-child of the woman's seed may become manifest.

[1] Or robbing.

214

66. For thus they do separate themselves as two enemies, and are continually opposite enemies one against another in the time of this outward life; for the judgment is given to the virgin-child against the introduced Serpent's child of sin. In the resurrection the virgin-child shall condemn the serpent-child into the fire of God; there the limus of the earth shall be proved and purged from the Serpent's ens, and again put upon the virgin-child.

67. Now saith reason, What pleasure hath God in this murdering of his children, can he not defend them from the enemy? Thus it must be: that the light may be manifest in the darkness, else the light would stand still in the darkness and bring forth no fruit. Seeing then the light receiveth into itself essence and perceivancy, also sensation from the darkness, viz. from the source of the fire, therefore one is set against the other, that so one might be manifest in the other: the joy against grief, and grief against joy; that it may be known what evil or good is.

68. For if there were no grief then the joy were not manifest to itself; but yet all is in the free will: as every thing doth introduce itself into evil or good, so it runneth on its course, and the one is but the manifestation of the other; for if there were no night or darkness then we should know nothing of the light or day. Thus the great God hath introduced himself into severation, to his own contemplation and sport of joy.

69. The like also is to be understood in the various diversity and severalty of men, touching evil and good. The evil must be a cause that the good be made manifest to itself; and the good must be a cause to manifest the evil in its wicked malicious subtlety and iniquity; that all things may come into their contemplation [and visible ken], and every thing might manifest its judgment in itself unto the great separation-day of the LORD of all beings, where every thing shall give in itself into its barn, for its usefulness and profit, that, in the eternity, the great God may be known in a creatural and formal manner, according to light and darkness.

70. For all things were created by the Word, and brought into a form. Seeing then God is an angry jealous God and a consuming fire, and also a merciful loving meek God of light and giving [or free grace], in whom there cannot be any evil at all, therefore he hath introduced fire and light, evil and good, one with another in the Verbum Fiat, into a free will, whereby the will may form[1] either in the evil or [in

[1] Or work.

the] good; and yet he hath created all things good, and to the light, and set them into the free will, to multiply themselves in the free will, to conceive in evil or good; and yet hath associated to each thing its likeness, viz. to a male its female, that so nothing hath cause to degenerate,[1] and to man he hath given commands what to do, and [what to] leave undone.

71. Thus all things stand to the judgment of the great God, and in this time they must be in contest, that one may be manifest in the other. But then in the great harvest every thing shall have its own seat in itself; when strife shall be taken up and cease, and all things must stand to the honour and admiration of the wonderful works of the great God, who alone knows whereunto every thing shall be good, and for what he will use it.

[1] Or fall from its place and order into destruction.

Shews how the Adamical Tree hath put forth and opened itself out of its Stock, and introduced itself into Boughs, Branches, Twigs, and Fruit; out of which Pullulation or Manifestation the Invention of all Arts and Governments[1] is Arisen

The Deep Gates out of the Centre of the Eternal and also the Temporal Nature, shewing how the Eternal Wisdom hath introduced itself into a formal [Visible and Ideal] Contemplation.

1. THE eternal divine understanding is a free will, not arisen either from any thing or by any thing; it is its own peculiar seat, and dwelleth only and alone in itself, un-apprehended of any thing; for beyond and without it is nothing, and that same NOTHING is only ONE; and yet it is also as a nothing to itself. It is one only will of the abyss, and it is neither near nor far off, neither high nor low; but it is ALL, and yet as a Nothing. For there is in itself no contemplation, sensation or perceivancy whereby it might find a likeness in itself.

2. Its finding is its own forth-proceeding, so that it beholdeth itself in the egress,[2] for that which is proceeded forth is its eternal lubet, sensation, and perceivancy; and it is called the divine wisdom. Which wisdom the unsearchable abyssal will apprehendeth in itself to its centre of lubet,[3] viz. to an eternal mind of the understanding; which understanding the free will formeth in itself to its own likeness,[4] viz. to an eternal-speaking, living [working] word, which the free will doth speak or breathe forth out of the formed wisdom of the lubet.

3. And the forth-breathing[5] is the spirit or mouth of the understanding in the formed will of the wisdom, which doth distinguish [or variously severise] the speaking Word, so that the mind, and the understanding of the mind, becomes manifest and revealed; in which

---

[1] Or Polities.   [2] Or proceeding forth.
[3] Or imagination, desire, or magia.   [4] Or express image.
[5] Or spiration.

manifestation the free lubet or wisdom is, in the speaking or forth-breathing, formed of the free will, by the spirit, into diversity and variety.

4. In which formation the powers of the divine properties do arise; so that it is truly said and declared concerning God, that he is the eternal will, understanding, mind, counsel, power, and wonder; in[1] which wonders of powers he hath moved and formed himself from eternity. In which formation consists the invisible spiritual world, wherein the Spirit of God hath melodised and sported with itself from everlasting, which also hath neither ground, limit, bounds nor original.

5. For it is the divine vision[2] of the formed wisdom. Its centre is the formed will, viz. the Word, forth-speaking out of all powers; and its life is the spirit which proceedeth in the speaking or breathing, which distinguisheth and formeth the lubet of the wisdom. So that the formed wisdom playeth before the life of the Deity, as little children play before their parents, who have begotten them out of their essence for their joy, and in them the parents take their delight and pastime.

6. Thus likewise are we to understand the being or essence of eternity; which being or essence the eternal free will hath, in the forth-breathing Word, introduced into a desire, viz. to an external comprehensiveness, in which comprehensibility the beginning of the corporeal being is arisen, viz. the centre of the formed nature; wherein the desire hath amassed, formed and introduced itself into properties, viz. into darkness and light, into pain and source, into joy and sorrow. And yet we must not understand any sorrow to be in the pregnatress; but the free will doth so form and conceive itself in the desire to the contemplation and manifestation of the wonders; that so the properties might be peculiarly manifested and revealed in each other.

7. For if there were no contra-will then there would be no motion in the properties; but seeing the free will hath introduced itself into love and anger, viz. into evil and good, a twofold will is arisen in these properties, viz. a wrathful [will], according to the nature of the fire and of the darkness, and a good love-will, according to the nature and quality of the light; in order that one might dwell in and manifest the other.

8. Not that this birth hath received only a temporal beginning: it is[3] eternal, and is the manifestation of the divine vision, sensation, and

---

[1] Or with.   [2] Contemplation.   [3] Or hath been.

perception. Only, in the creating of the creation this birth introduced itself into a compaction or external comprehensiveness, that it might have a distinct dominion to work in for its own sport and play.

9. Also we are not to conceive that in the creation the evil, proceeding from the darkness and fiery property, was separated from the good, and placed in a peculiar sundry working dominion, but the one *is in* the other. Yet the light shone through the darkness, and the darkness could not comprehend it. Every life in the creation proceeded forth from the fiery property, and the spirit of the rational understanding did arise from the light's property. In the creation every fiery life was brought forth, *in its beginning*, to[1] the light.

10. Moreover, the Creator of all beings hath given the creatures of the outward world, which hath a temporal beginning out of the eternal Word, a universal light for visible contemplation; also, every life in the creation hath received the light of nature out of the centre in itself, out of which the understanding ariseth, so that the creature can rule and govern itself.

11. And nothing was created evil, or to the dominion of iniquity; for though on one part it hath an ens of the wrath in itself for its life, yet on the other part it hath also an ens of the light and good virtue in itself; and it is set in the free will, to conceive [or work] in evil or [in] good; for there is nothing so evil but it hath a good in it, whereby it may rule and be predominant over the evil.

12. But man was in equal accord in his properties: no property was manifest above the other, for he was God's image; like as there is no evil manifest in God, unless he would himself manifest the wrath of the eternal nature in a thing: even so also the divine free will was given to man.

13. And withal, the command [was given to him] that he in his free will should not lust after evil and good, viz. after the divided properties; he should continue steadfast in the equal harmony of the properties, and rule with the light over the darkness; and then the properties of the wrath had stood in mere joy, delight and melody in him, and he had been a mirror and form of the divine wisdom, which had seen and beheld itself in him, according to the kingdom of joy.

14. But seeing that he did contemplate with the free will in the dissimility, how evil and good were each of them in its own peculiar self-full property, and brought his lust and longing thereinto, desiring to taste thereof in the essence; whereupon this same property did also

[1] In or for.

take him in his lust, and prevailed in his will, and also in the ens whence the will did arise to its own contemplation and dominion. And thus the first man, who was good in the beginning, became a stock or tree of the taste of the knowledge of evil and good, viz. a contending dominion, in which both wills, viz. the good and the evil, ruled in one another.

15. But seeing the fiery wrathful will so overcame the good which was from the light's essence, that the light's ens was taken captive in the wrathful ens, this image fell under the power and command of the outward dominion, which was evil and good; and also under the wrath of the inward nature, viz. of the fiery darkness; upon which image God had compassion, and did re-inhest[1] the Covenant of Grace into the captivated, disappeared and (as to the divine wisdom) blind ens of the holy world's being, and did incorporate the same as a Covenant of a new regeneration of a new holy will and life.

16. Thus now we are to consider aright of the stock of the human tree, how it hath spread forth and displayed itself in the properties, and introduced itself as a tree (evil and good) into boughs and branches; and from whence his [man's] temporal government of distinct and sundry offices and callings is arisen, which he did awaken in him when he lusted after evil and good, and thereby brought himself in subjection to nature, seeing he fell under its dominion.

17. And we see very clearly that Moses hath described and set down in his first book[2] how the human tree hath opened itself in evil and good, and introduced itself into boughs and branches for its fruit. Also we see how the fiery wrathful property hath always gone before, and first of all brought forth its fruit: we have a clear and plain understanding hereof in the names of those which the Spirit of God hath put by Moses in the lines of propagation.[3]

18. For first he setteth Cain, whereby is understood, in the Language of Nature, a source out of the centre of the fiery desire, a self-full will of the fiery might of the soul, viz. a sprout or twig out of the first Principle, in which branch or sprig the first Principle did, in an especial manner, prevail, and would sever itself into a self-fullness, and break itself off from the love-ens. Yet not as a dark source, but as a source of self-full lust, and also [of] fiery strength and might.

19. For out of the ens of Cain (as the same was in the centre of the begetting nature in the wrestling wheel of life) arose his will; and out of the will, the desire; and out of the desire, the substance; in which

---

[1] In-promise.   [2] Genesis.   [3] Genealogy.

substance the false mind is understood, wherein the dominion of the outward did form and fasten itself; whereinto the devil also, in the wrath of nature, crept in with his desire, and desired the lordship and domination of this world in selfhood. As the fallen devil doth always desire domination in the place of this world, in the inward eternal, and [in the] outward temporal nature.

20. But seeing the word of divine power and holiness had incorporated itself[1] with a Covenant of regeneration, into the woman's seed, viz. into the disappeared ens of the spiritual world's essence, that it would deprive the fiery wrathful will, proceeding from the centre of the dark world, of its fiery might of selfhood; thereupon after Cain there sprang forth out of the human tree a sprout out of the aim of the Covenant, viz. Abel, whose name, in the Language of Nature, signifieth an out-breathed angel, which, in the first will of the essence whence the soul ariseth, had formed and fixed itself in the centre of light, in the love-desire, and penetrated quite through the fire's centre. Whereupon the fiery desire did desire to cut off the earthly life, which hath its original out of the fiery desire as its property; for which cause Abel and all his posterity[2] became martyrs.

21. For this is the door of Christ, who must give himself into this death of the wrath, and penetrate the human centre (of the soul's original according to the fire-world), with the love-ens, viz. with the deepest love of the Deity, and change the fiery wrathful desire of the dark world's essence into love.

22. Adam was the stock of the universal human tree. But when Eve was made out of him then the tree was divided according to two Principles, not wholly in the essence, but according to the nature and quality of the centres of fire and light; for the centre of the light, viz. the ground of the love-desire, did stand in Eve's matrix; but in her fall it disappeared as to the creature; therefore the divine Word did re-inhest[3] itself therein to a centre of regeneration.

23. Now Cain and Abel were the two twigs which grew out of this tree from the property of both Principles, viz. of the fire, and of the light; and they were a type of the whole tree, with its fruit which it would bring forth. But seeing Abel was a type of Christ (who was to be conceived without the help of man, only and barely of the incorporated Word in the seed of the woman, who should suffer death for man), therefore Abel must pass through without branches and fruit. For the fruit which Christ should bring forth was to generate anew

[1] Or espoused itself.   [2] Or successors.   [3] Espouse, betroth or promise.

the human tree; and not produce other twigs out of his loins. Therefore Abel also, being the type of him, should not generate any twig out of his loins. For the line of the Abelical seed remained in the Covenant, and pointed at Christ, who should spring forth out of the Abelical line, and again manifest the spiritual world's essence.

24. Therefore Adam must bring forth another branch by his Eve out of the vital tree; which was to be like Adam in his image; viz. Seth. Which name doth signify, in the Language of Nature, a forth-running, or leap, where a glance or aspect of a love-will ariseth out of the fiery will; which, notwithstanding, is withheld and hindered by the outward world's being, essence and substance, viz. by the corrupt house of flesh.

25. Now Christ must come to help this captivated, forestalled and obscured will, which, notwithstanding, hath its first ground out of God's love, and free it from the band of wrath wherewith the divine ens was captivated, for this was Christ's office: not that he should beget, but give himself into the generation of Seth, and redeem Seth and his branches from the wrath, and regenerate him anew in himself. He was not to beget children to this world, but to bring forth Seth out of this world, and bring him in himself into the spiritual world.

26. Now in Seth the line of the Covenant went forth, in which Christ would manifest himself according to the human tree. But in Cain the line of the wonders, viz. of nature and its government went forth; for Moses saith, that unto Cain was born Enoch, and he built a city, and called the name of the city after the name of his son, Enoch (Gen. iv. 17). Now Cain was the first man born of woman, and Abel the second, whom he slew.

27. Now Moses saith that Cain built a city, whereas, indeed, if we would go merely upon reason, there were not men who might be able to build a city, and inhabit it; for the spirit in Moses doth here make a veil before the understanding, which lieth in the word city; for he saith, Cain's son was called Enoch, and also the city. Now this is verily true; but the spirit in Moses looketh upon the root of Cain and Adam; how the tree, evil and good, hath opened and displayed itself into its boughs and branches; for by the name of Enoch the spirit looketh upon the property of the branch, viz. of Cain's son, intimating what kind of people would arise from thence, viz. a city[1] and dominion of the outward world in selfhood; for in the Language of Nature it is to be understood in the name.

[1] Or commonwealth.

28. Enoch signifieth a forth-breathing of life, and a reassuming to a selfish contemplation; a child of self, which in nature doth introduce itself into a self-full dominion and will, so that it doth imagine and frame in its mind a dominion or region, country or city, desiring and aspiring in its will to be a tree or prince of men. For when the human life departed from the Spirit of God into selfhood, then it would be a peculiar selfish lord, which will's son was Enoch, viz. a city or amassed substance to a self-full domination and government.

29. From which government and dominion the branches or children were born, concerning which the holy spirit complained in Noah, that they would not suffer his spirit to reprove them any more (Gen. vi. 3), for they were a tree or branch sprung forth from the tree of self-fullness; from which the worldly principalities and superiorities have taken their rise and original. For when the human life fell unto the stars, and the spirit of the outward world, then the same brought the human life into its [the outward world's] own dominion, from the angelical into the astral and outward elementary dominion, according to its figure. This, the city of Cain, viz. Enoch, doth signify unto us, viz. the dominion upon the earth.

30. But now Enoch cannot be the ruler, but the city is he, that is, the branch or the country of the children of pride, who departed from God in their own selfish power and authority. Now the multiplicity of wills must have a judge, seeing they would not suffer the Spirit of God to rule them (1 Sam. viii. 7). Therefore the spirit in Moses saith, *and Enoch begat Irad* (Gen. iv. 18). This is now the governor who, out of their own essence, set himself up to be judge and lord over them, viz. a potentate and tyrant.

31. For the name is very pregnant in the Language of Nature, and signifieth a forth-breathing of life, where the life doth soon form[1] itself in the centre of the fiery property and strong might; viz. in the anger of God, which was become ruler over the life; the same took Irad, as a lord and tamer of the life, and set him over Enoch.

32. From this root the rulers of the world are arisen; for seeing that man would not have God for a ruler of his life and will, God gave[2] them the ruler in nature from among themselves; that they might lord it over and rule one another.

33. For God hath not given mankind any law or government among themselves, but made man to be lord only over all creatures, so that he should rule over all things. But God himself would rule with

---

[1] Or take.   [2] Or permitted.

his spirit over man, and govern the human life. But seeing that self-hood would not, then Irad (that is, the fire's strength and might) sprang forth forcibly out of the human tree, and set itself over the city, Enoch, upon the earth.

34. But now Irad must have something wherein and wherewithal to set up himself to rule and reign, for the fire's wrath and fury would not have suffered them; and also the government must be somewhat profitable and advantageous. Therefore Moses writeth now very right and exceeding wonderfully, and saith, *Irad begat Mahujael,* which intimateth very emphatically, in the Language of Nature, an assuming[1] of the outward and inward centre of nature, viz. of the outward and inward world; a self-conceived, bold, courageous, vainglorious, arrogant mind, which would possess the riches of the outward world in its domination and superiority, viz. all manner of creatures and fruits. And especially it denoteth a splendour of the inward assuming, viz. an earthly god, which externally sets itself in God's office. Out of this name, Babel, viz. the Beast with the Whore, was afterwards brought forth.

35. And Moses saith further: *Mahujael begat Methusael.* This is now the right wonderful name, wherein is signified how the life doth arrogate divine power to itself. For Methusael would intimate in the Language of Nature thus much, that is to say, Mine is the divine might: I am an angel, set therein by God, or, I am the ordinance of God. Which indeed is true, but [only] according to the first Principle, by the outward nature, viz. a natural power and ordinance.

36. Moreover, in this name there is hidden, under the angel, the praise of the children who should be subject to this might, and live under the same, as under the divine ordinance. But this angel's name in divine power doth first form itself in the fleshly selfhood; for the syllable Me-, which beginneth the word of the name, doth first form[2] itself in the outward world's birth, in the mine-hood; and sheweth that this ordinance doth not arise out of the kingdom of heaven in God's holiness, but out of the first Principle, which formeth itself in the third Principle, viz. in the outward world's nature, into such an order; and therefore it shall and must be abolished, and proved through the judgment of God.

37. And Moses goeth on to write, and saith, *Methusael begat Lamech.* Now in this name the hidden mystery of the divine ordinance

---

[1] Or apprehension, taking, forming or amassing to itself.
[2] Text, take or conceive.

by the angelical counsel is contained; and it signifieth in the Language of Nature in this place as much as a sending of the angel over the dominion of the humanity, viz. over the regions of the world, over the fleshly life, which should be subject to the supreme governing prince in nature.

38. For here the wound which Adam received is sought: in that two superior princes do reign over the human life, viz. the ordained good angel, and the incorporated evil angel in the flesh. Also hereby is understood the powerful assault of the evil angel from without and from within; for the inward spirit in the name goeth forth out of the Covenant of God, and passeth into the outward world. Which denoteth how man would become lewd and profane, and also vilify the Covenant of God, and yet with the assuming goeth again into self-hood, and formeth itself in the forth-proceeding angel's name. Which denoteth a hypocritical whoredom in an angel's form, which entereth again into the external, and at last casteth away the Covenant, together with the angel's name, quite from itself.

39. Further, Moses writeth, *Lamech took two wives: the one was called Adah, and the other Zillah* (Gen. iv. 19). Hereby is understood in the generation of the life's tree thus much, viz. that the human life knew the wound which was arisen in its stock;[1] and thenceforward took two wives, that is, a twofold essence and will, viz. Adah signifieth how the soul goeth with the will through the mind, and formeth itself with the desire in the first stock of Adam, and would fain be honest again. But the life had also taken to itself Zillah for wife of the pregnatress, viz. fleshly joy and pleasure.

40. The wife or will, Adah, would exercise a good dominion, and rule and maintain itself upon the earth according to God's command; and she bare Jabal: *Jabal* betokeneth the simple, plain man, such as are countrymen, and the like; for Moses saith, that *from him proceeded such as dwell in tents and such as keep cattle* (Gen. iv. 20).

41. But the other brother, saith Moses, was named Jubal, *who was the father of all those that handle the harp and organ* (Gen. iv. 21); for the other will proceeded from the spirit of the outward world into temporal pleasure and joy; and devised all kinds of joyful sport and pastime for the recreation of its life. And this signifieth Jubal, viz. an external jocund angel, with whom the inward spirit sported before itself in a likeness.

42. *And Zillah*, saith Moses, *she also bare Tubal-cain, a master in all*

---

[1] Stem or body.

brass and ironwork (Gen. iv. 22). That is, Zillah is the fiery desire which formeth itself in the human property into a substance of Sulphur and Mercury, and brings itself forth with its spirit out of the substance into a contemplation and visible ken, in which understanding man hath found out the arts of metals.

43. For *the sister of Tubal-cain was Naamah.* Here lieth the precious pearl, dear masters. Naamah is heavenly in her property, clothed with the external vesture, so that you do not know her, for the earthly man is not worthy of it; for her essence is virginal, a virgin of purity. It pointeth in one part at the inward new man, viz. the sister of the sulphurean man; and on the other part it signifieth the gross metal of the earth, and also the precious metal, viz. gold and silver.

44. For Tubal-cain is the brother of Naamah, they lie in one womb; but Tubal-cain is of this world, and Naamah is a virgin hidden under her brother; and herein the twofold earth is understood, viz. in a twofold property; one heavenly and the other gross earthly, viz. an essence out of the dark world's property and an essence out of the light world's property. And thus also it is to be understood in man; for by the property of God's anger, viz. by the dying of the earthly man Naamah becomes manifest.

45. Wherefore doth Moses add the name Naamah, and yet speaketh nothing either of any that she brought forth, or that she married? Answer: because that *in the regeneration the natural generation ceaseth.* The new virginity in the spirit of Christ doth not produce any creature more, but they must all proceed out of the first centre and stock, so that they may be all one tree; and by the fire the metal, viz. the virgin, which is Tubal-cain's sister, is made manifest.

46. The name Tubal-cain hath an excellent understanding in it, for it sheweth how the sulphurous mercurial wheel doth open itself in the birth and generation of metals, and also in the original of life. For God subjected all things to man, and gave him all things for his delight and play; therefore Tubal-cain must open and discover himself in the human tree, that so they might understand it. Hereby we have signified enough to those that are our schoolfellows.

47. *And Lamech said to his wives Adah and Zillah: Hear my voice, ye wives of Lamech, and mark what I say: I have slain a man to my wound, and a young man to my hurt. If Cain shall be avenged, sevenfold, truly Lamech seventy-and-sevenfold* (Gen. iv. 23, 24). This is a wonderful, strange and marvellous saying. Who would understand what the spirit signifieth here, without its own peculiar exposition? I do seriously admonish the

mocker to leave our work here uncensured, for he understandeth not our spirit and sense.

48. Lamech saith that *he slew a man to his wound, and a young man to his hurt.* This man is Abel, according to the outward humanity of the kingdom of this world; and the young man is the image of Christ, proceeding from the virginlike line out of the seed of the woman in him: the man he slew to his rebuke, viz. to an incurable wound, and the precious young man in the man to a hurt, which would gall and trouble him as an evil hurt, bruise or boil in the conscience of sin. For the wrath of God wrought in this boil, and the wound being a great and woeful hurt might not be healed; for the curse of the Lord went forth out of this boil into the wound, in which the earth was cursed, so that the human dominion became a valley of misery.

49. For Lamech saw the sore wound, and returned; and thereupon took two wives, that is, a twofold will into his mind for his government, whereby he would rule upon the earth, viz. one went forth from Adah into the grazing and keeping of cattle, and the hard labour of the hands for a temporal livelihood, wherein he found the curse and wound. And the other went forth out of the branch of Zillah into the earth after the metals, to make useful tools and instruments for the tillage and husbandry of the ground, and for other necessaries; and so he found in the metals the rusty boil and sore in their metalline nature; for the precious tincture or the fair blossom of the earth was hidden in the curse, viz. environed and beset with an evil boil and sore.

50. Now Lamech knew the woeful hurt, and said, *Hearken, ye wives of Lamech, and mark what I say.* He would fain express the hurt and damage; he saw back again into the tree of man, and considered the revenge of God, which had laid hold of man's life, and said, *Cain shall be avenged sevenfold, and Lamech seven-and-seventyfold.* For God said also to Cain, when he stood and cried, *Thou drivest me out this day from the face of the earth;*[1] *and it will come to pass that whosoever findeth me will slay me.* [But the Lord said to him], *Whosoever slayeth Cain, vengeance shall be taken on him sevenfold. And he set a mark on Cain, that none should kill him* (Gen. iv. 14, 15).

51. These are most wonderful and hidden sayings: *Cain shall be avenged sevenfold and Lamech seventy-and-sevenfold?* Wherefore shall Lamech be avenged seventy-and-sevenfold, and Cain sevenfold? Who hath done anything to Lamech? Here the spirit pointeth out of the

[1] Or from the land and country.

centre of the human life upon the time which was to come, intimating, how it would afterwards go with man, in this wound, when, as men should multiply and increase, and make unto themselves kings and princes, dominions and governments, that the wrath of God would also forcibly exercise itself in man's will, and even in the human life and dominion open and display itself.

52. Now, if a man would understand what Lamech saith concerning the revenge, then he must look upon the centre, for the life of all creatures consists in seven degrees or properties, as it is above clearly mentioned. Now Adam was the stock, for Adam and Eve are one tree, from the parting and division of which evil and good did arise. And Cain was the first twig which sprang forth from this tree, wherein the seven properties of life did put themselves forth out of the right divine order and harmony in the life, and destroyed the image of God; which was long of the devil, who egged him on also in the divided properties to the brother-slaughter, so that he slew Abel. Now God said, *Cain shall be avenged sevenfold, if any one slay him.* And he set a mark on Cain, that none should kill him.

53. The devil had folded up himself in the wrath of God, and cunningly insinuated himself into the seven properties of life, seeing they were departed from their mutual harmonious accord; and he would be lord in the place of the spirit of God in the life of man, and would wholly murder and slay the life, as to the kingdom of God. Therefore God set a mark, with the promise of the Covenant therein, so that none could slay it.

54. For Cain did not cry out only for fear of the outward life, but he feared that his right eternal life might be slain, that his life should be wholly blotted out from the face of God; for he cried also, and said, *Lo! thou drivest me out this day from off the earth; and I must hide myself from thy face; and I must be a fugitive, and a vagabond in the earth; and it will now come to pass that whosoever findeth me will slay me.* He cried out for fear of being killed, and was sore afraid. And yet there was no man besides him upon the earth, save only his father, Adam, and without doubt his sister, whom he took to wife.

55. Cain feared the spirits who had moved him to slay his brother, that they would also kill him; for he saith, *I must be hid from thy face.* Now this was not in any external manner, but in an internal, for God dwelleth not in the view of the outward eyes, but in the inward spiritual [vision]. Therefore God said, *Whosoever killeth Cain's internal life, vengeance shall be taken on him sevenfold.* And he set the mark of the

Covenant on his life, so that no spirit in the wrath could murder it; for he was a twig out of the tree of life.

56. Although the seven properties of nature in him were departed from their mutual accord in each other, yet he was not the sole cause of it, for he had so received his life from father and mother in the divided property. And therefore the grace passed as well upon him as upon Abel; except only that Abel proceeded out of the other line. But the centre of the soul was alike to them both. But the motion in the seed was unlike; for they were the two types of the world; viz. Cain the type of the selfhood in the wrath, and Abel the type of the resignation of life, where, from the resignation, another world springeth forth through death out of the centre.

57. Not that Cain was born to destruction, but that evil awakened property in the dissimility, viz. the soul of the outward world, brake forth forcibly in the seed; and took the [centre of] life into its power, and therein God set a mark, viz. his Covenant, that the murderers should not slay the soul's life.

58. But if it should so come to pass that the own peculiar will would give itself to the murderers, then the life of Cain should be avenged sevenfold, that is, through all the seven properties; and the free will which did slay the life of God (which was in the Word) should be rebuked and punished sevenfold through all the seven forms of nature, both temporally and eternally. And this is the meaning: whosoever killeth the life, [that is] what free will soever murdereth its life, vengeance shall be taken on it eternally in the seven properties of the dark world.

59. And in this place we are further to consider aright of the great mysteries; for the seven properties of the human tree, producing and manifesting the life of the wonders of God, had now spread forth themselves even unto Lamech. The dominion of the world was now wholly brought forth with Lamech in nature; for Lamech was the seventh man in the root of the wonders arising from the first stock. That is, Adam was the first; Abel belongeth not unto the line of the wonders, but unto the regeneration; Cain was the second in the line of the wonders; Enoch the third, Irad the fourth, Mahujael the fifth, Methusael the sixth, and Lamech the seventh.

60. Now Lamech did spring forth from Cain's root out of this line of the wonders of God; and he was an honest upright man; but was environed[1] with the spirit of the wonders. And he looked back upon

[1] Taken or beset.

the wound, and also upon the sign[1] of grace in the Covenant, and knew for certain that even now the spirit of the wonders should be fully brought forth and manifested in the human life; whereby all arts of the world should be found out.

61. And he saw also forwards, how it would fall out in these wonders of the world; how his children would introduce his life, which they should receive from him by propagation, into a Babylon of folly, and corrupt the same. And hereby also he looked especially upon the Word whence the human life was sprung; and how the life in the spirit of the wonders of the world would introduce itself into a seven-and-seventyfold word of languages and nations, as came to pass at Babel; and how the free will of nature would go astray from the only God, and be corrupt, and that it should be avenged seven-and-seventyfold. That is, every tongue and speech should be avenged in the anger of God, and therefore, because they would corrupt Lamech's life, which they received of him by propagation; and this the wrath of God would avenge in the free will of his children, divided into several speeches.

62. For the spirit saw forwards, how the free will would give up and addict itself to selfhood, and apostatise from the only God, and how the anger of God would seize upon and confound the natural spirit of the wonders in man, viz. the soul of the outward world, from whence the great Babylon of contention about God's being and will would arise; and this, the spirit said, should be avenged seven-and-seventyfold in Lamech.

63. For this was a seven-and-seventyfold Racha [or avengement] upon the word of the understanding in the human life; that out of one only tongue, out of only one speaking Word and vital Spirit, a seventy-and-sevenfold tongue (viz. a confusion of the understanding) should be made. Before, the understanding lay in one sound [voice or harmony], but now the Racha came into it, and confounded and shattered it into seventy-and-seven parts.

64. For the human wheel of the sound or understanding was turned round, and the ten forms of fire, wherein time and eternity doth consist, did open themselves in every form of nature; which was seven times ten, which makes seventy; whereto also belongeth the centre, with its seven unchangeable forms of the eternal nature; which is altogether seventy-and-seven parts.

65. And herein lieth the Grand Mystery.[2] Dear brethren, if ye

---

[1] Or seal. [2] Mysterium Magnum.

were not clothed with the garment of the contentious languages, then we would be bold to declare something more in this place unto you; but ye are yet all captivated in Babel, and are contenders about the spirit[1] of the letter; and yet have no understanding of the same. Ye will also be doctors and learned masters [forsooth], but yet ye understand not your own mother-tongue: ye bite and devour one another about the husk of the word, wherein the living Word doth form and amass itself, and ye neither desire nor understand the living Word. Ye speak only out of seven and out of seventy-and-seven, and yet ye have the Word in one number, wherein the whole understanding[2] is contained: ye have it moving upon your tongues, yet ye cannot comprehend it.

66. And the reason is, that you will speak only out of seven, and out of seventy-and-seven, viz. out of the wrath which hath divided the tongues; and doth avenge the life of Lamech seventy-and-seven times in your tongues and speeches. But if ye would go[3] unto the centre and open your eyes then you would see how the Babylonical whore leads you captive by her string, and how she hath set herself over the life of man, with seventy-and-seven[4] numbers; and hath wholly hidden our sister Naamah with the numbers; that the beast of the numbers might reign and rule in the wrath of God over the life of our sister Naamah.

67. But we have heard a watchman say: Away! the beast, with the whore, which stood upon the earth in Naamah's stead, is quite fallen, and given to the press of the sevenfold Racha[5] in the seventy-and-seven, &c. The Racha ariseth up in Lamech, and goeth through the seventy-and-seven; and this none can hinder. Amen.

68. For Naamah shall be manifested to all nations, tongues and speeches; and even then, out of the seventy-and-seven, there shall be but one word of understanding. For the life of man proceeded from ONE only Word of God, and hath formed and divided itself in selfhood, in the spirit of the wonders of the world, into seventy-and-seven properties of the only Word. Now cometh the time that the life's beginning shall again enter with the spirit of the wonders and speeches into the end, viz. into the beginning. And therefore the child of the wonders, which hath given itself forth in[6] the sight of God, must be made manifest in the unity.

---

[1] Or meaning. [2] Or the understanding of all things.
[3] Or enter into. [4] One copy hath it seven, seventy-and-seven.
[5] Vengeance. [6] Or before.

69. And seeing that the free will hath given itself into the vanity of the speeches and the multiplicity of the powers, and defiled and slain the life of the only Word, the Racha proceedeth forth from the murdering spirit through seventy-and-seven; until the beast, together with the harlot, be consumed and devoured with the fire of God's anger.

70. And then Tubal-cain findeth his sister Naamah in golden attire, and Adah rejoiceth in her son Jabal, who is a herdsman; for Lamech hath again found his children which he left in the Racha. And the pride of self, and also the craft, deceit and subtlety of the Serpent ceaseth. Then[1] every beast shall eat its own pasture. The time is near: Hallelujah!

[1] Or, for.

The Thirtieth Chapter

Of the Line of the Covenant

1. THE line of the Covenant is not so to be understood as if the Covenant fell only upon this line. No, the Covenant befalleth[1] the only life, which was in the Word before the times of the humanity. The line of Seth passeth only upon the manifestation in the flesh, in which line the Word in the Covenant would externally manifest itself in the flesh. But the spirit proceeding from the centre in the Covenant falls as well upon Cain's line as upon Abel's; yet in Cain's [line] in the spirit, and in Seth's in the external mouth [or manifestation], viz. in the formed and conceived word, that is, in the office and ministry of teaching and preaching. For Seth was sprung forth according to the spirit, out of the Covenant, where the spirit moved itself in the incorporated Word in the Covenant; and Cain was comprehended under the spirit of nature.

2. For by Cain's line the arts were brought forth to light, which were a wonder of the divine wisdom, contemplation and formation, viz. of the formed Word through and in nature. And in Seth the Word was brought into a formal life, viz. into a spiritual contemplation, wherein the Word of God did behold itself with the wisdom in a spiritual image;[2] and in Cain's line it beheld itself in a natural formed word; and both serve to set forth the wonderful deeds of God.

3. Not as Babel judgeth, that God, out of his purpose and determinate counsel, hath thus predestinated and chosen one part of men in his anger to condemnation, and the other part to life: they that so judge are yet under the number seventy-and-seven in the multiplication of the word; for the Promise was given to Adam before Cain was conceived. The Covenant touching grace rested in Adam and Eve; but the spirit of sanctification and regeneration by Christ, passed only upon the seed of the woman, viz. upon the seed of the kingdom of heaven which was shut up; that is, upon the light's tincture, upon the matrix of Venus, wherein Adam, when he was man and woman, should have propagated himself in peculiar desire and love; which, seeing it could not be [by reason of Adam's strong earthly imagination], was taken from Adam and made into a woman.

4. But when the woman became earthly, the heavenly part of this

---

[1] Passeth upon, belongeth to, or is entailed upon.   [2] Form, or figure.

matrix [which was to the producement] of the heavenly birth was shut up in death. Into which matrix the Word of God did again incorporate itself with the Covenant, to open and manifest himself in this matrix with a living and heavenly seed, and to destroy the power of death.

5. For the Word would not open itself in the formed word of nature, viz. in Cain's generation, but in the disappeared heavenly ens; and by the same revived and requickened heavenly ens, that is, by the woman's seed of the heavenly part bruise the Serpent's head, viz. the devil's introduced desire in the wrath of nature; that is, overcome the wrath [and curse of God] in the generation of Cain and Seth.

6. The Word in the Covenant did open itself in Seth and Abel, [it being] as a voice of the teacher, and Cain's generation should in its life receive this voice, and impress it into its life, so that it might produce the new regeneration. But that many of them have continued in death, and contemned this voice, is (see ch. 29, 52) long of the free will, which suffered itself to be held by the devil in the anger of God, and still to this day doth suffer itself to be held, in that the Cainical will doth love nature and self too much.

7. For if the free will of the soul will apprehend the word in the Covenant, then it must die to its natural selfhood and self-full will, and be wholly resigned to the own will in the Covenant, that it may, with its desire, follow the word and spirit in the Covenant, as the same doth lead, guide and move it.

8. And this Cain is very loath and unwilling to do; he will be a selfish lord, and with the desire doth figure and shape a monster and an evil beast in his free will, which doth not resemble the first image of the formed life in the word of God. Now against this beast the words of Christ are directed, when he saith, *Unless ye be converted, and become as children* (that is, unless you do depart from and utterly disclaim the will of the self-generated beast, and enter again into the form of the first life) *ye cannot else see the kingdom of God.* Also, *ye must be born again of the water* of the heavenly world's essence, *and of the same holy spirit* proceeding from the Covenant, *otherwise ye cannot see and behold God.*

9. This evil beast of the Godless form is predestinated to condemnation; but the Covenant is in the life. If the free will resigneth itself up to the Covenant, then Christ ariseth in his humanity, out of the Covenant, in the life; and even then the strange beast dieth in Christ's death, and the will formeth itself again into the first image, according as God created it. And this is not annexed only unto Seth,

but unto Adam's life, viz. unto the only life of man which was in the Word of God, and passeth from one upon all; as all branches in one tree do receive sap from the only root of the stock.

10. But the properties of nature, viz. of the natural life, have brought themselves out of Adam's stock into sundry boughs and branches, whence the multiplicity of nations, tongues and speeches is arisen. But the life is only one, and the Covenant in the life sprang forth from the root of life, viz. from the Word of God, out of which the life came upon all, even as the sin, viz. the fall and apostasy passed upon all, none excepted. For the children of Seth were concluded under sin as well as Cain's; but the Covenant, with its manifestation,[1] passed upon Seth; for his name signifieth, in the Language of Nature, a forth-breathing spring out of the life through the first centre of the soul, wherein the Word of God would open itself through the life.

11. And Moses saith, *Seth begat Enos, and then began men to preach of the Name of the Lord* (Gen. iv. 26): for the name Enos signifieth, in the Language of Nature, a divine lubet through the life, wherein the formed Word would behold itself in the sound and voice of the life. Therefore the spirit of God began to teach out of the Covenant through the life of man, concerning God and his being and will. This was the beginning of the divine contemplation through the formed wisdom in the Word, where the Word did behold itself through the wisdom of the formed human voice.

12. And as the life did form itself by Cain's line through the wonders of the formed wisdom in nature, with all manner of arts and works, and also dominions, governments and orders, and introduced them all for the setting forth of God's wondrous deeds and acts, viz. to a contemplation of evil and good, light and darkness; so likewise the spirit of God did bring forth, out of the line of the Covenant in the manifested Word, the wonders of divine holiness, truth, righteousness, love and patience; and by the preaching of the formed Word did declare what the holy and spiritual kingdom of God is.

13. In Cain the kingdom of nature was represented, and in Abel and Seth the supernatural divine kingdom. Both these arose together and went all along one in another to the remonstrance or contemplation of the divine lubet in the formed wisdom; and each put itself forth in an especial manner into its visible ken as a wonder.

14. For from Adam even unto Lamech, in the line of the wonders, there are seven generations; and in the other line, viz. in the line of the

---

[1] Or, the open and outward manifestation of the Covenant.

Covenant, from Adam unto Enoch are also seven generations. Enoch is the eighth, viz. a beginning of the prophetical spirit; for in the first seven generations the form of the spiritual kingdom proceeding from the life's tree was set forth.

15. Adam was the stock, for his life taketh its original out of the Word. But seeing the life of nature in him did predominate over the life in the formed Word, and would have the supreme dominion, and obscured the life proceeding from the Word, the Word itself freely gave itself with a Covenant to be a life therein; and set forth its figure in Abel, how the natural life should and must be broken, and the Word of the divine power again spring forth afresh out of the first life.

16. Thus Abel was the figure of the Second Adam, Christ, and therefore he must be slain for the Covenant's sake; for Christ should kill the exalted haughty natural will, and bring forth a new one. And therefore Abel also should not beget any natural child, else it had been strange to nature; for they should all proceed forth out of one stock; and the Word would spring forth anew through the only tree in the Covenant, that so the children of grace might be brought forth out of the tree of nature, as the dew out of the day-break.[1]

17. For thus also the figure of the new birth was represented out of the stem; namely, the line went forth out of Adam. He was the first, Abel the second, Seth the third, Enos the fourth, where men began to teach of the spiritual kingdom; Kenan[2] the fifth, which signifieth in the Language of Nature, a forth-going, re-conceived[3] lubet or desire of the divine contemplation, in which the taught word did form itself, viz. in prayer, and in the will's desire and also in their offerings.

18. *Mahalaleel* was the sixth, and signifieth in the Language of Nature an angelical form of an angelical kingdom, where the spirit did typify and portray the kingdom of Christ in this name.

19. *Jared* was the seventh. By this name is understood, in the Language of Nature, a priest or prince of the spiritual kingdom. For as Irad should be the regent or ruler in the kingdom of nature, so Jared should be the regent in the spiritual kingdom; for out of Jared came the office of Moses; and out of Irad proceeded the kingdom of worldly principalities, and framed governments and dominions.

20. But the Language of Nature sheweth very clearly that Jared is only a type of a spiritual kingdom; for the name carrieth forth the Cherub along with it through the word; for the spiritual kingdom

---

[1] Or morning.   [2] Or Cainan.   [3] Re-apprehend.

upon the earth was all along captivated in the wrath of God, until Christ, who destroyed the anger.

21. The office of this Jared is twofold, viz. externally it is the figure of the spiritual kingdom, bound with the wrath of God; and internally it is the true holy kingdom, which the penitent man receiveth or taketh possession of: outwardly it is Moses; and inwardly Christ.

22. From this outward kingdom the great mother of the Babylonical whoredom is arisen in the kingdom of Moses among the Pharisees; and in the kingdom of Christ among the verbal and titular Christians;[1] who do all only boast, and gloriously set up themselves in the figure as an idol, and appear as if they were the holy spiritual kingdom. But the Cherub carrieth forth the sound through their word, as a consonant of the wrathful anger of God.

23. And therefore they must contend about the kingdom of God's will; for they have not the spirit of the inward spiritual heavenly kingdom; but only the voice out of the figure, where evil and good are in contest. They have and use the letter, but as an empty, unprofitable instrument, as a figure of the spiritual form. For thus also the spirit did represent it by the name Jared, as a mixed kingdom upon the earth, whereby the inward spiritual new born children should be exercised and proved.

24. And by this form it did signify and foretell how that the greatest part in this spiritual office would be taken in the sword of the Cherub, and that their office would be cut off by the Cherub from God's holiness, and given to the spiritual eternal kingdom of the anger.

25. For as Lamech in Cain's line took two wives, viz. two wills, and confirmed his kingdom therein, and at last brought forth [or pronounced] the seventy-and-sevenfold Racha proceeding from the centre of nature (even from the seven properties) upon the murder of the free will, which would murder and slay his life in many: even so likewise Jared carrieth two wills in his nature's name, viz. one into God's love and mercy in the Covenant, and the other into the figure in which the anger of God ariseth up and carrieth the abominable idol (the belly-god) along with it; which is here deciphered and painted forth to the life.

26. And Moses saith further, *Jared begat Enoch.* Here the great and wonderful gate doth open; for out of Jared, viz. out of the kingdom of

---

[1] Text, the letter criers, or literalists.

the wonders, the prophet must arise: for the prophet is the mouth of the kingdom. He sheweth what the kingdom is, and how it is taken and apprehended in the evil and good, and what the issue and end of all things will be; also he declareth and pointeth out the means,[1] how the turba hath apprehended the life; and denounceth severe and earnest threatenings concerning God's anger; how the sword of the Cherub will cut off the false [man or prophet].

27. *Enoch* signifieth in its own speech as much as a forth-breathed breath of the divine good pleasure,[2] which hath in the time thus beheld itself with the out-breathing in a form; which power of the forth-breathing doth again draw the formed breath into itself, and doth only give forth its sound, as a voice of the divine will. And first it doth point at a twig, springing from the line of the Covenant, viz. out of the internal priestly office, out of the holy divine lubet of the wisdom of God, out of Jehovah. The spirit would comprehend the deepest love in Jehovah in one name and word, which is called Jesus. But in the meantime it did thereby play, in the time of the figure, in the holy wisdom, in the line of the Covenant, as with an internal hidden holy kingdom, which he would manifest in the fullness of time.

28. Secondly, it signifieth the power of the formed word, viz. the person or the body out of the limus of the earth, [viz.] of the heavenly part of the earth; intimating that this body should be taken into the holy word, and translated from this earthliness. As the light doth withdraw and swallow up the darkness, even so likewise the good part of the true humanity in Adam's first image shall[3] be translated [extracted or drawn forth] by the word out of the earthliness, and arise out of the earth: which Enoch's translation from this world doth point out and signify.

29. Thirdly, it signifieth and pointeth at the prophet, viz. the voice of the divine lubet, which did declare and set forth the kingdom of Christ, and also the kingdom of the wonders in their future trans-actions and junctures of time; for the prophetical voice did manifest itself again out of the translation. And did foretell and signify out of the essence of the spirit, viz. out of the most spiritual kingdom, that is, out of the human angelical kingdom, through the soul's spirit; and then also from the whole body of the kingdom, viz. from the nature of the wonders, from the limus of the earth and of the stars, [I say, it did

---

[1] Or the middle, viz. what hath been done and acted by the turba in the wonder of time.
[2] Or lubet.   [3] Text, should or is to be.

set forth both from the spiritual and from the corporal kingdom], how the outward kingdom of man should afterwards arise in this world's being, and what would happen and come to pass therein. This the inward holy omniscient spirit doth signify through[1] the outward, viz. through the wonders of the pregnatress [or mother] of the outward beings, viz. through the spirit of the outward world. For the inward spirit did view itself through the formed wisdom of God, and did contemplate and behold itself in the formed spirit of the wonders: this the name Enoch signifieth unto us.

30. Now the spirit in Moses doth further demonstrate, and saith, *Enoch was sixty-five years old, and he begat Methuselah, and after that he begat him he continued in a divine life three hundred years, and begat sons and daughters: so that the whole age of Enoch was three hundred sixty and five years. And seeing he led a divine life God took him away, and he was no more seen* (Gen. v. 21–24). Here the veil hangeth right before the face of Moses, by reason of the unworthiness of man; and the spirit signifieth very clearly in Moses (if we had but the eyes of our understanding open), when these mysteries should be manifested [or fulfilled].

31. But seeing the Most High hath freely granted us by his counsel to understand this, we will, so far as we dare,[2] somewhat unfold these mysteries to our schoolfellows, and shew the precious pearl unto the children; and yet withal suffer a bolt to lie before our description, that the false heart shall not enter into it: but we shall be sufficiently and fundamentally intelligible unto those that are ours.

32. Moses pointeth in each degree in the lines, only upon one person, which he also setteth into the line through which the spirit of wonders goeth. Afterwards saith Moses, *and he yet lived such a time,*[3] *and begat sons and daughters*; of which he saith nothing any further. Thereby he would intimate and signify unto us the spirit of the manifestation of the wonders of God in each line. Their age, which the spirit setteth down, denoteth the times how long each dominion and government, both the worldly and the spiritual [or ecclesiastical kingdom] should stand in its form and structure. That is to say, how long each prevailing[4] monarchy of the secular and worldly power and domination should continue; and so likewise of the spiritual monarchy.

33. And these monarchies[5] of the wonders are forthwith represented out of the first twigs, springing from the beginning of the human tree. That is, they are set forth in each line in seven numbers,

---

[1] Or by. [2] As we ought. [3] Or so long.
[4] Beginning, growing, arising. [5] Or monarchs.

from Adam through Cain even unto Lamech; and in the other line from Adam unto Jared. By which numbers and names the spirit pointeth in each line especially at seven of the forth-proceeding properties of the tree and powers of the wonders; intimating how the powers of the wonders should afterwards bring themselves into governments, and how one figure should arise out of the other, and how one should destroy and break down the other, and set forth out of the destruction another form, as it hath been brought to pass in the spiritual and worldly[1] governments. For always the worldly government is to be understood *with* the spiritual; for the outward formed Word in the dominion and regiment of nature doth evermore set forth its form *by, with, and in* the spiritual [or ecclesiastical] form [or manner of discipline]. Therefore observe and mark here, with precise exactness.

34. There are seven times appointed to proceed from the tree of life in the word of power. The first proceedeth from the pure life of Adam; for before the creature the life was in the Word, whence it was brought pure into the image; this continued until the fall. From this pure life there springs forth a twig in the inward [kingdom], this same was Abel; but seeing the fall hung on him externally, this same pure life was carried through death into the holy world. This signifieth and pointeth at the kingdom of Christ, who should bring us through death into the pure life.

35. The second time begins with Seth. For Moses saith, that *Adam was a hundred and thirty years old, and begat a son in his own likeness, and called him Seth*. Understand, he was such an image as Adam was after the fall, and was set in the spiritual line of the wonders; and Cain also with him, in a worldly natural line of the wonders, for both kingdoms[2] go together. Seth's time continueth till the deluge, and beareth the supremacy, even to the deluge, or Noah's flood.

36. The third time begins with Enos, under Seth's time, and carrieth forth itself all along as a spiritual ministry, or knowledge of God, under Seth's time, as a hidden kingdom; and continued till Abraham, to whom the Covenant of Christ was established in the flesh.

37. The fourth time begins with Cainan, which is the spiritual form in prayers and spiritual offerings, wherein the Word formed itself in the wisdom, and carried itself forth all along, under Seth's and Enos's time, and manifested itself with Moses. Like as Enos's time was

---

[1] Ecclesiastical and temporal.   [2] Secular, and ecclesiastical.

first truly manifested with Abraham, with the promise in the Covenant, this time of Cainan continued in its manifestation and dominion under Moses, till Christ in the flesh.

38. The fifth time begins with Mahalaleel, and 'tis the reception or formation of the angelical form, viz. of the new regeneration out of the Covenant; and goeth secretly all along under the ministry of Enos, under Seth and Cainan, in the Word of the Promise, through all the three times; and did manifest itself with the fulfilling of the Covenant in the humanity of Christ, where the true Mahalaleel and angelical image, which did disappear in Adam, was again manifest in the humanity of Christ.

39. The sixth time begins with Jared, which is the spiritual priesthood under the external, where outwardly Seth, Enos, Cainan, Mahalaleel were in their times in their orders [or outward forms], as the ministry and preaching of Enos concerning God and his being and will; so likewise the preaching of Abraham concerning the Covenant and circumcision; also Moses with the Book of the Law. Under all these the inward priest Jared went along hiddenly. Inwardly this spiritual priesthood is Christ in the new man; and outwardly in the self-elected priests it is Babel.

40. This sixth time began in the kingdom of Christ after the death of the Apostles, when as men chose themselves teachers out of favour and outward respects. That is, it did even then first open itself out of the hiddenness[1] of the shadow, and put itself forth in the churches of stone, where the church stood in stead of the holy temple of Christ: then indeed the holy Jared, viz. Christ's voice, ruled in Christ's children internally; but externally the Cherub with the sword [did alone bear rule]. For the outward authority which these self-elected priests do manage is the sword of the Cherub; which is signified in the name Jared; which powerfully forceth itself forth all along in the word, in the Language of Nature.[2]

41. This sixth time is hidden and manifest; it is known, and also not known: for Christ said, *My kingdom is not of this world.* So that this time hath been fain to pass away, as it were, in a mystery under Antichrist, where inwardly, in the children of God, Christ's kingdom hath been manifest. But in the rest (who have also lived under this time,

[1] Or veil.
[2] That is, in the word Jared the Language of Nature doth emphatically express, that the sword of the Cherub should domineer the whole time of the sixth Seal among the priests, who should have taught the love of Jesus: but by this sword they fall. Amen.

and have been called Christians) only Babel and the Antichrist hath been manifest, both in the priests, and [in] their hearers. For they which have been born of God have heard the true Jared, viz. Christ's voice in them; but the others have heard only the outward voice in Babel, viz. disputation and contention about Christ's kingdom.

42. For all war which the Christians manage, is only the sword of the Cherub proceeding from Babel. True Christians wage no war; for they have broken the sword of the Cherub in the death of Christ, and are dead with Christ, and risen again in him, and they live no longer to the external might and dominion; for their kingdom is manifest in Christ, and is not of this world.

43. This sixth kingdom[1] beginneth after the death of the Apostles, and continueth with its outward government even to Mount Zion, till translated Enoch doth again appear in spirit and power. For Enoch is the prophetical root, and holdeth in his dominion[2] Noah, Moses, and the sword of Elias. At the end of this sixth time the outward Jared falleth, and with him that same outward building, viz. the city, Babel.

44. The sign of the end is deciphered[3] with such a figure:

(This Figure was thus deliniated in the Authors Manuscript, and soe received, by Abr:von Somervelt.

And denoteth the time when the triple cross doth open and declare

[1] Or sixth Seal.   [2] Or regiment.   [3] Or stands with such a figure.

itself in the voice of Enoch, as a manifestation of the holy Trinity, to make known the same in the figure and similitude in all visible things. Moreover, it denotes the conquest of the sword of the Cherub in Babel, when the force and violence of the city, Babel, turns its sword with the point downwards. Thirdly, it denotes the great rod and punishment upon Babel, which rod doth mightily advance its power on high. Fourthly, it denotes the wrathful enkindled fire of God's anger, which shall devour the sword and rod. This will be the end of the sixth time. The threefold cross doth betoken the time when this shall come to pass [or be fulfilled]. When the kingdom of Christ shall attain such a number, then is the sixth time wholly past.

45. The seventh time begins with Enoch,[1] viz. with the prophetical mouth, who declareth the secret wonders of God under all the six times; laying open what should be [and have been] done, and brings itself all along quite from under the veil of Noah, Abraham, and Moses, even into the kingdom of Christ, where this same prophetical spirit is[2] translated in Christ's spirit, till the end of the sixth time; then he manifests himself in the number of the triple cross. When the triple cross doth manifest itself, then stands the right triple crown upon the cross. And even then the Enochian prophet's mouth doth express and speak forth the great wonders of the triple cross; that is, he speaketh no more magically [viz. in types and parables], but sheweth the holy Trinity in the figure, viz. the formed word of God in all visible things, and revealeth all mysteries, within and without.

46. And even then is the time when Enoch, and the children under his voice, do lead a divine life, of which the first life of Enoch was a type. And then there is a blessed and golden year, till Enoch's last translation comes. And then the turba is born, which, when it shall enkindle its fire, the floor shall be purged, for it is the end of all time.

47. Enoch begat Methuselah, who was the man of the longest age, and was translated three hundred years after. This intimateth and declareth, that the spirit which in Enoch did bring forth a twig, viz. Methuselah, who attained the highest age, shall rule in the last and highest age [of the world], and in the meanwhile hide itself before that time, and remain as it were translated; as Enoch was translated, and was no more seen.

48. His translation was not a dying, or a putting off of nature and creature, but he went into the Mystery, between the spiritual and the outward world, viz. into Paradise; and is the prophetical root, out of

---

[1] Read the 35th question of the *Forty Questions of the Soul*.   [2] Or, hath been.

the stem of Adam, in the line of the Covenant, out of which spirit the prophetical mouth afterwards spake.

49. This spirit was translated in Christ's living voice, when it spake in the flesh, and must be silent till the voice of Jared is finished; then he proceedeth forth again from his first root, through all voices, viz. through the voice of Noah, who denounceth the deluge of anger to come upon Babel, and through the stock of Noah, and the whole forth-spreading propagation of his tree through all the lines, viz. through the Heathenish, Japhetical, and Sem's line,[1] and through Abraham's, and Nimrod's children in Babel, through Moses, and the prophets; and lastly through the voice of the manifested Word in the spirit of Christ; and revealeth the whole mystery of the Tree of Knowledge of Good and Evil.

50. For through his voice all the forementioned voices of the wonderful lines, whence the kingdoms of this world have had their rise, shall be changed into one voice and knowledge, and transplanted into one kingdom, viz. into the first tree of Adam, which is no longer called Adam, but Christ in Adam. All nations, tongues and speeches hear this voice; for it is the first word, whence the life of mankind proceeded; for all wonders do join again together in the word into one body, and that body is the formed divine Word, which at first with Adam did introduce itself into one only stem; and through him into a tree of manifold boughs, branches and fruits, to the contemplation of the divine wisdom, in the wonders of the powers, colours and virtues, according to evil and good.

51. This high tree doth disclose and clearly open itself, what it hath been in time, and what it shall be eternally; and in its manifestation,[2] Moses puts away his veil, and Christ his parables in his doctrine. And then the prophetical mouth of this tree of wonders doth express in divine power all the voices of the powers of the tree, whereby Babel taketh her end: and this is a wonder. And in this same wonder all numbers and names are made manifest, and this no man can hinder.

52. For that which is lost in the spirits of the letters shall be again found, and the spirit of the letter shall be found again in the formed word of the creation; and in the creation shall be found and known the Being of all Beings; and in the Being of all Beings the eternal understanding of the holy Trinity. Even then the contentions about the knowledge of God, his being and will, do cease. When the branches shall know that they stand in the tree they will never say that they

---

[1] Through Ham's, Japhet's and Sem's line.   [2] Disclosure, or opening.

are peculiar and singular trees; but they will rejoice in their stem, and they will see that they are altogether boughs and branches of one tree, and that they do all receive power and life from one only stem.

53. And here Moses shall keep sheep, and every sheep eateth his own pasture. Therefore observe: when this approacheth near to be fulfilled, then Noah denounceth the deluge, and Elias brings the flaming sword upon the false Israel; and the turba in the fire of the wrath devours the wild tree, with its fruits and branches. Let this be told thee, Babel.

54. For as concerning Enoch's divine time, our speech is taken from us, seeing Babel is not worthy of it, and also shall not see it. And likewise we must be silent concerning the discovery of the times of The Ancient, whose number shall stand open in the rose of the lily.

The Thirty-First Chapter

Of Enoch's Wonderful Line

1. M OSES writeth, *Enoch begat Methusalah* (Gen. v. 21). This name signifieth, in the Language of Nature, as much as a forth-proceeding[1] voice, which intimateth and denoteth the spirit of Enoch; which voice doth form[2] itself into a body, viz. into nature, and goeth forth in strong might through the word; and when the conceived or formed word is proceeded forth, it doth then contemplate itself. For the syllable *-SA-* is a fiery glimpse of light; and the syllable *-LAH-* is the forth-proceeded word, which beholdeth the property, of what kind of ens it is, wherein the word hath formed (or comprehended) itself. The divine sound beholdeth itself in the human ens and word, contemplating how the free will, proceeding from the human ens, hath introduced the divine voice or breath into a form of the spirit.

2. Now saith Moses, *And Methusalah begat Lamech.* The spirit did now put itself forth by Methusalah, even out of the ens into another twig; and called it Lamech, viz. a contemplation and beholding of the great affliction and wound, that the human ens was corrupted. For like as Lamech in Cain's line did express the wound of corruption [and misery that was broke in upon mankind], and spake of a seventy-and-sevenfold Racha upon the free will which did corrupt the life, even so here the divine spirit said: *the human ens is Lamech*; that is, the wound is too great, it prevaileth. Although the strong and mighty breath of God in Methusalah proceeded forth out of the prophetical voice, yet the ens, in propagation, did form itself in the corrupted nature in Lamech; that is, in two wills, as Moses saith, *The first Lamech in Cain's line took two wives,* viz. *Adah and Zillah.* Even so here likewise it would not be otherwise.

3. Now Moses saith, *And Lamech begat Noah* (Gen. v. 28). With this name the spirit goeth forth out of the wound of Lamech into the end of time, and bringeth the end into the beginning; for *NOAH* signifieth in the Language of Nature, *End and Beginning.* Now the spirit findeth in the end the holy word, which had espoused and incorporated itself in the Covenant, and saith, *This same shall comfort us in our labour and toil upon the earth which the Lord hath cursed* (Gen. v. 29).

---

[1] Or outgoing.   [2] Frame, or comprehend.

246

4. For the comfort of man must come out of the beginning and end; for in the beginning is, and was, the Word of God, which is the beginning of all things; and in the end is also the Word of God, which is the comfort of all things; that the creature shall be delivered from the vanity. Whereunto the spirit looked, and said, *this same* (where he meant the Word which would manifest itself in the humanity) *shall comfort us in our labour upon the earth which the Lord hath cursed*; for Noah could not comfort men, for he preached to them the rebuke, punishment and perdition. But he that was in the beginning and end, he comforted mankind in their labour and toil upon the earth, which they had in the curse and anger of God.

5. In this name, *Noah*, the spirit in Lamech looketh forwards into the end, and backwards into the beginning; and conceives itself in the beginning and end into a form, and calls the same, *Noah*, that is, an ark of the wonders which were in the beginning and end, and [in] the whole time; and displayeth or putteth forth this same spirit of the whole form through Noah into three branches, which went forth out of the tree of wonders, viz. out of the prophetical ens of Enoch in the human property. And thereof Moses saith, *And Noah begat Sem, Ham, and Japhet*. These were the three twigs of the second monarchy, under which most excellent mysteries are given us to be understood.

6. *Sem* signifieth an out-breathing divine lubet [or desire] out of the line of the Covenant, out of the life of man, and a comprehension of the lubet, viz. a type of that which secretly passed forth afterwards under the lubet. It pointeth at the humanity of Christ in the flesh, the type of which was Sem, viz. a representation [or express form] in the same lubet; in which lubet also the Covenant was made with Abraham, concerning the seed of the woman, wherein the blessing should appear.

7. The other branch or twig the spirit called *Ham*, which signifieth a strong breathing out of the centre of nature, and a gross amassment or compaction into a flesh. Which denoteth the earthly, natural, fleshly man, which holdeth Sem captive in itself; [understand by Sem] the inward man, which shall arise from death out of the earth.[1] Understand, the man proceeded from the limus of the good part of the earth, which was in Sem formed according to the divine lubet.[2]

8. We do not hereby understand the totally spiritual man, which is only as a spirit, but that [man] which is from the limus of the good

---

[1] *Note.*—Concerning the Resurrection.
[2] Or taken into the divine lubet.

part of the earth, which lieth captive in Ham, that is, in the gross bestial flesh, and is as dead without the divine lubet, which the spiritual Christus, viz. the totally spiritual man, shall put on at the end of the days in Noah [that is, out of the beginning and end]. This inward hidden man, his gross earthly brother Ham, viz. the gross earthly flesh (which is nothing worth) (John vi. 63), doth devour and swallow up.

9. And from the lubet of Sem springeth forth the third branch out of the centre of nature, where the divine lubet doth behold itself through nature; and this the spirit called *Japhet*, which is, in the Language of Nature, an appendix of Sem, a birth out of Cain's line of wonders, where the divine lubet doth bring itself through nature into a form of the wonders of the divine wisdom. With Sem it introduceth itself into a contemplation of the spiritual wonders in the holiness of God, and in Japhet into a natural wonder, viz. into the septenary of the eternal and [the] temporal nature; understand, into a form of the sevenfold wheel,[1] or life's forms, in which vital sphere[2] the Spirit of God appeareth as a glorious glee, or gleam of the wonders.

10. Sem is a type of the light-world, and Japhet is a type of the fire-world, where the light doth through-shine. Japhet a type [or image] of the Father; and Sem a type of the Son; but Ham is an image and type of the outward world.

11. For the type and figure of the three Principles stood in the three brethren, and clearly pointeth out the second monarchy, even to the end of the world; and withal shews what kind of men would thenceforward possess the world, viz. a spiritual world, and a natural world of wonders, and a bestial world of folly. These are the three sorts of men, viz. out of the stock and family of Sem came Israel, and out of Japhet's the Gentiles, who governed themselves in the light of nature, but Sem's [generation were disciplined] in the Covenant and word of God; but Ham [both in Sem and Japhet] he ruled himself in the bestial brutish property, against whom the curse of God was pronounced through the spirit in his father, Noah; for Paul said, *that flesh and blood shall not inherit the kingdom of God.*

12. And Moses speaketh now further, thus: *But when men began to multiply upon the earth, and daughters were born unto them; that the sons of God saw the daughters of men that they were fair, and took unto them wives as they pleased. Then said the Lord, Men will not suffer my spirit any more to reprove them, for they are flesh; yet I will make their days an hundred and*

---

[1] Orb, or sphere.   [2] Or, life's wheel.

twenty years[1] (Gen. vi. 1–3). Here Moses hath again the veil before his eyes; for he saith that *the children of God looked upon the beauty of the daughters of men, and took unto them wives according as they listed, and would not suffer the Spirit of God to reprove and admonish them.*

13. The meaning of it is this: The children of God, in whom the Spirit of God did manifest itself, looked, in the lust of the flesh after fleshly women, although they were of the generation and lineage of Ham, without God's Spirit; yet if they were but fair and beautiful for their lust of the flesh, they introduced the seed of the holy ens into such bestial vessels, and afterwards brought forth such tyrants,[2] and fleshly-minded men, who would not suffer the Spirit of God to rebuke them, for they were only flesh, without divine spirit and will.

14. They should not have mixed themselves with the bestial daughters, but looked after those in whom the Spirit of God was, even those who feared and loved God; but they looked only at the lust of their eyes and flesh, and corrupted the holy ens in the Covenant, in which God had espoused[3] and betrothed himself. Against these the spirit here complaineth, that they would not be instructed and reformed, but follow the lust of the flesh.

15. We see this very emphatically set forth unto us in Sem, Ham, and Japhet: that it is so, that the spirit would not that the children of God should mix themselves with the very carnal or bestial people; for after the deluge the spirit divideth the three brethren into three families, and would that each family should remain apart by itself.

16. For therefore came the deluge upon the earth, and destroyed these mixed people, and afterwards made a separation amongst them, according to the nature of the three Principles; that each property might possess its choir and line in the nature of the wonders; but yet it would not do. So that at last the spirit divides them with the confusion of the languages at Babel, that so they might come into a several division; for the properties of the tree did there divide and spread forth themselves into seventy-and-seven, viz. into the wonder of the nature of the formed word.

17. Now saith Moses, *And the Lord saw that the wickedness of man was great upon the earth, and that all their thoughts and imaginations in their hearts were only evil continually. Then it repented God that he had made man on the earth, and it grieved him at his very heart. And he said, I will destroy man which I have created from off the face of the earth; both man, and beast, and creeping thing, and all the fowls of the air; for it repenteth me that I have*

[1] I will yet give them 120 years' respite. [2] Giants. [3] Incorporated.

made them (Gen. vi. 5–7). These are marvellous and wonderful sayings, that the spirit saith it repented God that he had made man, and the creatures. Who would understand this without divine knowledge; that anything should *grieve* the *unchangeable* God! Reason would be ready to say, Hath he not known aforehand what would be? How can his will, which is himself, grieve and *repent*?

18. Here we must go into the centre. In God there is no grieving or repentance; nothing can grieve or trouble him. But there is a grieving in his expressed formed Word; for it repenteth the formed Word in the devils that the ens of light is turned into an ens of darkness. It grieveth the devil that he did not continue an angel. Also it repenteth the wicked man eternally that he stood not in the divine ens in the formed Word, and hath turned the power of the Word into malice and iniquity. Also there is a grieving in the formed Word in nature, over all kinds of creatures, that the property of the wrath in the curse of the anger doth rule and domineer in the formed expressed Word. It grieveth the love-ens of the Word, that the devil and wrath domineereth in it, and corrupteth and destroyeth many.

19. Now when God saith *it repenteth him*, it is to be understood according to the creation of the *formed* Word, not according to the eternal-speaking Word, which is unchangeable, but according to the good property in the creation, that it must be laden with evil against its will. For the spirit saith in Moses, *And it grieved him in his heart.* Yes! it did truly grieve or trouble him *in his HEART*. The good ens of the earth, which went also along with it into a compaction, which is from the spiritual world's property, from the holy word, the same was in the sin [or fall of man] captivated in death, and shut up in the curse in the earth. Now the formed Word grieved at it, and troubled or affected the eternal-speaking Word, viz. God's heart.

20. For our soul crieth unto God's heart, viz. unto the eternal-speaking Word, and moveth, troubleth or affecteth the same, that it should move itself in us according to its love. Now the human word worketh in the divine; and stirreth the divine; so that the divine [word] entereth into our sorrow for sin, and helpeth us to repent of our sins. For the spirit in Moses said, when Lamech had begotten Noah, *This same shall comfort us in our labour.*

21. This was now the spirit of the beginning and end of all things; it repented through nature of the iniquity of man, and [grieved] at the captivity of the vanity of the creatures; and wrought repentance into the holy eternal-speaking Word. The spirit in the formed Word of the

whole creation of this world said, *It grieveth me, that I have brought me into such an evil property in the creatures*: And wrought repentance into the living eternal-speaking Word, from whence the out-breathed formed Word has flown forth and proceeded.

22. For that this is so, let us take an example on our repentance: We cannot work any repentance, unless our inward human soul doth repent that it hath made, formed or brought forth the beast of vanity in itself. But if it will repent, then its formed word must enter or make its earnest approach into the heart of God, and press the same with an incessant importunity, and move in it. And now, when this comes to pass, then presently the deluge cometh upon the evil man of the vain will, which must forthwith be drowned in its sorrow in the word of death. Here, then, God repenteth in man; that the evil beast, full of sinful desire, is born; and in this same divine sorrow it must be drowned in God's love, and die unto the wrathful evil life and will.

23. Now understand aright God's sorrow or repentance in the creature of the creatures. The spirit in the whole creation, even in every life which moveth in the fire and air, said, *It grieveth me, that I have figured this image of vanity on me*; and this sorrow of the formed spirit in the expressed Word grieved, that is, moved the eternal-speaking Word in it. Then said the eternal Word, *I will yet give them an hundred and twenty years respite* (for even so long the time in the dominion or government of Seth's spirit did continue), and then the turba in all flesh shall perish or be thrown down. For this sorrow was nothing else but that the Word in the Covenant did grieve at the misery and vanity of man, and would comfort mankind by the Covenant through Noah, which comfort did first open itself in Abraham, viz. in Enos, his manifestation.

24. For the comfort went forth in the love of the Covenant, and opened itself with its branch at its right limit or juncture of time; for God hath confined all things into a certain limit, when everything shall come to pass. And from the comfort of the moving Word in the Covenant proceeded forth the judgment, that the old Adamical man, with all his desires, concupiscences and lusts, should, in the Covenant (when the same should open itself in the flesh) be drowned and mortified in the same new humanity of Christ; and out of the comfort of the Covenant a new human spirit and will should arise, which should live in righteousness and purity; of which the deluge was a type.

25. For the grief or repentance came out of the Covenant upon the

formed Word in the life; and therefore, seeing the same Word repented of the vanity, thereupon the vanity of the creature must be drowned; for the will in the Covenant went forth from the vanity, and grieved the life of God, and moved the matrix of nature in the water's birth, and drowned the fiery wrath in the fire's nature.

26. But the spirit in Noah doth especially complain here against man, for their Sodomitical, bestial concupiscence and filthy lusts of the flesh, viz. against unchastity, and unclean lascivious wantonness; and also against the high oppressors and tyrants, who put forth and advanced themselves in their own lust, and would rule and domineer, and no longer suffer the Spirit of God to rule in them, and reprove them that they had intruded themselves, to compel and tyrannise over one another without command. All this was an abomination before God; and it grieved the spirit in the formed Word that it had brought forth such evil beasts, and would no longer endure them.

27. Even this same prophetical spirit, whose root did open and display itself in Enoch, which also by Enoch did propagate and put forth its line with its branches; which also by Noah did grieve at the wickedness and iniquity of mankind, and drowned them with the deluge, even this is he which now also doth grieve at the great sins and vanity of men: for his mouth is at present opened; he hath been translated in the Spirit of Christ. Now this Word which became man doth repent at the vanity and wickedness of men; that its children of the new Covenant will not give willing obedience to the Spirit of Christ.[1] Therefore this prophetical mouth doth now disclose and put forth itself, for it is the time of its manifestation, and proclaimeth the great deluge of God's anger, and the flaming sword of Elias, who also was translated into the Mystery; for he must draw forth his sword in the turba.

28. Let this be told thee, Babel: he complaineth mightily against thy bestial unchastity and tyranny; against thy own usurped power, force and violence wherewith thou art proud and wanton, and hast thereby set up thyself in God's government. He will drown thee with thy tyranny and bestial wantonness in the fire of anger. Seeing thou wilt not repent thee of thy vanity, therefore he repenteth through thee, with the turba; and will drown thy turba, that so his repenting may be made manifest in his children, and also his refreshing comfort and consolation might be manifested out of his repentance.

29. For without God's repenting there is in us no true sorrow or

_____
[1] Suffer the Spirit of Christ to draw them.

252

repentance for the vanity; for the natural spirit desireth not to repent, yea, if it could be more wrathful, malicious, evil and vain, it would please, love and delight itself therein; for it is nature's spirit, strength and might. But the Word of God, which in the creation did impress and give itself into the human ens for a sovereign powerful [and holy] life, the same [incorporated engrafted Word of life], if it be stirred and moved, doth repent and grieve that it hath such an evil beast in nature on it; that saith, *It repenteth me that I have created the evil beast in nature.*

30. But this sorrow is not a sorrow to annihilation, as if he would have no more to do with the creature, but it is a sorrow which saddeth and moveth God's heart, viz. the holy divine Word, and setteth the natural spirit a time for to repent, that so it might enter into divine sorrow; but if it doth not, then he will drown the natural spirit in its evil will and ways, as came to pass in the deluge.

31. God said, *The earth is corrupt, and full of perverseness; and the end of all flesh is come before me, I will destroy them.* Here again is a great mystery, in that God said, *the earth was corrupt before him; that all flesh had corrupted its way; and that the earth was filled with perverseness through them* [and lo: he would destroy them]. The earth was afore with Cain accursed according to the vanity's property; but now he saith also in this place, *all flesh hath corrupted its way, the end of all flesh is come before me.* This is not so mean and slight a thing as one would look on it to be; for the spirit complaineth against *all flesh,* that all things were become vain in his sight, and full of perveseness.

32. Now saith reason, a beast doth not sin, it doth according to its nature's property; how can any perverseness be attributed to it? So far doth reason go, and further it knows not; also it understands nothing of the divine Mystery. It understands nothing of the formed Word that hath formed itself through the nature of time. It saith only, God hath created and made: and considereth not that all things are created in the Word, that the Word hath introduced and com- pacted itself into an ens. Also it will know nothing of the eternal spiritual nature of divine manifestation; it understands nothing of the ground or original of the outward visible world, with its creatures; when it saith, God hath made all things out of nothing, then it meaneth that he hath so spoken it forth, and yet it is wholly blind and senseless in it. It looketh only upon the outward colour, and knoweth not from whence it taketh its original; thus it is only learned in the external colour, and prateth of the painted work of the

outside and shell; and concerning the ens whence the colour ariseth, it is dumb and senseless.

33. The spirit complaineth against all flesh upon the face of the earth, even whatsoever hath breath and sense.[1] The outward nature had corrupted itself in every kind of life, and brought the formed, expressed Word into an ens of vanity; this was the perverseness and violent self-willedness of the natural life. The spirit of nature, which taketh its original in the fire, had exalted itself in its fiery property, and introduced itself into a wrathful life, and driven itself even to the utmost end of meekness.

34. For the devil was an insinuating predominant prince in the wrath's property, which had incited and stirred up the centre of the outward nature in the fire's matrix, and had not only corrupted the natural life of man, but also the creatures; for he moved and acted man in God's anger, who used the creatures for their service and food, so that the curse and the vanity was also manifest in every life, that man in his conversation stood in the curse and vanity, and so came, in the vanity in the curse, even into the abyss, viz. into the end of this world. Therefore said the spirit, the end of all flesh, in its perverseness and violence, is come before me. Every life had, through the vanity of man, brought itself unto the end of the outward nature; and the throat of wrath was open in nature, and would devour and swallow up all things in the wrath.

35. For the kingdom of God's anger, viz. the dark world, had gotten the upper hand in its property, and brought the good part of nature even unto the end. Therefore the formed, expressed Word did move, or repent through every life of this vanity, that it should bear the abomination on it; and said, that it would destroy with water the womb or pregnatress of vanity proceeding from the fire's mother, and break its power and force.

36. For before the flood the fire's root was more strong and potent than the water's root, and that, from the original of the fiery motion; that is, the Fiat stood in the fiery property, and compacted the earth and stones. So that there was then a great wrath poured forth in nature, and that, by reason of the casting out or ejection of the hierarch Lucifer into the darkness.

37. And here, by the flood or deluge, the force and violence was taken from the wrathful fire root in the centre of nature. For the repenting or grieving of the formed Word was nothing else but a

---

[1] Text, liveth in the air and fire.

type of Christ, where the eternal living divine Word in the human property did repent and grieve in the formed creatural word, at our sins and vanity, and mortified the same vanity in his death in the creature;[1] and drowned the formed creatural word in the human property with the divine water of love and meekness in the holy heavenly blood.

38. So also in this place, the formed Word grieved at the vanity of the creatures, in that they were laden therewith, and brought the life of all the creatures into death; and in its sorrow moved the meekness of the water-source in nature, so that all the fountains of the deep did open themselves, as Moses saith, and devoured the fire-source in the water. This signifieth unto man the Baptism of Christ, where the fire-source of the soul in God's anger was, in the Word of Christ's Covenant, baptised with the regenerated water of the spirit (understand the spiritual water), which shall quench the fire of God's anger. As it was above mentioned concerning the seven times, that each time of the seven degrees of nature hath brought itself unto its end; and in the end there was a sorrow for the abomination; and in the repentance and sorrow the turba was broken and destroyed.

39. Now behold here aright: by Noah, with the flood, the second time, viz. Seth's time, was at the end; and with Adam, in the fall, when he lusted to eat of the vanity, the first time was at the end.

40. In Adam the Word repented, and gave itself with a Covenant into the life, to help comfort and restore the life. And by Noah the Word repented, and moved all the fountains of the deep in nature, and drowned the wrath, and opened the Covenant of grace.

41. And when the time of Enos was at the end, in the days of the children of Nimrod, the Word grieved at the vanity of man, that they would not know God, and drowned the understanding of the one only tongue, and divided it, and gave by[2] its repentance the certain understanding in the Covenant with Abraham.

42. And when the time of Cainan was at the end, that the children of Abraham's Covenant were compelled in the vanity of servitude, the Word grieved at the vanity, and destroyed Pharaoh; and afterwards all the men of the children of Israel in the wilderness, save Joshua and Caleb, and gave them, out of its sorrow and repentance, the Law of his Covenant: a true type of Christ, who should drown the abomination in his blood.

43. Thus also when Mahalaleel's time was come to the end, the

---

[1] Died from the vanity.   [2] Or, out of.

Word grieved in the deepest repentance, and brought the life of God in Christ Jesus into the formed creatural Word in the human ens, and drowned the turba in the human ens, with God's love and mercy, and gave them the spirit of comfort, and the Gospel.

44. Thus even now also, where the time of Jared is at the end, which hath been covered with Babel, even now, at this present, the Word doth repent and grieve at our great vanity, and will destroy the abomination with the devouring jaws of wrath: with sword, hunger, fire, and death; and giveth, out of its sorrow, grief and repentance, a lily out of Enoch's mouth, in God's sweetness.

45. And when Enoch's line shall be at the end, that the vanity doth again grow in the turba, then cometh the greatest grief and sorrow of all, upon the nature of the wonders; that it is at the end, and there is no more any remedy for it. Even then cometh the last motion with[1] the turba in the first Principle of the eternal nature, and swalloweth up the outward nature in the fire. Even then the formed Word shall be wholly freed from vanity, and giveth, by[2] its last repentance, the holy spiritual world. Amen.

[1] Or, of.   [2] From, or out of.

The Thirty-Second Chapter

Of the Covenant between God and Noah

1. GOD said to Noah, *I will establish a Covenant with thee, and thou shalt go into the ark with thy sons, and thy sons' wives with thee* (Gen. vi. 18). A great, pregnant and remarkable example we have here in Noah and his children. The Covenant was made with Noah; for his spirit was a discovery or beaming forth of the formed Word in him, in the beginning and end of time; and the beginning and end was the eternal Word, which had espoused itself in the Covenant. In which Covenant the soul of Noah, viz. the formed Word of the eternal nature, found grace, and obtained the confirmation of the Covenant of grace.

2. As his name doth properly and peculiarly signify, in the Language of Nature, a beholding of the beginning and end. In this same beginning and end, viz. in the eternal-speaking Word of the Father, which would manifest and open itself again in the human life, grace was opened and presented to Noah, so that God did establish and confirm the Covenant with him.

3. And here we have a very excellent, and an emphatical example, which is exceedingly worth the mentioning, in the three sons of Noah, which in their properties were sprung forth from the stock of Adam in a threefold line. For we see that three nations [several sorts of people] did arise from them, and that God did include them all three, with their wives, in the Covenant of grace, and commanded them also to go into the ark, into the second monarchy, and did not exclude the fleshly Ham.

4. This is first highly to be considered: that a gate of grace standeth open to all men, and that God hath not set any election or predestination in nature; but the election or choice doth arise out of the free will, when it turneth itself from the good into the evil.

5. Secondly, it is a type of the three Principles, viz. Sem is a type of the spiritual light-world in the Covenant; and Japhet of the fire-world, which should be a sojourner of the light-world, and a mirror of the great joy in the light-world; and Ham is a figure of the limus of the earth, to which the curse and the anger of God doth hang. All these three, God took into the Covenant with Noah, and brought them into the ark.

6. For every man hath these three worlds upon him, and in him; and the Covenant in the Word was therefore given, that the whole man should be redeemed.

7. For Japhet signifieth the fire-soul; and Sem the image of God out of the light-world, viz. the spirit out of the holy Word; and Ham betokeneth the limus of the earth, with the outward dominion or region of the air, and of the magical ethereal constellations, together with the body, which shall be freed by the Covenant from the curse, and arise again out of the earth. The three brothers were a type of these three Principles.

8. Not that one did wholly arise out of one Principle alone, No! Sem and Japhet had likewise Ham's property in them, as did plainly manifest itself afterwards in the Jews, who became so wicked and vile a people. Only, we speak here of the superior dominion or predominant property, of which Principle the creature hath had in the outward life in its figure.

9. Ham has the outward earthly elemental kingdom in the figure, which stood in the curse. Therefore his image [or person] was also cursed of his father, in the spirit; for the earthly image shall not inherit the kingdom of God; but he also had a soul from Adam, which stood in the Covenant; but the free will doth very seldom work any good thing in such a lodging, and very easily attains the curse upon the soul. As we see that the curse did afterwards come upon this generation; that Israel must destroy [them] by their entrance into the Land of Promise; albeit they did not wholly destroy [them] all, yet the curse was come upon them.

10. There is a very great mystery in the ark of Noah, which the Lord commanded him to build after that manner, and shewed him how high, how long, and how broad it should be, and directed also that it should have three several stories; also concerning the creatures which he commanded him to bring thereinto; which is such a mystery, that the wicked malicious man is not worthy to know it. And we also shall not mention it in the ground [or depth of its meaning]. For it hath its time, wherein it shall be opened, viz. in the lily-time, when Babel hath its end. But yet to set down somewhat for a furtherance and direction to our fellow-branches, to whom in its due time it shall break forth and grow out of our ens of this lily (which also shall be a rose in the lily-time), we will set it down in a hidden exposition.

11. The mystery of the holy Trinity: also the three Principles:

also the three sons of Noah: also the three men that appeared to Abraham in the plain of Mamre: also the vision of the great temple in Ezekiel: and the whole Revelation of John belongeth unto this figure: also the temple of Jerusalem.

12. Set before thee the figure of the ark, with its three stories, with its height, length, and breadth, and place it in the three Principles. And in the three Principles open the mysteries of the hierarchy[1] of Christ in the three distinctions of heavens, which yet are only one; but in three properties, as fire, light, and air are three, and yet but one. Place in these distinctions [or several differences] the three sons of Noah; and go out of their properties into their monarchy in the world, which continueth to the end of days. Also set before thee the formed Word according to all the three Principles; and so you will find the ground of all. Especially set before thee, Moses, Elias, and Christ, in their appearance and transfiguration upon the mount: the ark of Noah is the first type of all these figures; and the hierarchy of Christ is the fulfilling of them at the end of days. Enough to ours.

13. *And the Lord said, Come thou and thy whole house into the ark, for thee have I seen righteous before me at this time*[2] (Gen. vii. 1). The Scripture saith elsewhere, *Before thee none living is righteous, if thou wilt impute sin.* But here God saith, *I have seen thee righteous before me at this time.* The creature was not the righteous one, without evil; but HE, who at this time did in Noah open and manifest himself out of the Covenant, who grieved at the evil of this time, and introduced his sorrow into God's love and mercy, and so brought the righteousness of the mercy into the sorrow, and manifested the grieving mournful spirit in the ens of the Covenant in the creature. Thus Noah was righteous before God at this time, when the Covenant did move itself in him.

14. This time is [or signifieth] the motion of the Covenant, which made Noah righteous. For this was the time when Noah received life in the womb. The spirit looked with his first glimpse of life out of the divine ens of the formed Word into the beginning whence the life was come, and into the end which was the kingdom of Christ. In this aspect [or divine glimpse] the life of Noah receives the righteousness in the mark of the Covenant at this time, for that was the time in him wherein he was found righteous.

15. God brought eight persons into the ark, and of the clean beasts seven and seven,[3] the male and its female. The seven persons point at the seven properties of the natural life, that God will have

---

[1] Or, hierarchies.   [2] Or, generation.   [3] Or, seven pair.

children out of all the properties into his eternal ark. The eighth person was Noah, and in Noah was the Righteous One, that was the Covenant, out of which the kingdom of Christ should come; therein stood the ark of Noah. But the ark hath three stories, which are the three Principles in one only divine manifestation, for each property of the three hath its own peculiar heaven and certain choir in itself.

16. The seven pair of clean beasts are even the very same mystery, for the centre hath seven properties; and yet they are but one in the divine power. But according to the eternal nature there are seven of them as to the divine manifestation. Which signifieth unto us, that the creatures were brought forth into life out of this sevenfold ens, where each degree hath again seven in it, to its manifestation, whence the infiniteness, viz. the form of God's wisdom, doth appear and shine forth, and that in the formed wisdom, whose image and figure shall not vanish or perish. Although their life, and the creature, which hath a temporal beginning, doth pass away; but the form shall remain in the divine wisdom, viz. in the ens of the formed Word in the figure, to the praise of God's wondrous deeds. Indeed, not to a restoration of their creature, but for a visible mirror or looking-glass in the formed wisdom of God.

17. But of the unclean beasts God commanded Noah to take only one pair of each kind with him into the ark. Understand it thus: The unclean beasts have, on one part, their original out of the limus of the earth, according to the grossness, viz. according to the dark world's property. Although their spirit taketh its rise out of nature, yet we are to consider the difference in nature in respect of that which came forth, in the Verbum Fiat, out of the source of the dark world's property, into a compaction; whence such an ens doth adhere unto many an unclean creature. And it signifieth unto us, in the right understanding, that the dark world, viz. the unclean world, shall appear before the wisdom of God only in one manifest form, viz. in the darkness. But the properties shall be manifest only in the creatures themselves, each in its own peculiar self and nature.

18. For the formed wisdom as to the darkness is the heaven of them all, which is manifest only according to the darkness, wherein the property lieth hidden, according to which God calleth himself an angry zealous God. Out of this dark heaven every creature receiveth its power and virtue according to its property. According as its hunger is, so it sucketh with its desire from thence: and it signifieth unto us, that the unclean beasts, each kind of them in their form, shall

appear only in one form in the wisdom of the darkness, viz. in the figure, as they were created in the beginning, and not in seven properties according to the centre of nature in all properties according to light and darkness, as the rest shall; for they are in the figure of the first Principle, which in the pure heaven shall be manifest only in one property, viz. according to the burning [property] wherein the light is moved,[1] and the wisdom formed.

19. But here I will warn the Reader to understand our sense and meaning aright, and not to put me calves, cows and beasts, in their spirit and body, into heaven. I speak only of the eternal formed wisdom, whence evil and good hath been brought to manifestation.

20. Moreover, God said to Noah, *For yet seven days, will I cause it to rain upon the earth forty days and forty nights; and every living substance which I have made will I destroy from off the face of the earth.* Wherefore did God say, *after seven days* the flood shall come? Why not presently, either sooner or later; why doth he set even *seven* days? In this the seven properties of nature are contained mystically, in which the Verbum Fiat had introduced itself into an ens, viz. into the formed Word; that is, into the creation of the world; in which creation the formed Word repented at the vanity of all creatures, and moved itself through the generatress of nature in the formed Word, to destroy the turba.

21. Now the first motion and information of the Word in the creation, with the six days' works and the day of rest, being seven days, was brought into a form of time, and it yet stood so, in its form. Now then, when the Word (which said it would drown every life with water) did open, disclose and manifest itself through the seven properties of nature to the water's birth, it came to pass in the form wherein the Word had given in itself with the creation, viz. in the same sevenfold operation, which should open itself in its own peculiar order, and not enkindle or elevate any one property above the other; but if all seven would open and manifest themselves according to the water's birth, then the only fountain or head-spring of all the deeps in the centre of nature should break open. And seeing they came in seven days into their outward, formed, working dominion, the speaking Word did also proceed in the opening thereof in seven days unto the limit for its manifestation of that which it desired; as namely, to drown the turba.

22. And let none look upon this as a fiction, or laugh at it, for

---

[1] Movable and formable.

whosoever doth so, doth not yet understand our spirit and meaning at all. Nor hath [he] any knowledge at all of the formed Word, but hath only an external understanding of nature, like [a brute beast or] a bird that flyeth in the air, and knoweth not what the essence is.

23. Now saith reason, Wherefore did it rain just forty days and forty nights; could not God have drowned the world in one hour?

Answer: In the space of forty days the turba was borne in the human property, viz. Adam before his Eve stood in the image of God forty days and nights, which yet in the image of God were only as one day. There he wrought forty days in his desire, viz. in the Fiat, and brought forth the turba in himself, in his lust after the grossness of the earth: the good part of the limus of the earth, which was drawn, in the Verbum Fiat, into a mass, did hunger after the evil, gross part, which was of the dark world's property.

24. And even in forty days the grossness did arise in his imagination in the good ens, viz. a self-full will to the perception or intromission of the gross earthliness, in which evil and good was made manifest. And when this same will's spirit was arisen in the desire, it entered into its own self-full dominion, and in its fiery and earthly might strongly suppressed the holy spiritual ens in the word of power. Even then Adam fell asleep, viz. into an impotency and disability of the angelical spiritual world, and the woman was taken out of him; and both were in this turba formed[1] unto the outward natural life.

25. This turba is that wherein God did also set the curse, which with Noah was first at the end, which God said, *The end of all flesh is come up before me*. And out of this forty-days-produced turba, the fountains of the deep did arise in the water source, and drowned the turba in the flesh of these sexes.

26. For from the sin of Adam came the deluge over the world; and this forty-days-produced turba was the sin in the flesh. Otherwise, if the water-fountain had not opened itself, the fire-fountain had proceeded forth out of the turba in the wrath of God. Therefore God said, It repented him, that he had made the creatures; and his sorrow went into the turba, and drowned it.

27. And let the Reader be put in mind, that so often as he findeth the number forty in the holy Scripture, that it altogether, in the beginning, pointeth at the forty-days-produced turba. For instance,

[1] Text, figured.

the forty days of Moses upon Mount Sinai: the forty years in the wilderness: also the forty hours of Christ in the grave. Also the forty days after his resurrection, before his ascension, do all belong unto this; and all the numbers forty in the secret and mystical prophetical sayings of the prophets: for out of this turba the prophet is arisen, with his prophecy.

28. But in that I say, that if the water-fountain had not been opened, the fire-fountain would have broken forth: is also true. For the children in the turba would have also burnt Noah in the ark with fire, if the most high had not hindered and prevented them with the water: for the fire's turba was moved in them. This was the world's end, or the end of all flesh: for at the end all shall be purified and purged in the fire's turba; for it will enkindle itself.

29. There is a very great mystery in that which the spirit saith in Moses: *Noah was five hundred years old when he begat Sem, Ham and Japhet*, which otherwise is against the ordinary course of nature, to beget children in such a natural age. Also there is a very great mystery in that God said that he *would give the world an hundred and twenty years respite*; and yet the deluge came in the six-hundredth year of Noah, viz. in the hundredth year after the warning or notice thereof. And it signifieth the abbreviation of time in its natural course, and also the end of the world, how that there shall be an abbreviation or shortening of time in the circle of the conclusion of all beings, of which we will mention something in a Treatise by itself, if the same be permitted us.[1]

30. When Noah entered into the ark, Moses saith, *The Lord shut him in* (Gen. vii. 16). The intimate signification of the spirit here is: He shut up the second time or age of the world, which was at the end, seeing the fire would fain have moved itself. Therefore the Lord shut it up with water, and herewith also [he opened] the gate of his entrance to go forth in the third time, and begin the second monarchy in the outward world: for the first time was in Paradise; the second, under Seth's manifestation: in the third, Enos's manifestation should be opened and set forth.

31. And Moses saith further, *And the waters stood upon the earth one hundred and fifty days. Then God remembered Noah, and every living thing, and all the cattle that was with him in the ark: and God caused a wind to pass over the earth, and the waters asswaged. And the fountains of the deep and the windows also of heaven were stopped* (Gen. viii. 1-3). Moses saith, *God*

---

[1] Query: this Treatise by itself.

remembered Noah. Now reason thinketh, had he then forgotten him? whereas he is present to all things, and is himself through all, and in all things. The spirit in Moses doth here hang a veil before the Mystery, that the natural man doth not understand it.

32. God's *remembrance* here is the beginning of the third time, even the beginning of the second monarchy in the four elements with the creatures. For in the Covenant made with Noah the second monarchy was comprehended, which went forth out of the centre of the generatress through the divine wisdom in nature.

33. And Moses speaketh further: *When the waters were abated the ark set itself down upon the mount Ararat* (Gen. viii. 4). This name [Ararat] doth plainly hint unto us, in the Language of Nature, a mountain, or a compacting and an amassing of an essence out of the centre of nature, even out of the wrathfulness, seeing the anger of God had then reposed itself there. The ark stood upon the allayed anger. But the last syllable in this word Ara-RAT, doth signify that the wrath of the eternal nature proceeding from the centre hath betook or formed itself into an active dominion; and would thenceforward ride through nature, as a warrior, and mightily exercise its power and violence in the human property, whereby they would undertake wars, and advance themselves in pride, pomp and power, and butcher and slay one another, eagerly contending about this mountain of the wrath's might [or severe human authority].

34. This mountain, Ararat, denotes the houses of the great ones or domineering potentates upon the earth, viz. the great castles, forts and bulwarks, the mighty mountains of the power, violence and strength of the rich; and also the high nobility, sprung up from the mystery of the great world; upon which kingdom the ark of Noah hath set down itself. But the Covenant with Noah, viz. the kingdom of Christ, hath set itself to be an eternal Lord over this mountain of the warlike might and force of arms sprung up from the anger of God; which dominion and reigning power of Christ shall abolish and take away the kingdom of this mountain, and quite suppress it. And it denoteth unto us truly, fundamentally and exactly, that this power and authority upon the earth would take upon it, in its own power, the ark of Noah, viz. the divine Covenant, and carry it; yea, put it on as a garment, and proudly perch up itself therein, as if it had the kingdom of Christ in its own power.

35. [And also it shews and denotes unto us] how that this mountain of the wrathful anger of God in the human property [or in man's

nature] would beautify, trim up and adorn itself with the ark of Noah; and would proclaim it to be the holy ark of Christ; and yet it would be founded only upon the wrathful anger, and be only an antichristian kingdom. Which indeed would carry the ark, viz. the name of divine holiness in the mouth but its heart would be only this mountain, a vessel and confused heap of God's wrath; and yet it would make devout shows of holiness, and glory in having the ark upon itself, but the aim and intent of the heart would be set upon the strongholds, the preferment, power and riches of the world.

36. Furthermore, it denotes that the potent and mighty of the world would build the ark, viz. the service and worship of God, upon their heart and reason, with great stone houses, and churches, and that these houses thus built up of stone should be their God, whom they would serve in the ark; and they would wage war for the houses of stone of their own contriving and framing, and for their devices and opinions therein maintained, and contend about the figure of the true ark. And not consider that the ark standeth upon their mountain, that God hath set it above them, and that they ought to walk under God's dominion, in humility, and suffer the ark to stand upon them; and not usurp unto themselves the power of the Holy Ghost, or take it away, and bind him unto their feigned power and hypocritical forms, and command him to be silent, as they do, in that they cry with full mouth: lo! here is an assembly of divines: here is the true Church of Christ: this you must believe and do: this is the law and ordinance of the Church. No, the ark stands above them, they are under, as the mount Ararat was underneath the ark. Christ is the ark, and not the contrived heaps of stone [or any form of man's devised worship or opinion]. All assemblies, congregations, or synods are under the ark Christ, and not above [it], for the ark of Noah placed itself above the mountain: to signify that the mountain must bear the ark. We must bear the ark of Christ upon us, and have the temple of this ark within us.

37. Furthermore, it denotes how the figure of this ark, viz. the spiritual kingdom upon the earth,[1] would place itself upon the mountain of power, domination, and lordliness, and would rule with the mountain in the ark; and take upon itself to meddle with the worldly dominions and authority; and bring the mountain, viz. the power of the secular arm, above the ark: whereas the ark ought to stand upon

[1] Ecclesiastical, clergical priesthood.

the mountain, and Noah, with the Covenant, to remain in the ark, till the Lord bid him come forth, that is, till Christ deliver the ark to his Father.

38. And Moses saith further, *At the end of forty days, when the ark had set itself down, Noah sent forth a raven, to see whether the water was abated, but the raven flew to and fro till the waters were dried up from off the face of the earth* (Gen. viii. 6, 7). The raven denotes the earthly man, and shews how that he would first put forth himself upon the mountain Ararat, that is, advance himself in his selfhood and earthly lust, and build up his kingdom in the second monarchy.

39. And though he came forth out of the ark, yet he would fly to, and again in, the kingdom of his selfhood, and not return into the ark, from whence he departed in Adam, and would be only a covetous muck-worm, and a greedy devourer of fleshly temporal pleasure in his own will; and remain as the raven, and not return to the ark, desiring to enter into it, but mind only to possess the kingdom of this world in glory and state. Also it betokens that the generation of this raven would have the chief place, pre-eminence and government, in the second monarchy (like the devil in the wrath of God), as histories witness that it so came to pass.

40. *Afterwards he sent forth a dove from him, to see if the waters were abated upon the earth; but when the dove found no rest for the sole of her foot, she returned again unto him unto the ark; and he put forth his hand and took her to him into the ark* (Gen. viii. 8, 9). This set forth and denotes the figure of God's children; who soon after come also under the government of the raven's property, and are brought into the government of this world; for they are also with Adam gone forth out of the ark, to behold and prove this evil corrupt world, and live therein. But when their spirit can find no rest in the earthly dominion, then they come again before the ark of Noah, which is set open in Christ, and Noah receiveth them again in Christ, into the first ark, whence Adam departed.

41. Moreover, the raven betokens the sharp Law of Moses, in the fiery might under God's anger, which binds and slays man, and brings him not into the ark. But the dove betokens the gospel of Christ, which brings us again into the ark, and saves the life. For the mount Ararat doth, as an exact type and figure, point out unto us the kingdom of Moses; and the Ark, wherein the life was kept and preserved, signifieth the humanity of Christ.

42. *And he stayed yet another seven days; and again he sent forth a dove*

out of the ark; and it came to him about evening, and lo! she had plucked off *an olive leaf, and brought it in her mouth. And he stayed yet other seven days;* *and let a dove fly forth out of the ark, which returned not to him any more* (Gen. viii. 10, 11). The spirit in Moses sheweth by these three doves, and the raven, which Noah sent forth out of the ark, a great mystery, which albeit he doth not clearly unfold, yet for certain is couched therein. The raven doth also denote the Law of Moses in nature, which will remain in its selfhood, and will not return in true resignation and self-denial, under the obedience of God, but will enter in to God by its own strength, power, and ways.

43. The first dove signifieth the prophetical spirit, which arose under Moses, viz. under the outward Law and offerings, and pointed through the offering into the ark of Noah, and Christ. This prophetical spirit went all along through the office of Moses; it indeed flew under Moses, but it tended again into the ark with its prophecy, as the first dove which Noah sent forth flew indeed into the world, but came again into the ark of Christ.

44. The second dove with the olive branch, which also came again to Noah into the Ark, denotes the Word in the Covenant of Noah, which came forth out of the holy ark of God into this world, viz. into our humanity, and plucked off an olive leaf in the world, and brought it to Noah, that is, it plucked off a branch from our humanity, and took it into the holy Word, viz. the mouth of God, as the dove the olive leaf, and brought the branch to holy Noah, that is, to God the Father. But that it was an olive leaf, denoteth the unction of the holy spirit, that the same should anoint the humanity, and bring it again with this dove into the holy ark.

45. The third dove which Noah let fly, which came not again to the ark, betokeneth the kingdom of Antichrist upon the earth, which indeed is flown forth with its doctrine out of the ark, but its spirit remaineth only upon the earth, feeding upon the fat grass [upon the riches, honour, and beauty of this world], and so it stayeth only in selfhood [and returns not to the ark]; it indeed maketh devout shows of holiness to God, and giveth good words, but the man, with his senses and reason, will not forsake the world, and return again to the ark. They build themselves stately palaces without the ark, for the pleasure of the flesh, and are very zealous and devout in hypocrisy without the ark; they will be accounted children by an external imputation of grace and adoption; but they will not enter into the ark, but they say, Christ is in the ark, he hath purchased and paid all,

we need only to comfort ourselves therewith, he will bring us in well enough.

46. The other party saith they have Christ in their works of hypocrisy, they take the ark along with them when they fly out in their fleshly pleasure. All these remain without the ark in this world, and return not to the ark. This the third dove denotes: for the Antichristian kingdom walketh demurely in the shape of a dove, and as a sheep, but it is only a figure [and darksome shadow] of Christ's kingdom, which consists in the spirit in power, and is really in the ark.

The Thirty-Third Chapter

Of the beginning of the Second Monarchy, and of the Covenant of God with *Noah*, and all Creatures

1. AND Moses saith, *Then God spake with Noah, and commanded him to go forth, with every living thing, each with its kind. But Noah builded an altar unto the Lord, and took every clean beast, and of every clean fowl, and offered burnt offerings upon the altar. And the Lord smelled a sweet savour, and said in his heart, I will not henceforth curse the earth any more for man's sake; for the imagination of man's heart is evil from his youth; and I will not any more smite every living thing, as I have done. While the earth remaineth, seedtime and harvest, cold and heat, summer and winter, day and night shall not cease* (Gen. viii. 16 et seq.). Moses saith that God smelled a sweet savour, and said in his heart, he would not again curse the earth, or smite every living creature any more for man's sake. This is a figure or mystical type, as is before mentioned in the offering of Abel.

2. For his heart is the Word in the Covenant, which took the prayer and will-spirit of Noah through the holy fire in the offering, and brought it in the Word to substance; and withal smelled, in the divine power, the humanity of Christ, who was to resign himself in the Covenant into the Word of power; that is, it desired to have the humanity in his power and virtue, as a pleasant savour; and from this smell [or sweet savour of holy rest in the paradisical property] the spirit of God declared that he would not again destroy man and the creatures any more; so long as the earth should endure, these creatures should also continue.

3. For Noah offered all manner of clean beasts and fowl; and the spirit saith that God smelled herein a sweet savour [of rest]. Now [Moses doth not mean] that God took pleasure in the smell or savour of the offering, for all beasts are in his power, and are continually before him; but Moses spake it in reference to the hidden offering in the Covenant, which the inward world in the creatures did smell, which hereafter would deliver them from the abomination of vanity by its own peculiar offering,[1] and set their figure into the holy wisdom, viz. into the spiritual world.

[1] That is, the inward central fire, which shall purge the floor, and crystallise the earth into transparent gold.

4. When Noah offered, then the Lord (that is, God manifested in the offering by the unmanifest holy name JEHOVAH, through JESUS) did smell the holy disappeared humanity in Adam; that is, he did taste in the lubet or good pleasure of his wisdom how the same should be again manifest in the holy name Jesus. And then he blessed Noah and his children, and said, *Be fruitful, and multiply, and replenish the earth. And the fear and dread of you be upon every beast of the earth, and upon every fowl of the air; even upon all that creepeth upon the earth, and upon all the fishes of the sea; into your hands they are all delivered. Every living thing shall be meat for you; even as the green herb have I given you all things. But the flesh with the life thereof,[1] that is, with the blood thereof, you shall not eat. For I will require the blood of your lives, of every beast will I require the same; and at the hand of every man will I require the life of man, seeing that he is his brother; and whosoever sheddeth man's blood, by man shall his blood be shed; for God created man in his own image. And you, be ye fruitful, and multiply, and be industrious upon the earth, that you may increase abundantly* (Gen. ix. 1–7).

5. When God blessed Noah and his children through the offering proceeding from the Covenant, and bade them be fruitful, he gave them again the whole world, with all its hosts, in possession; all whatsoever that liveth and moveth should be subservient to them, and be their own. And he gave it them all in common, he made there no difference between Noah and his children, no lord[2] nor servant, but he made them all alike, none noble or ignoble. But like as many branches and twigs grow out of one tree, and yet all together are but one only tree, so also he established the human tree upon the earth, and gave them all beasts, fishes and fowls in common, with no distinction, restriction or prohibition, save only that they should not eat their life in the blood, lest they should become monstrous in their life with the bestial life.[3]

6. God commanded them to rule over all the beasts and creatures, but in this place he gave them no peculiar domination or ruling power over one another. For all domination, lordly rule and authority, whereby one man ruleth over another, doth arise out of Ararat, that is, from or through the order of nature, according to its properties, according to the constellations, and outward dominion of the princes under the constellations or astrum.

7. The true image of God hath no other dominion in its members

---

[1] Or which yet liveth in the blood.   [2] Master.
[3] Or with the eating the life of the beasts.

than the body hath in its members, or the tree in its branches. But the bestial image from the stars and four elements maketh itself a dominion and government, according to its mother, whence it taketh its rise, and wherein it liveth.

8. Also all laws and external ordinances which God hath appointed man, do all belong unto the order of nature, viz. unto the expressed formed Word. The same, God hath given man for a property, that he should rule therein with the inward spiritual man of understanding, according to the wisdom of God, and make himself [laws and] order (according to the spirit of wisdom).

9. Over which orders and ordinances of men, which they make unto themselves, he [viz. the Lord] hath set himself as judge, and thereupon hath appointed the Last Judgment, to separate wrong from right. And whatsoever proceedeth not from truth, righteousness and love, against that the judgment of God is set; for it is generated or hatched through the false spirits of darkness in turba magna, and introduced into the human property as a false lust and subtlety; and is a stranger or bastard wisdom, which shall not inherit the kingdom of God.

10. All royal and princely highness and excellency, together with all governments and dominions, do arise from the order of nature. In the image of God there is no compulsion [nor force, violence or oppression], but a mere free-willing, desirous love-service, as one member in the body, or as one branch of the tree, doth freely and readily serve each other, and rejoice in each other.

11. But seeing that man hath introduced himself into the outward formed Word, evil and good, viz. into the kingdom of nature; the kingdom of nature hath deprived him of the holy dominion; and hath placed itself with its power over the human property. Therefore, if he will have the same again, he must be born anew of God, and then he may rule with the new regenerated life in the spirit of God, over the kingdom of nature.

12. Indeed there are orders of princely angels or hierarchies in the spiritual world; but all without compulsion, in one harmonious delightful love-service and will; as one member in the body doth readily serve another.

13. All whatsoever that man in the kingdom of nature doth draw under his power, and abuseth it to superfluity and excess, and thereby withdraweth from his fellow-members, whereby they are put to want, poverty and distress, and their freely-given right and due is

wholly withheld from them; the same is imprinted [or compre-
hended] in turba magna, as an abomination of nature, and put into
the judgment of God, to the day of separation.

14. Nature requireth only order, and giveth distinction of places
and offices; but the turba bringeth its abomination from the dark
world's desire thereinto, viz. pride, covetousness, envy, anger and
falsehood.

15. These five vices or iniquities in the kingdom of nature are the
whore's brats, and shall not inherit the kingdom of God. God holdeth
the kingdom of nature for his order, and hath given the same into the
power of man, that he [as God's instrument in this world] should
sever the evil from the good, and choose himself a judge to pass
righteous judgment upon the iniquity and malice of the false desire
and lust [of man]. For he saith, *Whosoever sheddeth man's blood, by man
shall his blood be shed*, viz. by the order and institution of nature. Not
that any should revenge himself upon others by his own selfish
power [or force of arms], but through the order of nature, through
God's law [and appointment]; the same is the true avengeress; for
God said, *I will avenge your life's blood, and will avenge it upon every beast.*
Here he meaneth, by the order of his law, and its officers who officiate
in the right and due execution of the same.

16. Not that a prince or lord hath power to shed blood without the
law of God; if he doth so, then the law of God condemneth him also
to death. Here there is no peculiar self-full power given over man's
blood; let him be king or prince; for they are only officers over the
order of the divine law, and they ought not to go further than the
command of God gives leave. Indeed they have the law of nature
committed to their charge, as servants of the same; but they must
deal therein only according to righteousness and truth, and not do
anything through selfish [covetous, proud and envious] desire, for
God hath created man in his own image. Now the kingdom of
nature in its offices hath no power over this divine image to kill the
same, but the office or commission in God's order passeth only
upon[1] the outward image of nature.

17. Therefore if an officer of nature [viz. any magistrate] takes
away the life of a righteous man, him, nature appointeth unto the
judgment of God to the day of separation [wherein God will judge
all the unrighteous acts of man]. What then will become of the tyrants
who turn the truth into lies, and shamefully abuse and condemn the

[1] Or hath power over.

children of God for their divine knowledge and profession's sake, and stir up war and contention, to desolate and destroy country and people? All these belong unto turba magna, to the judgment of God; for they manage the sword of the turba in self-full lust and pleasure; unless the Spirit of God command them, and then they must do it for their office and charge's sake [and execute the just judgment of God upon those who have filled up the measure of their iniquity], as Israel was commanded to do among the heathen.

18. Whosoever sheddeth blood out of his own pleasure, to advance his authority, without urgent, absolute necessity, or God's command, he is moved, acted and driven by the wrathful fire of God's anger, and falleth at last to be a captive in the same kingdom.

19. Every warrior [or soldier] is a rod of God's anger, wherewith he doth, through his wrath and indignation, rebuke and devour the iniquity and malice of man. And it doth not belong at all unto the order [or ordinance] of nature, but unto the wrathful desire in turba magna, unto the order of the eager, fierce-devouring wrath, whereby God's anger doth overturn and lay waste countries and kingdoms.

20. Understand, it is the order of the dark world's property, which, by God's permission, advanceth its mighty force in the time of man's wickedness. And then it goes as the wrath will have it, until the same be well satiated in the blood of man.

21. For this is even the revenge of God's anger, of which he saith, that he would take vengeance for [or require] the blood of man; therefore he often taketh one man, and by him in anger slayeth another that hath deserved death.

22. When the great and potent rulers shed innocent blood, then cometh the anger of God, with its officers, and sheddeth their peoples' blood, and bringeth the sword of the turba upon them, whence war ariseth. But this is not from the divine order of the good nature, in which God governeth with his wisdom.

23. The wisdom of God desireth no war, but the anger of God, according to the dark world's nature, doth eagerly desire it, and effecteth the same in the vanity and iniquity of man.

24. If we lived as the children of God one among another, we need not have any warring and fighting. But that we wage war, we do thereby testify and declare that we are only children of this world, and fight for a strange inheritance, which yet we must forego, and thereby we serve the God of anger, as obedient servants. For no warrior or soldier shall inherit the kingdom of God, while he is such

a one; but [he that is] a child, new-born of the spirit of God, which forsaketh this world.

25. *And God said further to Noah, and to his sons with him: saying, Lo I, even I, establish my Covenant with you, and with your seed after you, and with every living creature that is with you, of the fowl, and of the cattle, and of every beast of the earth that is with you, even of all that came forth out of the ark; that henceforth all flesh shall not any more be cut off by the waters of a flood; neither shall there any more come a flood to destroy the earth. And God said, This is the token of the Covenant which I have made between me and you and every living creature that is with you, from henceforth for ever: I have set my bow in the clouds, the same shall be for a token of a Covenant between me and the earth; and it shall come to pass, when I bring a cloud over the earth, the bow shall be seen in the cloud. And then I will remember the Covenant, which is between me and you* (Gen. ix. 8–16). This Covenant with man is a type of the Three Principles of the divine being, viz. of the Being of all beings.

26. For the rainbow is the sign and token of this Covenant, that God doth here mind, and very intimately look upon, that man was created out of three Principles into an image, and that he should live in all three; and beheld now the unability and great peril of mankind; and set the sign of this Covenant before him, as a representation that his wrath should not any more be stirred so to destroy every life.

27. For the rainbow hath the colour of all the three Principles, viz. the colour of the first Principle is red, and darkish-brown; which betokens the dark and fire-world, that is, the first Principle, the kingdom of God's anger. The colour of the second Principle is white, and yellow; this is the majestical colour, signifying, as a type of the holy world, God's love. The third Principle's colour is green, and blue; blue from the chaos, and green from the water or saltpetre; where, in the flagrat or crack of the fire, the Sulphur and Mercury do sever themselves, and produce distinct, various and several colours, which betoken unto us the inward spiritual worlds,[1] which are hidden in the four elements.

28. This bow is a figure of the Last Judgment, shewing how the inward spiritual world will again manifest itself, and swallow up or avall into itself this outward world of four elements.

29. And this is even the sign or token of the Covenant of grace, which sign in the Covenant betokeneth the Judge of the world, viz. Christ, who, at the end of days, will appear in all the three Principles,

[1] Or world.

viz. according to the fire-sign as a severe Judge over the turba, and all whatsoever that shall be found therein; he will manifest the fiery judgment, and enkindle the turba, so that the first Principle shall appear in its fiery property, for all things of this world's being must be tried or purified in the fire of the first Principle, viz. in the centre of the eternal nature. And even then the turba of all beings shall be swallowed up in the fire.

30. And according to the light's sign he shall appear as a pleasant visage to all the saints, even in the midst of the fire; and defend his, in his love and meekness, from the flames of the fire.

31. And according to the kingdom of the outward nature of this world, he shall appear in his assumed humanity; and the whole outward mystery of the four elements, according to Sulphur, Mercury and Salt, even according to all the properties of the wonders of the expressed and formed Word, even all shall be made manifest before him according to light and darkness [viz. according to their good and evil].

32. Of this the rainbow is a type and figure, for it is a reflex [antitype] or contra-glance of the sun; shewing what kind of property [or virtue] there is in the deep. The sun casteth its shining lustre into the four elements towards the chaos, and then the chaos, whence the four elements do proceed, doth manifest itself according to the Principles, with its colours; and it denoteth and pointeth out the hidden or mystical ground of the four elements, viz. the hidden world, and also the hiddenness of the humanity. For in this hiddenness [or secret mystery] of the creation, God did set forth his Covenant, that he would not destroy its image any more with water; that the fountains of the deep should not be any more opened in the chaos, as came to pass in the Flood, and in the creation of the world.

33. The rainbow is an opening of the chaos in nature; and it may very well, if the sun be in a good aspect in the elements, produce and bring forth a wonderful birth, both in the vegetables and animals. Also there may thereby be a creatural living being produced in the deep, even according to the property of the sun's powerful influence; according as it findeth in the elements a property from the astrum or constellations, either to evil or good; as oftentimes to worms, flies, grasshoppers, and the like; and also to a good life, according as Saturn and Mercury are enkindled in their desire.

34. For when the chaos doth open itself, then the harsh-astringent Saturnine property doth attract, as a hunger or desire, unto itself, and

taketh the property of the chaos (wherein the hidden powers are contained) into its desire, and coagulates the same; and forthwith Mercury becomes quick in Sulphur, for the sun enkindleth the fiery Mars in its property, whereupon Mercury is stirred up or becomes active. This, Saturn frameth [amasseth] into a body, viz. into an ens. Now the saltpetre cannot agree or unite itself with Mars, and therefore there is a severation or motion; and seeing that they cannot get rid of[1] Saturn, viz. the fiat of the outward world; it becomes a flying life [or creature], according to the property of that same constellation.

35. Saturn [hath such a power or property in it as that it] may, if the sun be in a good aspect, take in the distilling dew out of the rainbow into itself, (understand, into the Saturnine property), which afterwards falls upon the water, which some fish do eat down, and coagulate in them, whence precious pearls may arise.

36. For the Paradisical property doth open itself all along in the chaos, if it be not hindered by evil malignant aspects; which Master Wiseling[2] will scarce believe. He can speak of the ground of nature exactly, and hath it at his fingers' ends, and yet is blind in the Mystery, and understands not either the inward or outward [part of nature]. For such I have not written anything, for I need not such animals[3] to the understanding of my writings, but good, clear, quick-sighted, illuminated eyes; unto all others they are dumb and absurd, let them be as wise and learned as they will.

37. The chaos is the root of nature, and yieldeth of itself nothing else but a good property; but if the constellation be evil, the evil malignant desire taketh the good property into itself, and changeth it into evil; as a good man among evil company doth change his good also into an evil.

38. And the rainbow is especially represented [or freely given] unto man for a token of the divine grace; so that he might behold and view himself, as in an open and perspicuous glass, what he is. For in the rainbow the sign of good and evil is manifest as a type of the centre of nature, out of which evil and good take their rise; over which the Son of Man was set by God, to be Judge.

39. For the type or form of the ark of Noah is also in the rainbow; if we were not blind it would plainly appear so unto us; also the Trinity of the Deity is therein portrayed: for the red colour betokeneth the Father, the yellow and white the Son, and the blue the Spirit.

[1] Or escape. [2] The false philosopher or sophister. [3] Text, calves.

40. And God hath set forth himself in a figure, according to his manifestation in the sign of the Covenant, that we should flee unto his grace, and receive his Covenant, and be always mindful of his revelation to come, where he will again manifest the spiritual world; as he hath set it forth unto us by way of similitude in the rainbow; [to the end] that we should see what is in secret [and how his Covenant is] eternally established [with us in secret], and standeth ever before him.

The Thirty-Fourth Chapter

How *Noah* cursed his Son *Ham*, and of the Mystical Prophecy Concerning his Three Sons and their Posterity

1. *And Noah began to be an husbandman, and planted a vineyard: And he drank of the wine, and was drunken; and lay uncovered in his tent. And Ham, Canaan's father, saw the nakedness of his father, and told it his two brethren without. And Shem and Japheth took a garment, and laid it upon both their shoulders, and went backwards, and covered the nakedness of their father; and their faces were backward, so that they saw not their father's nakedness. Now when Noah awoke from his wine, and knew what his younger son had done unto him, he said, Cursed be Canaan; a servant of all servants he shall be amongst his brethren. And he said further, Blessed be the Lord God of Shem; and let Canaan be his servant. And God enlarge Japheth, and let him dwell in the tents of Shem; and let Canaan be his servant* (Gen. ix. 20–27). This is an exact real type of the human property, according to the three Principles or worlds: for the spirit in Noah speaketh from the centre; and the three sons of Noah did now stand before the spirit in a figure; typifying what kind of people should arise from them.

2. By this figure the spirit of Noah prophesied or declared, from the very stock or root of the formed Word of the human property, what the second monarchy should be. Noah was drunk, and lay naked with his shame, at which his son Ham mocked, and also declared it to his brethren, that they also should do the like. Here the spirit intimateth and pointeth out whence the curse arose upon Ham, viz. from the shame of his father.

3. For this was even the abomination before God's holiness; out of which root Ham and his generation, viz. the man of vanity, doth arise, for in the image of God the shame is an abomination.

4. Therefore God commanded Abraham to be circumcised on this member, to shew that this member was not given to Adam in the beginning, and that it should be again cut off from the image of God, and not inherit the kingdom of God; upon which cause and reason also the soul's spirit is ashamed to uncover it.

5. But seeing that Adam did not stand in the image of God, when his Eve was made out of him, it was hung upon him for to propagate

in a bestial nature and kind; thereupon also this bestial tree, viz. the fleshly spirit of vanity, came to be propagated all along from this property, and adheres to man. The figure of this was Ham, and therefore he mocked his own property in his father.

6. The spirit of this property mocked its ens which it had from the centre of nature; it beheld itself in his father's shame, from whence it had its rise, as in a looking-glass of its selfhood. And thus this spirit [of fleshly Ham] forthwith brake forth as a life of vanity, and manifested what itself was, viz. a scorn [disdain or mock-god] of heaven.

7. Which the spirit of God's image in the formed Word of the good ens in Noah did well know, and did awaken in him the fire-centre of the soul in the wrath, and cursed this spirit of vanity, that it should not co-inherit in the kingdom of heaven. The scoff-spirit shall not possess the kingdom of God, but be cut off from the image of God, that is, from the outward image of the formed creature.

8. For the same property from whence the shame ariseth, is good in itself; but in Adam's imagination after the bestial property it became monstrous, bestial and strange in the image of God; and therefore this strange form and shape shall not remain for ever.

9. From this strange false shape the scorner or scoff-spirit did arise. The devil insinuated into the figure of Ham's strange spirit, and mocked at the heavenly generatress, that it was now even become a monster in the image of God; and therefore the spirit of Noah cursed the false scoff-spirit [in Ham and all his generation].

10. Not that we are to understand that Ham was accursed in his soul and soul's spirit, but according to the figure [he and all his were accursed] in the property of the reviling mocking spirit, which brake forth and manifested itself out of the monster; but he (that is, the earthly image of the limus of the earth) should be hidden with its own self-will in the image of God, and be only as a servant or instrument of the divine image proceeding from the holy ens; the earthly spirit should not rule, but the heavenly, viz. the soul with its spirit; the monster, that is, this vile reviling spirit, must not be manifest. But seeing the free will did awaken and stir up the monstrous spirit, which was only a scorner of the Mystery and hiddenness in the Covenant, Noah cursed him,[1] and said, He should be a servant of his brethren.

11. For he said, blessed be the God of Shem, and let Canaan be his servant: God enlarge Japheth, and let him dwell in the tents of Shem.

[1] Or it.

The God of Shem was he who had espoused or incorporated himself with the Covenant in the seed of the woman; the figure and type of this (in the spirit) was Shem; and Japheth was the figure of the poor soul captivated in the monster; God should let this Japhethical (or soul's) property, dwell in the tents of Shem, and enlarge it in Shem's figure.

12. But Ham's figure (according to the monstrous spirit) should not have any dominion or reign in the life of the new birth, but be only as a servant or as an instrument, without self-will or any peculiar life of selfness, [and] must serve and administer to the use of the spiritual kingdom; in manner as the night is hidden in the day, and yet 'tis really there, and yet so as if it were not; and it is the hand-maid to the day's operation and power.

13. Thus in like manner the spirit did express how the three properties of the humanity, viz. the woman's seed, and the creatural soul's seed, and the earthly seed in Ham's figure, should stand in their place order and rule in the regeneration in the spiritual kingdom; and thereby it did declare and point at the kingdoms of the world, intimating that this same figure would all along put forth itself in the kingdom and dominion of the humanity[1] upon the earth, and thus keep its figure externally, so long as mankind should live in the dominion of the four elements; as it hath thus fallen out.

14. For Shem's figure passed in the Covenant upon Abraham and Israel, among whom the Word of the Covenant was manifested and spoken forth; and Japheth's figure went along in nature, viz. through the wisdom of nature in the kingdom of nature; whence the Gentiles arose, who looked upon the light of nature, and Shem's lineage looked upon the light in the Covenant. Thus Japheth, that is, the poor captive soul which is of the eternal nature, dwelt in Shem's tent, viz. under the Covenant; for the light of nature dwelleth in the light of grace, and is a tenant or inhabitant of the light of grace, viz. of God's light, it is even as a form of framed substance of the unformed uncomprehended light of God.

15. And Ham's line passed upon the animal bestial man, proceeded from the limus of the earth, in which was the curse; whence the Sodo-mitical and almost wholly brutish people did arise; who esteemed neither the light of nature, nor the light of grace in the Covenant.

16. This signifieth and pointeth out the outward part of the soul from the spirit of this world; which, in the regeneration in the

[1] Or mankind.

spiritual world, shall be a formed and very fixed will; which may not or desires not to rule in the manner and condition of a selfish peculiar spirit; but shall be as a servant and minister of the creatural soul and God's spirit in the holy light's image; it shall not be manifest in any self-full arrogative understanding of selfhood, but remain hidden, as the night is hidden in the day; and yet it is really there.

17. For the animal soul shall not inherit the kingdom of light; although it shall and will be therein; yet it hath no dominion [or predominant virtue of its selfness]. As an instrument is a dead senseless thing in reference to the master, and yet it is the master's tool wherewith he maketh what he pleaseth; the same in like manner we are to understand concerning the animal soul in the regeneration.

18. But in the time of the four elements it will have the upper hand and sway, for it hath brought itself into a proper selfhood and imaginative life of selfish propriety; and therefore God hath accursed it, and condemned it to death, so that it must die to selfhood.

19. For when Adam in his desire did awaken the earthly properties out of the limus of the earth, so that they went forth out of their just accord and mutual harmony, each of them into its own self-will and lust, to behold and look upon its self as a peculiar self-life; the bestial soul was hereby brought to its predominant power and force. And this same is Ham's property, which God hath ordained to be servant under the angelical kingdom, and cursed its jeering scorning power, in that it did mock at the heavenly matrix, and set forth its own figure and form.

20. The spirit saith in Moses, *Shem and Japheth took a garment upon their shoulders, and went backward to their father and covered him; so that their faces were turned backward, and they saw not his shame* (Gen. ix. 23). O thou wonderful God! how very mystically and secretly dost thou carry thy works: who would know and understand thy ways, if thy spirit did not lead us, and open the understanding!

21. Both these brothers took a garment upon their shoulders and covered the father. Wherefore did not one do it alone? or wherefore did Noah drink himself drunk, and lay so naked with his shame? This, reason looketh upon, as if there were nothing more in it [but only a history of such an act]. But seeing that Ham was thereby cursed, and made to be a servant of his brethren, and not only he, but also all his posterity out of him, we see thereby very clearly what the spirit doth hereby signify, viz. that it is a type, character and figure of that which should afterwards come to pass.

22. The earthly spirit, which the devil had made monstrous, was a scorner and jeerer of the heavenly birth; it indeed saw the shame which it must bear upon it as a monster; but he went away as a beast, and mocked the new regeneration of the heavenly matrix. But Japheth, viz. the poor soul, and Shem, that is, the disappeared heaven's image, which was moved, stirred or quickened again in the Covenant, they took a garment upon their shoulders. This garment was the new humanity, which should open itself out of the Covenant, out of the angelical world.

23. And *they went backward, and covered the father's shame*. This intimateth and betokeneth that the free will of self must and shall wholly turn itself away from the bestial monster of self-fullness and ownhood, wherein the shame standeth open, and enter again into the resigned filiation or child-ship; and go no more forwards, but retire again backwards; and must take the garment of the new humanity, viz. Christ's innocency, merit and satisfaction upon it, and therewith cover the shame which our father Adam hath, with the monster, passed upon us by inheritance: This was the type which was here set forth.

24. And that Shem did not carry the garment alone, and cover the father, doth figure out unto us, that the soul, viz. Japheth, (that is, the inward kingdom) of the inward eternal nature, must help; for the soul is of the Father's property, and this, Japheth doth typify. And the soul's spirit, viz. the fair image of God in the light, which did vanish or disappear in Adam, and stood typically[1] in the Covenant, of which Shem was the figure, doth point out unto us the Son's property, who should open the Covenant. Thus also we are to understand that the Father in his will, who freely gave us the Son, took on one part the garment of our sins' covering, and this was typified by Japheth; and the Son, on the other part, who covered our shame with the Father's will, of this Shem was a figure.

25. For if Christ shall lay the covering garment upon our shame, then the soul must help, that is, it must give up and resign its will wholly thereinto; and go backwards with its will towards the bosom of the Father; and not any longer parley with itself in its own will and knowledge, how it goeth or will go; and so it must take the garment, in true repentance, upon its shoulders; and leave the other part upon the shoulders of Shem, viz. unto the true image of Christ,[2] which is the precious noble Sophia.

[1] Or in the image.   [2] Or God.

26. Both these take the heavenly garment, and go backwards to the Father; and though they cannot see how they go, yet they go in faith, trusting on God's mercy, and turn away their eyes from the shame, vanity and false will. For in this place going backwards and covering the shame signifies nothing else but to convert the selfhood naturally going forwards in its own will and way, and go back again into the ONE, out of which the free will departed and came into the monster, or shame.

27. Noah's drunkenness signifieth, that when Adam entered with his lust and desire into this world's property, he became drunk in the bestial property; and therein he uncovered his shame, that is, he disclosed and made bare therein the bestial lust. Now, when this was done, he stood before God in great shame; and then the bestial spirit in this monster of false lust and poisonful concupiscence brake forth, and reviled the precious heavenly image, and made itself master.

28. And thus Christ must, in our soul, and in our disappeared and again revived noble Sophia, cover the shame of our father Adam and his children; for he would therefore not be born of the seed of man; but out of the heavenly, disappeared ens, and brought his living ens of the holy world thereinto; that so he might cover with his heavenly ens our monstrous shame[1] of the soul's property, which Adam's lust had uncovered.

29. The corrupt nature which had opened itself now in Paradise, went along in all men; and though the image of God was again regenerate in the spirit of the saints, as in a figurative form until the fulfilling of Christ in the flesh, yet the monstrous image was propagated all along in all in the earthly property.

30. But seeing the first earthly world of the human property was drowned in the flood, and there the first monarchies ceased, the same figure did forthwith represent itself again in Noah and his three sons. So that now the spirit doth here signify from the very stock and root of the human property, how it should afterwards be, viz. the tree of man would in its properties introduce itself into boughs and branches; that is, spread forth itself into distinct nations and governments; and that they would not all know the only God according to the light of his grace; and how that God would represent unto them the light of grace in the generation of Shem.

31. For Noah saith, *Blessed be the God of Shem, and let Japheth dwell in Shem's tents.* By the God of Shem he meaneth the holy Word in the

---

[1] Text, seed.

Covenant, intimating how the same would manifest itself. And then the Japhites or Gentiles, which lived in the light of nature, should come to the light of grace manifested from the generation of Shem; and enter into Shem's tents, and dwell therein. This did point at the Gentiles, who before knew only of the light of nature, but when the Word did manifest itself in the person of Christ, with the gracious light of the Gospel, they came into the light of grace.

32. And even here Ham, viz. the fleshly lust-spirit, must be in its own property and selfhood a servant among the children of light, for the children of God do compel him to servitude and keep him under, and take away his reviling scorning will. For the spirit of Ham, which Noah cursed, doth intimate how this Ham's spirit would be great upon the earth, and go on only in its own proud monstrous and bestial knowledge, and scoff at the children of the light, account them fools, because they hope upon something else, which they do not outwardly see.

33. Thus the spirit in Noah pointeth out unto us three sorts of men; first it signifieth the children of faith, who nakedly and merely look upon the hidden light of God's grace, and have the same shining in their hearts.

34. The other would look upon the light of nature and reason, and would endeavour to fathom and search out the hidden light by the strength of reason, and that they would therefore contend, dispute, wrangle and jangle, and bring forth many wonderful strange monsters and conceits out of the light of nature, and set them up for gods, or God's light, as it hath so come to pass among the Christians and Gentiles.

35. The third sort would be of Ham's nature and generation; and know neither the light of nature nor grace; but walk as the beast, and be only titular verbal praters and literal children, and, moreover, mockers, scoffers, and fleering apes, who would also be called the children of God. But their knowledge would be only of the external stone church; a mere custom, and verbal round of a service of God,[1] where the mouth would use indeed the name of God; but the heart would only bring forth a bestial spirit to earthly pride, lust and pleasure.

36. Thus the spirit of Shem, Ham and Japheth would dwell together in one congregation. Shem's generation in faith hidden among the Japhites, as a poor, disesteemed, contemned, abject

[1] Or Divine Service as they call it.

people. But the tribe of Japheth would set forth themselves with great plausible words, with great and huge ostentation of God's service; but yet it would be but as an hypocrisy and seeming holiness, proceeding from the light of nature. But Ham's lineage would be full of gluttony and drunkenness, scoffing, and reviling, and they would mock at both, viz. the children of the Cain-like seeming holiness, and also at the children of the true light; and would live as the wild brute beast; and yet in their swinish life would be children of grace by an outward appropriation or adoption.

37. This Ham hath now the dominion in Christendom; he hath flattered with Japheth, so that he hath set him up by the light of nature an external specious divine worship, as a titular God. This titular God hath covered Ham, in his bestial Sodomitical spirit, with a very fair and glorious covering, under the purple mantle of Christ; and laid under his head great sacks full[1] of the light of grace; and these the bestial mouth-spirit of Ham must take along with it; and when it must indeed die, then it hath whole sacks full of the light of grace.

38. But the light of grace remaineth only in the sacks, and Ham's spirit remaineth in itself an evil beast; and cannot truly open the sacks and take out the light of grace. This Ham's spirit is accursed, and shall not inherit God's kingdom; unless it be really born again out of the light of grace; otherwise the sacks and coverings avail him not at all.

39. For a beast goeth into the sanctuary [or to holy service of God], and remains a beast when he comes thence. Thy seeming holiness and devotion, thy comforting, flattering and soothing up thyself, avails nothing, unless thou return again into thy first mother, from whence man is originally proceeded, and become as a little, new born child, and let Ham and Japheth go, with all their arts and pratings.

40. For Japheth obtains it not in his specious glistering kingdom; unless he enter into Shem's tent, viz. into the light of grace, so that the same may be born in him. Outward adopted children avail not in God's account; but innate children, born anew of the heavenly ens in Christ spirit; and whosoever hath not the same is already judged (John iii. 18).

[1] Or satchels full.

THE

SECOND PART

OF THE

Myſterium Magnum

Beginneth with the Propagation of the *Humane*
Tree through *Noahs* Children.

AND

The building of the Tower of *Babel* and Confuſion of the Speeches,
and their Diviſion into Severall *Nations.*

This is

The other Tree

Wherein the Powers of the Properties unfold and forme them-
ſelves into the Languages ; even out of *One* into *many*
Languages Tongues and Speeches.

Beginning with the X. Chapter of *Genesis* and the 35th Chapter of the *Mysterium Magnum* : and ending with the XXXV. Chapter of *Genesis*
and the 64. Chapter of the *Mysterium Magnum*, at the 5th verse.

Written by

JACOB BEHM

Teutonicus.

LONDON,
Printed by *M. Simmons* for *H. Blunden,*
at the *Castle* in *Corn-hill.* 1 6 5 4.

The Thirty-Fifth Chapter

Shews how the Human Tree[1] hath spread forth itself in its properties by the children of *Noah*; and how they were divided and severed at the Tower of Babel in their properties, by the confusion of the Tongues into distinct Nations

1. EVERY tree groweth first[2] (after that it shooteth out of its pregnant seed)[3] into a stock, afterwards into branches and boughs; and bringeth forth further out of its ens the blossom and fruit. Thus also we are to understand of the human tree, according to its virtue and manifestation of its hidden wonders of the divine wisdom, which lay hid in the human ens, and put itself forth in time out of each degree of the properties.

2. Adam was the first ens to the grain [or pregnant fruitful seed of mankind], and this same ens, which produced the human life, was in the divine wisdom in the Word of the divine power of the divine understanding. The spirit of God brought this holy ens out of the divine wisdom and lubet into the Verbum Fiat, viz. into the desire of the forming word, viz. into nature; and therein the spirit of God figured the ens of divine wisdom, through the speaking Word, into a formal life; and the nature of the three Principles into a body; into which body (understand the ens of nature) the spirit of God breathed this same figured, shaped, creatural life of divine understanding.

3. And hence man had his rise, and became a living soul, both out of the heavenly spiritual ens, and out of the temporal ens of the earth and four elements; both out of the constellation or astrum of the divine magic, and [out of the] natural magic; a complete, perfect likeness of God; a delightful tree of the life of divine wisdom and contemplation, engrafted into the Paradise of God, viz. into heaven, and into the time of this world, standing in both; fit to regenerate[4] and form his like out of himself: like as out of one tree many twigs,

---

[1] Or Tree of Mankind.　　[2] Gen. x.　　[3] Grain, kernel, pippin.
[4] Generate again, or propagate.

boughs, branches and fruits do grow; where every fruit hath a grain, kernel or pippin in it, fit to produce a new stock and tree: The like we are also to understand concerning the tree of mankind.

4. The inward spiritual ens grew in its power in Adam's life, until the outward earthly natural [one] overcame him by the infectious persuasion of the devil; and then the natural ens put itself forcibly forth in the powers of the wonders of nature; and brought forth its branches and boughs out of the essence of nature.

5. And though the holy ens of the heavenly world's essence and being did disappear in Adam by his infection and poisonful imagination, yet the Word of divine power did give itself again thereinto by Covenant; so that this ens of the heavenly world was propagated all along in this tree, until the time of its now springing forth in the ens of Mary, where the Covenant was accomplished [stood at its aim and limit].

6. Adam's spiritual holy stem grew until his fall, and there it stood still; and then the Word freely gave itself by the Covenant thereinto, as into a disappeared [expired] ens, to regenerate it again in its true entity; and the outward natural stem obtained the power and the self-growing life, in the fall, where then the elements, each of them in its property, became sensible and full of its own self-full power and operation, and grew so unto the flood, especially before the flood, in its boughs and branches, and did shew itself as a full-grown tree, according to all the properties in evil and good.

7. But the powers had not as yet unfolded and explicated themselves therein, for all men had only one language; the languages were not made manifest out of the properties before the flood.

8. They indeed understood the Language of Nature, viz. the formed word in its difference; but this difference or distinct variety was not as yet formed and framed into tongues, until the stock of the human tree, did, after the flood, bring its power into the branches. Whereupon the tree of mankind began to bloom and blossom forth out of the properties of the powers of the formed natural word, viz. out of the blessing, wherewith God blessed Noah and his children, viz. the branches of the tree, and bade them be fruitful, and fill and replenish the earth, and gave them the Covenant of grace.

9. For in Cain this tree was cursed, but in Noah it was again blessed, that the properties of the formed natural word should put forth themselves with the tongues through the property of nature, as a wonder of many words or gods in the only living Word.

10. The image of God in the formed word should bring forth the formation of the only Word, out of the first ens, into many formations or forms of tongues and speeches, according to the nature and manner of the princely dominions of the high spirits, which also are in their distinct degrees and differences in the formed word; and in the deep of this world do rule in the properties of nature above the four elements, yea, also above the operation of the stars in the soul of the great world; which also bear the names of God in the formed word of nature, as an instrument of God, whereby he, in a formal manner, ruleth in his dominion and love-delight or harmony.

11. That the Ancient Fathers[1] lived so long before the flood, was because that the powers of the formed word of the divine property were yet undivided and un-manifested and un-explicated in them. As a young tree, which is full of power, virtue and sap, doth excellently manifest and display itself in its branches and spreading growth, but when it begins to bloom, then the good power goeth into the blossoms and fruits.

12. The like also we are to understand concerning the first age of mankind. When the powers were couched in one property in the stock, then men did understand the Language of Nature, for all languages did lie therein; but when this tree of the one only tongue did divide itself in its properties and powers among the children of Nimrod, then the Language of Nature (whence Adam gave names to all things, naming each from its property) did cease, and the stem of nature became faint, feeble and weak, by reason of the divided properties in the word of the powerful understanding.

13. Thus they did not any longer live so long, for the true power of the human life, whence the understanding floweth, is come[2] out of the Word of God. But seeing that the understanding did divide itself into many tongues and properties, Nature grew weaker and weaker; and the high understanding of the properties of the spirits of the letters did fall, for the internal brought itself into an external, in manner and wise as a man relateth and speaketh of a thing which he hath by hearsay, and yet hath no right understanding of the same, also is not able to see it.

14. Of such a gift [as the understanding of the Language of Nature] mankind was deprived of at Babel, when as they so highly exalted nature, and would by the outward nature build them a tower, whose top should reach even to heaven; which hath a very subtle, hidden

---

[1] Patriarchs.   [2] Or proceeded.

and innate understanding; and it lieth very excellently and emphatically in the names of Noah's children, and childrens' children; which the spirit in Moses hath set down in the line of their forth-spreading generations; wherein the properties of the division of the only understanding and language may be understood, [for they do entirely intimate], how the properties of the understanding do give forth and unfold themselves one out of another, and how each mutually brings itself into a sundry particular speech, as into a peculiar selfly word.

15. For the names of the children of Noah, and their children (from whom the second monarchy had its rise upon the earth), are seventy-two; which the spirit in Moses doth point out; and herein lieth the great mystery of the Tower of Babel, viz. the division of the tongues.

16. For seventy-seven is the whole number of the divine manifestation through the formed word; seventy-two, are Babel, viz. the tongues of the wonders; the other five are holy, and lie hidden under the seventy-two, and they take their original out of JOTH, and the JOTH standeth in the ①,[1] viz. in the One, which is the eye of eternity without ground and number.

17. Through the five holy speeches proceeding from JOTH, the spirit in the formed word of nature speaketh holy divine words in the children of the saints; and through the seventy-two tongues he speaketh through the nature of the wonders, both from the evil and the good, according as the word doth form and amass itself in an ens.

18. The five speeches belong to the spirit of God, who speaketh by his children, when and how he pleaseth, but the seventy-two belong to man's selfness and particular ownhood, whence man's self-full understanding speaketh lies and truth. Therefore the seventy-two languages, viz. Babel, must pass through the judgment of God, and the pure shall be separated from the impure, and tried in the fire.

19. For him, who is taken under, and capable of this knowledge, we will give a short direction and manuduction, to trace out our sense and meaning, (which yet we in this place will keep to ourselves), and thereby intimate unto him, how he may search out all mysteries and secrets which lie couched under these names, which the holy spirit, in Moses, hath marked out.

20. The spirit in Moses sets down seven names in Japheth's line, viz. the seven sons which he begat; which are these: Gomer, Magog, Madai, Javan, Tubal, Meshech, and Tiras. Now Japheth is the first, and betokeneth the first Principle, and therein the kingdom of nature;

[1] ①.

intimating how, even out of nature, the seven free arts or liberal
sciences should be found under a natural philosophy; and these were
found out in this Japheth's line in a natural manner, by the heathenish
philosophy. For this was the twig which should dwell in Shem's tent,
as Noah foretold.

21. For the seven sons of Japheth signify and point out the seven
properties of nature, and under their seven names lieth the great
mystery of the Japhetical lines in the kingdom of nature, [intimating
to us] what kind of people and kingdoms should arise from them, even
unto the end of the world; concerning the manifestation and writing
of which our speech is stopped and taken from us; but it shall be freely
and fully manifested to our school-fellows in its time; and be wholly
made known and revealed.

22. After this the spirit mentioneth only two sons of Japheth which
begat children, viz. Gomer and Javan; he passeth over the other
children of Japheth in silence, and mentions not at all what children
they begat. And this is not without cause. The spirit pointeth at the
two sorts of men among the Gentiles in the kingdom of nature, viz.
under Gomer he setteth three names, Ashkenaz, Riphath and
Togarmah; these were the sons of Gomer, who do thus manifest
themselves in the Language of Nature, viz. they form [conceive or
amass] the ens of nature, viz. the formed word, into an ens, and bring
it into a contemplation, that is, into an acute speculating reason, and
make a figure out of it, viz. a dominion (or form of a government of
self will) according to the kingdom of nature, for temporal glory and
renown.

23. And under the other son, Javan, he setteth four names, viz.
Elishah, Tarshish, Kittim, and Dodanim; and he saith, that of these
fourteen names all the isles and languages of the Gentiles were filled,
and that they had their rise and original from hence. These four names
do intimate out of the properties of nature, thus much, viz. by the
first a good half-angelical will; by the second an introduction of the
good will into the wrath of nature, from whence an evil warlike selfness ariseth; by the third a false understanding, whereby the angelical
good will is brought in the selfhood of reason even to be a fool, and
sets forth itself with a strange outside lustre; and it signifieth the
heathenish idolatry whereinto they brought themselves through
reason, without God's light, and thereby did set up heathenish idols,
and made themselves great kingdoms; so that the spirit of nature hath
brought them under its power and might, into its own form. And

under the name DODANIM the spirit intimateth the kingdom of nature in selfhood with its selfly divine service, viz. an external visible God, which may be shewn by the pointing of the finger.

24. And under these fourteen names in Japheth's line the human kingdom of nature is wholly portrayed and typified; and we are in an especial manner to observe, that the angelical will is therein concluded, betokening the wise and deep understanding heathen in the light of nature, in whom the inward holy kingdom did behold itself, who (notwithstanding they lay shut up in the true divine understanding, and saw by an external light [or reflex]), in the restitution of all beings, shall, when the covering is taken away, live in Shem's tent, viz. in the formed word of nature, yet in their property.

25. Out of this fourteenth number of the fourteen names of Japheth came the prophetical and apocaliptical numbers. From which the spirit prophesied how the wonders of nature should open themselves one after another, and what should happen in each degree of their manifestation; which we will here pass over in silence, and mention it in its due place.

26. Under Ham, the spirit bringeth the greatest intimation of the kingdom of nature, for he fully sets forth the external form of reason, for he saith, Ham begat Cush, Mizraim, Put and Canaan. CUSH giveth, in the ens of the pregnant generating nature, a signification of a form of sudden conceived, swift ascending lust in selfhood, like to a running, or far and wide domineering and reigning might; and it is the root of the princely government according to the third Principle; but Japheth is the same ground [or work] according to the first Principle.

27. MIZRAIM signifieth a forth-driving power, which doth forthwith comprehend itself again in the lust, in which the centre of nature doth go forth all along in a strong through-breaking lust and desire, and breaks open the form of the lust. Intimating unto us the original of the divided tongues, and how the power of the only formed word of the understanding should be divided.

28. The name PUT sheweth forth, even from the ens of nature, a high city or place whereby the will [of these men] would advance itself on high, in contriving and framing how to build them a high tower. CANAAN signifieth a land of lowliness and humility; shewing that God would be found in the lowly and humble; and it especially signifies, that this high-flown aspiring will shall be overthrown and cast down.

29. Although the Reader may not be able to understand us in this tongue, yet I set this down only to the end that he may learn to consider and meditate on the great mystery which the spirit of God hath signified under these names, from whence such a purpose of a few men did arise, that it is even wholly a mere wonder whence the tongues and speeches do take their rise and original: for the spirit in Moses doth set down afterwards, that *Cush begat Nimrod, who began to be a mighty lord upon the earth; and was a mighty hunter before the Lord.* Who would now understand what kind of mighty lord and hunter he was before God, without the understanding of the Language of Nature? which, seeing it is not every man's gift to understand, we will only intimate the sense and meaning, even what the spirit doth thereby understand in the word of the essence.

30. *Nimrod became a mighty lord, and was a hunter before the Lord.* Now if I be able to see the spirit in its essence, in the formation of the word, then I see what a lord and hunter Nimrod was; for the spirit doth herein signify and point at the properties of nature, shewing how the same have opened themselves in man's nature, and brought themselves into an external form to a contrived framed government among men. The spirit signifieth by the name how the human free will hath formed itself in the nature of the understanding; and imagined such a model and platform into its mind, out of which imagination and fancy the outward work arose.

31. For the name NIMROD doth give a very clear signification, in open understanding, that he came from Cush, for he is in himself a taking, apprehending or an arrogation of power and might out of nature; intimating how nature doth form and frame itself into a government in the mind; and hath put itself forth with power, and hath hunted, suppressed and oppressed the inferior properties; therefore the spirit saith, *a hunter before the Lord*; for the nature is before the Lord, therefore the spirit speaketh here of a hunter before the Lord; for look as a hunter doth hunt, drive, take and tame wild beasts, even so the spirit intimateth, that out of this self-advanced human nature, such evil beasts would arise, who would live only to the outward nature.

32. Now out of the wrath of nature arose, over these foolish bestial men, the hunter, viz. the outward domination; which should hunt, catch, kill and keep them in awe, so that the hunter might tame them, and hold them under a government; else there would be only a general raving, raging, biting, tearing, devouring and eating up of

each other, among the bestial men. Seeing they would not suffer the Spirit of God to rule and guide them, they must suffer the office of nature to rule them; for otherwise what need hath the Lord of a hunter, that the spirit in Moses saith, that *he was a mighty hunter before the Lord*: that which hunteth before the Lord of all beings doth not hunt hares or other beasts.

33. Moses hath a veil before his clear shining eyes. The spirit doth hereby hint at the government of nature, shewing how the human government hath formed and contrived itself in the soul of the outward world; and how it should afterwards be among them; and what hunters would arise over them; and compareth the human dominion to a hunter, who hunteth for beasts to catch and slay them; and thus it would be also among them, that these hunters would hunt after men, to take them and bring them under slavery and servitude, and chase and course them to and fro by their bloodhounds; bite, tear, slay and devour them by war and murderous acts; and tame and bring under all, with force, fury and violence, and excellently well manage the government of the hunter in their own self-assumed power.

34. For man was fallen under the possession of God's wrath in nature; the same forced forth itself now with its desire, and formed itself into a government according to the outward constellations and the four elements, as they do build up and break down: even so did this hunter do with his beasts in his sport.

35. Here the world may take an exact looking-glass to behold itself in; it is the true original ground of the worldly dominion and rule.[1] And although the same ground of government hath an internal spiritual original, yet it is, in the outward form only, before God, as a bestial huntsmanship among the beast-men, who must be bound and tamed.

36. For the inward spiritual government standeth in great humility in an angelical form; whereunto God also created man. If he had but remained in Paradise, then he would have had no need of the hunter; but seeing he would be a beast, God ordained him also a hunter, who might keep under the wild unruly bestial men. And the hunter and [the] beast are both alike before God in this world's bestial property; but seeing it may not be any otherwise, God holdeth it for his natural order; for he hath given every thing its government [station and order].

37. But it is to be lamented that this hunter doth hunt, slay and

[1] Lordship.

devour the tame human beasts, which do not belong to his game. But what shall we say, or wherewith shall the children of God excuse themselves, or quit themselves of this hunter, before God? Seeing every man bears externally the hunter's hind on him, over which the hunter of nature hath power, the inward spiritual man must leave his outward beast unto the hunter; for his outward beast is also evil.

38. The spirit of Moses setteth under Ham's lineage twenty-nine names, which came from Ham. Which intimate the twenty-nine properties proceeding from the third Principle, viz. from the spirit of the outward world; hinting how the formed word would be manifested through the outward nature; both in tongues and properties, whence the governments and orders of countries and nations have had their rise; albeit each property hath again its extern birth, like as one branch or sprout of a tree doth produce and bring forth other twigs. Yet the spirit in Moses doth point at the chief head-root, and the properties under these names; shewing what kind of people would arise from thence, and what their alterations and their final conclusions would be; all this lieth hidden under their names.

39. Thus Ham hath twenty-nine names of his children, and he is the thirtieth, twenty-nine is the set number of his children and childrens' children, under which the number of the end lieth in Ham's government and dominion. Thirty is his whole number, whereof the prophet speaketh, that this Ham would sell the Righteous One for thirty pieces of silver; and give the same for a potter's field. As a pot is accounted of in reference to its maker, even so is the fleshly man Ham in regard of God. He taketh his thirtieth number, which he ought to bring into God's kingdom, and giveth it for an earthly vessel, which doth resemble a field, and in that, doth sell the Righteous One, who lieth hid under the thirtieth number in the Word of power. Thus the Righteous One, under the thirtieth number, doth, by the death or mortification of Ham's flesh, sever himself from the twenty-nine numbers of these properties, which have gotten the upper hand in Ham. For in the thirtieth year the Righteous One, viz. Christ, did separate himself unto his office, and in the thirtieth number lieth this same mystery. This is understood by our fellow-scholars, and only hinted at in this place.

40. Shem hath in his line of propagation twenty-six names, and he is the twenty-seventh. And the spirit in Moses speaketh very hiddenly, saying, that *he was the father of all the children of Eber; and Eber begat two sons, the name of one was Peleg, for at his days the world was*

divided; and the other was named Joktan[1] (Gen. x. 21–25). All whatsoever the spirit in Moses speaketh of the outward acts of the patriarchs, he hath under them a single inward eye upon the line of Christ; for he saith that Shem was *the father of all the children of Eber*. Although Eber be first in the third degree after Shem, yet the spirit looketh so punctually upon the Word in the Covenant, wheresoever it doth open itself in a line.

41. For EBER signifieth in the forming of the word, as much as a sound or manifestation of the Word out of the centre; and saith further, that he begat Peleg, and called him so by reason of the division [of the earth]. The spirit doth not only look upon the outward division of lands and countries, but much rather upon the line in which stood the limit[2] of the Covenant; for in Eber the limit of the Covenant did open itself in the Word, as in the sound or manifestation, and went all along in the seed upon Peleg. And the line of Adam and Christ did there sever itself in the two brethren; as afterwards it did among the children of Abraham and Isaac: with Isaac and Ishmael; and with Jacob and Esau. Thus likewise it was here with Peleg and Joktan. Externally the world was divided, and internally the kingdom of Christ, and the kingdom of the world. Not that we are to understand that Joktan did not remain in the Covenant; only the spirit doth here look upon the motion of the seed, in which line the limit or mark of the Covenant was to be moved, wherein the Word would again move itself in the disappeared humanity of the heavenly ens, and manifest itself in the humanity.

42. The names of Shem's children and grand-children are mere intimations and significations of the properties out of the wonderful line of the prophetical spirit of Enoch; where these same properties were brought forth out of the stock into boughs; but here into branches.

43. The spirit in Moses (Gen. x. 26–30) setteth fourteen names under Joktan's line, which are the wonderful number of this bough in the tree's property, being the kingdom of Christ according to the property of nature. And of Peleg he saith no more but of one son, which he calls Reu, whom he begat when he was thirty years old (Gen. xi. 18). Intimating and pointing at the line of Christ, wherein the main limit and eye-mark of the Covenant stood. The spirit denoteth only one, for by One the Covenant should be opened; for the spirit looked with the one upon the kingdom of grace; and with

---

[1] Or Jaketan.   [2] Or mark.

his brothers' fourteen names it hinted at the human kingdom.

44. And in that he saith, that *he begat Reu, when he was thirty years old*, the spirit therein looketh forwards upon Christ, who should arise and come forth out of this stock, and manifest himself the thirtieth year of his age in his office; as also likewise all the ages under the line of Christ, which Moses hath set down, have a very certain intimation and prophecy, and point at the times of the motion in the Covenant; as [may be seen] through the prophets and other saints in whom the Covenant hath moved itself.

45. The spirit of Moses setteth five names of the children of Shem, which came forth of his loins. And though he did beget more for Moses saith that *he begat sons and daughters* (Gen. xi. 11), yet the spirit mindeth only the properties of the formed Word in the Covenant of the human property. These five names do figure out and set forth, as in a type, the five head speeches of the spiritual tongue through the formed word, proceeding from the high name of God; out of which tongues the prophetical and apostolical spirit speaketh.[1]

46. And though we could set down a form of the same, yet we should be but as senseless or dumb to the Reader who understands not the Language of Nature; and therefore we have but given a hint of it to our school-fellows. For the spirit doth also, under the names, point at the kingdoms and dominions, and they are God's, who with his name doth order, govern, guide and lead every kingdom, according to the property of his name. As the property of each kingdom is, even such is the tongue, language, phrase, and manners of the same; as it is written, *Such as the nation is, such a God it also hath.*

47. Not that there is more than one God; only, we understand therein the divine manifestation, how God doth give himself forth, in his manifestation in the formed Word, to all nations, according to every nation's and people's property; so that every nation and people doth use or bear forth the same only Word according to its property; the external form and division of which is Babel; for (Gen. xi. 6) all people had only one tongue and language, and dwelt together.

48. The only tongue was the Language of Nature, out of which they all spake; for they had it in one form, and understood in the language and speech the sense, viz. the ens, even how the will formed the ens; for so also was the spirit in the ens. Of which we will give a short intimation and manuduction, to the understanding and illuminated mind to consider of, to prove, exercise and make trial of it in

[1] Or spake.

himself; not that a man can express it, and bring it into a certain form. No, that cannot be, for it is the spirit of the wisdom of God, his manifestation.

49. The spirits of the letters in the Alphabet are the form of the one spirit in the Language of Nature; the five vowels bear forth the holy tongue of the five holy languages out of the name Jehovah, from whence the Holy Spirit speaketh; for the five vowels are the holy name of God, according to his holiness. For the name Jehova hath nothing in it, save only the five vowels A, E, I, O, V. The other letters signify and express the nature, even what the name of God in the formed word is in nature, both in love and anger, in darkness and light. But the five vowels do signify only and alone what he is in the light of holiness; for nature is tinctured with the five vowels, so that it becomes full of joy and delight.[1]

50. But that the ancient wise men, skilful in this tongue, did interpose an H in the name JEOVA, and called it JEHOVA, the same was done with great understanding, for the H maketh the holy name with the five vowels even manifest in the outward nature. It sheweth how the holy name of God doth breath forth and manifest itself even in the creature. The five vowels are the hidden name of God, who dwelleth alone in himself; but the H signifieth the divine lubet or wisdom, shewing how the divine lubet doth breath forth itself out of itself.

51. The inward understanding in the five vowels is this:

I is the name JESUS.

E is the name *Engel*[2] (Angel).

O is the formed WISDOM or lubet or the I, viz. of JESUS, and is the centre or the HEART of God.

V is the SPIRIT, viz. the SUS[3] in JESUS, which proceedeth forth out of the lubet.

A is *der Anfang*[4] *und das Ende* (the beginning and the end), viz. the will of the whole comprehension, and it is the FATHER.

52. And these five do fold themselves up with the comprehension or formation into three, viz. into such a Word, △/, that is, A, O, V,[5] Father, Son, Holy Ghost. The triangle denotes the Trinity of the properties of the Persons, and the V on the triangle denotes the spirit in the H, viz. in the breathing, where the universal God doth manifest himself spiritually with his own proceeding forth or procession out of himself.[6]

---

[1] Text, a kingdom of joy.   [2] Germ. Engel.   [3] Viz. the sweetness.
[4] Germ. Anfang.   [5] △/ A. O. V.   [6] יְחֹוָה

300

53. The other letters without the five vowels, do all proceed from the name TETRAGRAMMATON,[1] viz. out of the centre of the eternal nature, out of the Principle; and do denote and speak forth the differences[2] of the formed wisdom, viz. of the formed word in the three Principles, wherein the whole creation lieth; they are the sense of the creation, viz. the property of the powers, and the true revealed God in the word of nature. Understand this further thus:

54. When as the lubet of man, viz. the free will of man, doth conceive or form itself into a desire, then it conceiveth the whole Alphabet; for the desire is the Fiat, and the lubet to the desire, is the contemplation of the free will, viz. the formed word of wisdom, wherein the free will doth behold itself, and contemplate whereinto it will introduce the lubet of the wisdom, either into evil or good; and when the free will hath thus beheld itself, it doth conceive with the lubet in the letters, viz. in the sense of nature, and composeth the senses of the letters together, and formeth the lubet into a word; the same standeth in an internal form, viz. in a conceived thought.

55. And even then the free will taketh the H, viz. the spirit of the forth-breathing, and bringeth the formed thought before the counsel of the five senses, who behold the formed word, and prove the same, whether it be apt or not; if it doth but please them, then the H, viz. the breathing spirit, taketh the word, and brings it upon the tongue into the mouth; there is the chief framer, viz. the Fiat, which is the divine instrument, and figureth the senses of the properties out of the letters, as the free will hath set and composed them into a substance to the sounding or pronouncing, manifestation or expression.

56. Now mark and observe us here, very exactly; how every word is formed or brought in the mouth to substance,[3] viz. to the expression; how the chief worker and contriver, viz. the Fiat which is in the senses, doth shape and figure it; and how the tongue co-operates or frames itself therewith, when it takes it; and by what way it brings it forth, whether through the teeth, or above, or with open mouth; also how the tongue doth frame itself in the conjunction of the word; which sense it doth again draw back, and will not wholly cast forth, as there is many a sense which is not half put forth, but many, fully, and many again are drawn half backwards towards the heart. And now as the word was formed, so is also the thing in its form and property which is named by the word, (provided that the free will giveth it also

[1] Τετραγραμματον.   [2] Varieties.
[3] Note, when a word is formed or expressed, it is brought to substance.

a right name, and doth not impose a strange name on it, out of malice or ignorance); so it is externally noted, and internally in the compaction of the senses it hath such a virtue, or ill malignant property.

57. Now whosoever hath the understanding of the senses, viz. of the spirits of the letters, so that he doth understand how the senses are set or compounded in the lubet, he understands it in the framing of the word, when the same is formed or brought forth to substance; and is able to understand the sensual [natural or essential] language of the whole creation, and understands whence Adam gave names unto all things; and from whence the spirit of God hath prophesied in the Ancient.

58. This is now the ground of the head languages. When as all people spake in one language, then they understood one another. But when they would not use the natural[1] genuine tongue; then the true and right understanding was put out in them; for they brought the spirits of the genuine tongue of sense into an external gross form, and framed the subtle spirit of the understanding into a gross form, and learnt to speak out of the form only; as at this day all nations speak only from this same form of their contrived sensual tongue.

59. Now no people do any more understand the language of sense, and yet the birds in the air, and the beasts in the fields, understand it according to their property.

60. Therefore man may well think and consider, what he is deprived of, and what he shall again obtain in the new birth; although [perhaps] not here upon the earth, yet in the spiritual world; for in the language of sense all spirits speak one with another; they use no other language, for it is the Language of Nature.

61. Our learned ones do term themselves doctors and masters, and yet none of them understands his mother tongue. They understand no more of the spirit than the country man doth of his tool to the tillage of his ground; they use only the bare contrived form of the gross compounded words, and understand not what the word is in its sense; hence ariseth the contention and strife wherewith men contend and jangle about God and his will; men will teach what God is, and yet understand not the least of God.

62. The five holy speeches in the language of sense are God's Word; they are his operation through the sense tongue, viz. through the properties; as it cannot be denied that God giveth power, virtue and life to all creatures and vegetables, for his holy name is through

[1] Text, sensual.

all. And Adam had this holy name as a proper possession, working, ruling and sensibly efficacious in his senses; and even this jewel he lost; which is now again restored and enkindled in the holy name JESUS.

63. Therefore none can with right be called a divine, or learned in the holy Scripture, much less a doctor of the same, unless that he understands the sensual tongue, and knows how the Holy Spirit hath spoken by the sensual tongue in the holy penmen of the Scripture. If he understands not the divine sense in the holy Scripture, let him not undertake to be a master over it, to censure or interpret it, he is not at all learned therein; he is only a changer of letters [a chop-logic in the Scriptures], and understands not one letter in its sense.

64. Thus understand us herein concerning the children of Noah, viz. Japheth, Shem, and Ham, and their children and grand-children. They had lost the sensual language, and had made themselves a formed contrived one; and so spake in a formed language which they themselves understood not in the true sense. Therefore God was hidden to them; for they understood no more the voice of the Holy Spirit in their language, viz. the mental tongue of the five vowels.

65. And they looked about or imagined where God should be; and supposed that he must needs be something with form, and dwelling apart from them; and seeing they could not understand anything of God upon the earth, either what, or where, he was (and yet had heard so much of God spoken by their forefathers), thereupon they thought that he must needs dwell on high above the stars, and thought them not able to reach thither; therefore they undertook to build them a tower, whose top should reach to heaven, that so they might ascend up to him. Also they would thereby make themselves a great name, that [it might be said] they had built a tower even unto heaven.

66. Such a knowledge the formed understanding had of God; as still to this day such doctors are to be found, who know and understand no more of God's habitation and being, than these builders of the tower knew; and build in their art altogether (except the true genuine understanding ones) upon this high tower, and can never ascend up to God, and therefore they contend about the building. Every one saith how it might be built sooner and better, and yet they could never agree; for they have all built themselves even to death thereon, until the Lord sendeth a watchman, and shews them that it is

in vain; that they shall not find him on high, but that he is even among them, under the letter, and they have not known him.

67. At this we do exceedingly rejoice, that the time is born that we are lead from the Tower of Babel, and are able to see the holy God in the sensual language, Hallelujah! The Tower is broken, and fallen down at which our fathers have built themselves to death; and yet have not built it up; the foundation thereof shall not be any more laid, while the earth standeth: saith the spirit of wonders.

68. The hidden mystery of the Tower, and the divided languages, is this: Mankind had framed the sensual language of the holy Spirit into a dumb form; and used the formed word of the human understanding, only in a form, as in a contrived vessel or vehiculum; they spake only with the outward contrived vessel, and understood not the word in its own proper language of sense; they understood not that God was in the speaking Word of the understanding; as at this day the like comes to pass, and is.

69. But seeing God had, in the beginning of the creation, incorporated himself with his word into man's image, viz. into the properties of the senses, and would not be without sense, or in one only conceived form: and likewise seeing that all things do stand in growth, seeding and harvest, even now was the time of the human tree's blooming, where the spirit of the senses did put forth itself in its properties with blossoms; and manifested the properties through the blossoms, and out of the blossoms brought forth the fruit; and like as every blossom doth open and put forth itself at the outmost part, or highest of the stalk or branches of the tree or stock, even so the spirit [of nature] drove the children of men to the extremest height, that they also would build them a high tower, like to a high tree or tall stalk; for it would manifest its blossom, and fruits also, in the highest of the stalk; and upon the tower which they would build up unto heaven the sensual spirit opened itself with the blossom.

70. For man's will was, that they would ascend up to God; and the God of [nature, or] sense put forth himself in the same desire and will, for they sought him only in a circumscribed [local, outward] manner; and even so he applied himself to them in a conceived form of sense, out of the contrived formed tongues and languages, wherein notwithstanding they were dumb and knew him not.

71. They were entered with the sense, viz. with the mental spirit,[1] into nature, and nature had captivated them in the understanding.

---

[1] Or the spirit of their mind.

Therefore God also manifested himself to them with the sensual spirit in the contrived form of the tongues, out of the seventy-two properties, through the three Principles, viz. through a threefold sensual Alphabet, according to the three worlds' property; viz. through three times four and twenty letters; and they brought the sensual spirit of the letters, in their contrived form, through the tongue out of each letter, through the three Principles, viz. into three properties of tongues and languages, according to the property of the Trinity of the Deity.

72. And hence arise seventy-two languages out of one only sensual tongue, wherein all speeches and languages are contained, and each tongue and language fell upon its people; according as every family of the stock of the human tree had a property out of the formed word, even such a language befell them out of their sense, viz. out of the same property of the formed word.

73. For the sense of man's speech, that he is able to speak, doth come unto him originally out of the divine Word, which introduced itself with the Verbum Fiat into a creation. Now this Word brought forth itself through the compacted properties according to their compaction, nature, kind, form and property; for so distinct and various also are the senses in the quality even in the place of this world; far otherwise in one country than in another. And even so God did likewise form the languages according to the property of every land and country.

74. For seeing that people were to be dispersed into every country and climate, he opened to each people a language, according as it should be in a land; which did apply itself unto the same quality [of sense], and accord therewith; so that the quality of the country did not introduce the turba into it, if they, with the word of their voice, agreed to the sound of the formed spirit in the soul of the great world in that place.

75. For, as the manifestation of the formed word was in the spirit of the world in every place, even so the spirit of God did form, through the nature of the properties, the language and speech in every country. First the seventy-two head languages out of nature, and afterward the collateral affinities,[1] proceeding from the senses of every head language; as we plainly see, that a man doth scarce find, in any place of the world, among all the head languages, one and the same sense in any head language, within the compass of fifteen or

---

[1] Or dialects of language.

eighteen miles:[1] they alter and change almost every fifteen or eighteen miles, all according as the properties of that pole, or elevation, are: [Look] what kind of property the lubet hath in its predominant constellation, even such a property the vulgar people have in their language and speech.

[1] Fifteen or eighteen miles. According to the elevation of the pole, climate, or zenith and nadir.

The Thirty-Sixth Chapter

Of the Antichristian Babylonical Whore of all Nations, Tongues and Speeches; shewing what is contained under the Languages and Tower of Babel

AN OPEN GATE OF THE MYSTERY
OF THE GREAT BABYLON

1. COURTEOUS reader, I desire to warn thee in love, that thou wouldst not understand our sense and meaning according to partial affections, to detract, revile, or especially to contemn or despise any, as from us; much less to set upon them, in their office, function and dignities, out of passion; but we shall speak in general. Let every one prove himself; he shall indeed find the great mystery of the Babylonical tower in himself; and also the number of the false beast. Let him but read our meaning with patience, and take himself along, as to his evil innate hereditary property, under the same, as really the earthly mortal man in all men belongeth unto this text.

2. We will here write what the time hath brought forth and manifested, and if it were not manifest by man, yet the beasts should be driven to manifest the same; for the time is born,[1] and nothing can hinder: The Most High accomplisheth his work.

3. Moses saith, Nimrod, Ham's [grand-] son, began his kingdom at Babel, and was the first lord upon the earth after the flood, and was the first erector of the tower, and the city Babylon (Gen. x. 8–10). Yet we are not to understand that only Ham's children would build the tower, but also Japheth's and Shem's, for they were yet all together as one people, and would build them a tower, whose top should reach even unto heaven, that they might thereby make themselves a great name (Gen. xi. 4).

4. This tower, on which the tongues were divided, and where the great city, Babel, stood, is a figure of the fallen earthly man who is entered into selfhood, and hath made the formed word of God in him unto an idol; for the nature of the tower was even this, viz. that it should there stand as a great wonder, which men had made in their

[1] Or fulfilled.

307

own contriving fancy, whereupon they would ascend up to God; and signifies that man hath lost the right understanding of God, and his habitation and essence.

5. Man had compacted [or framed] his understanding, through the desire of self-elevation and exaltation into the sensual tongue, and contrived or conceived the same into a selfly propriety, in which conception or comprehension the spirit of the mental tongue of the five vowels was departed from him.

6. Not that we are to conceive, that this spirit was departed from its creature; only the free will of man had, in the formed word of the consonants[1] (wherein the spirit of the five vowels, viz. the unformed Spirit of God, did manifest itself) brought itself forth, as a peculiar god, out of the resignation to the unformed Spirit, into a self-fullness and self-willed weening and fancy; the type whereof was the tower, where the men of Babel would come and climb up to God in their own conceived will and thoughts. They themselves were gone forth from the Spirit of God, and would through their own power and ability take the kingdom of God to themselves in selfhood; they would enter with their own will, self-born in evil and good, into the property of God's holiness. This denotes and declares the divided tongues, where every property had brought itself forth out of the universal sensual tongue into a selfishness and a peculiar selfly understanding, so that they did not any longer understand one another; where the understanding was compacted and brought into a propriety out of and according to the three alphabets.

7. This compacted formed tongue the Holy Ghost did open on the day of Pentecost in St Peter's sermon, where Peter, from the opened sensual tongue, spake in one language all languages; and this was also Adam's language, whence he gave names to all creatures.

8. Thus understand us aright, what Babel and the tower of Babel doth typify and point out. The city Babel is the Ham-like man, who buildeth this city upon the earth; the tower is his self-chosen god, and divine worship. All reason-taught, from the school of this world, are the master-builders of this tower. All those who have set up themselves to be teachers, and are chosen thereunto by man, without God's spirit, they are the master-workmen at this tower, and the idol of the world, none excepted; they carve and frame altogether only stone and wood for this tower.

9. For the name Nimrod sheweth us very clearly, also in its own

---

[1] Or speechless, dumb letters.

308

sense of the formed word, that it is a self-contrived, formed, amassed and compacted lust, which did advance itself on high as a selfly god; the type whereof was the tower. God suffered them in their confounded understanding to set forth the figure of their property, as a type of what man would be in the presence of God.

10. Now saith reason, wherefore did God suffer it to come to pass? Answer: Thus must it be; that the wonders of the wisdom in the unformed Word of the five vowels might introduce themselves, through the formed word of the three Principles, into a form or external contemplation, as a counter platform, draft, portraiture or formation. For the dark world of God's anger was become manifest in man, whence the gross earthly property was generated, which also had wholly captivated man; and the same did here likewise represent its image as a selfly god.

11. Now then, the tower was a type of the dark world, where man would behold God in the dark selfhood; and denotes the earthly man, who standeth in God's sight as this tower, and is an image and resemblance of divine contemplation[1] according to evil and good, as a painted life; for the true human life was the formed life, which became, in own-desire to selfhood, such an image, before God, as this tower.

12. All men, even from Adam, who have taught of God, without [having] the divine vision of the spirit of God in them, they have all spoken and taught from this tower of the confounded tongues. And even hence hath the strife arisen about God, and his will and essence; so that man hath in selfhood contended and jangled about God. One hath said, they must bring bricks to the building of the tower, another stone, a third lime, a fourth wood, water, or other needful materials; and their chief masterbuilders have been manifold, every one according to the property of his own tongue: every one hath desired to build the tower upon his own foundation and proper ground; one hath had, in the property of his country and climate, stone for the building thereof, another lime, the third chalk or clay, the fourth wood; and every one hath thought good to build the tower alone for himself, out of the material of his own property, for a great wonder, that all the world might look and behold that which he hath built.

13. And then, when people of other countries have seen what that hath built, then they have contemned it, and said, that the property of the material of their country hath been better for the erecting the

[1] Or God's contemplation.

tower; and have begun to reject it, and to build the tower for themselves, and praised that also; which likewise hath again been despised of others, who have accounted the material of their country better, so long till they have fallen quite out, in pride and contention, and have left off from the tower, and have fallen upon one another, and persecuted, slain and murdered one another about the knowledge of the tower of Babel; and that party which hath then got the victory, that hath again built the tower out of its own property; till other people have also risen up and accounted their own matter and stuff for the best.

14. For the speeches of the understanding were confounded and divided, therefore the people neither knew nor understood one another's property; and each people or nation hath supposed and looked upon the other to be strange in the power of the understanding in the formed word; from whence the contempt of religion, viz. of the knowledge and confession of the word hath arisen; for the sensual [intelligible] tongue was compacted according to the multiplicity of the properties.

15. And thus the wrath of the eternal nature (and also the prince who dwells therein, viz. the devil in his legions) doth satiate and recreate itself in the strife and contention of man in the compacted word of the tongues; and thus the Antichrist, who is the tower of Babel, viz. the self-will of the Ham-like man, domineereth in the temple of God, and there hath set himself up in the place of the Holy Spirit.

16. For the temple of God is the formed word of the human languages and tongues in man's understanding; as it is written, The word is nigh thee, namely in thy mouth and heart (Rom. x. 8); and the seat and habitation of the opposite adverse devil is the monstrous property out of the dark world.

17. In this formed word of divine understanding, the Antichrist, viz. the will of self out of the properties of nature, hath set up and established himself, and pranketh and set forth himself with his property of nature, as if he were God, and yet he is the condemned accursed son chosen to death, which cannot inherit the kingdom of God, for he was not made a creature out of God's will but out of the will of self; as the devil, who was an angel, yet became a devil from the will of the dark world which advanced itself in him.

18. The like also we are to understand concerning the Antichristian Babylonical beast of reason's self-will, which termeth itself

divine, and is only a monster of the true man which died in Adam to the holy image of God's spiritual world, and shall and must be born anew in the Word, which did again manifest itself in the human property in Christ; or else it cannot see the holy Word, viz. the unformed divine Word of power.

19. This same holy Word must again enter into the compacted sensual tongue, and bruise the same, so that the whole and perfect understanding of all tongues may be again manifest in one; as Christ said of the corner-stone that it should be a rock of offence; upon whomsoever it should fall, him it should bruise (Rom. ix. 33; 1 Pet. ii. 8).

20. Thus understand us now what the Antichrist or the Babylonical whore with the dragon-beast is, as may be seen in the Revelation: Every man which is not born again of God hath the mark of the beast and the false whore in him.

21. The beast is the animal [natural] earthly Ham-like man, who is from the limus of the earth, according to the earth's grossness and malignant malice, which ariseth out of the dark world, and standeth in the curse of God. This beast did arise in Adam and Eve, when they did imagine after evil and good; and came into its self-fullness, away from the divine power and will; and is before God only as a beast. This beast, the devil hath infected with his desire, and made it wholly monstrous, and insinuated his desire thereinto, so that it only lusteth after vanity, as a cow doth after grass.

22. But the whore of the beast is the poor soul, captivated in vanity; which soul had its rise in the formed Word of the three Principles, which was God's image; but now, by the lust of the beast, it hath begotten to itself an own self-will, which is departed from God into selfhood, as a self-willed, self-born creature, which doth what it pleaseth, and not what God's spirit willeth. This self-will, revolted and apostatized from God, is the whore of the beast, which whoreth with itself in the pride of selfhood.

23. But now the poor captive soul lieth in this gross beast, and is captivated in its own self-born will, viz. in the whore, and longeth after God, from whom it proceeded and was inspired into the created image; and looketh about on all sides, where its true native home of rest should be, and it findeth that it is clothed and covered with this whore; and then it bringeth its desire into this whore's will, and seeketh the place of God for rest; and then the whore's will taketh the poor captivated soul's desire into itself, and thereby doth exalt and set

up itself; it persuades itself that it, in the soul's desire, is the fair child of God which shall possess heaven, and gives out that it is holy, and sets forth itself as a god, which men must honour and adore.

24. And seeing this bastard, viz. the false will of selfhood, cannot see or behold the place of God, either what or where God is, then the false will goeth on in the way of its property, and betakes itself unto, and appropriates to itself, the manifested word of the letter, viz. the formed voice of God's children, who spake from the living Word, and setteth its contrived form of its own conceived ens into the literal word, and clothes itself externally with the literal word, standeth forth with boldness and self-achieved confidence, and saith, Here is the place of God; here is heaven; here is God manifest. But it is only a bastard, and is predestinated[1] to condemnation; for God hath not created it; but it was born and brought forth out of the lust of the soul, when it did turn its face from God into the centre, and would taste and prove evil and good.

25. This harlot's brat sitteth upon the bestial monstrous man, and rideth upon him as upon its horse, and is half devil, and half brute beast, which shall and must die, or else the soul will not be redeemed so as to see the face of God again.

26. This whore hath taken its power and understanding out of nature, viz. out of the compaction of evil and good, that is, out of the dark and outward world, and hath swallowed up [or avalled] the precious image of God in itself, which, after God, was created out of the heavenly ens.

27. Here is the swineherd, as Christ said, who had consumed his father's inheritance with the swine. He meaneth the poor soul, which hath devoured, spent and consumed its heavenly goods in the heavenly ens with this whore of the evil self devilish-will; so that it standeth in God's sight as a tattered patched swineherd, and keepeth the fruit of the evil whore, viz. of the devil's fatted swine upon the earth, which are the wicked ones in their fruits.

28. Thus we understand what the Antichristian Babylonical whore in man is, which hath arisen out of the divided properties, viz. out of Adam, in whom the properties departed out of their mutual and equal accord, each into its own desire and lust to selfness, whereby Adam became earthly and mortal; out of whom afterwards the tree of the multiplicity of tongues and speeches did arise out of one only tongue.

[1] *Note.*—Predestination.

29. Now know this: that the multitudes or variety of faiths are generated out of the divided tongues; so that almost every nation hath brought itself into sundry, several and peculiar opinions of God's being and essence, and therein consists the confusion, viz. the mystery of the great Babylon; concerning which the spirit of God did prophesy and declare out of the prophetical root, both out of the line of Christ, how Christ should come to restore and remedy the poor captive soul, and regenerate its right true life, and also out of the turba magna, how this beast, together with the whore, should be cast from the face of God into the fiery furnace.

30. With this whore of self, all the false spiritual ones[1] [or priest-hood] have clothed themselves; who set up themselves to be teachers of the mystery of God's kingdom, without God's spirit. Outwardly they have covered themselves with the prophetical and Apostolical word, and pleaded the testimony of the Bible. But they have introduced their own sense out of the whore's ens thereinto, and have hung, in their heart, to the Babylonical fleshly whore, and have not understood the prophetical and Apostolical tongue [in its sense].

31. They have spoken from the sense of their own bestial selfhood, through the prophetical and Apostolical word, and have brought and used Christ's words to their own selfish Babylonical harlotry, and committed whoredom; and likewise have adorned and trimmed up their bastard, under Christ's purple mantle, with silver, gold, and precious stones, and also with worldly dignities, honours, favour and riches.

32. After these, men have run, and have even adored and esteemed them as gods, falling deeply in love with their bastard; although their hearts have never agreed, or stood upon the only true ground, [but have been at variance with each other]. And this is that of which the prophet Daniel speaketh, saying, *they shall honour a god, whom their fathers knew not, with gold, silver and precious stones* (Daniel xi. 38, 39); and unto those that help them to strengthen their [strange god] Maüsim,[2] they will divide the land for inheritance. This whole chapter doth belong hereunto.

33. Now, when we consider aright what this Babylonical tower is at present, in Christ's kingdom upon the earth, and what it was under Moses, and among the Gentiles, then we find very clearly, that among all three it is of one property; and so also among the Turks and present Jews: every nation builds it, out of its own materials, for in the right

---

[1] Clergical and ecclesiastical.   [2] God of forces.

universal sensual tongue (if it be manifest in one) we are altogether but one only people and nation, even from Adam.

34. But the very cause that we are divided, and brought into opinions, is by reason of our master-builders and founders, viz. of the high schools, priests, popes, bishops, doctors, also the rabbis and masters of all nations, who are set as workmen to the building of the tower. All these have judged from their own language and natural understanding, viz. from their conceived and formed sensual tongue, from the outward letter; and have indeed neither known God nor the light of nature; but have been blind and dumb as to both; both the Jews and Gentiles; and also the self-made teachers of the Christians.

35. Whosoever have run, devoid of God's spirit, without divine understanding, either among Jews and Gentiles, Christians and Turks, they have built only this tower in their own essence; and the same is even a tower of the great wonders of God, of divine contemplation both according to light and darkness, life and death, joy and sorrow.

36. Not that we are to understand that this tower is not at all profitable before God; it is even the great mystery of God's manifestation according to love and anger. As God hath created out of the great mystery all manner, kinds and sorts of beasts, birds, worms, trees and herbs, evil and good; and that, all to the manifestation of the great wonders; thus likewise the human tree hath brought forth such wonders out of its sensual tongue, out of the multiplicity of the properties, and introduced them into a substance for its growth [and glory], viz. to the great harvest of God; where each property of love and anger, light and darkness, shall reap in its own fruit, and every thing shall possess its heaven in itself, in its own formed and conceived ens, out of the only Word of God, which hath given forth itself to every life (even unto every life and being, according to its own proper quality and virtue, according to, and out of, its Principle) as a universal Word, to the glorious manifestation of eternity.

37. Now, when we further consider of this beast, with the whore, what it is in itself, within and without, then we find that it is the formed compacted word of the spirits of the letters; for men are all of one only property as to their life; all are begotten out of one flesh and soul; and have all but one only kind of life; as a tree in many boughs and branches, where the boughs and twigs do not perfectly and wholly seem alike, or the same in form, but all have one only sap and virtue: so likewise the creature of mankind, among Jews, Christians, Turks and Heathen.

38. And the only difference is this: the spirits of the letters in the formed word do sever us in the understanding; else we live all alike in the four elements, and eat of the fruits of one mother, and remain in her, when we die to this outward life.

39. The compacted sensual tongue, which is divided in the spirits of the letters, doth [confound us and] make us to err; so that we do suppose we are strange one to another; and yet we are all but one only tree, which the devil hath poisoned with his desire in Adam, so that the equal temperature or accord was brought into distemper and discord; whereupon the spirits of the letters were [variously] made manifest, so that we speak from many speeches; that is, we have introduced the powerful word of God into the multiplicity of the divided properties; and have made, in each tongue's property, a self-hood, or a selfish desire to arrogation, self-apprehension and assumption.

40. Hence arise the contrarieties, differences, and opinions,[1] in that we have introduced the unformed word into [the form of our own self-made] image. Now we contend and strive about these images [and conceits]; and every one supposeth his own to be best; and when we bring all these images [and several semblances] again into one language and speech, and mortify them, then the only quickening Word of God, which giveth power and life to all things, is again manifest; and strife ceaseth, and God is all in all.

41. Therefore we say, as we have found it in the grace of the One, that all men's imaginations, opinions and knowings of God, his being, and will, without the divine light [or illumination of the spirit],[2] are this same whore's beast, which is flown forth and arisen from the compacted spirits of the letters; whereby men contend about the spirits of the letters.

42. We have lost the five vowels in the Alphabet; which do introduce all the spirits of the letters into one pure harmony; and the five vowels are as 'twere senseless or dumb, in reference to the other letters; and yet they are the life of the rest, for there cannot any word be formed but there must be a vowel.

43. Now there is no better way or remedy to bring us into union, that so we may become ONE again with one another, one people, one tree, one man in soul and body, than to destroy and kill all the images or forms of the letters in us; and suffer none of them at all to have its own self-life; not desiring to know or will any more of God, save only

---

[1] Text, images.   [2] The undoubted Unction of the Holy Ghost.

and alone what God willeth to know in us and through us; and also that we do immerse or resign the soul's hunger and desire merely, only, and nakedly, without any other knowing or willing, into the five vowels; and therein the great holy name of JEOVA or JESUS (viz. the living Word) is manifest; which giveth life unto all things, and [that we should] not, according to the property of nature, desire and will the different variety of many things, but give up ourselves into the one only love-sun: therein is he manifest.

44. As the outward sun giveth life and power to the whole world, so likewise this only name, in its power, giveth life and understanding to all the letters; and understand us aright what we mean by the whoredoms of the letters.

45. The letters, viz. the properties of the sensual tongue, have introduced themselves into an external form, or self-full will and understanding, and brought themselves with the vowels into a compaction [self-comprehension or particular formation]. And when this was done, then JESUS, viz. the holy name JEOVA, died [or disappeared] in the sensual tongue in the letters with the five vowels of the one only holy mental tongue; that is, the spiritual man, which was resigned in [and to] God, died to the divine understanding and will.

46. Now there is a self-willed beast of selfishness and ownhood brought forth out of the spirit of the other letters, which doth only kill, and bring forth dead fruit. For Paul saith, *the letter killeth, but the spirit maketh alive* (2 Cor. iii. 6). Understand this thus:

47. The divided sensual tongue killeth us, sets us at odds and variance, and leads us into Babel. But the spirit of the vowels, viz. the holy name of God, doth again revive and quicken us in him. Therefore the holy word of the five vowels did again (when as the spirits of the letters were divided and brought into the selfhood of the wonders of God) espouse and incorporate itself forthwith in Paradise with the precious Covenant, into the letter, viz. into the natural man; for to manifest itself again with a motion in the compacted tongue, and to introduce the holy sense again into the sensual tongue.

48. Thus understand us aright: The literal form in the sensual tongue is now the evil beast, which will domineer in its own power. Now into this evil beast the spirit of the five vowels, viz. the name JEHOVAH (which with the H, hath breathed the JESUS thereinto) hath given in itself, and killed the evil beast, viz. the self-will, and hath again tinctured the spirits of the letter, viz. the right natural man, with the tincture of the holy name of the vowels, or JEHSUS;

and with the love hath slain the death or deaths in the letters, and destroyed their self-will; so that the spirits of the letters cannot any more introduce themselves into a self-full compaction of the sensual tongue; for they are dead in their own will; and the spirit JEHOVAH in JESUS is become their life; so that they live no longer to their self-hood, viz. to the nature of the wrath; but in that they live, they live to God (Rom. vi. 11).

49. Thus now the beast of the whore is in us outwardly, viz. in the mortal man; and inwardly is Christ in the immortal man, who is passed through the death of the letters and hath turned the death into life (John v. 24).

50. Now it behoveth man, and his main happiness depends thereon, that he also die unto the images of the letters in him; and disclaim or depart from all reasons, scholarship, or knowledge of nature, and all Babylonical master-builders, however they be called; and enter into the one only life, JEHSUS; and not at all dispute about the way, where it is; but only think[1] that it is in him; that he must forsake all, whatever he hath, either art, wit or skill, etc., and become one barely and nakedly in himself, bring himself into the ONE, viz. into God's will, and be freely willing with whatsoever it will work or do with him. He must give up himself will-less; and leave himself wholly in God's mercy; and bring all his learnings into this one only thing; that he, in his teachings and learnings, will not do or speak anything but what God willeth through him. And thus all images [opinions and conceits] do die in him; and the soul's life falleth into the only living Word, which hath manifested itself again in the humanity.

51. For this is the great beast of the Babylonical whore in us: that we bring ourselves into the images and forms of the letters; and make opinions to ourselves: that opinion is a beast.

52. Also we must not desire to know and will, ourselves; but die continually with our own self-will; and in all things give God the honour; and give him again that which he giveth us, viz. whatsoever understanding, wisdom and skill we have; and acknowledge that it is not our own, but that the divine sun shineth out of and through us, and worketh in us as it pleaseth.

53. Thus likewise we must diffuse and give out again, universally to all, our power and virtue, which the divine sun worketh in us, without any gain, advantage or hire from any; whosoever shall help to

---

[1] Or consider.

maintain and nourish our life, unto him we must be thankful, and not flatter any for his authority's sake; or receive his false glance, show or lustre into this sunlight; but all must be in general or common, as the sunshine doth give itself universally, and gives no strong, great or potent thing any more, but its purity and brightness; it tinctureth the earth and its children with one only power and virtue, and giveth life and strength to all things.

54. Herein now we shall know whether one be a teacher sent of God, or whether he hath his rise and original only out of the spirit of the letter. If he be born universally out of the love, then he hath the light of divine knowledge, viz. the sensual divine understanding, a tongue, tinctured from the divine ens of the five vowels, and speaketh from the spirit of God, rebuketh and teacheth powerfully without respect of any man's person, and hath no image [or mental idol] in him; for he teacheth from the spirit of God, even what the same [spirit] teacheth in him.

55. But if he be a master-builder of the tower of Babel, born of the spirit of the letters, viz. of the disharmony [or diversities], then he is a hypocrite and flatterer, a glozing fawner that will say anything to please those that are gainful and advantageous to him; a soother of those that do help to honour his Maüsim, and adorn his letter-god in the divided tongues; a scorner, evil speaker, and bold censurer of those that do not honour him in his form [and sect of religion]; a self-applauder, ambitious, proud, and under a glistering show of religion and seeming holiness, a covetous, malicious, envious one; putting forth himself with ostentation, that so he may be known and honoured; he will be applauded and set by, of man; attributes to himself understanding and wisdom; and boasteth of wisdom and a rectified judgment and understanding, and yet hath none of them; but he is only a builder on the tower of Babel, viz. of an external figure and form; a painted Christian; he will undertake to teach others, and yet he himself was never taught of God. He teacheth only from the form of the compacted spirits of the letter, which have compacted themselves in evil and good; he taketh these into his own power and ability, and compacts and sets the words together into an opinion.

56. And that opinion is the tower of Babel, and they which run after him, and associate, gather and bind themselves with him in the opinion, are the city, Babel, viz. the children of Nimrod; who will climb and ascend up to heaven upon this tower, and are continually a climbing up, their whole life, yet come not to heaven in the opinion;

but when the time of the outward literal constellation is out, then this built tower falleth down, viz. the outward man, together with his opinion, and all shatters and breaks to pieces, even to the only soul, which then standeth naked and bare before God.

57. Here is now no remedy, unless that it hath the one only spirit of the sounding letter, viz. the enformed Word of God in it, so that it is able in its desire to attract and draw the same to itself, and clothe itself therewith, that the same doth cleave and break in pieces all the formed, contrived, compacted tongues and images of the letters, and introduce them into one only tongue and will, which is God, all in all. All things must enter again into the ONE, viz. into the universal; in the multiplicity there is nothing but strife and disquietness, but in the Oneness there is an eternal rest, and no enmity or contrary will.

58. Now when we do truly consider again what the tower and the city, Babel is, in its formed image upon the earth, and what and where it is, then we find it clearly portrayed before our eyes, that it is the great houses of the churches, cloisters, fortresses, and also the strong walls and towers of the cities upon the earth, wherein men hide themselves from force and power, and in the opinions play the hypocrites before God in the churches, cloisters and strongholds; and cry unto him that he should receive and accept of them in their contrived, framed and received opinion of the letter.

59. What is all this? An idolatry and hypocrisy, an Antichrist, with show and glistering glory. What do men bring into this glozing, hypocritical Babylon? Nothing but images [mental idols], and self-contrived opinions, forged out of the form of the letter. What do men carry home with them from this hypocritical, specious house? Only the images of the letters. Into these images [and conceits] the poor captive soul doth wrap itself, which notwithstanding is full of fear, doubting, and trembling, by reason of the conceived and received image [or opinions]; and is continually in fear lest another people might break in upon its received, framed images, and destroy and overthrow these its received images. Therefore men have made fortresses, bulwarks and towers and strong walls about their cities and churches; that so they might defend themselves, lest the tower upon which they would ascend up into heaven should be destroyed.

60. Now saith reason: these are indeed houses of meeting, where men do teach and instruct the simple and ignorant, where men sing and pray. Lo! externally, in and among the literal men, they are only

the tower and city, Babel; but internally, among the children of God, in whom the Temple of God is, where the images [and mental idols] are destroyed, there, is Christ: that is, in those who have pulled down and broken all images and opinions in them, and are entered through the conversion from images and conceits only and alone into the only mere naked grace, mercy and free compassion of God, and esteem themselves as wholly unworthy, empty nothings, and become as 'twere dead in themselves, willing or desiring nothing else save only the mere purity of God in his love-will, and account themselves too unworthy of attributing or taking anything to themselves; and freely fall, in deepest humility, into God's tender mercy, as if they were not: and wholly cast their desires and wills into God's compassion; so that, what he wills and doth in them, that they also will, and nothing else. In these, I say, it is a house of teaching and a house of hearing, a Temple of God, where the spirit of God teacheth, heareth, singeth and praiseth in the soul; for they are dead to all selfhood, and self-willing and weening, and do melodise with unity and oneness of spirit in the praise of God, in the knowledge of the Holy Ghost: these are the Church of Christ.

61. But the rest have only the tower at Babel in the opinion, in their [conceits and] images; these idols they carry with them into the houses of stone, and glory in them, worship them, and carry them again home with them; and fight for them, as if they had the living God in them; and wage great wars for these images; laying country and people waste and desolate; and yet they are more foolish than the birds in the air, which do all praise and honour God in one tongue and understanding; for they are all without any images; whatsoever the great God doth with them, therewith they are content.

62. The human tree is one only tree; if they continued in the one only God who hath created them, and did not make unto themselves images, who would set them at odds and variance about God? They indeed are and live in the one only God (Acts xvii. 28), and yet they contend and jangle about God.

63. Wherefore do they contend? For the idols of their heart, for the stone-houses of the churches, and for the pride of the images [and forged opinions]. Every one will honour his image, and set it up aloft as a high tower, that so he might have great respect in the city, Babel. And therefore they build themselves strongholds, and make great bulwarks and walls to defend and keep the image; and flatter themselves in hypocrisy, and understand and mean, by the contrived

and painted image, the god Maüsim, viz. the fat belly [god], and pleasure of the beast, viz. of this whore's image. They set the image upon the tower for the show of their holiness, and therewith they are very devout in glistering appearances before God, as with a peculiar self-born god. But they immure the beast within their stone-houses, that it may be secure, and there fat itself.

64. What is now this beast with the whore? It is half devil, which hath its kingdom upon the earth, and it is half beast; this evil beast hath devoured man, viz. the image of God.

65. And for this cause God became man: that he might destroy, slay, and nullify the works of the devil. And we must put on this divine humanity, and destroy the devil's kingdom in us, and mortify all images; otherwise we cannot see God: the living Word must mortify the literal image.

66. The living Word is therefore become man, that the literal image might die, and the first man, which was formed out of the living Word, in God's image, might be regenerated anew in Christ's spirit, viz. in the living Word; and if now he be born, then all the image-teachers are more prejudicial than beneficial to him; for they introduce only their images into the Temple of Christ, and destroy the image of God.

67. And here let this be declared concerning the children of Nimrod, and the tower of Babel; as the spirit hath so given us to know. And we do admonish the Reader, in love, to prove and examine himself: he shall find where he is. This is not written to reproach any. But thus the spirit speaketh with open mouth, and sheweth what all things are, from whence they come, and into what end they shall go.

68. But the reason why so much is written of the beast and the whore of Babel, is because it is at its end, and shall soon be broken in pieces; therefore it must be revealed, that men may see and know it. For Babel falleth not: unless that all whatsoever hath made the images doth likewise fall. All images [opinions and sects of religion] together with the beast and whore must fall; else there is no cure or remedy.

69. Men have for a long time been a patching and piecing of it, and have verily thought to have made a virgin of the whore. But her whoredom hath thereby been only adorned, trimmed up, and made the greater. If this whore shall fall, then all sects, which are only the images of the whore, must fall down and come to naught, together with the beast upon whom she rideth. Every man must break down

and destroy the images and idols in himself: and where they will not do it, there the seal of the Lord doth it.

70. How very finely doth the whore at present perk up its head, and seeing it heareth that the spirit doth intimate [great and glorious things] of Zion, viz. of the adorned holy bride of Christ; then it thinks that it is the fair child which God will bring into a golden temple, wherein there shall be a brave golden time, and mere joy, pleasure and delight; and it looketh about to see from whence this fair temple of God should come, into which it should enter, and become a virgin; it hearkeneth continually from whence these holy people should come, who, as it supposeth, should make a golden world.

71. But it thinks not to leave off from its covetous voluptuous whoredom, and be converted. No! it groweth worse and worse; and more unchaste and abominable, full of blasphemies; so that there is scarce any good at all in it; and it standeth before God, as an arraigned condemned whore.

72. Hearken, thou adorned and crowned Babylon, full of evil and wickedness in the sight of God and his angels; we have heard a watchman say: Away! the city, together with the tower of the whore and the beast, is fallen, and judged of the Most High. Thou shalt not see the city of God for ever, unless that thy children do put off and cast away the defiled garment, full of shame; and fall down wholly naked and bare, without any image, at the feet of the Most High; and turn unto him. Such as these may indeed see it; but as for others, who hope for golden mountains, and seek for temporal honour, money, and pleasure of the flesh; not any of them. Amen.

73. Reason will here, (in the above-mentioned text, where it is mentioned that a true Christian must die to all images [opinions] and self-knowledge, and be wholly annihilated in himself), begin to speculate, cavil, and say, that we do forbid man the natural knowledge and external rational wisdom, whereby men do govern the life and all things of this world, and if this were so all understanding would be abolished.

74. Unto him we declare, that nothing is hereby taken away or abolished in man; neither understanding, skill nor art, for all these arise out of the divine wisdom. We do not nullify the expressed Word of the formed wisdom, but only the beast, which will rule in divine contemplation, viz. the beast-like will of self and selfish ownhood and propriety, which is departed from God, which honoureth itself as a

false selfly god, and cannot believe or trust in God (this is even the Antichrist, which hath set himself up in God's place, 2 Thess. ii. 4). And we withal do teach, that man must wholly die to the Antichristian image, that he may be born again in Christ, with a new life and will; which new will hath might and ability in the formed word of nature to see and behold with divine eyes, all the wonders of God both in nature and creature, in the formed wisdom.

75. For if the Antichrist dieth in the soul, then Christ ariseth from death; for he resteth in the five vowels in his grave, viz. in the mental tongue, which died in Adam, and lieth captive in Antichrist. When this same ariseth from death in the mental tongue, and is made alive, then he openeth all the treasures of the heavenly wisdom in the sensual tongue; so that man doth far more clearly understand the spirits of the letters, viz. the formed word of nature, in all the three Principles, than he did before in the Antichristian whore's child.

76. For the new birth is indeed effected and brought to pass in the mental tongue, viz. in the disappeared image of the heavenly humanity; but it tingeth and casteth away the false Antichristian image of the natural humanity, viz. of the spirits of the dumb senseless letters, and doth make them all senseless and dead in their selfhood, and gives them their own life; so that they do behold themselves in the new humanity, and make all their assumptions and formations in the new humanity.

77. These new assumptions and formings are effected and wrought forth in the divine will, in resignation; and they are the heavenly images and formings, which are formed and shaped in the Holy Ghost to the honour of God.

78. For if the holy name of God be not in its power, in the forming of the words, viz. in the spirits of the letters, which are the formed word, and helps to form the word in the sensual tongue, then the false Antichrist speaketh only from his own self-assumption of the literal form.

79. For the spirit of God doth form and imprint into the word of the mouth (when as the sensual tongue takes it) righteousness, truth, faith, love and patience, viz. divine power and virtue; but the Antichristian child doth coform in the conception of the word out of the Serpent's ens, lies, falsehood, tales, unfaithfulness; pride, covetousness, bitter stinging envy, anger, backbitings, revilings, and all whatsoever is against God, and maketh the formed word of the letter

to a beast and wicked bastard, which is rejected from the face of God, upon which the judgment passeth.

80. The like is also to be understood concerning the external wisdom and art. If the divine wisdom worketh therein, then the understanding and the art is very good, and grounded in the divine wisdom; but if it be otherwise, it standeth in mere Antichristian false image [and fancy], to the judgment of God.

81. Therefore let a man prove and try himself what falls in and suggests itself into the sensual tongue in the formation of his words; if it be truth, righteousness, faith in hope, love in patience, an earnest, full, unfeigned desire to speak and do the truth, and that for God's sake, in hope of eternal life, then it is well with him; let him continue steadfast in such exercise, and work more and more effectually and powerfully therein; and his precious pearl-tree stands in its growth and increase.

82. But if the contrary be found in him, that when he will speak, that then lying, a proud look, great words for pomp and ostentation, also envious bitterness, false speaking against his neighbour, false-hood, anger, a revenging desire, false and evil interpretings, and wrong harsh censurings do fall in and imprint themselves into the formings and fancy of his words; then he may certainly and really know, that he hath the Antichristian Babylonical whore, together with the false wicked dragon-beast, sitting in his heart; which doth introduce and insinuate and imprint such will and desire in his words, for the forming and building up of the hellish images; for these false insinuations and suggestions are all brought to substance in the formation of the sensual tongue.

83. Therefore know, O man! (and prove thyself) that thou art the image of God according to the divine Word and understanding: if thou speakest, willest and dost righteously, then thou art that same image of God, wherein God dwelleth, speaketh, willeth and worketh; but if otherwise, and the contrary is found in thee, then thou art the apostate rebellious Lucifer, in his generation and train; and dost, willest and desirest even that which he willeth and doth.

84. And though thou desirest not hell-fire; Lucifer also did not desire it; but there is no other reward for the false image, seeing it forms itself out of the abyss, it must verily enter into its father's country.

85. For the speech and understanding of man doth not befall him from the stars and elements; for then other creatures could also speak

and understand: Man hath the same, originally, from the incorporated formed Word of God; it is the name of God, which he must not
abuse, upon pain of eternal punishment. This incorporated Word man
hath, out of all the three Principles, in himself; and hath a free-own-
peculiar-will to form a substance out of which Principle he will; and
thereupon also follows the separation, and reaping in, of every thing
into its receptable [or appointed place].

Of *Abraham,* and his Seed, and of the Line of the Covenant in its Propagation; and also of the Heathenish Gods

1. IF we look upon the history of the acts of the ancient holy patriarchs, with right eyes of understanding, then we see therein mere wonders; for the lines [or races] of the children of God are like unto a tree, which groweth into boughs and branches, until it bears fruit. Thus also the line of Christ grew in the stem of the promised Word in the Covenant, from branch to branch, even into the height of the twigs, unto its right age; until the power of the tree, that is, the Word in the Covenant, put forth itself with the glorious sovereign fair blossom.

2. Out of which blossom the holy image of God is again grown in flesh and blood, viz. in a holy body. We see its boughs and branches so fair and excellent, that the soul doth most exceedingly rejoice [at this contemplation], and truly desires to bud and grow forth along with these boughs and branches, to the great praise of God in our angelical tree of the hierarchies of Christ, in[1] the holy Paradise.

3. God made a Covenant with Adam after his fall, when he died to the heavenly ens in him, that God would quicken him again, and regenerate him anew. And this Covenant was the root in the disappeared ens which grew in this line of Adam from Seth and his children and posterity, even unto Noah, in one stem of the tree;[2] and with Noah God renewed the Covenant.

4. For the undivided sensual tongue, wherein the spirits of the letters did rule in one harmony, continued until the flood, so that all men spake in one tongue, in which tongue the divine spirit of the five vowels, viz. the divine understanding, moved.

5. But seeing they had introduced the image and beast of vanity into the sensual tongue, and fell wantonly in love with the Babylonical whore of selfhood, therefore God complained against them, that they would not suffer his spirit any more to rule them, and said, that *it repented him that he had made man.*

6. For as the sorrow to destruction did manifest and open itself,

---

[1] Text, of.   [2] In the stock or body of the tree.

even so also the sorrow of repentance to the new regeneration out of the Covenant. Thus the sorrow of the formed Word in the only sensual tongue destroyed every life and being which lived in the air, that is, in the manifested spirit of God, viz. in the third Principle; and the word of the sensual tongue did, after the flood, put itself forth in a compaction of the spirits of the letters.

7. For God said to Noah, *the men are flesh, and moreover vain and wicked, even from their youth.* Thus the holy Spirit would not any more manifest himself in the evil contrived sensual tongue, but left them to follow their own fancy; seeing they refused to follow him: he suffered the power and force of nature to manifest its wonders out of evil and good, viz. in images of the dark and outward world, where their images were trimmed up and set forth in the [glory and] light of the outward nature, wherein evil and good are mixed together, to the contemplation of the wonders of God, according to love and anger; from which ground the heathen's understanding, with their idols, did arise and spring forth.

8. For the understanding of the spirits of the letters did bring itself into the formings of many speeches, and in those formings of self the images were brought forth in the understanding, wherein the outward nature did behold itself; and also the devil did, from God's wrath, introduce his imagination and desire into men, thereby to lead them from the true understanding into images; so that they did not know the true God.

9. For all the oracles of the heathenish gods do take their original out of the outward and inward nature of the dark world, as a figure or understanding of the soul of the outward and inward dark world, like a peculiar selfly god, understand, a nature-god; for as the sensual tongue was become such a nature-god, and understanding, which did play the hypocrite with itself, and formed the images in itself, so God suffered it to be that nature did likewise represent itself to them as a god in the oracles, and spake through the images.

10. For the heathen worshipped the stars and four elements; seeing they knew that the stars and four elements governed the outward life of all things. Their understanding of the compacted sensual tongue, viz. the comprehended word of the understanding, did also enter into the formed compacted and amassed word of nature in them, and one understanding moved the other, namely the human understanding, in their desire, moved the understanding in the soul of the outward world of the expressed and formed word out of the

inward dark and fire world, and out of the outward astral and four elemental world, in which soul the meaning of the sphere of time is in the understanding.

11. Through which understanding of the soul of the outward world the prophetical spirit hath signified, from the spirit of God, how the formed and expressed word of nature and time should afterwards bring itself into forms of pulling down and setting up among the nations, viz. into the building and rearing up of kingdoms, and of their destruction and ruin; in which soul of the outward world all things stand in time, limit, measusre and weight, like to a clock or horologe, of which the Scripture speaketh much.

12. From this soul, viz. from the horologe of the understanding of nature, the heathen were answered by their images and idols, viz. through the sense of the astrum, which their faith (that they powerfully brought thereinto) did move and stir up.

13. And not wholly by the devil, as the calves' eyes judge, who know nothing of the mystery, and say, only devil, devil, and know not what God or devil is: they are themselves idols and men-devils, and serve their image-god Maüsim [and Mammon] in selfhood, and are as much conterfeit images and idols, as the heathen were.

14. And they have at present made the turba in them a false god, which will even bring the deluge of fire upon their necks; of which they have no understanding or faith; and say continually, there is no danger [a brave time of Reformation], whereas they have brought the horologe of nature to its set limit to destruction: for the withheld spirit of the wonders is at the end and limit of its imprisonment, and manifests itself out of the great horologue of the inward and outward nature, with the mental tongue, through the sensual compacted tongue; and this is a wonder, which none can hinder.

15. Now as we are to understand and consider thus, of the sensual compacted tongue of the formed understanding of the Gentiles, who were of Ham's and Japheth's generation, the like also we are to understand of the mental (yet compacted) tongue in the Covenant, which in the manifestation of it from Shem's children and generation fell upon Abraham, where, after the flood, the first spiritual holy oracle did open itself out of the mental tongue of the five vowels, out of the holy name of God in the Covenant, viz. out of the holy fire of the love of God; through which fire the divine voice was made manifest.

16. And we see very excellently and fully how the spirit in Moses doth intimate and declare it in the genealogy, even in the names,

how all the ten forms of fire,[1] viz. the ten properties of the holy tongue to[2] the fire-life (understand to the fiery tongue), are set forth, in the names of the children of Noah, even unto Abraham.

17. For in Abraham the spirit of the fiery tongue [viz.] of the holy understanding of the mental tongue did open itself out of the Covenant, and set forth also its figure out of its compacted formed mental tongue, viz. the circumcision and the offerings [or sacrifices], which figures did all point at Christ, who should open and unloose the band of the mental tongue to the divine understanding, and again enkindle the light of grace in love, even in the formed word in the letters of the sensual tongue, and destroy the beast of the formed tongue, in which the devil sported, and set himself therein as God.

18. This guest the holy flaming tongue, viz. the spirit of Christ, did drive forth in the opening and manifestation of the Covenant; and took possession of the throne of prince Lucifer in the human property in God's children.

19. Moses setteth down ten names from Noah to Abraham in the line of the Covenant, viz. Shem, Arphaxad, Salah, Eber, Peleg, Reu, Serug, Nahor, Terah, Abram: and he sets down very wonderfully that Terah begat three sons, viz. Nahor, Haran, and Abram. This is even a type of the three Principles, intimating how all three should be opened in this holy flaming line of the Covenant, through the holy fire, and be severed from vanity; and how the whole man should be born anew and formed to the image of God, through the holy fire in the Covenant. As indeed the names of the three brothers do represent and hold forth so much in the tongue of sense. If a man doth but introduce the true mental understanding thereinto, then he seeth it in the form of the composed spirits of the letters; which although we could well give a hint of, yet the unilluminated reader would not understand it; but to our school-fellows we need not decipher it, they have it already in the understanding.

20. By the ten forms of fire I understand first the formed word in the seven forms of nature, and the eighth, ninth and tenth forms are the inward world, which is unformed. The eighth number is the fire of the eternal nature of the divine manifestation, also the strength and omnipotence, which at the end of days shall purge the floor. The ninth number is the heavenly tincture of the fire and light; and the tenth number is the love-fire, viz. the triangle of the holy Trinity

[1] Read the 1st Question of the *40 Questions of the Soul*.
[2] Of, or producing the fire-life.

in the majesty: signified enough to those that are our school-fellows. It is explained at large in the *Forty Questions of the Soul*; even the philosophic discourse at the beginning and entrance of the same [Questions].

21. Out of these ten properties of the names in the line of the Covenant the oracle, viz. the divine voice, was made manifest in Abraham; and therefore the spirit of the Lord commanded him to go from his own country, and from his kindred; for the voice of the divine manifestation with the Messiah, or Christ, should not come forth out of his kindred, viz. out of his own blood, but out of God. But yet in him lay the vessel, viz. the ens, in which the divine voice would manifest itself; and therefore, because another seed should be introduced into his own seed, viz. a heavenly ens (John iii.), he commanded him to go from his kindred and father's house.

22. For the possibility and ability to the divine manifestation did not stand in man's ens, but in God's; but man's ens must come thereunto, that so Adam's heavenly disappeared ens might be quickened in Christ's living ens, and in Christ arise from death. Therefore God said to Abraham, *Get thee into a land, that I will shew thee.* Here the spirit signifieth that he should not see God in his father's country, that is, in the earthly man, but in the land which the Lord would shew him, in his seed, which was another seed, out of the divine ens. In this strange seed he would bless his own seed, that is, tincture it with the divine tincture of the ninth number in the sacred Ternary, even with the tincture of the holy spiritual world.

23. For thus said the Lord to Abraham: *Get thee out of thy country, and from thy kindred, and from thy father's house, into a land that I will shew thee: And I will make of thee a great nation, and I will bless thee, and make thy name great; and thou shalt be a blessing: I will bless them that bless thee, and curse them that curse thee* (Gen. xii. 1, 2). The great name which he would make him in his seed, that was not to be understood only as to the kingdom of this world, for Abraham was only a stranger upon the earth, and must wander [up and down] from one place to another, and possessed no princedom or kingdom, as the great names of the Gentiles out of the sensual compacted tongues; for he was to be a stranger and pilgrim upon the earth in the promised seed and blessing, for Christ said also, *his kingdom was not of this world.*

24. But the great name which should be a blessing, wherein God would bless all nations, was the hierarchy of Christ in the Covenant, which would open itself in Abraham's seed. This was an eternal great

name of a royal hierarchy of an enthroned Prince in divine power and omnipotence, which should rule over the curse; for God said, *he would curse them that cursed him*, viz. the apostate revolted devils, and all wicked men, who would curse this holy seed and blessing; upon their head this seed should tread.

25. And here, under Abraham's great name and blessing, the person of Christ is wholly to be understood; for he said, *In thee all nations shall be blessed, and thou shalt be a blessing*. Now all the families of the earth could not be blessed in the outward mortal man of Abraham; for Abraham died, and his children and grand-children were a long time strangers, servants and bond-men in strange countries; as in Egypt for three hundred years and upwards, and had no sceptre till under Moses; who also was no king, but a prince of God [which princedom] continued unto King Saul; where they would indeed have a king against God's command and will; whom notwithstanding God did afterwards reject, and set up David to be king (out of the prophetical spirit in the compacted mental tongue) under Christ's person, who should bring forth and manifest the great name, and eternal blessing.

26. But here now we are rightly to understand what the person of Christ should be, under this name and blessing; not wholly a stranger [or another person] which should not be out of Abraham's, and Adam's seed, as some do err concerning it, and install or set Christ only in the promised seed, viz. in Abraham's promised seed; wherewith the poor captive soul would be little benefited; also hereby the resurrection of the dead out of these our present bodies would be wholly nullified.

27. For if Christ were wholly another, then also another [or wholly a strange person] must be born in us out of Christ's seed and flesh, which would not be I [or my self], but wholly another man, as some do err; that we are so born of Christ, as the dew is out of the morning, which indeed is true, but my I-hood [or personality] which was created in Adam out of the divine ens, (viz. out of the good part of the ens of the earth, which came forth also out of the heavenly world's being, as to the good ens into a coagulation) must also be therewith joined, as the like is also to be understood in Abraham.

28. For God said, in thee all nations shall be blessed. He said not, alone in me, but he said, I will bless thee, and make of thee a great nation, and make thy name great, and thou shalt be a blessing, thou

thyself shalt be it; that is, Christ should become Abraham, and Abraham Christ.

29. For the seed which disappeared in Adam and died to the mental life, into which God engrafted or incorporated the limit or aim of his Covenant, with the quickening Word, the same is that into which God would introduce his blessing, viz. the living divine heavenly ens, and would bless Abraham and Adam and their children in this re-quickened ens or disappeared seed, and make them truly alive. The living ens of the Word in the Covenant, and the Adamical dis-appeared ens in Abraham, should become one person and body; for the same are one kind of ens.

30. But the poisonful malignant sensual desire, which the devil had made monstrous, had shut up this holy ens in Adam in death, and covered it with the gross earthly property; like unto a fair piece of gold which was changed into lead, so that one would say, the gold is dead and gone. And 'twere truly so indeed, if the artist did not again redeem it.

31. Thus likewise the heavenly artist would not reject Adam's disappeared gold, and make clean another new thing, but he took his own tincture, and of his own gold, out of which he had made Adam's gold, and tinctured Adam's gold with his own gold, [even] with his tincture, that is, with the Word, viz. with the power of God, and with the essence of the Word, viz. with the heavenly corporality.

32. So that Christ became a God-man, and Adam and Abraham in Christ a man-God; God and man one person undivided, according to and out of all the three Principles of eternity and time, according to and out of body and soul; with every property of man, and every divine property: except the Serpent's property which Adam lusted after, took in, and imprinted on himself; the same he did not assume; but the ens, understand the human ens, whereinto the devil had sown his seed, that he must assume, and therein bruise the head of the devil, and of the insown Serpent's ens, and destroy the prison of death, which held the heavenly ens shut up; and spring forth afresh; as the dry rod of Aaron, which budded and bare green almonds, was a lively representation of this: and this is the true understanding of the seed of Abraham and his Blessing, as he meaneth.

33. Abraham in the spirit of Christ should be a blessing, for Abraham's ens, and Christ's ens, hath blessed all nations. Under-stand, the line of the Covenant, in which the promised Word stood in the aim or limit of the Covenant, viz. the spirit of the five vowels,

the great name JEOVA, which God, by the motion of the Covenant in Abraham's seed, made to [be] JEHOVA, or JEHOVAH, as an inspired or inbreathed God, who should bless the whole Alphabet of the sense-all tongue,[1] understand, the formed compacted word, viz. all nations, tongues and speeches: a blessing of the Jews and Gentiles.

34. For he said, all nations shall be blessed in thee, no nation or people excepted, but all, even all; not only the line of the Covenant, but Adam in his children; the line of the Covenant should bless the line of Japhet and Ham; for Japheth should dwell in Shem's tent, that is, in Christ, viz. Japheth should be received into Shem's line.

35. But the gross earthly Ham (understand the gross flesh) is accursed in Ham and Cain, and shall not inherit God's kingdom (John vi. 63). Not Ham in soul and body [is cursed], but the Serpent's man, whose figure according to the outward, Cain and Ham must represent, so that all properties might be manifest in an external figure.

36. Therefore we admonish the Jews, that they learn to know their Messiah. For the time of their visitation is at hand, wherein they shall be redeemed from the captivity of their misery, and be made free again.

37. Also we admonish those that are ours, that they grant Mary to be the daughter of Abraham, and Adam, and Christ's mother as to the soul, and Adam's created image, and not according to the Deity, or according to the ens in the Word of life which came from heaven. For that was not her propriety. Indeed it stood in her, but [it was] in the Word of the promise in the eye-mark of the Covenant (which was accomplished, or) at the limit, [in her].

38. But she is not the mother, which hath brought forth or born God, as the Jews and Turks do say that we so teach; but God hath brought forth and blessed the same in her seed; she in her seed received the power of the Holy Ghost in the Word, and brought forth the creature which was God and man.

39. And not the property of the Deity, which hath neither beginning nor end, also doth not possess either time or place, but is through all, and in all, from eternity to eternity, and hath only manifested itself in the humanity as the fire doth through-heat and iron, and changeth it wholly into fire; and yet the iron remaineth iron still. So also the man or the humanity which Mary brought forth out of her

---

[1] Or tongue that expresseth the sense of all languages in one.

essence, and out of God's essence, in one only essence, is to be understood.

40. She brought forth the humanity, and God the Father hath from eternity brought forth the Word which did manifest itself in the humanity, and filled the humanity, as the fire doth through-heat an iron, and the sun doth illustrate or through-shine the water or glass.

41. She indeed hath brought forth the heavenly body, but not from the power of her ens or seed, but from the power and ability of that ens which did manifest itself in her seed; as the essence or being of eternity manifested itself through time, and yet the time was not able or capable to receive the essence of eternity into its own might; but the essence of eternity assumed or took on it the essence of time; as the inward heaven and world hath brought forth and assumed the outward heaven and world: so likewise the eternity assumed the essence, that it breathed into Adam, which died or disappeared in the seed of Mary, understand in her own human seed.

42. And this is the great name of Abraham in Christ, and the blessing of Abraham, wherewith God blessed Abraham and his children, and not a strange person, as some erroneously conceive, who understand not the three Principles.

43. The person was strange, but it is become an indweller in us. The heaven took on it the world, and made the world in it to heaven, and yet each remained dwelling in itself, viz. the formed word of the body, a creature, in itself; and the unformed Word in itself, God over all, and in all, and through all. Thus also we are to understand and consider of the heavenly living essence, which gave itself into Adam's and Abraham's ens, as filling all, in the person formatively, and without the person at once through all, and with the Word of power as a habitation or mansion of the power also through all, or everywhere, but not to be comprehended of anything; as the sun's power and influence, and the air, do penetrate through all things, and give life to every being: the like is here to be understood.

44. We must by no means abolish the creature in Christ's person, for that which he assumed, both from the soul and body of man, the same is creature; but that which he introduced out of the Deity into the humanity, that is neither nature nor creature, yet in our humanity formatively, but immense, uncircumscribed, not particular: like as the air and sunshine is whole or entire, so likewise it is here. And we are in like manner to understand it, as if the sunshine did introduce itself in something, into a form, and yet were wholly one thing with the

334

shine or light without the form: thus likewise Christ's heavenly divine ens, which he introduced into our humanity, is to be understood.

45. God did often appear to Abraham, and spake with him as one man speaks with another. Therefore reason saith, How was it done? did God assume the form of a body? God appeared to Abraham in the ens and essence, wherewith he would manifest himself, in his seed, viz. in Christ's person, and spake from the Word of the Covenant in the limit, in Abraham's seed, even unto the mental tongue of Abraham, which moved itself in the Covenant, and this the sensual spirit in Abraham did understand.

46. For otherwise Abraham was not able to see God; but in the formed ens of the heavenly essence Abraham was able to see in the spirit of the Covenant, viz. in the same spirit which would manifest the represented type and essence in the human essence.

47. For it it written in Gen. xviii. that God appeared to Abraham in the form of three men, and told him of a son which should proceed forth out of his loins, whom Sarah should bear unto him, upon whom the Covenant passed. Now what did the appearance of these three men typify? Nothing else but the Trinity of the Deity, and the manifestation of the divine formed word through the three Principles. Therefore the divine image was represented in three men, for it is a threefold ens, but one only essence, viz. three worlds, and yet in one another as one; but differenced in three Principles, viz. with the dark wrathful fire-world, and with the holy light-and-love-fire-world, and with the outward visible world.

48. Out of these three worlds man was created, even into an image of the divine manifestation; therefore God shewed himself to Abraham in the same ens and essence, as in the form of the angelical message, and yet spake of himself.

49. For the represented ens, through which God spake, was angelical and human: it would become human, for Christ, as to the person of the creature, should be a prince or an angelical hierarchy; so likewise God appeared to Abraham in this ens, essence and property with his own indwelling voice.

50. Very exceeding wonderful is the history concerning Abraham, for the kingdom of Christ is therein wholly represented. Not only the kingdom upon the earth in the time of the four elements, which also is portrayed and set forth under it, but yet only as a pilgrimage, which should not be the right kingdom, for Abraham must continually wander up and down, and also his posterity. And yet God promised

him the country wherein he was a pilgrim for his propriety, that he and his children should eternally possess the same.

51. For so God said to Abraham, *Lift up thine eyes, and look from the place where thou art, northward, southward, eastward, and westward; for all the land which thou seest, to thee will I give it, and to thy seed for ever* (Gen. xiii. 14). But now they obtained possession of this land a long time after; and were first brought in by Joshua; and Abraham and his grand-children lived not to obtain it, and they were very often driven out from thence; and yet God said he would give it to Abraham and his children for an eternal possession.

52. But we see at present that they have it not in possession; for the Turks have now possession of it; and Abraham's seed, viz. the Jews, have at present neither land nor princedom, but are almost in all places only as captives. But now the purpose of God must stand, his word must be true: Abraham in his seed shall eternally possess it, for eternal is not temporal only.

53. Therefore also God spake of the place, and sheweth the same to Abraham, that he might see it with his eyes. And even here lieth the Great Mystery; for Paradise was in the world, and Adam lost Paradise; but in Abraham's seed, viz. in Christ, Paradise was again restored, not according to the mortal man, but according to the heavenly.

54. Now we see at present that Christendom hath not these lands or countries in possession; and so likewise the Jews have them not; and now seeing that Abraham shall eternally possess them in his seed, viz. in the holy seed, thereupon we are to consider of the place of the holy Paradise aright; as the prophetical spirit in Ezekiel, and Daniel, and others of them do signify and declare; but especially St John, in the *Revelation*, concerning the holy Jerusalem, which cometh down from God out of heaven, as a bride prepared and adorned to her bridegrom; and in all, thus much is signified: that Christ in Abraham's seed shall take in his kingdom.

55. For with the dissolution of the four elements, when the four elements shall be in equal weight [or brought into the true temperature], and the earth crystallised like a glassy sea, as may be seen in the *Revelation* (Rev. iv. 6); even then that which was promised to Abraham concerning the eternal possession shall be performed; for Christ said, My kingdom is not of this world. But now the kingdom of this world was shewn and promised to Abraham; therefore we must thereby understand the heavenly kingdom, and even that very place

which was shewn unto Abraham, when Paradise shall be again made manifest, and Abraham in Christ shall appear to the eternal possession.

56. For although at present, according to the four elements, the Turk hath it in possession, yet Abraham in Christ hath it with his seed in possession according to Paradise, viz. in the Paradisical world. Abraham is arisen in Christ, and possesseth his promised land in his Principle: He is in Paradise, and the Turk is in the outward world.

57. Paradise is in the world, yet not in the third Principle, but in the second; the one doth not confound the other. When Abraham's children in Christ do part from the earthly body, then they take possession of this promised land, according to the spiritual man, and possess the same eternally.

58. And this is that which God so often said to Abraham: That he would give him the land to an eternal possession; for when he promised it him, then he commanded him to go away from that place, to signify that he did not mean the external kingdom, but the eternal; and set him forth a figure in the stars of heaven, [saying] that even so his seed should be multiplied and increased; and as the stars have a pure clear body in comparison to the earthly bodies, so likewise the seed of Abraham should be a heavenly eternal one.

59. But that Abraham's children, viz. the Jews, are at present cast out from thence, and dispersed into the whole world, the reason of it is, their blindness and obstinacy, until the time of the Gentiles be accomplished. They have not known the Lord of glory, but have rejected him; but when they shall know themselves, they shall be planted again into the root.

60. Not that they are cast out of the root, but they must be blind, that their light might shine to the Gentiles; until the Gentiles also become blind in this light of Abraham (as indeed they are at present really blind); and even then the light of Abraham shall again arise out of its own root and stem, and shine unto all nations. Even then Japheth shall dwell in Shem's tent, and Israel shall be brought together unto the open grace-fountain of all nations: concerning which all people are as yet blind.

61. But the time is near, and the morning star is appeared; if any be able to see: But the Babylonical whore hath blindfolded all; so that all nations walk in the night. Her abominable whoredom is come before the Most High, who will blot out her shame, which hath defiled the heaven. This thou shalt soon find by experience, in thy drunkenness, saith the spirit of wonders, from its own root.

The Thirty-Eighth Chapter

A clear Manifestation of
The Beginning of the Heathenish War:
How *Abraham* delivered *Lot*, his brother's Son;
And of the Royal Priest *Melchizedek* of Salem,
To whom *Abraham* gave Tithes

1. HERE[1] we see very clearly what the imaginations, purposes, intentions, and undertakings of men have been, even from their youth upward; how they have brought themselves out of the image of God, into half bestial and half devilish properties, viz. into pride, covetousness, and self-full domination, in like manner as the devil desired the same, and therefore was cast out from his kingdom.

2. For here the Gentiles, and the children of Ham at Sodom and Gomorrah; and in the whole region thereabouts, did now begin to exercise their domineering power; among whom Abraham was only a stranger, and dwelt in the plain of Mamre, as in a wilderness, where he kept cattle. But the Gentiles did tear and rend for the kingdom of this world, and for the external might and power, striving how one people might rule over another, whose will and dominion hath continued even to this day, and hath received its beginning from the heathen, and the children of Ham, viz. from Babel, from the divided tongues.

3. When the powers of the formed word, viz. the properties of nature, did divide themselves, and each introduced itself into a selfishness, then strife and enmity did arise among them. For the centre of the nature of the dark world hath obtained his dominion in the fallen property of man; for men were as dead to the kingdom of God, viz. in the love and humility, and lived at present to the outward stars and the four elements.

4. Also the devil had built his stronghold in the Serpent's ens in man; therefore they sought only after that which made them great and potent in the world. And yet we may see how the devil did only fool and ape them, in the wrath of God, so that they slew one another, and esteemed temporal pleasure higher than their life, which is the

[1] Gen. xiv.

greatest folly under the sun, that man should bring his life into death's danger, for a poor silly pride's sake, whereas yet he knows not whether he shall hold and possess that for which he murdereth, killeth, and slays.

5. And we see how soon the devil, in his envy and pride, ruled in them; for though they had the whole earth before them to possess, and many countries and islands were uninhabited, yet they undertake war, that so they might but domineer over one another, and rob and plunder one another. Thus the devil, as man's enemy, brought them into his pride, that they might serve him.

6. 'Tis not in vain that Christ calls him a prince of this world: he is a prince according to the property of the wrath of the dark world therein; in and according to the same property he ruleth man in body and soul, in will, and mind.

7. For all war and contention doth arise out of the nature and property of the dark world, viz. from the four elements of the anger of God, which produceth in the creature, pride, covetousness, envy, and anger. These are the four elements of the dark world, wherein the devils, and all evil creatures live; and from these four elements ariseth war.

8. For although God bade the people of Israel to drive out the heathen, and wage war, yet the command was wholly from the angry zealous God, viz. from the fire's property, for the heathen had stirred up the wrath and indignation which would devour them. But God, so far as he is called God, desireth no war; yea, he cannot desire anything that is evil or destructive, for he is, according to the second Principle, viz. according to the light, alone good and giving, and giveth himself to all things.

9. But according to the dark world's nature he is an angry zealous God, and a consuming fire, if his wrath be awakened. According to this property he desireth to consume all that moveth and enkindleth itself therein; and from this property God bade Israel fight, and smite the heathen. For his anger was set on fire in them; and they were as wood cast into the fire, which the fire desireth to consume.

10. Therefore the wrath of God bade one nation slay another, that it might even out of his wrath be taken away. Otherwise the fire of his anger would have enkindled itself, as happened to the five kingdoms of Sodom and Gomorrah. Thus the wrath of God did satiate itself in the life of the wicked, which it devoured into itself, in that they slew one another.

11. As it yet nowadays so comes to pass, that oftentimes men cry unto God for to give them success and victory against their enemies, that they might murder them; but God giveth them not victory therein, but the sword of his anger, which they awaken with their prayers [fierce desires] and will. Were they true men, and children of God, they would need no war, for the holy Spirit doth not wage war, but he only loveth and giveth. But according to the property of the anger he consumeth all ungodliness and wicked doings, and is thereby more blown and stirred up [in indignation].

12. For the more a man addeth wood to the fire, and stirs it, the more it doth elevate and inflame itself, until it devoureth whatsoever it can reach. The like also is to be understood concerning the zeal of God: this enkindled anger-zeal of God was set on fire in Adam; and it did devour his image of the holy world, and passed from Adam upon all men.

13. For they which were in the line of the Covenant had the enkindled zeal, according to the first Principle, viz. according to the soul and body, also in them; the one not better than the other; the Serpent's ens lay as well in Abraham and his children, according to the enkindled soul, and according to the gross bestial property of the mortal, as in the Gentiles; except the line of Christ in them, which was not the sinful man's selfhood, but it stood in God's power; as the heaven standeth in the world, and yet the one is not the other; and as the heaven stands in hell, and hell in heaven, and yet the one doth neither confound or comprehend the other; or as the night is in the day, and the day in the night; or as the light of nature dwelleth and shineth in the darkness.

14. Thus we are to understand how the children of the saints have waged war against the crew of wicked men, and drove them out, viz. in the anger's property, which managed its sword by them, to destroy the heathen, and the generation of Ham; for Abraham went out with his whole house and people, against the heathen, who had carried away Lot, his brother's son, captive, and he smote the heathen, and delivered his brother (Gen. xiv. 14–16). This was done in the zeal of God, which thus delivered his children through the might of his anger; for what conduceth to the wicked for destruction, the same conduceth to the holy men for life and deliverance.

15. But that those who will be called Christians (who ought in and with Christ to be dead to the anger and wrath of God in Christ's death) do wage war, they do it not as Christians, but as heathen. No

Christian warreth; for if he be a Christian, then he is dead in and with Christ's death to the four elements of God's anger in self; and born a new man in Christ's spirit of love; who liveth in righteousness, in love, and patience, and liveth not to himself, but to God in Christ.

16. For a true Christian leadeth his conversation and will in heaven, in the life and spirit of Christ; as St Paul saith, *our conversation is in heaven*. But when the Christians do wage war, they do it from the heathenish property, and not from Christ's property. For a Christian is not of this world; his kingdom is in heaven; and he is dead in Christ to the world, according to the new spiritual man in him. The heathen-man, viz. the half-devilish man (who hath his kingdom in this world, who never hath room enough upon the earth, but liveth in the four elements of God's anger, viz. in pride, covetousness, envy and wrath), the same desireth in the Christians to war, fight and slay.

17. St Paul saith, *Give your members to be weapons of righteousness* (Rom. vi. 13). *For why do men fight* (James iv. 1)? For the kingdom of this world; and yet as Christ said, *his kingdom was not of this world* (John xviii. 36). So also his children's kingdom in him is not of this world. Now then if we give up our body and soul for weapons of God's anger, and seek only thereby self [interests, liberties and privileges of Mammon], and slay one another for the kingdom of this world, I think we are herein Christians indeed in the mouth, but the heart and soul is a heathen, and not born out of Christ's spirit.

18. When Abraham had smitten the heathen, he desired nothing of the goods which he took, but restored to the king of Sodom what the heathen had taken from him, and was only zealous in the Lord. He did not fight for country and kingdom, but to deliver his brother [Lot]; this was a true zeal, which the Lord drove in him; he did not stand up and fight for country or city, and albeit he obtained it, he desired it not, but went again unto his own place.

19. And here the spirit in Moses speaketh very wonderfully and saith, that when Abraham returned from the slaughter, that the king of Sodom met him; and Melchizedek, king of Salem, brought forth bread and wine; who was a priest of the most high God, possessor of heaven and of earth, and blessed Abraham, and Abraham gave him tithes: And though we find almost nothing elsewhere in the holy Scripture of this priesthood, yet the same was really in the figure of Christ; for the spirit saith, in another place, of Christ, that he was a High Priest in the order of Melchizedek.

20. Thus the spirit of God doth very secretly and mystically

represent the figure of Christ by Abraham; and calleth him a king of Salem, and a priest of the most high God, viz. a priest of salvation and the holy unction, as it intimates in the sense-all tongue; that is, Christ hath blessed Abraham, and brought him forth bread and wine, viz. his flesh and blood; and is the high priest before God, that makes atonement for Abraham and his children.

21. For Abraham had managed the sword of God's anger against the heathen. Now came Melchizedek, and blessed Abraham again (lest the sword of the turba should lay hold on him), and he gave him forth bread and wine, that is, the heavenly ens, which he would introduce into Abraham's seed, and change it into flesh and blood; and here he appeased the Father's anger in the Covenant, as in the type.

22. For this priest with Abraham is really to be understood in a spiritual manner; for although Abraham might have externally a priest after the same manner with him, under the figure of Christ; yet Moses saith, he was a priest of God; and said to Abraham, *Blessed art thou Abraham unto the Most High, who possesseth heaven and earth;* who hath shut up thine enemies into thy hands. Here is none other to be understood but Christ, who very often appeared to Abraham in the figure, and blessed him always; for the spirit in Moses calleth him also a king of Salem; which is nothing else but a king of salvation.

23. And Abraham gave him tithes: indeed he might have such a priestly order with him, to whom he gave tithes; but this king and priest was he of whom he preached; to whom Abraham gave tithes, viz. the tenth property of the human properties of the fiery tongue of the soul; and the priest gave his bread and wine, and his blessing thereinto, viz. the love-fire, the tincture of the light, together with the heavenly substantiality; that so Abraham, in this bread and wine, might receive the light's tincture into the soul's fiery tincture, and become again a complete image of God; which was separated in Adam with the woman. Therefore Christ, viz. the woman's tincture, gave him again the light's ens, that so the male and female property might become one image or person. This the spirit doth here signify in Moses, under the royal priest of Salem.

24. For Esdra, when he dictated the lost Bible,[1] in the knowledge of the spirit of God, to his scribes, saw this very well; and therefore the Holy Spirit doth so set it down: and we see very exactly, how Esdra wrote the histories of Abraham in the vision of the spirit; for

---

[1] *Note.*—Esdra dictated the Bible that was lost. 2 Esdra xiv.

the whole history of Abraham is delineated under Christ's person, and is an image or type of Christ.

25. Abraham saw in the spirit this priest of Salem; and when Abraham offered sacrifice, then this priest was in the offering, and offered to God; for he was to make reconciliation for the world with an offering; therefore he was a priest of God.

26. He brought Abraham's will-offering, viz. his prayer and desire in faith, into the holy ens of God, and in the same ens, viz. in the divine essentiality, heavenly bread and wine was brought to Abraham's soul, that it might eat at God's table, till this priest became Abraham; that is, did manifest himself in Abraham with the heavenly corporiety, viz. with the soul's food in the right bread and wine.

The Thirty-Ninth Chapter

How God appeared to *Abraham* in a Vision, and established the Covenant with him in his Seed; and how *Abraham's* faith laid hold of the Covenant, which God accounted unto him for Righteousness; and how God commanded him to offer Sacrifice: and what is thereby to be understood

1. MOSES saith, *After these things it came to pass, that the word of the Lord came to Abraham in a vision, and said, Fear not, Abram, I am thy shield, and exceeding great reward. But Abram said, Lord God, what wilt thou give me, seeing I go childless; and the steward of my house hath a son, this Eliezer of Damascus? And Abraham said further: To me thou hast given no seed; and, lo! this son of my servant will be mine heir. And, behold, the Lord said unto him, He shall not be thine heir; but he that shall come forth out of thine own bowels shall be thine heir. And he commanded him to go forth, and said, Look towards the heaven, and number the stars, canst thou number them? And he said unto him, Even so shall thy seed be. Abraham believed God, and that was counted to him for righteousness* (Gen. xv. 1–6).

2. In this portion of Scripture lieth the root of the Christian faith, for God said to Abraham, that he was his shield and reward, that he would give him the seed out of his loins: God would be Abraham's reward; and give him a son of his own, whose seed should be as the stars in heaven, which are innumerable; and his steward's son should not be heir, viz. the animal human-seed, full of the Serpent's ens, shall not inherit, but God's reward, God's ens. He would give in his reward into his seed, viz. into the power of his loins, which should be a seed, like unto the stars of heaven. He looked upon the seed in the Covenant, viz. upon the eternal kingdom, which should be as the stars in heaven, so pure, bright, clear and innumerable; and this Abraham believed, and it was imputed to him for righteousness.

3. Believing here is this much, viz. he received and laid hold of the Word; he took it into his desire, viz. into the human ens. The

aim in the Covenant in the formed compounded word, viz. in Abraham's nature and property, received the speaking Word of God, viz. the promise; and both these were formed into one, and in this one Abraham's faith was right; for God counted the Word, which Abraham received into his faith's desire, unto him for righteousness, for propriety, and for justification.

4. For this received or intaken Word justified the creatural word, viz. the expressed, created word. Understand, that word which had formed itself in the human property, and brought itself into a creature, and put itself forth out of the three Principles into an image, in which image the self-will had, through desire and lust, elevated itself with the dark world's property, viz. in the fire of God's anger, and introduced itself into an earthly grossness; into which gross image the devil also had introduced, by the Serpent, his ens, will and desire.

5. Now the living eternal-speaking holy Word came forth out of the light's and divine love's property to help this ens, this compacted word and created image, and became its reward. This same, Abraham's natural word and power received into itself; and this same Word of God, intaken and fixed in the desire, justified Abraham's corrupted word. It was his righteousness: the same destroyed the anger, and ruinated the devil's desire and will; understand, in man's ens, viz. in the formed word, this was effected.

6. For there is no faith without God's Word and power; therefore Abraham did now take God's power and promise into his ens in him, and formed or conceived the same into a substance of his spirit: this was the faith of justification; that God's Word, and the human will and desire, came into one spiritual substance. Thus God accounted the received or inspoken apprehended Word unto Abraham for righteousness, viz. for propriety. And this is the ground and root of faith; that he took in or imprinted God's promise into his desire, as his very own; and let not the same pass from him in doubt. As Jacob [also] did, who took the Word of promise into him, and said, *I will not let thee go until thou dost bless me*, and wrestled the whole night with the Word of power, until he obtained victory; so that the promised Word gave in itself to him, for propriety, viz. to a blessing, or a great reward, as here in Abraham.

7. Thus understand us very accurately: The incorporated Word of the Covenant in Paradise, which God promised to Adam concerning the Bruiser of the Serpent's head, did here at present wrestle, through Jacob's formed word of the human property, with the new

promised word, viz. with the living Word [which did at present move itself in him], and would that the corrupt human ens might be blessed with God's love, that the wound might be healed. And it did long and pant after the fulfilling of the Covenant, that God would be pleased forthwith to introduce the holy ens of his heavenly essentiality into man's essence, that Christ might be born out of God's and man's essence. Therefore let Christendom know, that faith is not only a history or knowledge [but a real substance].

8. Faith is nothing else but the uniting of one's will to God, and the receiving of God's Word and power into the will, that so both these, viz. God's will and man's will, become both one substance and essence; that the human will be even God's will. And even then Christ, in his suffering, death, and resurrection, is accounted unto his own humanity for righteousness; so that man becomes Christus[1] [or the Anointed]: understand, according to the spiritual man. And thus we put on Christ in Abraham's faith, and are twigs, shoots and branches in his vine, and the temple of God. He that teacheth and believeth otherwise is yet in the compacted, uncontrite or uncloven tongue of unbelief, in the whoredom of Babel.

9. This is the true, real ground of our Christian faith; that as Abraham put on Christ in the faith, so we also at present do receive, and, in our heavenly part of the humanity, put on Christ in his humanity, according to the heavenly world's essence; in the same flesh and blood which Melchizedek represented and brought to Abraham in the heavenly bread and wine, viz. in the type thereof; yea, wholly receive it into our ens of the heavenly world's essence, which died in Adam, and [we] become alive therein, and arise from death in Christ, and dwell very essentially with our spiritual man, in him. And even then he is our own righteousness, we in him, and he in us, only one Christ, one God, one faith, one tree in the Paradise of God, in the stem which is God, and in the power and virtue thereof, which is Christ, and in the branches of the tree, which are we Christians, wholly one tree, not two: We understand not herein the gross bestial man, full of the Serpent's ens, which shall not inherit the kingdom of God (John vi.), but the true man, which God created in his image.

10. Let Master Sophister or wiseling of Babel look us right in the face, and see what spirit's child we are. We understand not the beast, but the man Christ, which died in Adam, which was again regenerated

[1] Viz. Christ.

out of Abraham's seed, and deprived death of its might, and destroyed hell in man, and slew the death in us, and arose again from death, and liveth for ever. The same we mean by a right Christian, and not calves and oxen, dogs, adders, serpents, toads, and the like, who would with their beasts of vanity be outwardly adopted, and regenerate children of God. No such beasts cometh into heaven; only and alone [and none else but a Christ, viz.] a child of Christ, which is born of Christ's flesh and blood: without are dogs (Rev. xxii. 15).

11. Therefore let it be told thee, O Babel, thou ridest upon the dragon of thy own contrived half devilish, and half bestial tongue in thy own words and will, and hast not Abraham's faith, viz. in the received and formed Word, which became man; but thou howlest with the dogs; and wilt, with thy [snarling, jeering, contentious] dog's will, in a strange child, be Abraham's heir.

12. But God said to Abraham, *Thy servant's child shall not be thy heir, but he that is begotten out of thy loins,* who is born of the faith of righteousness, he shall be God's heir, and not the son of the bondwoman, viz. the strange introduced gross bestial Serpent's ens.

13. And God said to Abraham, *I am the Lord that hath brought thee out of Ur of the Chaldees, to give thee this land to inherit it. But Abraham said, Lord God, whereby shall I know that I shall possess the same? And he said unto him, Take me an heifer of three years old, and a she goat of three years old, and a ram of three years old, and a turtle-dove, and a young pigeon. And he took all these, and divided them in the midst, and laid each piece one against another: but the birds he divided not. And when the fowls fell upon the carcases, Abraham drove them away. And when the sun was going down, a deep sleep fell upon Abraham; and lo! an horror of great darkness fell upon him. And he said to Abraham, By this thou shalt surely know, that thy seed shall be a stranger in a land that is not theirs, and they shall be compelled to serve, and be afflicted four hundred years, but I will judge the nation whom they must serve; and afterwards I will bring them out with great substance. And thou shalt go to thy fathers in peace, and be buried in a good old age. But they shall come hither again after four generations: for the iniquity of the Amorites is not yet full. Now when the sun was gone down, and it was dark, lo! a smoking furnace, and a fire-flame passed between the pieces* (Gen. xv. 7–17). Here the right figure of Christ's offering for the humanity is represented; and also his suffering and death, his persecution, and also his victory [is deciphered herein]; and likewise the man of sin and vanity, intimating, how he must fill up his measure, and whereunto each is appointed.

14. God gave Abraham the sign how it should go with his seed, in that Abraham said, Lord God! whereby shall I know that I shall possess the same? Then God set the figure of the seed before him (for he had comprehended it in his faith, which was made his righteousness), and shewed it him in a figure: for the offering signifies the offering of Christ. The three sorts of beasts, viz. the heifer, she goat, and ram, each three years old, betoken the part of the outward humanity of the time, viz. out of the limus of the earth.

15. But that they must be three years old, betokens the whole outward threefold man, of the Sulphur, Mercury and Salt, viz. the three properties of the three Principles, which lie in the earth in one essence or substance.

16. And that Abraham divided these three beasts, and laid one right over against the other, signifieth the twofold limus of the earth, viz. the gross property out of the dark world's property; and then secondly, the limus out of the heavenly world's property, which lieth in one compaction in the earth, whence man was created as to the body.

17. But that Abraham divided them, signifies that the grossness which Adam's desire introduced must by death be separated from the pureness of the humanity; and one must lie right opposite to the other, and be divided from one another, each into its property; as light and darkness are divided, and yet are near one another.

18. The turtle-dove betokens the poor soul captivated in this bestial property; and the young pigeon signifies the inward disappeared humanity of the poor soul, which shall become young again in the offering, viz. a new birth.

19. But that the two doves were not divided, but offered whole, signifieth that nothing shall be taken from the soul, and from the inward man of the heavenly limus; they shall remain whole and entire in their substance, and be offered whole to the angry fire of God in Christ, and be brought quite through the fire of anger, through death, viz. through the great darkness and horror of death and hell, as this was the figure thereof.

20. When Abraham had set forth his offering he fell into a deep sleep, and horror and great darkness did encompass him. The sleep signifieth the death of Christ, and the horror, the wrath of God, viz. the abyss of hell, and the darkness, the dark world; into this the Word, which had given in itself into Abraham's faith to be a seed of the children of God, should enter with the offering in the whole

humanity (both with soul and body), and reisgn itself up wholly to the anger of the Father to be devoured.

21. And the enkindling of the fire, which passed between the pieces, was now the holy fire of God which came forth out of the holy burning, viz. out of the love-flaming Word, which gave in itself to Abraham's faith in the humanity of Christ in soul and body, when he stood in the Father's anger, in the death and darkness in hell, and cast the humanity in soul and body unto the anger, and changed the anger into love-fire; for the wrath of the Father, according to the eternal nature of the dark world which was enkindled in the humanity, must in the humanity receive such a holy ens wherein the anger might, in its fire, be changed into a light- or love-fire.

22. This holy ens in the Word of faith must enter into the great horror of God's anger; for in its property the soul stood therein essentially. It is out of the Father's fire-property, out of his strength and omnipotence, viz. out of the first Principle. And here the second Principle, viz. the love-fire, came to help it; therefore it must enter again into its own root from whence it came to be a creature; and be tinctured in the power of the love-fire in the divine light, and be changed into an excellent pure divine gold: of which this offering was a type.

23. And that the fowls fell upon the carcasses, which Abraham drove away, signifieth the hungry essence of the wrathful property of the anger of God in man, which hungered after the humanity, and would devour the same into itself. But the Word in Abraham's faith drove away the devourer from thence; it should not be devoured, but be offered; that so one essence might enter into another, and overpower the other.

24. The offering of Christ (viz. the humanity of Christ), did indeed give itself wholly as an offering or sacrifice into the Father's anger, into his fire's essence; but the love-spirit of God hindered the wrathful essence of the fire, so that the fire could not devour the humanity of Christ. It took only the self-will of the humanity, and brought it again into the first universal entire will; out of which man's will was given him, which had corrupted him, and brought him to selfhood. Here it was again introduced into the Father's will, viz. into the first root; for so also Christ said (when he in this condition or trial on the Mount of Olives sweat blood), Father, not my will, but thine, be done (Luke xxii. 42).

25. The divided word of man's property, which had turned itself

away from the universal perfection, viz. from the ONE, into a self-hood, must enter again into the ALL, and be tried, purged and purified through the fire of God; and live and move in the One, viz. in the Father's only will.

26. The figure of the servitude in Egypt signifieth that Christ in his members should be only a pilgrim and stranger in this world, and that the outward man (which is of this world's essence) should be subject to the dominion and power of this world's essence; and be plagued, and always accounted only as a carpenter's axe, whereby men do build the house.

27. For a Christian man is even as God's hatchet, wherewith God builds his house for a habitation; both as to the holy children, and also to the wicked. They must build both. Inwardly from God's spirit they build God's temple, and outwardly with their hands they must be in servitude; for the outward kingdom (wherein they dwell) is not theirs, but the heathen's, which have their heaven therein, and work therein in God's anger.

28. As it was very fully and mystically told to Abraham that he should be subject to servitude in his children, until the iniquity of the Amorites was full. So that herein we see very clearly how God's children must serve the Amorites, viz. the Gentiles, until they also obtain their inheritance in the wrath of God, and also wholly accomplish their works in the anger of God for a building of the dark world; for God said they should serve the Egyptians, and have only plagues for their reward, until they had accomplished and filled up their measure. Thus the wicked must wholly finish their works; and the children of God must be embroiled also in servitude with them.

29. Therefore, dear children of God, albeit you oftentimes must serve wicked lords and people, and be accounted as bond-slaves, as it yet at present so falls out; yet think that ye also serve God therein; for as ye in your hearts and mouths do build God's kingdom to your possession, so you must likewise with your hands help your masters to build their hellish seat; for ye are God's instruments, fit enough for all kinds of structure. You must not do it from your choice and well-liking, but from the command of God you must do it.

30. For in that the potent do compel the poor, and force them into servitude and slavery, that he doth from his god, viz. from the kingdom of nature, from the stars, and from selfhood, wherein he buildeth up the house of his wonders to the kingdom of nature. This is his office, whereunto his god useth him; and it is also a great wonder

before the eternity; but it ariseth from the divided tongue, where the properties entered into selfhood, each in itself; over which the strongest domineer. Unto all these, viz. to the kingdom of nature, the earthly man must be subject, understand the outward man, else he resisteth the kingdom of nature, viz. the formed word.

31. Now it doth not belong to the children of God to resist or oppose, but to do all for God's sake, whereto alone God will use them; they must think that they in this world, and in the eternity, are God's servants, and will serve him in his order [or ordinance].

32. We do not hereby judge or condemn the worldly magistracy and order; but we shew the ground of all mysteries. Dominion and rule ariseth out of the kingdom of nature, and may indeed enter into God's kingdom, if it manageth its authority and power as a servant of God in the kingdom of nature, and not as a self-willed god, who will do what he please. If rulers acknowledge and behave themselves as God's stewards and officers in his kingdom of nature, and transgress not the order of nature, and do not advance themselves higher than the office of nature sets them, and so make themselves petty gods [to command and impose what their will and lust leads them to, then well and good; but if it be otherwise], they shall find it as God said to Abraham, *This people, whom they must serve, I will judge.*

The Fortieth Chapter

Of the History, and exceeding wonderful Typification of God's Spirit concerning *Hagar*, *Sarah's* Maid, and her Son *Ishmael*, and his Rejection from the Heirship and Inheritance of *Isaac*

1. WHOSOEVER will read the acts of Abraham, Isaac and Jacob,[1] and rightly understand what the spirit of God doth signify and mean by the same, he must not look upon them only as a history, as if nothing else were couched therein than an outward achievement or relation of an act or thing done: The whole kingdom of Christ, together with the kingdom of nature, is therein set forth exactly; not only the work of man's redemption, but also what men, how or what in man, shall possess and inherit God's kingdom; not as the Jews boast, that they alone are God's people: No, it is far otherwise, God looketh not upon one sort or generation of mankind, but upon the stem or root of the tree.

2. In the two brethren, viz. in Isaac and Ishmael, both kingdoms are typified, viz. in Ishmael the kingdom of nature, and in Isaac the kingdom of grace. And thus also in Esau and Jacob; for at present two lines went forth out of Abraham, viz. Japheth's and Shem's. Ishmael was the first, as Japheth among Noah's children. And so likewise Cain among Adam's children; these point at the kingdom of nature, which hath its original out of the Father's property, and must always be the first, if a creature shall be brought forth [or to the producing of a creature].

3. Afterwards comes the kingdom of grace, which taketh in the nature; as first there must be a fire ere there be a light; the fire begetteth the light, and the light maketh the fire manifest in itself; it taketh the fire, viz. the nature into itself, and dwelleth in the fire.

4. The like also we are to understand concerning the two properties of the humanity, viz. in the two Principles, according to fire and light; viz. according to the Father's, and Son's property, according to the anger, and according to the love, both which are in one essence.

[1] Gen. xvi.

5. But seeing man's will had subjected itself to the kingdom of nature, the kingdom of nature did now also represent its property in man's image, to the highest God, especially in this wonderful man Abraham, in whom the Spirit and Word of God moved itself. Now the figures of the eternal Principles, viz. of both wills, were represented out of one man to the Word of God, which had brought forth and formed all essences, viz. the revolted disobedient [will] in Ishmael, and the holy obedience, which sprang forth from the power of the received Word of faith, in Isaac.

6. Two types were here set forth, viz. in Ishmael the poor, sick, distempered, evil, corrupted Adam, fallen from the will of God; and in Isaac the image of Christ [was represented], which was come to help the poor corrupt Adam, and to introduce his apostate will into death and mortification, and purify the same again in the fire of God; and regenerate it anew in the love-fire, and in the first only eternal will of God, where the Father and the Son are one only will and essence in the wrathful anger-fire and in the love-light-fire.

7. For with the motion of the divine property, when God moved the nature and created the creatures, the two properties, viz. of the love and the anger in nature, did sever themselves; so that the mystery of God, viz. the invisible spiritual world, might be manifest, and come into a wrestling [love-striving] sport, in the strife and counter-will.

8. For if there were but one only will, then all essences would do but one thing; but in the counter-will each exalteth itself in itself to its victory and exaltation. And all life and vegetation stands in this contest, and thereby the divine wisdom is made manifest, and comes into form to contemplation, and to the kingdom of joy; for in the conquest is joy. But one only will is not manifest to itself, for there is neither evil nor good in it, neither joy nor sorrow; and if there were, yet the one, viz. the only will, must first in itself bring itself into a contrary, that it might manifest itself.

9. The like also is here to be understood concerning Isaac and Ishmael: for Christ must be born of Abraham's seed; and the corrupt man must also be born out of this Abraham's seed, whom Christ should help and save.

10. For Christ, viz. God's Word and Will, took unto him, on his holy heavenly ens, man's revolted ens and will, and brought the same in him into the mortification of selfhood, even into the root, whence man's revolted apostate will did arise in the beginning of his creation,

viz. into the wrath of the eternal nature, into the Father's property, as to that nature; and regenerated the revolted human will in the same fire through the love-fire, and united or atoned God's love and anger, viz. the divided nature, in the human will; which nature, in the creation of the world, had introduced itself into a contrary, to the manifestation of the wonders.

11. Now understand us here aright, according to the very acute depth; Christ must be the king and hierarch, viz. the human prince in the eternal kingdom; and the kingdom was his own peculiar. Now his subjects, viz. his servants, must be other persons than he, all which must introduce their will into him, as into one stock. He must be the tree, which should give to his branches, viz. to the rest of mankind, sap, power, and will, that so they might bring him forth fruit. But seeing the branches on his tree, which was himself, were become evil, he gave himself into their evil essence, and put forth his power and virtue in them, that so they might become good again, and flourish in him.

12. And that this might be effected, the tree, and the branches of the tree, must be distinguished or severised, that so the wonders of the formed wisdom of nature in this tree might not cease and come to naught; for which [wonder's] sake God had moved himself to the creation, and severed the will of nature, viz. his formed word, into a contrary.

13. Isaac was conceived in the ens of Christ, viz. in the apprehended or formed word of faith, of Abraham's ens in the faith, and stood in the figure of Christ; he was not wholly and only out of the heavenly ens, but out of both together; out of Abraham's Adamical ens, and out of the conceived or apprehended word of faith; and Ishmael was out of Adam's ens, of Abraham's own nature, according to the corrupt property; he was wholly out of the essence of Abraham's soul and spirit, but not out of the apprehended word of faith which passed upon Isaac.

14. Now Ishmael was even as his father Abraham, before the conceived word of faith; and should also take or receive that same word of faith in the desire out of Isaac's heavenly divine innate or inbred Word, and bring it to a substance of faith in him. For God anointed the humanity of Christ, and the humanity of Christ anointed his boughs and branches, viz. those who also bring their desire into him; and so they also come even to the same unction, wherewith God anointed Abraham's seed in his faith's desire.

15. Thus the figure of Christ was represented in Isaac, and Adam's figure in Ishmael; and in Abram God and Adam did stand as 'twere opposite. God received Adam again in Abram into his Covenant, word, and will, and out of this same Covenant, word, and will, which Abraham received of God, in which Abram was justified, Christ was born; who received Ishmael, and all the poor corrupt children of Adam (who do but introduce their desire into him) into his word and heavenly ens, and delivered them to his Father, viz. to the bosom of Abraham, into which his Father had imbosomed or immersed the eternal holy Word of divine love, wherein standeth the compassion over us the children of poor Eve.

16. Thus understand us now aright in this, concerning Abraham's bondwoman, and concerning the free, what that doth mean which was said to Abraham, *The son of the bondwoman shall not inherit with the free* (Gen. xxi. 10; Gal. iv. 30). It was not spoken concerning the outward inheritance only, but concerning the eternal inheritance of the adoption or filiation of God.

17. The rebellious self-will of nature was in Ishmael, which he inherited from his mother Hagar, and from Abraham's natural Adamical will, which was a mocker of the new birth.

18. For the devil had introduced his will into the human will, inclined to selfhood in the Serpent's ens, which will did only mock and scorn the new birth; just as the devil is only a scorner and contemner. When he is told how that the anger, viz. the wrath of the eternal nature, of which he is a prince and possessor, shall be changed in man again into love, the same seems ridiculous to him. This false spirit was a reviler and mocker, in Ishmael; of whom God said, *Cast out the son of the bondwoman*, viz. this scoffer; for the scoffer's spirit and will shall not inherit with the free, viz. with the only will of God.

19. But now we are not to understand this concerning the whole person of Ishmael; as if God had rejected him out of his purpose from the divine adoption. No, no; the contrary plainly demonstrates itself; for when Hagar waxed proud, seeing that she had conceived, and not her mistress; and lightly set by Sarah her mistress; and Sarah reproving her sharply for it, she fled from her. Then the angel of the Lord met her, and said unto her, *Hagar, Sarah's maid, whither wilt thou go? Return again to thy mistress, and humbly submit thyself unto her, I will so multiply thy seed that it shall not be numbered for multitude.*

20. *And the angel of the Lord said further unto her, Behold, thou art with child, and shalt bear a son, and his name shall be called Ishmael; because the*

Lord hath heard thy affliction. He shall be a wild man; his hand will be against every man, and every man's hand against him; and he shall dwell in the presence of all his brethren. And she called the name of the Lord who spake with her, Thou God seest me: for she said, Here I have seen him, who hath looked after me. Therefore she called the well where this was done, the well of the living who hath looked upon me (Gen. xvi. 8–14).

21. Understand this figure thus: Hagar fled in the will of self, viz. in disobedience, that is, in the will of nature, in which the devil, according to the wrath's property, desires to be a prince. This will would not humble itself under the Covenant, and obey the free one, viz. God's only free will: In the figure, Hagar fled away; for the will of selfhood must fly away, and wholly die, and not inherit the Covenant, and the adoption. But the angel of the Lord met Hagar, and said, *Whither wilt thou go, Hagar, Sarah's maid? Return again to thy mistress, and humble thyself under her hand. Behold, thou art with child, and shalt bear a son, whose name thou shalt call Ishmael; because the Lord hath heard thy affliction. The meaning of it is this:*

22. Thou poor miserable man, captivated by the kingdom of nature; nature hath indeed brought thee forth in its contrariety, in its wonders; and the devil hath poisoned thee, so that thou must be a wild man upon the earth, to the opposition of God's children, so that they must be tried and exercised by thee, and be brought into tribulation, that so they also might powerfully put forth out of the holy ens the sap of their root of salvation, and in the pressure, move, act, and penetrate with the ardent desire, through the love ens, which is wholly meek, soft, and still; so that in this contrariety and contest fruit might also grow upon the divine One. Thy wild will must indeed be cast out and mortified, but return again to the free, viz. to the only will of God, and humble thyself before the free one; for I have looked upon thy misery and affliction, and have not cast thee from my presence, but [have cast forth] only the wild property, viz. the will of the natural selfhood.

23. But I must have it also in the time of this world, for it shall dwell in the presence of all its brethren, and exercise them in the fear of God with its opposition. But return thou only in repentance unto the free. I will so multiply thee that thy seed shall not be numbered.

24. Why must even the mocker be thus done unto? Because in him lay the kingdom of the wonders of God's manifestation out of nature, viz. out of the fire-world, out of God's strength and omnipotence; which he will again introduce in Christ into the love, viz. into the

only free One. But Hagar, viz. the will of the fire-soul's nature, must be converted and enter into repentance, humble itself before the free, viz. the only merciful love-will, viz. before the Covenant and seed in Isaac, and cast away the rebellious will from itself.

25. And therefore the Lord sent his angel to meet her, and manifested himself unto her with his voice, and she called the name of the Lord *Thou God seest me: Here I have seen him who hath looked after me.* That is, the contrary or rebellious will ran away from the free, viz. from God. But God looked again upon the poor miserable and captive soul, and called it again. And then said the soul, Certainly, here I have seen him who hath looked after me, after that my will of self, viz. of nature, was run forth from him; which is thus much.

26. When as the mocker, viz. selfwill is gone forth in its nature, and hath brought itself into an opposition against its brethren[1] (who sometimes will not work in their heavenly allotted ens), and set itself against them with contempt and scorn; and performed its office of nature given unto it for the exercise of the children of God; then God looketh also upon the mocker, as his instrument to the exercising of the soul, and wills not that the soul should perish. He looketh on it again, instructeth it, and calleth it, and draweth it also in man's conscience unto himself; this now is the meaning: *he hath looked after me,* even when I had almost accomplished the work of nature in the will of self.

27. Hagar being thus seen of God, when she became disobedient to her mistress, and ran away from her, and without doubt in an opposite will against her mistress, the same did much trouble, move and affect the woman. Thereby her mistress, viz. Sarah, was also exercised, so that she was earnestly moved in herself, and called and prayed to God, that he would take away her reproach; in that she was barren, and bless her, and make her fruitful; that she also did purify the house or vessel wherein she should receive the holy seed of Abraham in his blessed seed, and not introduce any human wantonness of nature into Abraham's blessed seed; but desired she might have a right divine desire in her, wherein she might take the seed of Abraham.

28. And even therefore God made her barren, even to her old age, lest the bestial lust should be predominant in her, and mix itself in Abraham's blessed seed; for she should give all her human power (viz. the woman's seed in the Covenant, which did move itself in her, as to

---

[1] Understand, the powers of the soul; and also all holy men in whom the light prevails.

the kingdom of nature) into the seed of Abraham; not out of the wantonness of bestial lust, but out of the desire of the nature of the formed word. Therefore the bestial lust, introduced by Adam (in which lust the devil had made his murdering den), must be first even as quite mortified in her, that so the inward nature might yet stand only in the desire, viz. the formed word's ens as to the creature.

29. For the promised Word in the Covenant with Abraham should give itself out of Abraham's seed into Sarah's seed, viz. into the woman's matrix in Venus's tincture, and take unto it the female ens out of the love-tincture, which had parted itself from Adam into a woman. Indeed, not according to the manifest life of the holy heavenly ens shut up in her, which disappeared in Adam and Eve, which was first made manifest in Christ, but according to the kingdom of the formed word of nature, in which the heavenly ens lay shut up, until the motion of the Covenant in the ens of Mary, where the limit or eye-mark stood at the end of the Covenant.

30. Thus Hagar and her son Ishmael (who as to the will of self, viz. as to the devil's introduced desire and his outward constellation, was a mocker of his brethren, and did exercise them) must be an instrument of nature, whereby God manifested his wonders.

31. But as God will not eternally cast away the nature from him, but thus useth it in time in a contrary, to the opening of his wonders of wisdom out of love, and anger, as a generatress of his wonders [in good and evil], the like also we are to understand concerning the evil innate property in man, which cannot judge the soul.

32. But the free will which it hath if it therewith continueth in the iniquity in selfhood, that condemneth it. For it will not enter again into the One, viz. into the quiet Rest. Its condemnation[1] is in itself, and not without it; it maketh its hell in itself, that is, it awakeneth, out of the centre of the eternal spiritual nature, God's wrath in itself, viz. the property of the dark fire-world. In which it is not the child of God's love, but of his anger, of which substance and essence itself is.

33. For if the soul dieth to self-will, then it is dead unto hell, viz. to the kingdom of the wrathful nature. Now it cannot do this in its own self-ability, unless God look upon it again, as here happened to Hagar, when she said, *Thou God seest me.* And therefore she called this place or fountain, *the fountain of the living and seeing.* For the fountain of life did even there manifest itself in her, and brought her again to conversion.

[1] Note.

358

34. For she should not be cast out with her son from the purpose or election of God, but God did only set forth the figure of both kingdoms in their seed, viz. in Ishmael's, and Isaac's: For thus said God afterwards to Abraham, *Moreover, concerning Ishmael I have heard thee: Behold, I have blessed him, and will make him fruitful, and multiply him exceedingly; twelve princes shall he beget; and I will make him a great nation* (Gen. xvii. 20).

35. Now what God hath blessed, that the Bishop with his reason shall not unhallow or make execrable. He[1] hath set him[2] up to be a ruler in the kingdom of nature, that he might manifest the wonders of nature, and not predestinated him to condemnation, as Babel judgeth; in whose hand a shepherd's crook were more comely and fitting, than to expound the mysteries of the Scripture with earthly eyes [or apprehensions], and make conclusions therein; which indeed serve the devil, and make men lewd and profane.

36. For though Ishmael was afterwards cast out with his mother Hagar, so that he attained not to the inheritance of Abraham's goods; the same hath far another figure than reason seeth in it. God set Ishmael to be a prince in the kingdom of nature; and Isaac to be a prince in the kingdom of grace. Ishmael must possess strange [or another sort of] goods, because he was not sprung forth out of the line of the Covenant; and Isaac was of the line of the Covenant; and therefore God gave Isaac Abraham's goods, viz. the blessed inheritance, because he was born of the blessing, and out of him the Lord of the goods should come. Therefore he in the meanwhile should be a possessor of the same dominion, until the Lord should come; and Ishmael must be a servant and minister of the same Lord [who was to come after].

37. For the children of nature are servants in the kingdom of grace, not lords in self-will; they must not with the own self will enter upon the inheritance of the kingdom of Christ; for it lieth not in any man's own willing, weening, running or going, to will and take the same in their own self-will's ability; but it lieth in God's mercy (Rom. ix. 16). It is a kingdom of grace, not a kingdom hereditary to one generation of men only. But God gave it of grace to Abram in his seed.

38. The mocker Ishmael must be cast from the blessed inheritance, for he was not born of the line of inheritance, viz. out of God's special gift, as Isaac was, who represented the person of Christ. For Christ

---

[1] God.   [2] Ishmael.

alone should be the heir of God's blessing, who had the same out of the right of nature; all the rest, one with another, must be as his sojourners: for Japheth must dwell in Shem's tent, not as a lord and master of the tent, but as a servant.

39. For the person of Isaac also, according to his innate Adamical nature, was no otherwise therein than as a servant; but that he was chosen to be heir, the same was from God, who bestowed it on him as a vicar or deputy of his Lord, who should spring forth out of him; whose property, given of God, he did carry in himself, as in the place or mansion of the Covenant. Understand, he bare Christ in himself in the Covenant of God, and to him alone the goods did belong, out of the right of nature, for he was God's child by divine nature, and an heir of all whatsoever God had created.

40. But unto all others the heavenly goods did not belong out of a natural right, for they had lost the right of nature in Adam, and attained thereunto only by the free gift and gracious donation of the giver, even by the mercy of God; therefore Ishmael was cast out from the inheritance of Abraham's peculiar goods; for the figure of Christ's kingdom to come was here represented.

41. And we may yet see this clearly, sufficiently and fully set forth, in that Abraham lay with an Egyptian strange maid, and begat a son of her out of his seed, viz. out of the essence of his body and soul, and yet afterwards rejected this son from the inheritance; so that we plainly see here the figure of the right children's inheritance, that none can come to the adoption [or true childship of God], unless he be born out of this Covenant, out of Christ's flesh and spirit.

42. The old Adamical man, as to its own self-will out of the Serpent's ens, is wholly rejected and cast away; he is nothing profitable [or wholly unfit] for the kingdom of God, he is only an instrument, whereby God proveth and exerciseth his children, as a besom wherewith the house is swept.

43. The soul must forsake its own will unto all eternity, and must have a new body born or generated in it out of the heavenly ens, which heavenly ens did disappear in Adam as to God, and was introduced again thereinto out of Christ's spirit.

44. The gross introduced bestial property is also alike rejected from the kingdom of God in all men who are born of Adam's sinful seed, as well in Isaac and Abraham as in Ishmael; but the ens in the Covenant shall live for ever, and at the Last Day it shall again put on the true man created in Adam out of the limus of the earth, which is of

the kingdom of this world's essence; yet not the grossness of the earth, but the ens of the formed word, which hath given forth itself into a creation.

45. The inward ens of Christ (which the soul putteth on it for a heavenly body out of Christ's spirit, and out of his flesh and blood) is spiritual. It is a spiritual body, which dieth not at the death of the outward man; yea, it is not buried; neither doth it arise again; but in Christ it is dead and buried, and risen again, for all, and in all, and liveth eternally, for he is passed from death to life.

46. And therefore Ishmael came not to the inheritance of his father's goods, for he had not yet put on Christ in the flesh and spirit. But Isaac had put him on in the Covenant, viz. in the incorporated Word, and had Christ now in the Covenant from God's gift, as a natural right in himself; not from his own power and ability, but from the power of the Giver, even from the power of the Covenant.

47. But now Ishmael must put on the Covenant from Christ, and not from the inherited adoption or childship, as Christ, who had it from God in a childlike [or filial] right. And now Ishmael must do this for the obtaining of it, viz. he must behold himself in the fountain of the seeing and living, as his mother Hagar did, and return again with the lost son to the Father; and fall down before Abraham's feet, that is, his heir, Isaac, in Christ; and pray that he would receive him into his house (which is Christ's humanity, viz. the spiritual world), as a servant and day-labourer; for he hath had no more any right to his inheritance; he hath been begotten and born only as a step-brother [or son in law] of a strange mother, viz. of the kingdom of nature.

48. And for their sake Christ came, that he might have mercy on them, for he himself also said, when he was in the flesh, *He came not to seek the righteous, but the* poor *sinner*, his brother in Ishmael and Adam, not his line in Isaac; for the *whole hath no need of the Physician, but the sick*, wounded, poor sinner (Luke v. 31, 32).

49. And we will not herein conclude so blindly concerning Predestination, and Election of Grace, as Babel doth, which teacheth that God hath ordained a certain number and company to damnation, and the rest to salvation.

50. If this were so, then nature must needs be limited, confined, and determined, when it should beget and bring forth a child of God, and nothing would be in the free condition or liberty; yea, God must then confine and shut up his unchangeable [one, infinite] will into a beginning and limit, and nothing at all could be free in the human

property, but whatsoever any one did, that must unavoidably so come to pass, let him rob, steal, murder, or blaspheme God, and live as he pleased, it must so be. If this were true, then the Ten Commandments, and all doctrines, teachings and laws were to no purpose, and none need repent, unless God compelled him thereunto.

51. I say, whosoever teacheth so, he useth and taketh the name of God in vain, and horribly profaneth the holy name of God, which is free, from eternity, and offereth itself to all poor sinners, and bids them all come unto him (Matt. xi. 28).

52. The Covenant was indeed established[1] in Isaac, viz. the divine might and dominion; but it was given to no man in the line of the Covenant, but only and alone to the Man, Christ, so that none came, out of a peculiar right, to God, but all in the grace of the One; and God did declare his mercy and compassion in Christ unto all, and without him there was no door of grace to the Jews, viz. Abraham's seed, and also to the Gentiles; all are only children received out of grace, and new born in him; and none, either of the Jews or Gentiles, without the life of Christ [are received to mercy]; all men who have pressed [or earnestly come] into God, viz. to his grace, those he hath all received in the grace which he offereth in Christ.

53. Therefore Christ also prayed for his enemies, which knew him not, but crucified him, that God would forgive them in him, and receive them to favour; in which access all nations who knew not Christ in the flesh, but fly to God's grace, have an open gate, and are taken into God's mercy.

54. For, besides[2] Christ no man cometh to the childlike inheritance; to him alone the goods do belong, viz. the hierarchy of men; as he himself also said, *Father, the men were thine, but thou hast given them me*, and I give unto them the life eternal (John xvii. 6). And therefore it belongs unto him, because he is God's Son, born of his essence, from eternity.

55. Adam was also God's natural son, which he created out of his essence. But he lost the childship and the inheritance, and was cast out, and with him all his children; as Ishmael was cast out from the childlike or filial inheritance.

56. For in Abraham the inheritance of the true sonship was again manifested; but Ishmael was not born of the inheritance of the sonship, but of the rejected seed. But now God offered again, out of free grace, his holy inheritance in Abraham, that he would generate the

---

[1] Set forth.   [2] Without.

rejected seed in this new mother, which gave in itself into Abraham's seed, again in himself to a childlike seed.

57. Not that the rebellious runagate Adamical will in the selfhood in Ishmael should be received into this mother; no, the same is wholly cast out with Ishmael in all respects from the filial inheritance. He cannot be born anew, unless he die to his self, and [to his] own willing, and come, in a converted will, to God in Christ, as the lost son, who neither wills nor desires anything from a natural proper right, but only that the Lord of the goods would have mercy on him, and receive him again to be a day-labourer. This converted will God doth take in,[1] to his gracious, free-given inheritance, viz. into the goods of Abraham in Christ, and maketh it to be heir in Isaac's goods, viz. in Isaac's freely given inheritance in Christ.

58. Ishmael was cast out from Abraham's, viz. from God's, goods, that he might come unto his son, to whom he gave the whole inheritance, and entreat him for the filial inheritance; for the natural Adamical man had lost it; and that which was lost was again freely given to the Covenant of Abraham, viz. to the blessed seed, that is, to the man, Christ; and he now doth freely give it unto them who come unto him.

59. All men who come unto God the Father, and pray unto him for the eternal adoption,[2] unto all them he giveth the adoption in his son, Christ, unto whom he hath freely granted the whole inheritance, viz. the hierarchy of mankind, viz. the possession of the throne of the angelical world, [even] in the place of this world; and given unto him all the power of rule and dominion; as he said: *All power in heaven and in earth is given to me of my Father* (Matt. xxviii. 18).

60. For God the Father ruleth the place of this world in his Son, Christ; and all men who now come unto God, they come to him in Christ, who is the Lord, viz. the mouth of his Father.

61. Christ is the staff, wherewith God [guides and] feeds his sheep: in Christ's voice all poor sinners who turn to God are born to a new will and life; and in the filial birth in Christ's voice they die wholly unto the own will of selfhood in Christ's death.

62. For Christ is dead to the human selfhood in the Father's anger, and buried with the will of self in the eternal death; and is risen again in his Father's will, and liveth and ruleth to all eternity in his Father's will.

63. God the Father introduced his voice and word, viz. his

---

[1] Text, engraft, or in-linage.　　　[2] Or sonship.

manifestation, into the seed of Abraham, viz. into man's will of self; and brought that will of the human selfhood, with his own introduced voice, into the death and into hell, which death and hell were manifest in the selfhood of man's own will; and in the power of his manifested voice, he did destroy the death and hell in the voice and word of man's selfhood; so that man should not any more will to himself, but what he now willeth, the same he must will in the manifested voice of God.

64. So long as Ishmael willed[1] in the voice of his scorning con-temning self, he could not be heir of these introduced, free-given goods: but when he hath turned to God, and forsaken the will of self, then God also sendeth the angel to him, even while he is in his mother's womb; and saith, *Return again to the free; and humble thyself under her hand, and thou shalt live* (Gen. xvi. 9).

65. For Ishmael was run away from God in the womb; which signifies the fugitive runagate nature of man in selfhood; and in the mother's womb God sent him an angel to recall him. Noting, that all wicked men are called inwardly by the voice of God while they are yet in the womb, and also the time of their whole life, in their own essence and being; only, the natural will of selfhood stoppeth its hearing, so that the voice of God is not manifest therein.

66. That is, like as the sun shineth all the day long, and giveth itself unto every essence which will but receive its power; so likewise the voice of God soundeth through all men, to recall [and reclaim] them, the whole time of their life: so soon as the seed is sown in the womb, the voice of God is sounding [or working] therein to a good fruit. But on the contrary, also the voice of God's anger soundeth in the essence of man's selfhood; there is a continual combat betwixt them; as with heat and cold; that which gets victory, of that is the fruit; this strife continueth as long as man liveth in this world.

67. Therefore we declare with good ground, that men ought not to make conclusions concerning the children of God's saints; as if God had so, out of his purpose, begotten one to condemnation, and hardened him that he could not come to the adoption; and chosen in himself another, that he could not be lost; it is a mere groundless fiction. [There is no footing or foundation at all for it, either in the book of nature or in the holy Scripture, it proceeds from the abyss and bottomless smoky pit of darkness and hypocrisy.]

68. By the tribes[2] of the saints (in whom the divine Covenant hath opened itself, viz. by the patriarchs, as Adam, Noah, Abraham, Isaac,

[1] Or, would take the inheritance.   [2] Or, the stems.

and Jacob) there are always two figures represented, viz. Christ, and Adam, a good, and an evil man.

69. Cain, Ham, Ishmael and Esau, were types of the corrupt man, and Abel, Shem, Isaac and Jacob, were types of Christ, who opened himself in this line, and set himself forth before the corrupt children of Adam as a light and preacher, to convert them.

70. For *God hath not sent his Son to condemn the world* (John iii. 17), viz. the poor corrupt man, but he hath therefore sent him into the world among the Godless crew of evil men, to teach and call them; and those who have a willing desire to hear he will save. Even those that have but a sparkle of the divine ens in them, which is capable of hearing, the quickening and renewing voice of Christ doth cry and call in that little spark which is in all these; that is, it bloweth up that little spark, that it may become a divine fire.

71. And that we may open wide the eyes of the blind, self-named Christendom, and also of the Jews in their boasting, that they may not so brag, and stand upon their knowledge, as if they alone were the children of God, because they know the name of God, and flatter themselves with the knowing it, and condemn other people, who are deprived of knowing as they know, and have introduced another knowledge, as they, alas! do most blindly; in so much, that one nation and people doth exercise [or evilly entreat] another: Know, that Cain, Ham, Ishmael and Esau, are the types of the Turks and heathen, whom God blessed in Ishmael; and gave them to possess the princely dominions in his kingdom of this world, and cast them out in their own contrived knowledge from the knowledge of the adoption[1] of Christ; as he cast out Ishmael; but recalls them in the womb, by the angel of the great counsel, unto the free, viz. to God's goods, that they should return to him.

72. For they lie shut up under the veil of Christ, as Christ did under the Levitical priesthood under Moses; and as the Children of Israel under the Law were not justified through the Law, but through him who was hidden under the Law, and thus they are now hidden under the true knowledge, and lie as it were shut up in the mother's womb.

73. But the angel of the great counsel calls them by their mother, Hagar, viz. by the kingdom of nature; that she (the mother and her child) should return home to Sarah, viz. to the free, that is, to the one only God, who hath born his Son of the free. Thus they come as it

[1] Or, sonship.

were under the veil in the mother's womb to the free, viz. to the one only God; who hath born unto them, of the free [woman], the true Lord, (unto whose goods they, being strangers, are received in grace), as sojourners.

74. For as Ishmael did not go to Isaac for the inheritance, which did of right belong to Isaac (because the Lord was in him, who freely bestowed it upon him, and set him as a steward), but would have it of the Father; even so the Turks have turned themselves from Isaac, viz. from the Son, to the Father, and will have the inheritance of God from the Father.

75. Now the Father is manifested [to us] in the Son; and when they now do call upon the Father, he heareth them only in his Son, viz. in his voice manifest in the human property, and they yet serve the Son in the Father.

76. For we men have no other God at all without Christ the Son; for the Father hath manifested himself towards us with his voice in the Son, and heareth us only through his voice manifested in the Son.

77. Now when the Turks worship the Father, he heareth them in the Son, and receiveth them to adoption only in the Son, in whom God hath only alone once more manifested himself in the human property, and in no other property besides.

78. Now saith reason, how can they attain to the adoption of Christ, when as they will not have the Son to be the Son of God, and say, that God hath no Son. Hear, O man, Christ said, *Whosoever speaketh a word against the Son of man, to him it shall be forgiven; but he that blasphemeth the Holy Ghost, to him it shall never be forgiven* (Matt. xii. 32): that is, as much as if he should say:

79. Whosoever reproacheth the humanity of Christ in ignorance, [considering of it] as his own flesh, to him it may be forgiven; for he knoweth not what the humanity of Christ is. But he that blasphemeth the Holy Ghost, viz. the only God, who hath manifested himself in the humanity, wherein Father, Son, and Holy Ghost, are one only God, he hath no forgiveness for evermore. That is, he that rejecteth the only God, he hath quite broken himself off from him, into an own-hood of self.

80. Now the Turks do not blaspheme the Holy Spirit, who manifested himself in the humanity, but they reproach the humanity, and say a creature cannot be God.

81. But that God hath wrought, and done wonders[1] in Christ, that

---

[1] Or miracles.

they confess, and blaspheme not the Spirit which hath wrought in Christ, viz. in the humanity. Blindness is happened unto them, so that they walk under a veil.

82. Now saith reason, God hath taken away the candlestick from them, and rejected them. Hear, O man, what was the cause that God (as he threatened by St John) did take away the candlestick from them, and shut them up under the veil. Thinkest thou that it was done without his foreknowledge, without his will? No, it was done with his will.

83. He permitted the kingdom of nature to give them a doctrine of reason; seeing Christendom became blind in their reason, in respect of Christ's person, and did wrangle and jangle about Christ's humanity, and put all manner of scorn, reproach and disgrace upon his person; as it fell out among the Arians, when they denied his deity, and the bishops in their covetousness did apply his merits in his humanity for the belly's sake to their belly orders, and did practice all manner of lewdness and profaneness, even with swearing, cursing, and juggling and sorcery by his suffering and holy wounds; so that there the holy name of God, which had manifested itself in the humanity, was abused; thereupon God did hide himself from them in their understanding, so that first they became blind with the Arians in respect of the deity of Christ.

84. But afterwards, when as they would be only blind beasts, he hid himself also from them in respect of the humanity by the Turkish religion,[1] so that they were wholly deprived of the candlestick of the world, and it went with them, as the prophet said to Israel under their king: *Ah! I must give thee judges, as in former times* (Isa. i. 26).

85. Thus the king of light in the humanity was withdrawn from them, and the judicature of nature was given them again for a guide and governor; so that they returned again into the mother's womb, viz. into the root, out of which man was created, that is, to the only God; so that the name and knowledge of the holy humanity of Christ is yet put out with them.

86. And that they might not use the same so vainly, and uneffectually for swearing, and false defence [or covering], they must again enter into Hagar, as into the mother's womb; and have now verily been a long time a people run away in their mother Hagar from Abraham's house, viz. from the humanity of Christ.

87. But know and declare this as a word of the Most High, known

---

[1] The doctrine of Mahomet, or the Alcoran.

in the sound of his trumpet, which he hath prepared to awaken all nations, and to visit the face of the whole earth: That the angel of the great counsel, viz. the holy voice of Christ, is not departed from them, eternally to forget them, so little as a mother can forget her child, that she should not have pity upon the son of her womb, albeit he were disobedient to her.

88. For as the angel came to Ishmael [being yet in the womb] when his mother fled from Sarah, and did enrich him with a blessing and worldly dominions, and bade the mother with the child return to Sarah; thus likewise when the Eastern Countries entered again into the mother's womb, with their knowledge of religion, God gave unto them, in the kingdom of nature, power and authority over the princely dominions of the world, for to possess and rule them under the light of nature, till its time; and then they shall come in again with great joy, and with great humility, to Abraham, viz. to Christ.

89. And not in the form of the Babylonical, formal, literal Christendom, in their invented and contrived orders, which are only letter[1] Christians (so that a testimony [or some outward footsteps] of Christ and his kingdom have still continued upon the earth), but they shall be born in spirit, and in power; for they are the lost son, which is wandered away from the Father, and is become the swineherd.

90. But when the angel shall bid them return, they come in the humility of the lost son returning to the Father. And then there will be great joy celebrated by Christ and his angels, that the dead is made alive, and the lost is again found, and the true golden jubilee-year of the marriage of the Lamb ariseth up among them.

91. And albeit the elder brother (who hath continued in the letter) doth grumble at it, in respect of the different form which he hath made to himself (for the most part for his belly and honour), yet they are not moved at it; they are merry with the Father.

92. Now then, if we truly compare counterfeit[2] Christendom and the Turks together, and look upon them aright, then we see that they (since the Turks departed from them) have been but one people, before God in righteousness and holiness, with different names.

93. And they are the two sons, to one whereof the Father said, *Go and do this; and he said, Yea, but did it not; and to the other also, Do this, and he said, No, but did it* (Matt. xxi. 28–31). Which doth so highly advance or set forth the Turks in the kingdom of nature, which the blind Christian world doth not understand.

[1] Verbal, outside.   [2] Painted.

94. Not that we justify the Turks, and say that they should remain in their blindness. No, but to the counterfeit[1] [verbal] Christians we declare, that they are alike [with the Turks] before God, in that they are as blind as to Christ's kingdom as the Turks. As it plainly shews itself, in that Christendom is full of strife and contention about Christ's deity, and humanity; and abominably profaneth the holy name in his humanity; and uses it only for a form and custom to swear [and covenant by] also to idolatry [and hypocrisy], and is gone from the sword of the Holy Spirit, unto a bloodthirsty confounding sword, wherein is nothing but contending, and contemning one another; and the whole titular Christendom is turned into mere sects and orders, where one sect doth despise and brand another for unrighteous. And thus they have made of Christendom a mere murdering den, full of blasphemies about Christ's person; and have bound the spirit of Christ, (in which a Christian should live in deepest humility), to the forms and orders of disputation; and have set foolish reason to be a master of the understanding[2] above Christ's kingdom.

95. But ought we to speak so of Christendom and the Turks as if they were alike? Thus we say, The Turk is openly an Ishmaelite, and a mocker of Christ's humanity, and holdeth him not for the Son of God and for the son of man, jointly; for he understands not the heavenly ens in the person.

96. But the sects of Christendom do indeed cover themselves with Christ's mantle, but do attack him in his humanity and deity, and revile him in his whole person; tear and rend one another [with words, and swords] about his person; the one will have it this way, another that way, every one will be master over his words and spirit; and deride Christ in his members, and are as revolting rebellious and fugitive Ishmaelites as the Turks, and live in their selfish will; and serve the kingdom of nature in their selfhood, and worldly interests and pleasure.

97. A Christian should be dead with Christ to self; and be risen again in Christ; and be born anew of Christ, and put on Christ; that so he might be a Christian in Christ, in the spirit and heavenly flesh of Christ, according to the internal spiritual man.

98. But instead hereof men have put on Babel and the Antichrist; and do boast themselves of their ordinances [and of the divine orders

1 Painted.
2 Or, to judge what the meaning of the Holy Spirit is in the Scripture.

in the performances of devout duties in lip-labour and much prating],
and in the stone houses of the churches, cathedrals and cloisters of
Christendom; where indeed they do counterfeit somewhat of Christ,
seeing that they there read the writings which the Apostles left
behind them; but afterwards in their preaching, for the most part
they foist in the kingdom and government of nature, with brawling,
and disputing; and spend the time with disputing, confuting, and
contending about sects [and their different mental idols and opinions],
in so much that one party is brought wholly to condemn another, and
the ears [and hearts] of the hearers are so infected with gall and bitterness that one sect wilfully opposeth another, and cries it down for
devilish; whence nothing but wars, and disdainful provocations do
arise, to the desolating of countries and cities.

99. Thus they are alike before God, and lie as it were shut up in
Hagar, in the dead reason; except the true children of God, which
verily are here and there to be found among all nations and sects, but
wholly simple, and despised; also covered under Christ's cross, to the
reasonwise world.

100. For as the four elements receive the powerful influence of the
sun, and we see in the substance the body, but not the sun, although
it worketh therein; so likewise the spirit of Christ is hid in the children
of God. But as a herb springing from the earth doth by the virtue of
the sun put forth a fair blossom and fruit, so also God's children out of
their disregarded form [or homeliness, to the lewd world's or prating
hypocrite's eye, do bring forth the fair fruits of humility and piety].

The Forty-First Chapter

Of the Seal of the Covenant of Circumcision, and of Baptism

I. WHEN God had made a Covenant with Abram,[1] and blessed him, and made him a father of many nations, which should be blessed through him, viz. by Abram's blessing in the Covenant, then he gave him the seal of the Covenant, viz. the sign and the figure upon what ens the blessing passed; and shewed him in this figure, what in man should inherit and possess the eternal blessing; that is to say, not the gross earthly bestial man, which is conceived and born in the lust of the flesh, out of the bestial lust of man and woman; which did involve or insinuate itself into Adam, according to the brutish and bestial property of the divided life's essence. Upon this the Covenant and blessing doth not pass; but upon the ens of the Word formed out of the heavenly world's property, out of the limus of the earth; not upon the introduced Serpent's ens out of the dark world's ens and property; but upon the soul, and its right body, which was created to it in Adam.

2. And we here see by the circumcision the types that the bestial copulation of man and woman is an abomination before the holiness of God, which yet is borne withal, by divine patience and permission, seeing now it cannot be otherwise with man, he having lost the magical birth of Paradise. For here God set forth the figure in the circumcision, that every male must be circumcised on this member of the propagation of the masculine seed, in that man soweth his own will out of the property of nature in his seed; therefore God set forth the figure with the circumcision, both of the earthly seed, and also of the member and will. For the spirit in the Covenant must cut off, through Christ's death, this figure in the inward spiritual man, together with this bestial will and desire.

3. For the bestial gross earthly seed of the man or woman shall not put on the Covenant and blessing, as Christ also said; but he who is not born of the will of man, nor of the flesh, but of God (John i. 13). The bestial birth, with its members, must be cut off through the temporal death; and die in the spiritual birth through Christ's death, and be buried in the eternal death, viz. in the nothing.

[1] Gen. xvii.

4. But seeing the Covenant of God had incorporated itself in Abraham's seed to a propagation, God did here set before him by the circumcision the person of Christ, in whose death this beast and monster should die, and out of his death a new angelical form should come forth. For the circumcision was not the atonement, but the apprehended [or conceived] ens of faith was the atonement; out of which ens of faith Christ should be born; but the circumcision was the sign that the ens of faith in the Word of God, should cut off the earthly seed.

5. For the living Word of God looked into the Covenant; and in the Covenant the human seed of the heavenly part lay disappeared; and in the disappeared ens stood the aim or limit of the new regeneration in Christ's motion, where the Word of the divine tincture and power would again move itself in the true humanity created in Adam; and also it did move itself in the spirit of the children of faith, so that they were received and accepted of God in the spirit (upon the promise of the motion or manifestation of the shut-up ens) as dear innate children.

6. Not that they had put on Christ in the flesh before his manifestation, but indeed the same ens in their faith; and this same received or intaken ens of faith was the circumcision, which circumcised the heart and mind, and rent in twain the sinful veil; and pointed at the cutting off of the earthly introduced Serpent's ens in Adam, viz. of the earthly seed, and the earthly members to the bestial propagation; it shewed that Christ (when the incorporated ens of faith should manifest itself in the humanity) should and would cut off this beast, and destroy the life of death and hell therein.

7. We must not look upon the circumcision only and barely as a sign or figure, for it is the seal of the Covenant, which stood as a seal imprinted on the ens of faith, for the spirit of the promised word to the new birth was in the seal, as among the Christians it is in the seal of Baptism.

8. And therefore God said, that soul that shall contemn this Covenant shall be rooted out from among his people, and commanded the natives and strangers to be circumcised, although they were not of the seed of Abraham, to signify that the Covenant passed upon all people who would but receive the ens of faith; even there the circumcision should be done.

9. For that was not the right circumcision which was done outwardly on the flesh, but it was the sign only of the circumcision; the

true circumcision was effected in the ens of faith, in the Covenant, in the power of the Word and Holy Spirit, where the Word, in the spirit of Christ, doth cut off the Serpent's ens from the right human ens of the heavenly part; viz. it cuts off the ens of the dark world, introduced and insinuated through Adam's evil desire, and the devil's in-flying poisonful desire.

10. The baptism of the Christians, and the circumcision of the Jews hold wholly one and the same right. Among the Jews the circumcision was effected or performed in the Word of power, the Holy Spirit baptised them with the holy fire's baptism, understand, it baptised their true man, corrupt [and withered] in Adam, the same was tinctured with this baptism, viz. in the ens of faith; for the ens of faith was the baptism of the Jews, where the Holy Spirit did inwardly baptise them unto Christ's humanity.

11. But now seeing this same word of faith (viz. the ens of faith) hath put on the humanity, and quickened it in itself to life; this same spirit doth now baptise with water, pointing at the humanity of Christ; for the water of eternal life, viz. the heavenly world's substance, was disappeared in Adam, and made alive again in Christ's heavenly ens, (being also the water of the heavenly powers) introduced into our (in him assumed) humanity; therefore the humanity of Christ was the first-born from the dead.

12. And with this same heavenly water, which God's word and power introduced into the humanity of Christ from heaven (understand from the holy spiritual world, viz. from the second Principle) the Holy Spirit of Christ doth baptise the Christians in their baptism of water; which externally is also but a sign of the internal seal, in which seal the Holy Ghost baptiseth.

13. And therefore Christ hath appointed the seal of the circumcision into a baptism of water; seeing the fire-baptism in the Covenant is become manifest in the water of life in the humanity; so that this fire-baptism, viz. the flaming love-word, is made flesh. Therefore Christ said, We must now be born anew through the water and spirit, else we shall not see God (John iii. 5).

14. For in the water wherein the flaming love-Word in the ens of the Covenant hath manifested itself in our heavenly disappeared water (which is become incarnate) all the children of Christ must be new born, and take this water in their faith's desire; in which water the eternal flaming love-Word of God hath incorporated itself. This same water baptiseth the inward man which disappeared in Adam to

the new regeneration; and the earthly bestial half-serpentine-and-devilish man to mortification and death;[1] it circumciseth the poor captive soul, and putteth the Covenant and humanity of Christ upon it in the inward spiritual man, now disappeared or withered as to the kingdom of heaven.

15. Understand it aright, ye Jews and Christians; you have but one only baptism; the Jew is baptised inwardly on the soul in the ens of the Covenant, and circumcised on the disappeared ens of the right heavenly humanity, viz. the Serpent's ens is cut off from the heavenly ens in the power of the Word, and the flaming love-spirit in the ens of the Word tinctureth the true humanity, and baptiseth it with the in-taken or conceived ens of faith; the faith, in the spirit of God, baptiseth it with its heavenly water.

16. And the Christian is baptised even with the same very word and water in the faith; it is wholly one and the same; only, this is the [external] difference: that God hath appointed and established the Covenant of circumcision in the baptism of water; seeing that this fire-baptism hath manifested itself in Christ's humanity in the water of life.

17. And that you may yet see, that they are both one, Christ was circumcised as a Jew, and was baptised as a Christian; thereby to declare that he, in his love, revealed in the humanity, had manifested the fire-baptism in the water, viz. in great meekness and long-sufferance, and changed them into one.

18. The ens of faith was not yet become incarnate among the Jews, therefore God gave them the sign of the inward circumcision by the cutting off of the outward foreskin, that so they might have a sign that the Holy Spirit, in the ens of faith in the Covenant, would cut off their sinful birth; whereby they were the children of grace in the ens of faith.

19. But this same ens of faith was first made flesh among the Christians in Christ's humanity, and is also now incarnate in the children of faith in their true man. The Christians do now in their faith's desire put on Christ (viz. this ens of faith, which the Jews did also put on in the flesh) in the heavenly flesh, viz. in the heavenly living water in the divine manifestation.

20. This water is the heaven, wherein the only holy element is the motion and essence; it is Christ's, viz. God's, holy corporeity, viz. the formed wisdom of the forth-breathed or formed word of the divine

[1] Note how we are baptised into death.

374

powers, God's living, eternal-speaking Word, which is a spirit, and the divine understanding; which again attracteth to itself its own forth-breathed essence, viz. the forming of its wisdom.

21. The Father's will draweth the soul, which is a fire-breath out of its fire-spirit, unto itself; and the Son's will draweth the noble image created out of the wisdom, viz. out of the heavenly essence, to itself; and the Holy Spirit draweth the whole moving human understanding to itself, so that it is a God-Man, and a Man-God, God made manifest in an image; and this is the image of God. And thus also the circumcision and the baptism is to be understood, which in both is the ground and chief cornerstone to the new birth, among the Jews, and Christians.

22. Now in that the males were to be circumcised,[1] and not the females, and yet all are to be baptised among the Christians, is thus to be understood, as followeth. Mark it aright, ye Jews and Christians, and all other nations, we tell and declare it unto you all, for ye are hereby called; the time is come about that the Antichrist must die.

23. Adam was the image of God, he was man and woman, and yet neither of them before his Eve, but a masculine virgin in peculiar love, full of chastity and purity. The tinctures, viz. the power of the fire and light, according to the property of the Father and Son, were both in each other as one, in an incessant conjunction of desire, wherein stood the peculiar fiery love-desire.

24. But seeing the devil assailed the property of the fire's tincture, and brought his false desire thereinto, so that the fire's tincture was divided in the properties of the eternal nature, each property on the centre gave itself forth into its selfhood, whence the selfly revolted will and the false lust did arise; which lust desired to prove the dark world's essence, viz. the earthly essence out of the dark world's desire, and to taste in itself how the same would relish, if evil and good (each manifest in itself) were together, viz. in the dis-temperature without the divine One. Hereupon the false fiery desire shut up the property of the light's tincture with the introduced vanity of the devil's desire, and with the earthly hunger after the vanity (proceeding from the dark world's essence) in the earth, and in the elements, so that the heavenly female or right virgin-like life was extinct in the ens of the light.

25. For the Holy Spirit departed from the introduced vanity; and so the holy matrix, viz. the heavenly generatress, disappeared, and the

---

[1] *Note.*—Why males alone circumcised. Why males and females both baptised.

mother of the outward nature, viz. the outward natural woman, (understand the property of the woman), got the upper dominion in the birth: so that Adam must now be divided and figured into a man and woman.

26. But seeing the fiery property of the tincture (which now hath the dominion in the man, and is called man by reason of the Father's property) was the cause of the poisonful infection; so that the tincture of Venus, viz. of the woman, or the light, was mortified; and seeing he introduced in himself the abomination of lust into the woman's property, (whereby afterwards the woman, viz. his Eve, did so eagerly lust after evil and good, and began the earthly eating). Thereupon we are here to consider, that this same fire's soul, viz. the man's tincture, must be baptised again with the divine love-fire, that so it might not introduce the ens of the devil and Serpent, insinuated into the masculine seed, so poisonful, into the woman's matrix; it must be tinctured and baptised again with the divine love-tincture, viz. with the holy love-ens, which came to pass in the ens of faith, in the promised incorporated Word of the power of God.

27. But the woman, viz. Adam's virginity, was now transformed or formed out of Adam's nature and essence into a woman or manness, and in her the holy virginity disappeared as to God, viz. the tincture of the love and light did still remain, but as it were dead or disappeared; for the outward mother, viz. the elementary mother, lived now in its stead in her, and was the generatress of nature, which must receive Adam's, viz. the man's, seed into itself.

28. Into this disappeared heavenly tincture of the light, viz. into the true holy virginity, the eternal holy Word of the power of God, which had created Adam into an image of God, did promise in-hest, and incorporate itself, with a Covenant, to bruise the head of the devil and the Serpent's ens.

29. Thus understand us here very accurately. Like as the Father generateth the Son; and as out of Adam (who betokens the Father's property) the woman, viz. his love-tincture, was taken; and as before, while the woman was in the man, the fire's tincture penetrated into the light's tincture, and loved itself therein; and as man and woman are one body—so likewise the fire-baptism of the circumcision went forth out of the man's fire tincture into his female tincture in the woman. God baptised the fire's tincture in the man, and out of the man's seed cometh both the male and the female sex.

30. Thus the man's Covenant and baptism entered into the

woman, viz. into the female property, for the woman's tincture had in it already the holy ens in the Covenant, that God's Word in the Covenant would become man, in her shut up [barren] ens, and quicken again therein the disappeared virginity.

31. Therefore the woman must not put on the seal of baptism in her own peculiar will or desire, but have it from the man, seeing she was taken from the man; that so she might become a right woman [or manness] in the man's baptism, that so the image of God in her might obtain the fire's baptism and tincture from the man.

32. For St Paul understood this very well, when he said, *The woman shall be saved by bearing of children, if she continues in the Covenant, and in the love* (1 Tim. ii. 15). For the woman hath her soul from the man's soul; and when she is given to the man, then she is one body with him, and brings forth children to the man; she is his woman, his instrument, a half-man; and the man a half-woman.

33. And that the man's property might again obtain the perfect love, viz. the female ens, and the woman the masculine ens, the Holy Spirit baptized the man's, viz. the fire's tincture, with the heavenly holy virgin-like tincture; and the man baptised the woman's essence in his seed with the fiery and also divine tincture. Therefore God commanded the males alone to be circumcised.

34. For in the Jews' fire-baptism the Spirit alone baptised, without water, but among the Christians the Spirit baptiseth through water; the Jewish women could put on the Spirit indeed in the man's fire-tincture. But now, seeing this same fire-wood[1] is become flesh, they ought now of right also to put on Christ in the flesh, and be baptised; for their heavenly disappeared virginity must also put on Christ's introduced heavenly virginity, so that they might be true manlike virgins in the spirit and essence of Christ.

35. Now reason asketh further, Wherefore must the male children be circumcised just on the eighth day? Why must it not be either sooner, or later? Did it not lie in man's choice and power to delay the same, if it were weak? Herein is contained the mystery and wonder. Dear brethren, cease from the contention of the letter, and learn to understand the hidden mysteries; we shall deal with you in a child-like manner; do but look us in the face, from whence we come, and whence it is that we know and understand all this.

36. God commanded the boys to be circumcised upon the eighth day, and wherefore? Six days are the man in nature, the seventh is

[1] Burning, ardent.

the day of rest in him, viz. the heavenly disappeared ens, wherein the six spirits of nature do work; as God made the creation in six days, viz. out of the six properties of nature, and brought them to rest into the seventh, viz. into the emanation or flowing forth of the heavenly ens, which God hath co-imprinted into the compaction of the creation, which is the rest, and right life, of the six properties.

37. Thus man hath gotten seven days for his own, the seventh is his day of rest. Understand, the seventh property is the heavenly nature, which died in him, whereby he came into disquietness; therefore the eighth day came out of mere grace to help him, and gave itself again into his seven working days, viz. into the seven properties of his own essence; and this day is Christ, in the circumcision and in the baptism.

38. For God in this process holdeth the order with the regeneration of man, in manner and nature as he created him out of seven days. Understand, in six days his natural life was brought into an image out of the six properties of the inward and outward nature, and the seventh property was the Paradise, viz. the Saturday,[1] in which the six spirits of nature (in their operation) were reconciled and atoned, for it was the spiritual world.

39. And hence arose that command unto the Jews, that they should sanctify and rest, even externally, on the Saturday, viz. the Sabbath, to signify the inward holy eternal Sabbath, in which the spirit of God worketh in man and every creature, in each according to its property; for every created being resteth in him.

40. And therefore he commanded the male children to be circumcised on the eighth day, viz. in himself, for he himself is this eighth day which circumciseth. For before Christ's humanity the process went in the form of nature; but seeing now Christ hath fulfilled the nature of man, and given himself into the seven days of man's property, children may now be baptised every [or any] day.

41. We see here a very excellent figure, by the beginning [or first institution] of the circumcision and Covenant of the fire-baptism, against the makers of the reason-conclusions upon the letter, who will needs have it, that some children are damned from the womb, and even therefore, because they are taken and born out of the corrupt ens of nature: For Ishmael, who was by nature a mocker, and captivated in the poisonful and corrupt Adamical ens, even he must be

---

[1] Text, The Sun-evening, or the evening of atonement, according as the word will bear it. See ch. 16 of this book, par. 16, 17 etc.

the first man which Abraham circumciseth; who was baptised in the Covenant.

42. Ye reason-wise, I pray you set this looking-glass before your eyes, and think what you do with your conclusions concerning predestination! We shew it you in humility. If you will not see, it shall be shewn you with fire, which is certainly known. For Christ came for Ishmael's sake, and for those that are like to him, to help, and save them, if they would themselves. But in Isaac shall the seed be called, viz. the eighth day, which is come to help the other six days, and introduce them again into the seventh, viz. into the day of rest.

43. Dear brethren, be instructed aright: The God of love, he will not the death of the poor corrupt man, but hath poured forth his best treasure (which he had in himself, and is himself) in grace over all men; like as the sun doth shine unto the good, and evil. But the wicked doth corrupt and spoil the treasure in himself,[1] and will not receive it; but taketh in the ens of the Serpent, full of vanity, and is baptised with the fire of God's anger in the will of self.

44. But if he went with his own will into the death of Christ, and desired from the bottom of his heart to die unto his selfhood and own will, in God's mercy, and cast his whole trust and confidence in God, and thought that he had nothing of his own, in this earthly cottage, but that he was only a servant and steward of God and his neighbour in all that he hath and possesseth, and forsook the propriety [and selfish interest] thereof in his mind, he would soon be baptised with the Holy Spirit, and put on Christ in his will.

45. But these mischievous earthly temporal goods, temporal honour, and pleasure of the flesh, captivate him in the ens of the Serpent, so that he is not capable of the baptism of the Holy Spirit.

46. Also the self-elected, unfitted, and unprofitable teachers [trained up in the school of the disputing reason, and chosen by the favour of man] are wholly blind herein, and teach only of the husk or outward vessel of the regeneration. They will needs be outwardly adopted children [forsooth! by an external imputation of grace], albeit they live only in the will of self; they will preach the Holy Spirit into the beast of self will, which yet is no ways capable of the [Holy] Spirit. They understand nothing fundamentally, either of the baptism, or the Lord's Supper; the new birth is strange unto them; they deny the divine essential in-dwelling in God's children, viz. the Temple of God, and so stand before the Jews, when they should

[1] His precious image.

declare unto them, What Christ is IN US, and what baptism and the Lord's Supper is, just as pictured Christians, or as idols.

47. For the Jews know that God hath spoken with their fathers, and given them the circumcision, and the Covenant: there they stick. But could the Christians fundamentally demonstrate to them what the Covenant and circumcision is, essentially and effectually, together with their offerings,[1] they would forsake the sign, and enter into the substance.

48. But that it hath so fallen out, that both the Jews, and also the Christians, have walked in blindness, even till this last time, and so also the Turks, who, by reason of the blindness, contention, and ungodliness of the Christians, have turned themselves unto reason and nature. God hath therefore permitted it, because the Christians and Jews, both in the Old and New Testament, received and appropriated to themselves the Covenant, and the seal of the Covenant in the outward shell only, viz. in the vessel [or literal notion and apprehension], and lived only to the outward earthly mortal man. They always minded and provided for the earthly kingdom and life, more than for the eternal.

49. They would understand in the husk, viz. in the outward letter, what God hath spoken; and chose to themselves reason-wise people, which were gifted in the outward, formal, logical and notional understanding of the letter, who had not the spirit and power of God's Word and life in the new birth in them; but only the spirit of self, pride, and the earthly belly-god, contriving thereby how they might be rich, in Christ's poverty, upon the earth. These men have blinded them, so that both among the Jews and Christians men have minded and loved only the earthly ens' life.

50. Therefore God hath permitted that the wonders of nature in the power of his anger should be opened [and brought forth in them], and that they should thus stick in blindness, yet in controversy and contests (so that the name and memory of his Covenant might not quite be extinguished), and one nation hath by reason thereof exercised and evilly entreated another in the contention and contrariety; whereby oftentimes a fair green twig hath sprung from the [right] understanding, which hath been strange unto them, by reason of their received opinion, and they have contemned and persecuted it; for the earthly man in self is not worthy of the holy Covenant and seal.

[1] Sacrifices.

51. And seeing God knew very well that they would run of themselves without being sent of him, and would abuse the holy ens in the Covenant; thereupon the veil of Moses hath beset the Jews, and the Tower of Babel, with the Antichrist (viz. the outward Christ instead of the holy ens in the Covenant, that is, God's presence), the Christians; so that they have been evermore seeking, in this Antichrist, what God is, in his Covenant, will, and essence.

52. Thus they have been exercised in contention and persecution, in that they have persecuted one another, yet so, as that God's children have sprung forth in the cross, and Christ hath been inwardly manifest to them; but outwardly Babel hath yet stood both among the Jews, Christians and Turks. The Antichrist is only the same among all, for he is the titular or letter god, wherein the self-will seeketh and worshippeth God in the husk.

53. Hear, therefore, ye Christians, Jews, Turks and Heathen, even all nations of the earth, what now (yet once more for a farewell in this world's being) is freely tendered unto you, in the visitation of the merciful God in the voice of his trumpet, by his love-will and spirit. The sound of the trumpet concerns you all; let it enter into your ears, and do but open your ears and hearts a little from self, and then you shall hear the sound in you: it soundeth through all, even to the ends of the earth, but no self-will hears it.

54. The only divine way, wherein man may see God in his word, being, and will, is this: that man become wholly one in himself; and in his own will forsake all, whatsoever he himself is or hath, let it be authority, might, power, honour, beauty, riches, money, goods, father, mother, brother, sister, wife and child, body, and life, and become wholly a nothing to himself. He must freely resign up all, and be poorer than a bird in the air, which yet hath a nest, the true man must have none; for he must travel away from this world, that so he be no more to himself in this world. He must be a nothing to the world's self [and interests]; for the substance of this world which he possesseth for a propriety, is the Tower of Babel, and the Antichrist, wherein men will be their own god; and with this self-made god they will ascend upon the Tower to heaven, and place themselves for God.[1] Understand it thus:

55. It is not meant that one should run from house and home, from wife, children, and kindred, and fly out of the world, or so to forsake his goods as not to regard them; but the own self-will, which

---

[1] Or, with God.

possesseth all this for a propriety, that he must kill, and annihilate.

56. And think, that all that of which he is a master, is not at all his own; let him thrive or go behindhand, gain or lose, be rich or poor, wise or simple, high or low; let him have something or nothing. Let him esteem all these things alike; a fair garment as a coarse patched one; the prosperity of this world as the adversity; life as death; his authority as a servant's place; a kingly crown as an old hat; and forsake it all in his mind, and not account it for his own.

57. But think, and wholly resign up his will thereinto, that he is but a servant of all whatsoever he hath; and is only a steward in that calling, profession, office and order wherein he is; that it is God's and his brethren's in common, that he only serveth God and his brethren therein. And let him look that whatsoever is conferred and put upon him, be so received of him and managed by him, as that it may conduce to the general brotherly order and profession, that God may make such orders in this world, as a figure of the angelical world, that so he might serve him therein.

58. And not at all insinuate his mind into selfhood, as to think (let him be either king, counsellor, or judge of the people) that he is therefore better before God, or before man. He must continually look upon his naked bosom, and think, that one naked man doth always resemble and is like another; and also that his gown of state, and office over which he hath charge, is the brotherly society's.

59. And all whatsoever is bestowed and conferred upon him, either for honour, power, wealth and goods, to return and give it back again to God his creator, and say [unfeignedly] in his mind: Lord, it is thine, I am unworthy to have command over it, but seeing thou hast placed me therein, I wholly and fully resign up my will unto thee; govern and work thou by me as thou pleasest, that it may be done in thy will, and conduce to the profit and service of my brethren, whom I serve in my calling, as thy command. Do thou, O Lord, all, through me, and say only in me, how and to what I ought to direct the works of my hands; to whom I should give and bestow money, goods, power and honour. And thus [he should] continually think how he, in his place, may please and pleasure, not himself, but his brethren.

60. But if he be a servant, then let him think that he serveth God in his will, and men in God's, and the general brotherly function; and that, in that little which God hath given him in this cottage for food

382

and raiment, [he] is as rich as a king. For if he looks upon himself naked, he seeth the truth.

61. And when man bringeth it so far, that all is one unto him [that he is able to esteem all things alike, and be content with any condition, as St Paul teacheth], then he is [as] the poor Christ, *Who had not whereon to lay his head* (Matt. viii. 20); and rightly followeth Christ, who said, He that forsaketh not house, court, monies, goods, brethren, sisters, wife and child, and denieth himself, he is not worthy of me (Matt. x. 37; xix. 29).

62. And for this self and unworthiness' sake God hath turned away his holy countenance from the nations, so that they have known him only through a dark word and shadow.

63. But he that entereth into this total resignation, he cometh, in Christ, to divine contemplation, so that he seeth God in him, and speaketh with God, and God with him, and understands what God's word, being and will is. This man is fit to teach, and none else; he teacheth God's word from him; for God is made known and manifest to him in his Covenant, of which he is a servant and minister; for he willeth nothing save what God willeth through him.

64. He teacheth, when God commands him; let it be either to friends or foes, in their season, or out of their season; he thinks that God must do in him as he please, and albeit that he must therefore suffer scorn, yet 'tis all one unto him; if he be honoured and respected of men, he humbleth himself before God and his brethren, and giveth God and his brethren the honour, and takes it not at all unto himself; but if they curse him, and smite him on the face, he thinks thus: Now I stand in Christ's estate of persecution, it shall turn unto the best for me, and for my brethren.

65. Lo! loving brethren, this is a Christian. And such a kingdom God now offers to you, by the wonderful sound of his spirit's trumpet. And there must and shall be such a kingdom soon manifest and come into being, for a witness unto all the nations of the earth, of which all the prophets have prophesied.

66. On the contrary, he offers to all wicked, unwilling, stubborn men, his anger, wrath and hardening, to devour them, and to make an end with Babel. This say not I, but the spirit of the wonders of all nations.

67. Therefore truss up thyself in armour and lay lustily about thee, thou Antichristian Babylon, and devour much blood, for thou thyself art even he that destroyeth, and quite ruins thyself. For thee, there is

no remedy [thou wilt take no counsel, thy own Cain-like fury in hypocrisy doth harden thee], also there is no repentance in thy will. But for the children of God under thee we have written this, as we have known and seen it.

68. Now saith Babel, Whence shall this people come that shall know the Lord, and live in God? Hear, O Babel! among thy brethren in the time of thy affliction and tribulation, they are brought forth in their disrespect and misery; and thou callest them fools, and knowest them not. Let no man wait for another's coming; the time is already come about; the voice of the caller and hearer is already present, the covering is put away from this voice. Thou art not at this time called under a veil, but with open mouth, very clearly.

69. This voice of the Crier openeth God's clear countenance in his children, and in the ungodly the angry countenance, seeing they desire fully to purse up all in covetousness into self, viz. into the Antichristian bag, and to bring the whore of self even to the very top of the Babylonical tower.

70. The sign of this image, and its destruction, is the covetousness and envy; its sign stood before in silver and gold; that was the banner and standard of Antichrist. But now the banner hath changed itself into copper, seeing Mars is the soul in copper, viz. the man or husband; so that this Mars[1] is given to Babel for a banner and ensign, which shall rule till Babel hath an end; and no wicked man shall know this, and though he carry the sign in his hands, yet he calls it only [his] loving companion.

71. But upon the kingdom that is, and is not, and yet is, shall the glorious ornament of gold be put, for the prince of the powers of the earth hath given it to them. Amen.

[1] Or, sword.

The Forty-Second Chapter

Of the Three Men which Appeared to *Abraham* in the Plain of Mamre, who went towards Sodom, and set the Cities of the Children of *Ham* on fire from the Lord

THE MEANING OF THIS FIGURE

1. AT first, while Abraham was called only Abram,[1] God appeared to him in the vision as One; and when he had sealed the Covenant with the circumcision, he called him Abraham, viz. a company or multitude of nations. A forth-breathed manifest people of God, in whom God had forth-breathed or manifested himself; and he appeared to him also afterwards in the manifestation of the holy Trinity, viz. in three men, which were only one, wherein the manifestation of the holy Trinity in the Deity was set forth and represented in man's image, how the whole Trinity of the Deity would now manifest itself in this Covenant in the humanity, that the Trinity of the Deity should be seen in the flesh.

2. And hereby is declared the great humility in the Deity, viz. in Christ, how Christ would visit mankind, and take care of man, and [also] condescend to be entertained by man; as he came, in these three men, to Abraham, and suffered his feet to be washed, and did eat and drink. Which betokens, that men must cherish or lovingly entertain the poor Christ, who is poor in this world, in his members and children, who also would be poor, contemned and despised people. And what men do unto them, that they have done unto these three men, viz. to Christ, the holy Deity in the humanity.

3. The words of this figure run thus, *And the Lord appeared unto him in the plain of Mamre: as he sat in the door of his tent in the heat of the day; and he lift up his eyes and looked, and, lo! three men stood by him: and when he saw them, he ran to meet them from the tent door, and bowed himself towards the ground, and said, My Lord, if I have found grace in thy sight, pass not away, I pray thee, from thy servant. Let a little water be fetched, I pray, to wash your feet, and rest yourselves under the tree: And I will fetch a*

---

[1] Gen. xviii.

385

morsel of bread, that you may refresh your hearts; after that you shall go on: for therefore are ye come to your servant. They said, Do as thou hast said. And Abraham hastened into the tent unto Sarah, and said, Make ready quickly three measures of fine meal, knead it, and make cakes upon the hearth. And Abraham ran unto the herd, and fetcht a calf tender and good, and gave it to a young man; and he hasted to dress it. And he took butter, and milk, and the calf which he had dressed, and set it before them; and he stood by them under the tree, and they did eat.

4. *And they said unto him, Where is Sarah thy wife? And he said, Behold, in the tent. And he said, I will certainly return unto thee again, as I live;*[1] *and, lo! Sarah thy wife shall have a son. And Sarah heard it as she stood behind at the tent door. Now Abraham and Sarah were both old, and well stricken in age; and it ceased to be with Sarah after the manner of women. And therefore she laughed within herself, and said, Now I am old, shall I have pleasure, my lord being old also? And the Lord said unto Abraham, Wherefore did Sarah laugh, and say, Is it of a certain, that I shall bear a child, which am old? Is any thing too hard for the Lord? At the appointed time I will come unto thee again, as I live, and Sarah shall have a son. Then Sarah denied it, saying, I laughed not; for she was afraid. And he said, Nay, but thou didst laugh* (vv. 1–15).

5. O thou great and wonderful God! how plainly and simply dost thou represent and portray the kingdom of thy Son in the humanity; how lively and fully are the greatest Mysteries delineated herein; and indeed they are so plainly represented in such entire singleness and simplicity, as Christ, who, notwithstanding [he] was the King of Israel, did ride into Jerusalem upon an ass. Here the proud world may have a very true looking-glass, and see if they be the children of this simplicity.

6. The great love and humility of God in Christ's person is fully represented in this figure, how God came in the deepest humility and simplicity into the humanity, when the humanity was inflamed with highest heat of the wrathful indignation of God's anger, as the figure here denotes.

7. The three men came before Abraham's tent in the very heat of all the day. This signifieth, that God did first incorporate [or betroth] himself with his Love-Covenant, and also with the fullness of time touching the Covenant, when the human day, understand the six properties of the days, were most of all inflamed and set on fire in the wrath of nature in man; that is, in the fall. And afterward, in the full-

[1] Or, in that manner. As our translation, According to the time of life.

ness of time, when the humanity of these six days was in the very exceeding burning heat of vanity and the bestial property, he did manifest himself with his tender humanity out of the ens of the holy Covenant, and came in three persons of the Deity before the earthly man's essence, or earthly cottage, viz. the soul's tent, and appeared to Abraham, that is, to Adam in his children, viz. to the human essence.

8. And here is fully set forth the type and image of Christ: When Abraham espieth these men he goeth to meet them; and boweth himself towards the earth; and runneth away from the door of his tent unto them; and prayeth them to rest under the tree, until he should do that for which they came.

9. We must look upon this figure thus: When the divine voice had represented itself to Abraham, in the ens wherein it would become man in three persons, then Abraham's apprehended ens of faith set itself forth also to this image, viz. to the triune humanity in the figure. For the ens in the Covenant in Abraham's faith was surrounded with the great heat of God's anger, when the human day was grown hottest in the human essence.

10. But when he looked up, and saw the type of the triune Deity standing before him, this faith's ens, in deepest humility in Christ's person (being that which was to become Christ), did bow itself before the Trinity of the Deity, which was come unto him; which would in the fullness of time give forth and manifest itself with the voice (which now spake in these three men with him) in this ens of faith (being the humanity of Christ before his Father), and said, Lord, if I have found grace in thy sight, pass not away from this ens of faith, viz. thy servant.

11. For Abraham was now in the spirit, and spake from his faith's ens in Christ's humanity, and before him stood the type and image of Christ's Deity; and said, in the great humility of the humanity of Christ, Let a little water be fetched, and wash your feet. This is the great humility of Christ, who washed his disciples', viz. his children's, feet (as these three men here were washed), signifying and pointing out that Christ should wash with his blood the feet of God's children, who should be born of these three men, viz. of the Trinity of the Deity; whereby they might come to God.

12. And he bade the three men rest under the tree. This now signifieth the Tree of Life, under which God's children should sit down; and then he would bring them a morsel of bread to refresh

and comfort their hearts; and afterwards they should go, that is, when Christ hath washed his children's feet with his blood, whereby they are able to go to God, viz. the holy Trinity, then he giveth them a morsel of bread, that so they may recreate and strengthen their hearts; that is, he giveth them the bread of life, viz. his heavenly flesh for food, so that they wax strong, and are able, in the divine power, to go from Abraham's earthly tent through this world in God's anger, to meet the Lord, and bow themselves before him, as this figure signifieth.

13. And he saith further: For ye are therefore come to your servant. Understand it thus: The Holy Trinity was here at this time represented in an image of our humanity, and Abraham stood in the type of the humanity of Christ, even as Christ and his children are in reference to each other; the holy Trinity leadeth the children of Christ in the divine drawing to the humanity of Christ; and now these three men stood there in our stead before Christ, viz. before the figure; for the Father draweth them to Christ, and through Christ to[1] the Father; they are washed and atoned in Christ, therefore now said Christ to the three men, which God represented to him in his person: Even therefore are ye come to your servant.

14. For Christ must be our, viz. these three men's, servant; and God bringeth his three men, viz. us, who approach unto him, in himself, viz. into the will of the holy Trinity, unto his servant the Man Christ; that so he may wash and feed them; and then they are able with boldness and confidence to come unto the holy triune Deity.

15. And the men said to Abraham, Do as thou hast said. That is, Christ offereth himself to his Father, viz. to the three-one God, for a Servant. Understand, the Word, which the three-one God did inspire into Adam concerning the Bruiser of the Serpent's head, offereth itself for a servant unto the three-one God, viz. unto the children who should possess the kingdom of heaven. Now, the triune God saith, Do with these, thine and my children, as thou hast said. That is, with these children which are now set before thee, for they shall be angels, and thou shalt thereunto help them, for I am therefore come in them unto thee: now do as thou hast said.

16. Here God fully gave the Man Christ to accomplish the consummation with them, as he had said. And the whole, entire, excellent and holy figure of the new birth is therein emphatically and lively

[1] Or, in.

set forth. And it shews how the holy Trinity doth delight itself with figures concerning the Word incorporated and inspoken into Adam, and now opened in Abraham's ens of faith; and sets it forth with types, and playeth in figures with this Christ, who was to come; where God representeth in Abraham the person of Christ, and the children of the new birth, whom Christ should beget anew, in the person of the three men, viz. in the three-one Deity, which bringeth them through Christ into itself, and placeth them in the angelical choir; as these three men did appear in the form of three angels, and also in the person of the holy Trinity; signifying that the holy Trinity would dwell in these angelical men, and that they should be the image, viz. the manifestation of God.

17. Abraham commanded to take three measures of fine meal, and to knead it, and bake cakes, that the men might eat; what doth this mean? These three men had no need of any such eating. It is the figure of man's regeneration: The three measures betoken the three Principles, viz. the three worlds in man: the fine meal pointeth out the heavenly humanity, viz. the divine heavenly substantiality, that this heavenly and divine substantiality's property should also be kneaded, and mixed with ours, [which had] disappeared in Adam; and a divine cake, viz. sweet bread for food of God's children should be baked thereof, understand, in the fiery heat.

18. When Christ stood in the fire of his Father's anger, viz. in hell, then these sweet cakes were baked for God's children, which they should eat; and the three measures are now the three worlds (viz. the whole man, without the Serpent's, and beast's property) which shall be mixed with the divine ens into a lump,[1] and cakes baked thereof. This is now Christ's flesh, which he hath joined or mixed with our humanity; and giveth us now the sweet cakes thereof, to eat, viz. the heavenly flesh: Here the Holy Spirit did play therewith in the figure.

19. And Abraham ran to the herd, and made ready also a calf, tender and good; that is, he gave it to his young man to dress it. O thou wonderful God! how much doth simplicity please thee? how plainly and simply dost thou represent the great mysteries unto us? I thank thee, that thou shewest me, unworthy man, such things, wherein the whole world is blind. O God, open thou their eyes, I pray, that they may see, and turn unto thee, and enter into humility.

20. The tender calf, which was made ready for this meal, is the

1 Or, batch.

limus of the earth, viz. the outward man, which, before God, is as a beast. Understand, it is a wonderbeast,[1] like as the whole outward world, before the divine understanding, is only as a beast, wherein God formeth himself with the holy spiritual ens into an external body, to the manifestation of his deeds of wonder, both of love and anger. Which figure of the outward world, viz. the divine beast, shall not be wholly turned into nothing, but the vanity alone shall be separated from the good into the kingdom of darkness.

21. In like manner, God will not wholly cast away the divine beast on man, which indeed dieth here, but only the introduced Serpent's ens, and the vanity of the dark world's essence. The divine wonder-beast, which is the servant of the divine spiritual image, and shall be so in eternity, the same shall arise at the last day, and be proved through the fire of God; where it shall be made very pure, as a crystal, in which the angel, viz. God's right image, shall dwell; in which angelical image God is primely manifest, and thence shineth through the beast, as the sun through a crystal. This now is the signification of this tender and good calf, which was dressed for this meal, and shews that the outward man, according to his right image created in Adam out of the limus of the earth, shall be brought upon God's table.

22. But that Abraham saith he gave it to the young man to dress, that is, [to] the servant, doth betoken that this heavenly beast-man is the instrument of the angelical man, who is prepared to be a servant of this angel's image.

23. And Abraham took butter, and milk also, and set it all before these three men, and came before them under the tree, and they did eat. When Christ hath fed his people with his body and blood (and even while he feeds them) he cometh in his power in his children, before the holy Trinity, and waiteth in his children upon these three men, and giveth them from this prepared food, wherewith he feedeth his children, praise and spiritual food.

24. These three men, viz. the holy Trinity, do eat these holy spiritual meats, out of the power of Christ's body; for man's will giveth itself wholly, peculiarly and fully, to these three men, for a food of praise, with a holy voice and prayer of thanksgiving; and this voice of praise eateth the power of God into itself, in manner as a man willingly eateth the tune, harmony or pleasant air of a delightful music into his hearing, and is therein merry and pleasant. Even so

[1] Marvellous or wonderful.

God doth awaken or manifest himself in his power in his word of hearing, or divine sense, with man's pure humble voice or melody of praise.

25. For thereunto God hath created angels and men, viz. to his own joy. And know, that we speak from the true ground, and not from conjecture or similitudes,[1] but from the open seal of God, as we really see: do but understand it aright.

26. And now, when God had delighted and fed himself with Abraham in the heavenly ens, which he would, by the opening of the living Word in the seed of the woman (being also the heavenly ens), manifest and introduce into the ens of the Covenant; and had sported in the ens of Abraham's faith, viz. in the power of the praise of Abraham, viz. in his humility; then God asked after Sarah, whom he well knew, but Sarah knew him not; that even the Lord should be in such a form; then he said to Abraham, Where is thy wife Sarah? That is, she was not yet in this play, until she had received Abraham's ens of faith, and then this play would awaken itself in her; therefore she laughed at this; for she knew not the Mysteries; they did at present only manifest themselves in Abraham's spirit, where the ens of faith lay; and he said, She is in the tent; that is:

27. She is in the human tent covered with the earthly tent, that she doth not see who now is with me. And the Lord said, I will come again to thee, as[2] I live, and lo! Sarah thy wife shall have a son. That is, I will come again to thee with the motion of thy seed: and when Sarah shall conceive, then I will open and unloose her in her shut-up seed, and come into thy seed, that is, move; for, to come, signifieth to move: when God cometh, then he moveth man, and cometh or goeth in and with man.

28. But that he saith, *As I live*, this is spoken after an essential manner; for God told him how he would come; not before him, as at this time he did; but *as*,[3] that is, as the lightful influence and power of the sun giveth itself into a fruit, which when it cometh doth not step near to the fruit, but *as*;[3] that is, it penetrates essentially with the *as* into it; for *as* is, *as much as*, thus *I will see into it* [or open my love-aspect in the ens of its life]. *As I live*.[3] Hereby we are not to understand, as if he had said, *If I yet live*, but he would live in the *as*; he would come in the *as*, viz. essentially, and not figuratively and typically [as at this time he did].

29. For when God cometh, then he comes no otherwise, than

---

[1] Or, parables. [2] Ger. *so* signifies, as, or if. [3] Or, if.

as,[1] that is, like the sunshine into the fruit. This is understood in the Language of Nature, essentially, with emphatical excellency; for if God speaketh of his own coming, then he speaketh only essentially, in nature and manner of the uncompacted tongue of sense.

30. And Sarah laughed at this. She thought that she should bring forth a son from Abraham's lust only, from the human cohabitation in the concupiscence of the flesh; therefore she said. Shall I, now I and my Lord are both old, take pleasure? The bestial world-spirit laughed at its youth, in that it was now weak; and should now again become youthful; and thought with itself, This were a sport, if thou couldest. As if one should tell an old man, Thou shalt become young again, and receive such a desire and lust as when thou wert young. At this, nature would laugh, and think, yes indeed, would that were true; as if doubt and hope were coupled together. Thus it was also with Sarah: for the world-spirit understands not the Mysteries of God. It is before God only as a beast; and seeing the world-spirit did now hear that it should so come to pass, then it thought, Thou shalt be the work-master; oh that thou couldest, thou wouldst very fain; and laughed at itself, that it should become young again.

31. The natural man understands even as much of God, as a beast; when it sees the hay, then it thinks, now there is somewhat for me to eat; but if it sees nothing, then it hopeth for it out of custom. But Sarah had now hoped until she was ninety years old; and thought it to be very wonderful, that God would do somewhat unto her above the ordinary and usual course of nature; and imagined it unto herself after the manner of human pleasure.

32. But the Lord said, Wherefore did Sarah laugh at it? And she was afraid, and said, I laughed not. But the Lord said, It is not so, thou didst laugh; should any thing be too impossible for the Lord to do? Here is the type of Eve; when she had turned her vain curiosity into self lust, to eat of the forbidden tree, and God afterwards asked her wherefore she had done so, she denied also her own lust, and laid it upon the Serpent.

33. And seeing that now God had here alluded with Abraham concerning the new birth, he also doth the like with Sarah concerning the lust of Eve, which this woman's seed should slay as a lie. For Sarah must here therefore tell a lie, that she did not laugh, in that Eve also lied. God did here represent before him the lie of Eve, and that he would confound it with the eternal truth, and reclaim her;

1 Or, if.

as he did to Sarah, and convinced her so of her lie, that she must be ashamed of it.

34. And here we are to understand that God hath represented or delineated the whole process, how he would regenerate anew the true man which he created; and how the same should come to pass, and how he would burn the Serpent's ens in the eternal fire, and how he would put the lie of the poor soul to open shame and death on the cross; for we see this here very excellently in the type.

35. After that God had set forth the process of the new birth, these three men went towards Sodom; and would burn Ham, viz. the evil Ham-like fleshly property, with fire from the Lord, as it also came to pass; so that we see it very emphatically, how the judgment of God begins at the house of Israel; how Christ is set to be a Judge of the devil's ens and will, who shall burn the devil's essence with fire; as this following figure signifieth.

The Forty-Third Chapter

Of the Ruin and Destruction of Sodom and Gomorrah, how the same was foretold of God unto *Abraham*

1. AND the Lord spake to Abraham,[1] when he had blessed Abraham, and had said that he would command his children to walk in the ways of the Lord, and that he would also bless them, as is before mentioned: *Behold! there is a cry of Sodom and Gomorrah, which is Great, and their sin is exceeding grievous; therefore I will come down, and see whether they have done altogether according to the cry which is come unto me; and if not so, I will know. And the men turned their faces from thence, and went towards Sodom.* God said, *How can I hide from Abraham that thing which I do, seeing that he shall become a great and mighty nation.* And thereupon shewed him what he would do.

2. The un-illuminated reason looketh upon this figure very wonderfully, that God said: He would come down and see if the cry were true, that he might know whether it were so or no. Reason supposeth with itself: Is he then circumscriptive,[2] or dwelleth he aloft alone and above, doth he not know all things before? Doth not the Scripture also say of him, Am not I he who filleth all things? Also, the heaven is my throne, and the earth my footstool. Would he then first come down like unto a circumscriptive[3] being, which was separate from time and place?

3. Much more is reason incapable to search out the cry which came up before him. And hereupon the creatural reason thinketh, that God dwelleth only on high above the stars, in a heaven, alone, and looketh down here beneath, as the lustre of the sun looketh and shineth from its body upon the earth. So far reason reacheth, and further it knows not what God is, or where he dwells: it knoweth not that he is every essence,[4] and dwelleth through every essence or being, and possesseth no locality, also needs no place or space for his habitation; and yet that he (so far as he is called God) is no essence,[5] but is as a nothing in

---

[1] Gen. xviii.
[2] Comprehensible or measurable.
[3] Concluded in a place severed and apart, by himself.
[4] The whole Being, Substance, or Essence.
[5] Substance, thing, or being.

reference to the essence; and yet he is even through all things, and giveth in himself, in an energetical working manner, to [every] essence, as the powerful influence of the sun [giveth itself] to the fruit; but [he] worketh with the creature and its life, not from without into it, but from within out of it, to his own manifestation; and that the nature and creature is his manifestation. If reason did but understand this aright, it would here make no further question [but be undoubtedly satisfied in itself what God is].

4. Now, understand the sum of all briefly thus: God dwelleth in himself, both according to the love, and according to the anger; each property seeth only into itself, and is not manifest in the other with its own property; as ye have a similitude of this in the day and night, viz. in the light and darkness. The light dwelleth in the darkness, and seeth it not; also the darkness seeth not the light; and as the light dwelleth in its great meekness in the fire, and yet receiveth not the source and pain of the fire to itself, but remaineth only good, without any feeling life of the fire, and yet it ariseth through the consuming of the fire, viz. through the dying of the essence:[1] in like manner also understand the being of God.

5. God's love-eye doth not see essentially into the wicked rebellious apostate soul; neither also into the devil, but his anger-eye seeth thereinto; that is, God, according to the property of the anger or fire of wrath, seeth in the devil, and in the false soul.

6. Therefore God said, There was a cry come up before him. There he understood, before his manifested Word, viz. before the voice in the divine revealed ens of these three men. It was come before the ens, and before the hearing which had now in the promised ens represented itself, in three persons, unto man, concerning the humanity of Christ.

7. For the judgment over all the devils and wicked men was given unto this Word or hearing; for it was the moveable[2] Hearing whereby God the Father heard in the humanity, and whereby he would separate the evil from the good.

8. Now this Hearing, viz. the Hearing which would manifest itself in Christ's person in the humanity, heard the voice of the Sodomites in itself, viz. of the children of Ham; that is, according to the property of the anger; and brought the hearing before the infinite Hearing into the first Principle, viz. into the original of nature and creature. For the Sodomites, viz. the children of the flesh, do all live

---

[1] Material substance.   [2] Affective, or effective.

in the hearing of this world, viz. in the expressed formed Word, in the figure of the Deity, where evil and good are manifest together in one essence.

9. Now understand us here very punctually and acutely. The angelical world is called[1] *above*, and the formed outward is called[1] *below*; in manner as we may say when a fire is enkindled, then the light is above, and the substance [or matter] below. When we speak of God's [being] *above*, then we mean and understand *within*, for the [being] within, without the substance,[2] is the [being] above; for without the substance [or matter] there is all above, no below; that which is under the substance is also above.

10. Now the cry of the Sodomites was come before the *above*,[3] viz. before and into the first Principle, where the *above*[3] doth conceive or comprehend itself out of the Nothing in the first eternal beginning; viz. to a nature and formation of the powers or Word; and God's formed Word or voice, out of the Father's and Son's property, out of love and anger (which had betrothed itself by promise to be a Christ to man, and formed itself into a divine ens) heard the cry in the property of the anger, wherewith he is a judge of the wicked ens, or ungodliness.

11. Therefore said the Father, *I will come down that I may see whether it be so or no.* That is, he came down, that is, out of the above,[4] with that formed Hearing of these three men in the ens, which God had formed to be judge of the world, which was to become the Christ.

12. For this ens was to be creatural in the person, therefore it was formative, in an angelical manner, in the conceived Word of the promise; and therewith it came from above, that is, out of the above, viz. out of God; out of the unchangeable God; and with his love heard first in Abraham into the ens of the Covenant, into the aim or limit of his Covenant. And with the anger, viz. with the hearing of the fire, he heard into the iniquity and vanity of man; and saw with the anger what they did; that is, his wrath saw essentially into the iniquity and vanity of man, in manner as an incentive fire should arise in any piece of wood [or fuel], and would devour the wood. So likewise God looked with his anger-eye in the formed ens (through the same judicial Word in Christ's ens, wherein he will judge the world) into the wicked infection and will of the children of Ham at Sodom and Gomorrah.

---

[1] Or, is said to be.   [2] Extra substantiam.   [3] Or, highness.
[4] Or, from on high.

13. For when God had set before him, in Abraham, the new birth of his holy children out of his love ens; he also set before him the judgment in his anger ens, how he would, through this Christ, prove the wicked in the fire.

14. And the judgment upon Sodom is a figure of the Last Judgment; as the three men which came before Abraham were a figure of our new angelical humanity, where God dwelleth in man; so was also his anger in the wicked. And we see here, that God will judge the devils, and all wicked men, by the children of the saints; as he now did represent the figure of the judicial office in a humanity of three, and destroyed Sodom and Gomorrah from the world.

15. Also God said to Abraham, *How can I hide from Abraham the thing which I do?* It was hidden unto the earthly Abraham, but unto the heavenly, out of God's ens, God would not hide it. And here he set forth the figure of his love, and his anger, viz. the humanity of Christ in the great humility and love, and his truth and righteousness in the two angels.

16. For thus saith the text in Moses: *And Abraham stood yet before the Lord* (viz. before these three men, which he here calleth only one), *and came near to him, and said, Wilt thou also destroy the righteous with the wicked? Per-adventure there be fifty righteous within the city: wilt thou also destroy them; and not spare the place for the fifty righteous that are therein? That be far from thee to do so, to slay the righteous with the wicked; and that the righteous should be as the wicked, that be far from thee: that thou, who art the Judge of the whole earth, shouldst so judge* (Gen. xviii. 22–25).

17. This is now the very excellent and pregnant figure; how Abraham (in the ens of faith in Christ's person and spirit) cometh before God, viz. before the triune God, before the severe righteousness of God; and will reconcile and atone the Father; and prayeth for his children, which dwell among the company of the wicked; that his Father would be pleased to spare that place (where yet righteous people dwell) from rebuke, and draweth his mercy into his righteousness, and saith, *Thou wilt not so judge, thou who art the Judge of the whole world.*

18. This figure is nothing else but God in his righteousness, and God in Christ with his mercy. Here the two types stand both together; what else should it mean, that a man would withhold God from doing what he please?

19. The man Christ doth withhold God's righteousness and severe judgment from falling on the crew of wicked men, else they

had been devoured at the first disobedience in Paradise. This is he which cometh before God, and into God, viz. into God's anger, for he is of God, and therefore he can come before God [draw near to, or intercede with, God].

20. That is, the formed Word, viz. the creature, standeth before the judgment, and sits in judgment, and suffers not the anger to judge, so long as there are righteous people; as is here to be seen; if there had been but ten righteous persons, God had spared them. Indeed there were but three persons only which were righteous before God, viz. Lot, with his two daughters. His wife was also not fit [or capable of this mercy], therefore although she went out of Sodom, yet she remained still, and was turned to a pillar of salt, as shall afterward be cleared and expounded.

21. Abraham, that is, the spirit of Christ, entreateth so far with God that God would spare all these places for ten persons' sake. But they were all revolted and gone astray, save his brother's son, who was a stranger among this people, whom God first brought out, before he enkindled the wrath.

22. The spirit here speaketh very covertly and hiddenly in Moses and Esdras,[1] who wrote again these Acts in the Spirit of God, after that they were lost among the children of Israel. And we here see very fully and pregnantly, how exactly and punctually the spirit here aimeth at the figure in Abraham, and pointeth out what thereby is to be understood.

23. For at the appearance unto Abraham he speaketh of three men; and here he speaketh of two angels, which went towards Sodom, and destroyed the cities; to signify that the person of Christ is the third, which went not along; for here only two went, viz. God's truth, and God's righteousness, viz. the judgment, and the truth: the judgment remained in[2] Sodom, and the truth brought Lot out.

24. *And when both these* [angels] *at even* (when their time was out, and their day passed) *came to Sodom, Lot sat at the Gate, and when he saw them, he arose up to meet them; and he bowed himself with his face towards the ground; and he said, Behold now, my lords, turn in, I pray, into your servant's house, and tarry all night, and wash your feet, and ye shall rise up early, and go on your ways. But they said, Nay; but we will abide in the street all night. And he earnestly entreated them; and they turned in unto him, and entered into his house; and he made them a feast, and baked them unleavened cakes, and they did eat* (Gen. xix. 1–3).

---

[1] *Note.*—Esdras wrote the Book of these Acts, viz. Genesis, etc.   [2] Upon.

25. If we should declare and explain this in its right understanding, then we would express it after this manner: The cry of the
Sodomites was the curse which Noah laid upon Ham, when he cursed
him (by reason of his unchaste, wanton, bestial eyes and desire); this
same cursed, bestial spirit had propagated and bred up itself in the
malicious, profane, wholly earthly and serpentine property, in the
flesh and soul of this generation of Ham, so that it had established itself in a kingly dominion, under which they lived more like to beasts,
than true men.

26. This cry of the cursed Serpent's ens, grown up to its full
height in the anger, was made manifest, and sounded aloud in its
mother, viz. in the anger of God in the dark world's property, and
had awakened the judgment upon and in itself. And now God sent
his judgment upon the Serpent's ens. This was now the time of Enos,
his hidden, and at present opened seal (as it is before mentioned
concerning the seven lines[1] [or general junctures of time]) where his
mystery was at the end; and was now revealed as a sound of his
preaching in the Word of power, both in love and anger.

27. As in Abraham in love: for here the formed word, which
began to be taught in the days of Enos, did now manifest itself in the
formed pregnant and grown ens or being in Abraham, with the
promised and holy seed of faith. And in the children of iniquity, who
were of the generation of cursed Ham, the property of the anger did
here manifest itself out of Enos, his preaching, wherein he threatened
God's judgment and rebuke: this same was now grown up in the
children of iniquity, and brought to substance.

28. And now, seeing the seal of this Enos did open itself, seeing
his mystery was at the end, and was forthwith to be manifest according to love and anger, thereupon each property set forth its substance
to the divine contemplation; viz. whatsoever the word in the love
ens had wrought under the sound or voice of Enos, and also what the
sound of the denunciation of the anger of God had wrought: Here
now the essences of both properties did open themselves, and set
themselves into the judgment, to the final sentence of the righteousness of God. Now in this final arbitration or determination of the
divine justice, viz. in Abraham, there stood Christ in the judgment of
Enos, his preaching of repentance; and in Enos, his threatenings of
plagues and punishment, the earnest and severe judgment of God,
viz. prince Lucifer, did there stand (in the judgment in the children

[1] Ch. 30 of this book, v. 36.

of the curse in Ham), to execute the same in the wrath of God, as a servant of the house of darkness.

29. For God said to the people of Israel on Mount Sinai, *I will visit and punish the iniquities of the parents upon the children, even unto the third and fourth generation* (Exod. xx. 5), which is here to be seen in Ham, Noah's son. Here came first the curse of Noah into judgment.

30. And here two angels were sent (that is, in the power and might of the judgment) in Christ's stead, seeing Christ was not yet in the flesh, and in office; for Christ's office continued in Abraham before the Lord, and prayed for the rebellious men of Sodom and Gomorrah.

31. But when they were tried in the judgment (viz. in the office of the love of Christ before the Lord), whether there were any men of Sodom who were capable of the office of Christ, in the love, and yet none were found, then the office of Christ in Abraham remained behind, and went not unto Sodom. But the office of divine righteousness and truth went in the form of two angels to Sodom, and looked very intimately into their essence and being, and proved the same in itself, as it is to be seen, that as soon as these two angels came into the city, the property of the people did open and manifest itself, and they would have these men brought forth among them.

32. For these two angels had stirred up or moved their properties, and set them in open view before the Lord, to see what was in them; and they found that they were only bestial, unchaste, lewd murderers; which brought them into judgment; and now they must be judged according to their essence.

33. But that the spirit in Moses signifieth, that Lot sat at the gate, and knew these angels, and entreated them earnestly to turn in unto him, that so he might wash their feet, and bake them cakes, and that they did eat; and yet at first did deny to turn in unto him. The same is a very hidden mystery, for it is the spirit of truth and righteousness, which Lot knew very well, for it was moved in the essence, and entered first with the trial into Lot; and when as he humbled and bowed himself before the Lord, he was proved and found upright in himself.

34. But the truth did first refuse to go into his house with the righteousness, viz. with the judgment, and would remain in the street, for it was because of Lot's wife, who, when she was proved, and the judgment passed through her, was cast as to her temporal

life. For she continued in the judgment, as a first matter,[1] viz. as a Sulphur, Mercurius, that is, an impressed[2] matter of the judgment, as a transmutation into the first essence out of which the body was created.

35. Yet not so soon before the execution of the judgment. But when Lot went with her out of Sodom, and the judgment began, she drew the judgment back again on her, as is to be seen in the judgment, which then laid hold on her, for it had taken her in the probation.

36. Yet the command was given her not to look back, and so she might have overcome, if she had forthwith entered into repentance, and broken the evil earthly will, and fallen down with Lot, at the Lord's feet: and this was the cause that the two angels refused to turn in unto Lot.

37. And by Lot's wife the earthly matrix is signified, which shall not go along through the judgment, although it must help to work and bring forth fruit, as an instrument. Yet it is not in its outward form chosen unto the kingdom of heaven; for it was adjoined to Eve in the sleep in Adam's fall, and shall remain in the judgment, and be changed again into its first matter out of which it was created. It is not condemned into the abyss, but it shall pass into the mystery, viz. into Sulphur, and Mercurius, which in the Grand Mystery[3] is a Salt-spirit, viz. a cause of all corporality; as it shall be mentioned hereafter concerning Lot's daughters, who for this very cause were to be gotten with child of their father.

38. Thus understand the figure further, internally: Lot baked cakes of unleavened dough, and made them a feast, and they did eat. Now the angels do not use any such food; but they were only *formed angels* in an angelical shape, for Abraham and Lot also called them, *Lord*: it was God's judgment, and truth.

39. This feast was eaten in manner as the offerings of Abraham, and Moses, as is before mentioned; for the will's desire formeth[4] itself therein into a substance: God eateth only the word of the will, but the food is consumed in the outward spirit in which it is wrought.

40. For Lot's faith's desire was the divine food of these men; but with the feast, which Lot gave them out of his good love-will, Lot's will was formed into a substance that so he might be preserved in this judgment outwardly as to the earthly life, and inwardly as to the will of faith.

[1] Prima Materia.   [2] The hard astringent.   [3] In Mysterio Magno.
[4] Amasseth, conceiveth.

41. For these angels did eat of Lot's food as if they had eaten of his body and spirit, which was therein apprehended, in manner as it is to be understood in the offerings;[1] as is before sufficiently explained concerning the offerings[1] of Cain and Abel. For the unleavened cakes were (or did signify) the informing [or impression], as may be seen everywhere in Moses, and they denote the Body of Christ, whereinto the imagination of God entered, as into a type, and yet was only conceived or apprehended in the faith.

42. Furthermore, the spirit in Moses saith: And *before the men lay down, the men of the city, Sodom, came and encompassed the house round about, young and old, even all the people from every quarter; and called for Lot, and said unto him, Where are the men that came in unto you the last night? bring them out that we may know them* (Gen. xix. 4, 5).

43. This is now the figure, as it is before mentioned: The judgment (after that it had bound itself with Lot in the feast) did now penetrate and press in the probation of their essence and being, into all; that they came pell-mell on heaps, running as mad enraged people, driven, forced and compelled to the judgment.

44. For the zeal of the Lord, which longed after them, drew them to itself. It hungered earnestly to devour their vanity; therefore they ran altogether, young and old, and would know the mouth which hungered after them, for they in their blindness knew not what they did; thus the anger drew them to itself.

45. *And Lot went out unto them at the door, and shut the door after him. And said, ah! I pray, dear brethren, do not so wickedly. I have two daughters which have never known man; let me, I pray you, bring them out unto you, and do with them what seems good in your eyes: but unto these men do nothing; for therefore came they under the shadow of my roof. But they said, Come hither, thou art the only stranger among us, and thou wilt rule; well, we will deal worse with thee than with them.*

46. Here the ground of their sin is finely deciphered and laid out in its colours, wherein their cry was come before God; as, namely, uncleanness, lasciviousness, tyranny, self-willed perverseness; and the greatest of all was the contempt of God; for Lot had told them of the punishment which God would bring upon them. And then they said, *Thou art the only stranger among us, and wilt go about to rule and judge us, we will yet plague thee worse than those*; to signify, that God had before sent them warning by the messengers of his mouth, and that they had only plagued and contemned them. Therefore they said also to

1 Or, sacrifices.

THE RUIN OF SODOM AND GOMORRAH

Lot, Wilt thou govern us with thy threatenings, and contemn and nullify our works, we will serve thee worse than them.

47. For when they understood that men [of God] were come in unto Lot, who threatened them with ruin and destruction, they made an uproar against them, and would kill them. As the mad blind world hath always done, when God hath sent them messengers, who have rebuked and reproved them; then the Babylonical whore hath cried out, Run, run, there is a new heresy, which would teach us other doctrine, and reprove our way which we go in.

48. Thus it was here: the self-full rebellious devil's will, in his Serpent's ens, would be uncontrollable, unreprovable; and seeing these men were come, they cried out, *Mordio*;[1] and said there were false prophets and teachers come, to rebuke and contemn them, as the Babylonical whore hath always done; for she will not hear what the Lord speaketh through his children; but that alone must be accounted sacred, which she speaks from the Serpent's ens.

49. This whore hath covered herself with the literal word, and gives forth herself for holy, and boasteth much in a strange attire; but her heart is only Sodom and Gomorrah. When she seeth these two angels come from Abraham, that is, from Christ, to her in her Sodom and Gomorrah, and lay open her shame, then she makes the whole city of an uproar, with a cry of murder; so that all people, young and old, come running together, and think that there is some strange wonderful beast arrived.

50. And when they can perceive no new strange thing in God's messengers, and hear that they do only teach and reprove, then they think, O! our minister and pastor calls him a new upstart, a heretic and false prophet, there is a fool [and a frantic fellow, sure enough he is worse than out of his wits]; and they begin to wonder at him [like birds] at an owl, and assault him, and his house, his wife, and his children, with scorn, reproach, and contempt, as the Sodomites did Lot; every one thinketh, that he doth well if he can but jeer and revile these messengers.

51. And although he knows no other ground or reason [in the world], but only that the high priest[2] (who hath put on the whore of Babylon) doth set him at nought; yet he is very raging mad, and suffers a false wind (viz. the spirit of the Babylonish whore) to drive him, and raveth in misunderstanding, as here the Sodomites did, who (both young and old, small and great) do force upon Lot, and the

---

[1] Murder.   [2] Or, some noted minister.

two men which were come in unto him; that they might know them, that they might plague them, scorn, revile and reproach them. For thus the anger of God doth drive itself into a fire, for its own enkindling. And thus made also must the people be, when the punishment shall come, that they must all make up the measure of their iniquities.

52. And we will not hide from thee, thou unclean, lascivious, rebellious, self-willed, lewd, idolatrous, murderous Babylon, full of all vices, sins, and abominations; that now also these two angels, viz. God's truth and judgment, are come into thee; and declare unto thee, now, at the end of Enoch's seal, which was hidden (but at present is opened in its sound and voice), thy destruction and overthrow. For the time of thy judgment is at hand. And behold thyself aright; and observe it very narrowly: thou hast at present cast scorn, reproach and contempt upon Lot, and the two angels, as the Sodomites did; and therefore thy punishment hangeth over thee. And observe it: when the two angels shall carry forth Lot under the opened seal from thee, then the day of thy destruction is at hand, which now thou wilt by no means believe, but must be forced to find it so by sad and woeful experience, saith the spirit of wonders.

53. We may see very fully what was the Sodomites' vice and great sin, the cry whereof was come up before God; for Lot would bring out his two daughters, which were yet virgins, unto them, that so they might but cease from the raging uproar against these angelical messengers, for he knew well enough that they were wholly drowned in uncleanness; if so be they might satisfy their desire.

54. The inward figure in the spirit, giving us to understand what Moses doth hereby typify, is this: The judgment begins at the house of God, as here in Lot; the children of God must be first brought into judgment, and proved; to see whether there be children of God in any place which may withhold the anger, so that the punishment may be kept back; then the spirit taketh the children of God, and proveth them in the same vice and sin of that city or country, [to see] if they be capable of the same lewdness.

55. Lot must set his two daughters with entreaties into judgment; he would give them to the unclean lascivious people to be tried; for that which he said was so directed by the spirit, which had the two daughters of Lot in the judgment, and had brought the proba or trial into their essence, and hereby signified and laid open the sin and shame of the city, viz. that they were only unclean harlot's beasts.

56. But when these two virgins were not capable of this vice, the spirit, viz. the two angels, defended them; understand, God's truth protected them from the judgment of this people, and also from the sin of uncleanness. For Lot did not speak so of set purpose, as if he would suffer his daughters to be defloured and defiled; but the spirit did set forth its figure.

57. And know for certain that this first book of Moses was written wholly from the prophecy of the spirit, intimating what each act or sentence of the history holds forth in the figure. And whosoever will read, and rightly understand these acts [of the patriarchs], he must modelise or represent in his mind the old and the new man; and set Christ and Adam one against the other; and then he may understand all; and without this, he understands nothing hereof but a child-like history; which yet is so rich and full of Mysteries, that no man, from the cradle unto the longest age, is able to express them; although he had obtained the knowledge and understanding thereunto in his childhood. And we in our gifts do also give but some glances and hints thereof, albeit we have obtained the apprehension and meaning of them from the gift of God; yet we cannot express all, and the world were not able to receive it.[1]

58. And Moses saith, *The men of the city pressed sore upon the man, Lot, and when they drew near together to break the door, the men put forth their hand and pulled Lot into the house to them, and shut to the door. And the men which were before the door of the house were smitten with blindness, both small and great: so that they wearied themselves, and could not find the door* (Gen. xix. 9–11).

59. This figure was achieved[2] thus externally, so that they were thus blind with visible eyes, and could not see the door, and did not hurt, neither to Lot and the two men with him, nor his house either. But in the spirit, the figure stands thus:

60. When God sendeth these two angels, viz. his truth and judgment, into a man's spirit, viz. into the house of his heart, as here it came to pass in Lot (in whom also the spirit, viz. God's truth and judgment was manifest, and therefore he rebuked Sodom, for which cause they did encompass him about, to slay and murder him), then the judgment passeth first upon this man, who is represented unto the Sodomites, as if he were a fool, whom they must vex, plague and perplex, and they also do without intermission revile and rail at him, and condemn him for false.

[1] Understand or apprehend it aright.   [2] Acted or done.

61. But he must reprove, rebuke, and teach them, and he hath no external protection of man, they all cast the dirt of their mouths upon him; and they that should hinder it do but laugh at it. Let him look where he will, he hath no deliverer. Then, supposeth the common people, God rebukes and punisheth him on this wise.

62. But these two angels are with him in his heart, and stand in his person, as in their vessel and instrument, even amidst the enemies. But the common people do eagerly labour and bestir themselves to destroy him and his house.

63. And when it comes to the trial, in earnest, then these two angels do put forth their hand upon the wicked malicious men's hearts, and strike them with blindness, that they are confounded, and know not how they should get by[1] this Lot and the two angels; one casteth forth this, another that; one saith he is honest, another reviles him and saith all evil of him; so long till they cannot find the door, wherein they would break in unto him, and do him mischief. For these two angels do shut him up in themselves, that they cannot see the door of revenge. As may be seen here in Lot, how God doth deliver the messengers of his mouth, and hides them from the enemies; and this pen[2] hath so found it by good experience.

64. *And these men said unto Lot, Hast thou here any besides? son in law, and sons and daughters; and whosoever belongs unto thee in the city, bring them out of this place: For we will destroy this place, because the cry thereof is waxen great before the Lord, who hath sent us to destroy it. And Lot went, and spake to his sons in law which were to marry[3] his daughters, and said, Arise, get ye out of this place; for the Lord will destroy this city. But he seemed unto them as one that mocked* (Gen. xix. 12–14).

65. This is now an excellent mirror, how God also gave warning unto these men, and would have spared them for Lot's sake, if they would but have followed him. But the wrath had captivated them, and wholly hardened them; that they did but laugh and jeer at him; and as it were said unto him, What is happened to the fool? he thinks the sky will fall.

66. The inward figure stands thus: God's truth in the love drew these men, Lot's sons in law, and would deliver them; but the wrath was stronger in them, and had captivated them in the probation of their hearts. They continued in the judgment, as Lot's wife, whom notwithstanding Lot brought forth with him before the city, yet the wrath drew her back again into judgment; so that she (seeing she

---

[1] Or, at.   [2] The Author.   [3] English translation, which married.

was for Lot's sake freed from the fire-sword) must go into a trans-mutation, until the Last Judgment, which is a terrible example.

67. In this figure this present world may behold itself, and take warning; for as certain, and as true, that the preaching of Lot was true, and the punishment followed thereupon; so certainly also shall the punishment[1] of the sixth seal's time (which seal is even now at hand, and hath already opened itself) suddenly follow.

68. But that the warning hereof came so long ago, declareth that the time of the sixth seal, in its manifestation, is the most wonderful of all the six seals; till the seventh number,[2] which is yet more wonder-ful; for it is the end of this world, and the Last Judgment.

69. Let this be declared unto thee, Babel, ͰͰͰ[3] under the voice of the open seal of this sixth time, although thou contemnest and deri-dest it, it hitteth thee, and hath already strucken thee with the obdurate obstinacy of wrath, which hath thoroughly sifted thee in the appearance of the message of these two angels, and shall now be hinted only to some few, which shall go out, and be delivered with Lot's daughters.

70. The hardened, surprised and apprehended crew is already judged; for the doleful sifting sword hath taken hold of them; they run now in a raving raging manner, as mad people, in pride, cove-tousness and envy, and contemn what the angel's trumpet soundeth.

71. The cry which the angel's trumpet soundeth is this; Go out from Babel; Go out from Babel; Go out from Babel. She stands apprehended and captivated in the flaming sword. Amen.

[1] Or, judgment.   [2] Or, seal.
[3] A mystical mark whereby the Author shews to Babel the pouring forth of the sixth seal in wrath on the mystery of iniquity, and also the time.

END OF VOL. I

Printed in the USA
CPSIA information can be obtained
at www.ICGtesting.com
LVHW041643080124
768453LV00040B/288